More Praise for *Nervosa*

"Unflinching and heartrending and at the same time caus⸺ The inventive visual metaphors and obvious pleasure in language show us that art and creativity can be a path to hard-won hope."
—Matt Madden, author of *Ex Libris*

"Funny, cruel, moral, austere, decorative, despairing, and triumphant. Comics were invented so that Hayley Gold could write *Nervosa*."
—Seth Tobocman, author of *War in the Neighborhood*

"With sly wit and sleek rendering, Hayley leads readers down the surreal rabbit hole that passes for medical treatment of anorexia."
—Sabrina Jones, author of *Our Lady of Birth Control*

"With equal parts humor, horror, and self-knowledge, this book teaches us that there are no commonsense answers to the paradoxes of mental illness."
—Jason Little, author of *Shutterbug Follies*

"I couldn't put it down. This powerful memoir shows how eating disorder patients are denied agency, and how healing only starts when one is finally able to express their voice."
—Sarah Mirk, author of *Guantanamo Voices*

"Structurally brilliant and darkly humorous, this revealing graphic memoir is an excellent read for anyone who is looking for companionship in this experience, or a window into living with this disease."
—Rachel Lindsay, author of *RX: A Graphic Memoir*

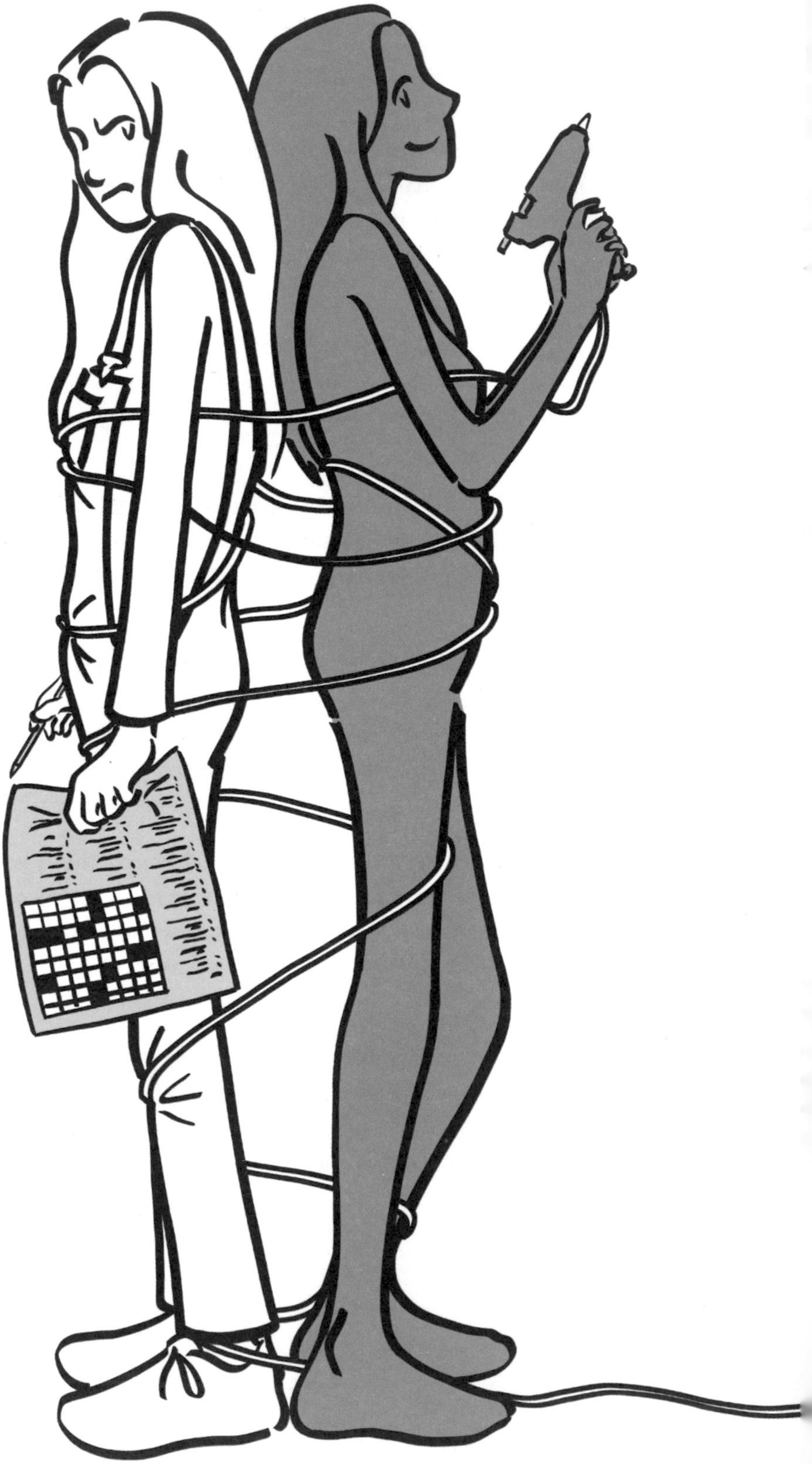

Nervosa

by hayley gold

Street Noise Books • Brooklyn, New York

Emily Dickinson poetry in the public domain:

"A word is dead," in POEMS: THIRD SERIES, edited by Mabel Loomis Todd (Boston: Roberts Brothers, 1896).
"Hope is the thing with feathers," "I'm Nobody! Who are you?," and "Will there really be a 'Morning'?" in POEMS: SECOND SERIES, edited by T. W. Higginson and Mabel Loomis Todd (Boston: Roberts Brothers, 1891).
"The butterfly obtains," in THE SINGLE HOUND: POEMS OF A LIFETIME, edited by Martha Dickinson Bianchi (Boston: Little, Brown, 1914).

All other Emily Dickinson poetry:

THE POEMS OF EMILY DICKINSON, edited by Thomas H. Johnson, Cambridge, Mass.: The Belknap Press of Harvard University Press, Copyright © 1951, 1955 by the President and Fellows of Harvard College. Copyright © renewed 1979, 1983 by the President and Fellows of Harvard College. Copyright © 1914, 1918, 1919, 1924, 1929, 1930, 1932, 1935, 1937, 1942 by Martha Dickinson Bianchi. Copyright © 1952, 1957, 1958, 1963, 1965 by Mary L. Hampson. Used by permission. All rights reserved.

Song Lyrics:

LOW

Words and music by Tramar Dillard, Montay Humphrey, Korey Roberson, Howard Simmons, and T-Pain. Copyright © 2007 Sony Music Publishing (US) LLC, Mail On Sunday Music, Top Quality Publishing, Universal Music - Z Songs and Nappypub Music. All rights on behalf of Sony Music Publishing (US) LLC, Mail On Sunday Music, and Top Quality Publishing administered by Sony Music Publishing (US) LLC, 424 Church Street, Suite 1200, Nashville, TN 37219. All rights on behalf of Nappypub Music administered by Universal Music - Z Songs. International copyright secured. All rights reserved.
Reprinted by permission of Hal Leonard LLC

BAD ROMANCE

Words and music by Stefani Germanotta and Nadir Khayat. Copyright © 2009 Sony Music Publishing (US) LLC and House Of Gaga Publishing Inc. All rights administered by Sony Music Publishing (US) LLC, 424 Church Street, Suite 1200, Nashville, TN 37219. International copyright secured. All rights reserved.
Reprinted by permission of Hal Leonard LLC

CALIFORNIA GURLS

Words and music by Katy Perry, Bonnie McKee, Lukasz Gottwald, Max Martin, Benjamin Levin, Calvin Broadus, Mike Love, and Brian Wilson. © 2010 WHEN I'M RICH YOU'LL BE MY BITCH, HIPGNOSIS SFH I LTD., WHERE DA KASZ AT?, PRESCRIPTION SONGS LLC, KASZ MONEY PUBLISHING, MXM, SONGS OF PULSE RECORDINGS, MATZA BALL MUSIC, MY OWN CHIT MUSIC, and IRVING MUSIC, INC. All rights for WHEN I'M RICH YOU'LL BE MY BITCH administered by WC MUSIC CORP. All rights for HIPGNOSIS SFH I LTD and WHERE DA KASZ AT? administered worldwide by SONGS OF KOBALT MUSIC PUBLISHING. All rights for PRESCRIPTION SONGS LLC, KASZ MONEY PUBLISHING and MXM administered by KOBALT SONGS MUSIC PUBLISHING. All rights for SONGS OF PULSE RECORDINGS administered by CONCORD COPYRIGHTS c/o CONCORD MUSIC PUBLISHING. All rights for MATZA BALL MUSIC administered by CONCORD AVENUE c/o CONCORD MUSIC PUBLISHING. All rights for MY OWN CHIT MUSIC administered by SONY MUSIC PUBLISHING (US) LLC, 424 Church Street, Suite 1200, Nashville, TN 37219. All rights reserved. Used by permission.
Reprinted by permission of Hal Leonard LLC and Alfred Music

DROP IT LIKE IT'S HOT

Words and music by Calvin Broadus, Chad Hugo, and Pharrell Williams. Copyright © 2004 by Universal Music - Careers, Raynchaser Music, EMI Blackwood Music Inc., My Own Chit Music, and Pharrell BMI Pub Designee. All rights for Raynchaser Music administered by Universal Music - Careers. All rights for EMI Blackwood Music Inc. and My Own Chit Music administered by Sony Music Publishing (US) LLC, 424 Church Street, Suite 1200, Nashville, TN 37219. All rights for Pharrell BMI Pub Designee administered by Warner-Tamerlane Publishing Corp. International copyright secured. All rights reserved.
Reprinted by permission of Hal Leonard LLC and Alfred Music

UNDER THE SEA from THE LITTLE MERMAID
Music by Alan Menken. Lyrics by Howard Ashman.
© 1988 Wonderland Music Company, Inc. and Walt Disney Music Company. All rights reserved. Used by permission.
Reprinted by permission of Hal Leonard LLC

ISBN 978-1951-491-24-6

Edited by Jisu Kim

Printed in South Korea

9 8 7 6 5 4 3 2 1

First Edition

Table of Contents

nervosa

¹nervosa \ˈnər-ˈvō-sə\ *n. (Psychiatry)* : a centrally based disorder, such as of the nerves or mind, as opposed to one based in the peripheral or external : NEUROSIS, HYSTERIA

²nervosa *adj.* 1 [Latin]   a : of or relating to neurons, nerves or the nervous system : NEURAL
b : characterized by unease of mind : NERVOUS, ANXIOUS
c : marked by strength of thought or emotion : SPIRITED, POWERFUL

2 *(Botany)* a : SINEWY, TOUGH
b : full of life : ENERGETIC, VIGOROUS

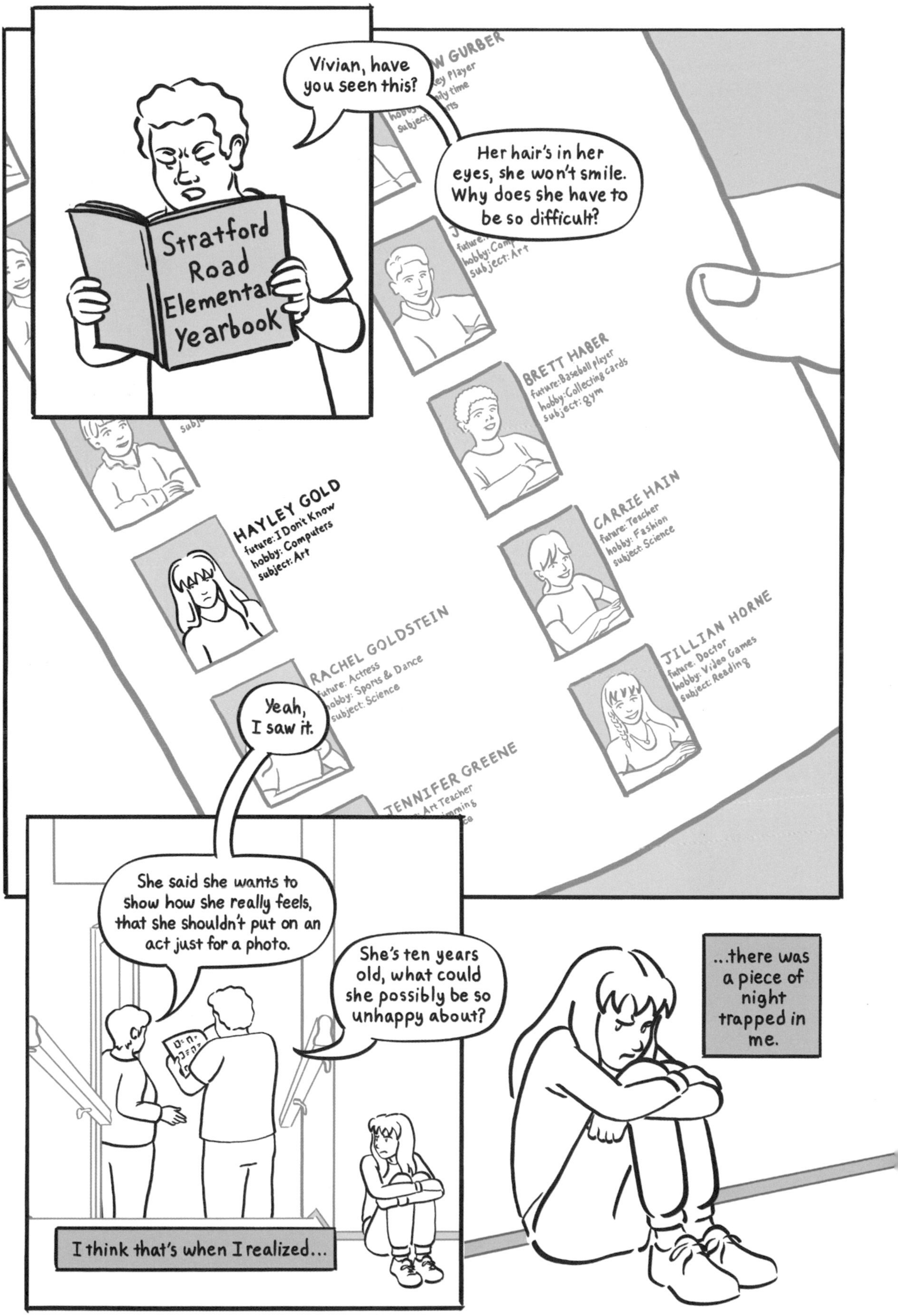

Vivian, have you seen this?
Stratford Road Elementar Yearbook
Her hair's in her eyes, she won't smile. Why does she have to be so difficult?
BRETT HABER
future: Baseball player
hobby: Collecting cards
subject: gym
HAYLEY GOLD
future: I Don't Know
hobby: Computers
subject: Art
CARRIE HAIN
future: Teacher
hobby: Fashion
subject: Science
RACHEL GOLDSTEIN
future: Actress
hobby: Sports & Dance
subject: Science
JILLIAN HORNE
future: Doctor
hobby: Video Games
subject: Reading
JENNIFER GREENE
Yeah, I saw it.
She said she wants to show how she really feels, that she shouldn't put on an act just for a photo.
She's ten years old, what could she possibly be so unhappy about?
I think that's when I realized...
...there was a piece of night trapped in me.

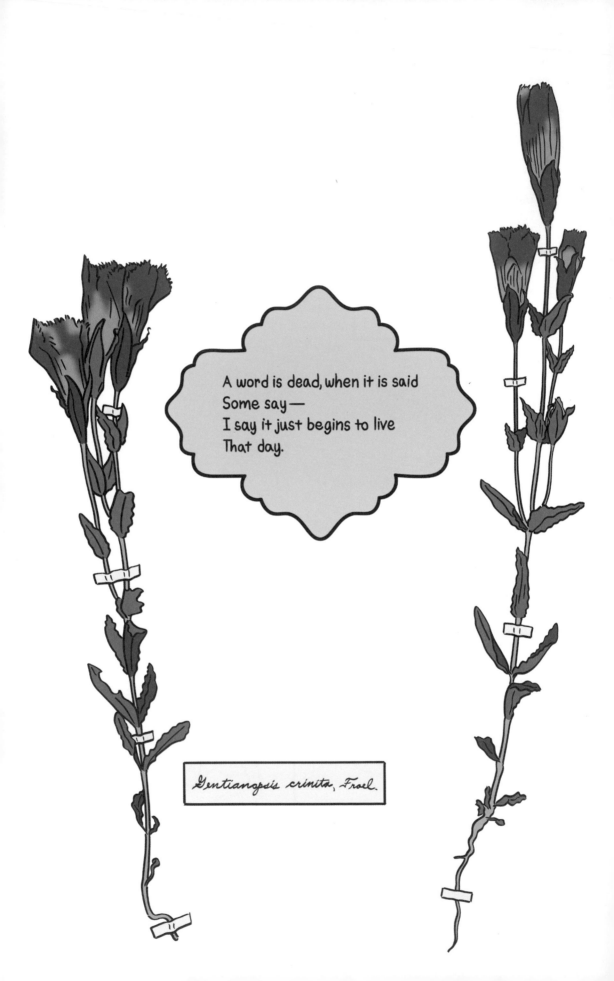

A word is dead, when it is said
Some say—
I say it just begins to live
That day.

Gentianopsis crinita, Froel.

Chapter

1

All the
Colors

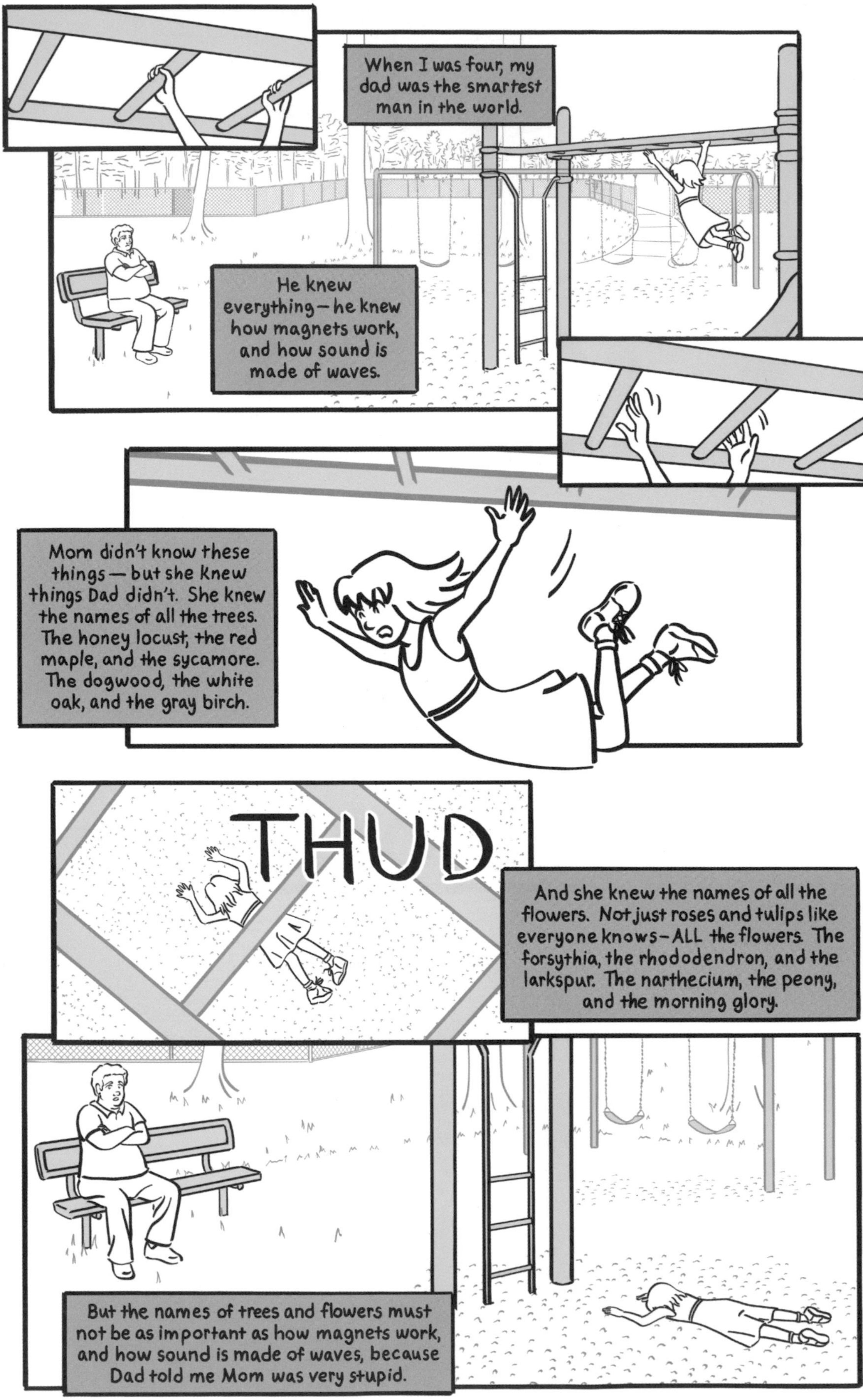
When I was four, my dad was the smartest man in the world.
He knew everything—he knew how magnets work, and how sound is made of waves.
Mom didn't know these things — but she knew things Dad didn't. She knew the names of all the trees. The honey locust, the red maple, and the sycamore. The dogwood, the white oak, and the gray birch.
THUD
And she knew the names of all the flowers. Not just roses and tulips like everyone knows—ALL the flowers. The forsythia, the rhododendron, and the larkspur. The narthecium, the peony, and the morning glory.
But the names of trees and flowers must not be as important as how magnets work, and how sound is made of waves, because Dad told me Mom was very stupid.

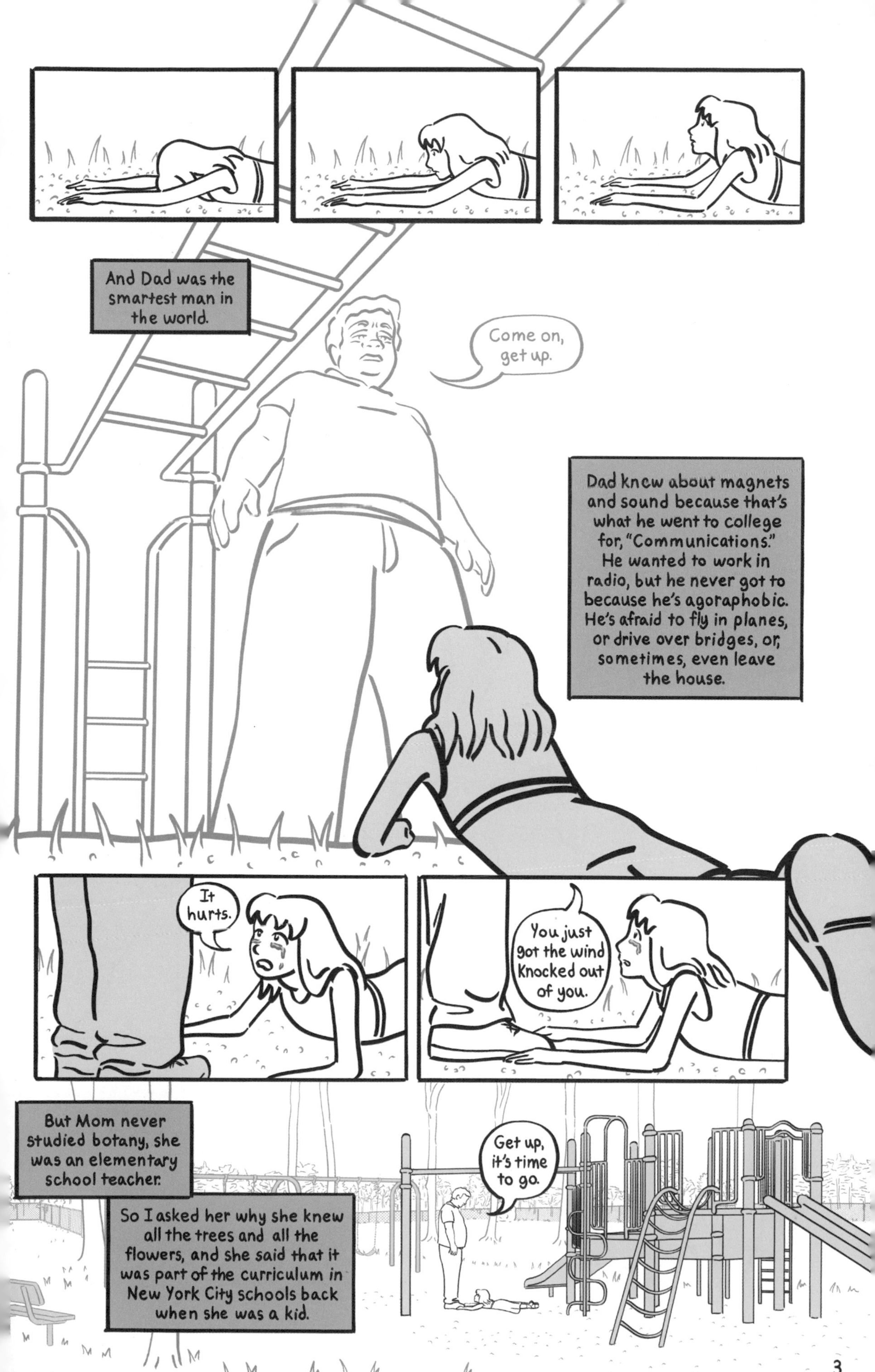

And Dad was the smartest man in the world.
Come on, get up.
Dad knew about magnets and sound because that's what he went to college for, "Communications." He wanted to work in radio, but he never got to because he's agoraphobic. He's afraid to fly in planes, or drive over bridges, or, sometimes, even leave the house.
It hurts.
You just got the wind knocked out of you.
But Mom never studied botany, she was an elementary school teacher.
So I asked her why she knew all the trees and all the flowers, and she said that it was part of the curriculum in New York City schools back when she was a kid.
Get up, it's time to go.

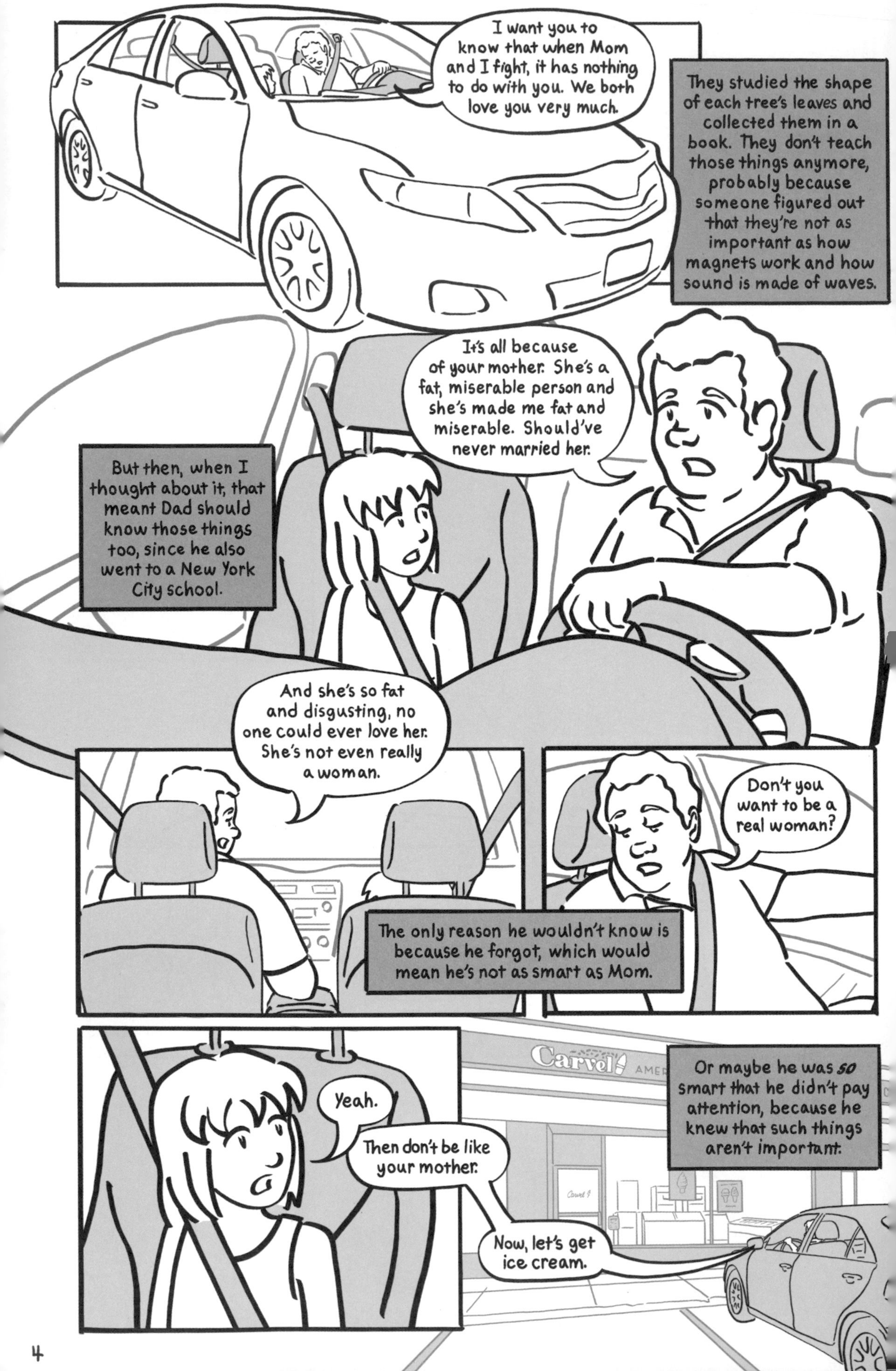
I want you to know that when Mom and I fight, it has nothing to do with you. We both love you very much.
They studied the shape of each tree's leaves and collected them in a book. They don't teach those things anymore, probably because someone figured out that they're not as important as how magnets work and how sound is made of waves.
It's all because of your mother. She's a fat, miserable person and she's made me fat and miserable. Should've never married her.
But then, when I thought about it, that meant Dad should know those things too, since he also went to a New York City school.
And she's so fat and disgusting, no one could ever love her. She's not even really a woman.
Don't you want to be a real woman?
The only reason he wouldn't know is because he forgot, which would mean he's not as smart as Mom.
Yeah.
Then don't be like your mother.
Carvel
Or maybe he was *so* smart that he didn't pay attention, because he knew that such things aren't important.
Now, let's get ice cream.

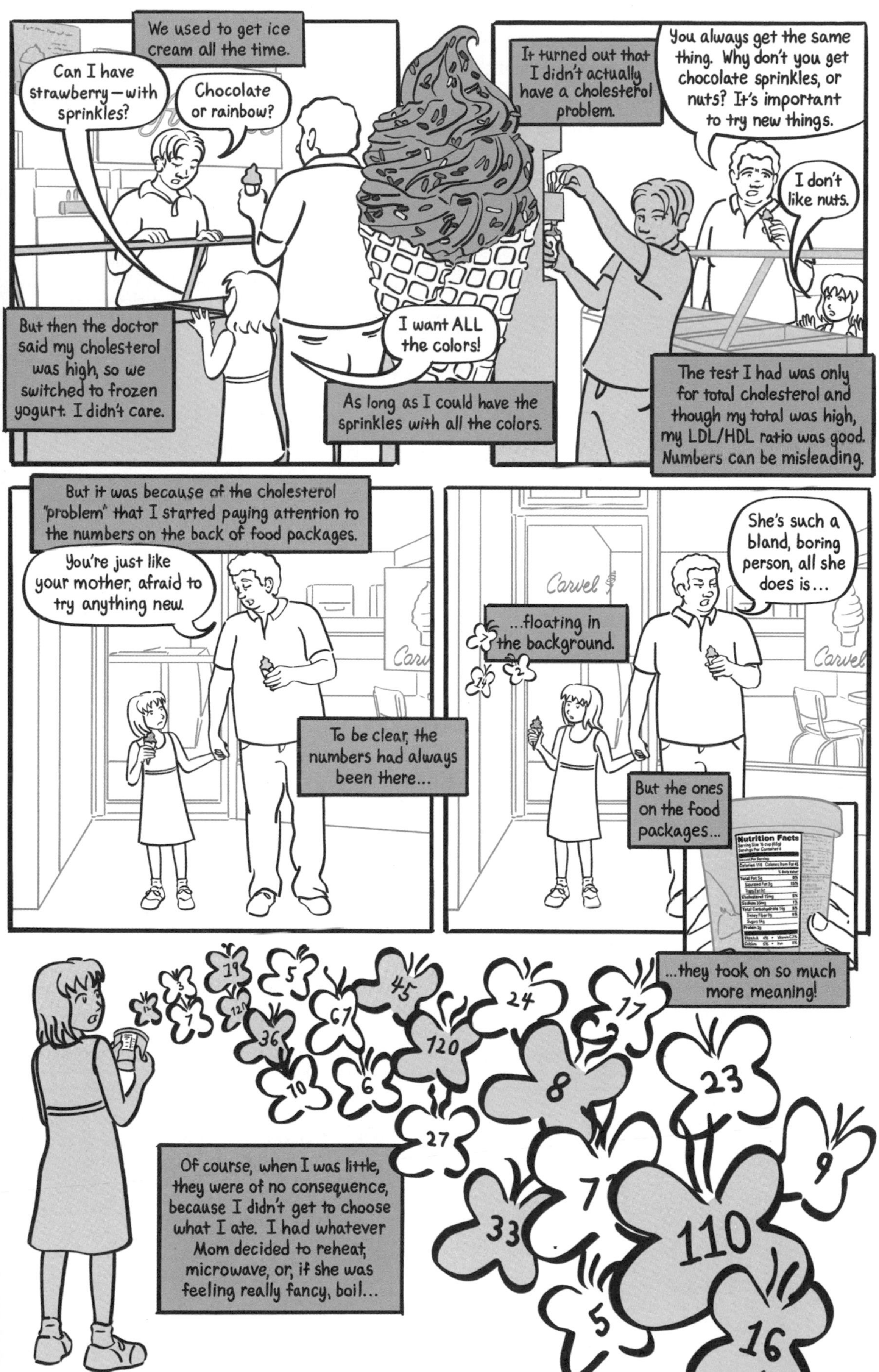
We used to get ice cream all the time.
Can I have strawberry—with sprinkles?
Chocolate or rainbow?
I want ALL the colors!
But then the doctor said my cholesterol was high, so we switched to frozen yogurt. I didn't care.
As long as I could have the sprinkles with all the colors.
It turned out that I didn't actually have a cholesterol problem.
You always get the same thing. Why don't you get chocolate sprinkles, or nuts? It's important to try new things.
I don't like nuts.
The test I had was only for total cholesterol and though my total was high, my LDL/HDL ratio was good. Numbers can be misleading.
But it was because of the cholesterol "problem" that I started paying attention to the numbers on the back of food packages.
You're just like your mother, afraid to try anything new.
Carvel
To be clear, the numbers had always been there...
She's such a bland, boring person, all she does is...
Carvel
...floating in the background.
7
2
14
But the ones on the food packages...
Nutrition Facts
...they took on so much more meaning!
19
5
45
3
7
120
67
24
17
36
120
10
6
8
23
27
9
7
33
110
5
16
Of course, when I was little, they were of no consequence, because I didn't get to choose what I ate. I had whatever Mom decided to reheat, microwave, or, if she was feeling really fancy, boil...

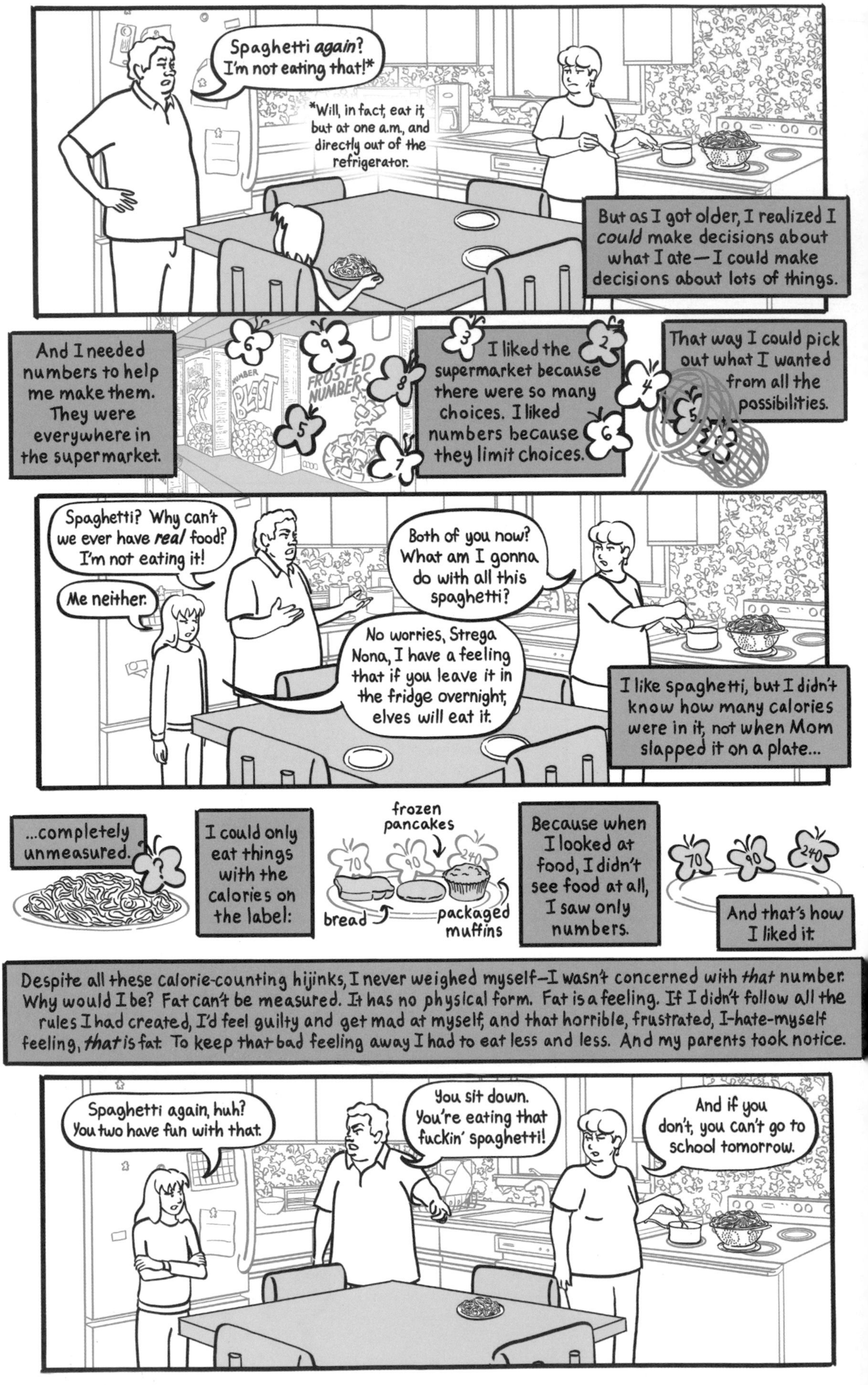
Spaghetti *again*? I'm not eating that!*
*Will, in fact, eat it, but at one a.m., and directly out of the refrigerator.
But as I got older, I realized I *could* make decisions about what I ate—I could make decisions about lots of things.
And I needed numbers to help me make them. They were everywhere in the supermarket.
6
9
FROSTED NUMBERS
NUMBER BLAST
5
3
8
7
I liked the supermarket because there were so many choices. I liked numbers because they limit choices.
2
6
4
5
That way I could pick out what I wanted from all the possibilities.
Spaghetti? Why can't we ever have *real* food? I'm not eating it!
Me neither.
Both of you now? What am I gonna do with all this spaghetti?
No worries, Strega Nona, I have a feeling that if you leave it in the fridge overnight, elves will eat it.
I like spaghetti, but I didn't know how many calories were in it, not when Mom slapped it on a plate...
...completely unmeasured.
?
I could only eat things with the calories on the label:
frozen pancakes
70
90
240
bread
packaged muffins
Because when I looked at food, I didn't see food at all, I saw only numbers.
70
90
240
And that's how I liked it.
Despite all these calorie-counting hijinks, I never weighed myself—I wasn't concerned with *that* number. Why would I be? Fat can't be measured. It has no physical form. Fat is a feeling. If I didn't follow all the rules I had created, I'd feel guilty and get mad at myself, and that horrible, frustrated, I-hate-myself feeling, *that* is fat. To keep that bad feeling away I had to eat less and less. And my parents took notice.
Spaghetti again, huh? You two have fun with that.
You sit down. You're eating that fuckin' spaghetti!
And if you don't, you can't go to school tomorrow.

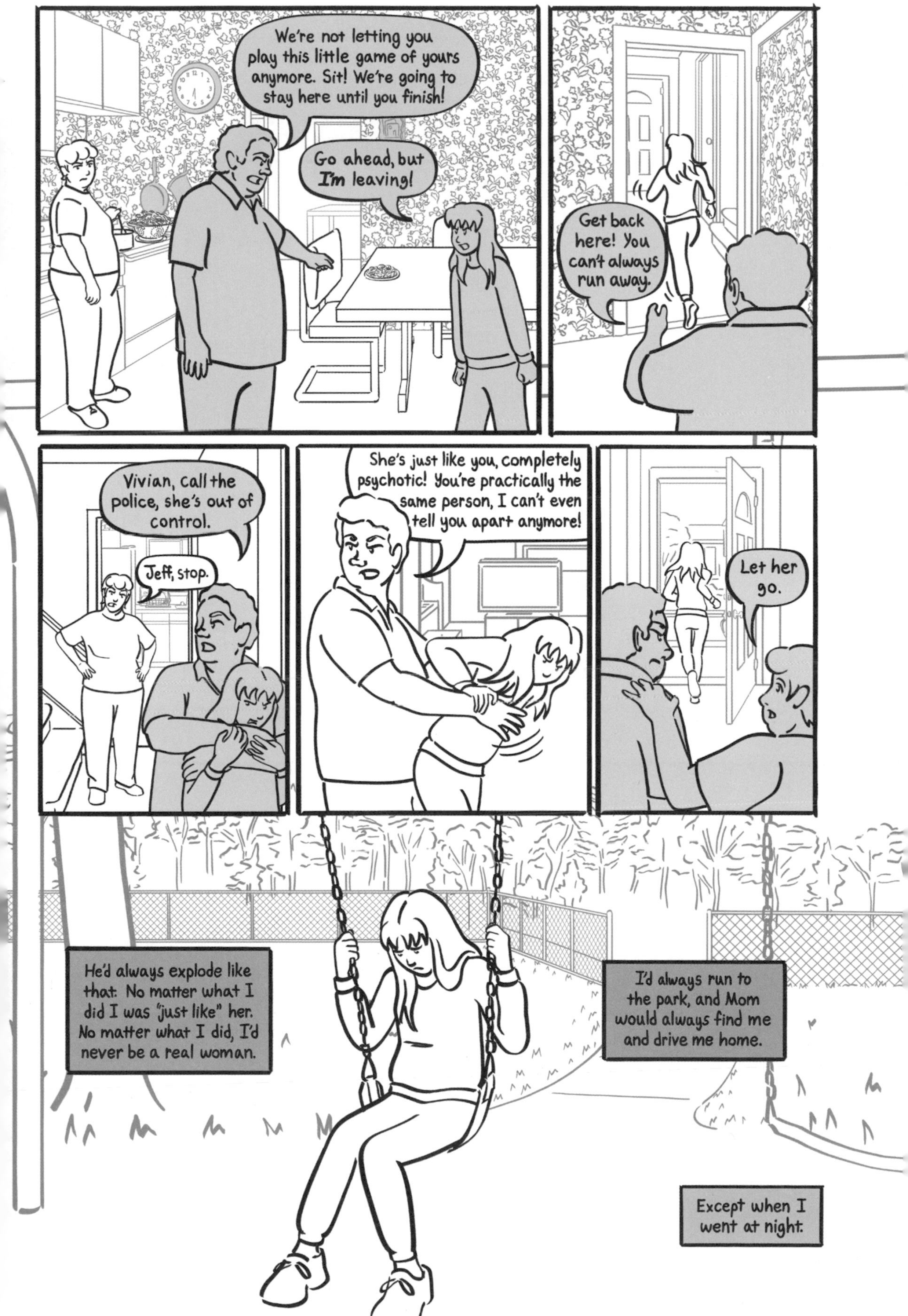
We're not letting you play this little game of yours anymore. Sit! We're going to stay here until you finish!
Go ahead, but I'm leaving!
Get back here! You can't always run away.
Vivian, call the police, she's out of control.
Jeff, stop.
She's just like you, completely psychotic! You're practically the same person, I can't even tell you apart anymore!
Let her go.
He'd always explode like that. No matter what I did I was "just like" her. No matter what I did, I'd never be a real woman.
I'd always run to the park, and Mom would always find me and drive me home.
Except when I went at night.

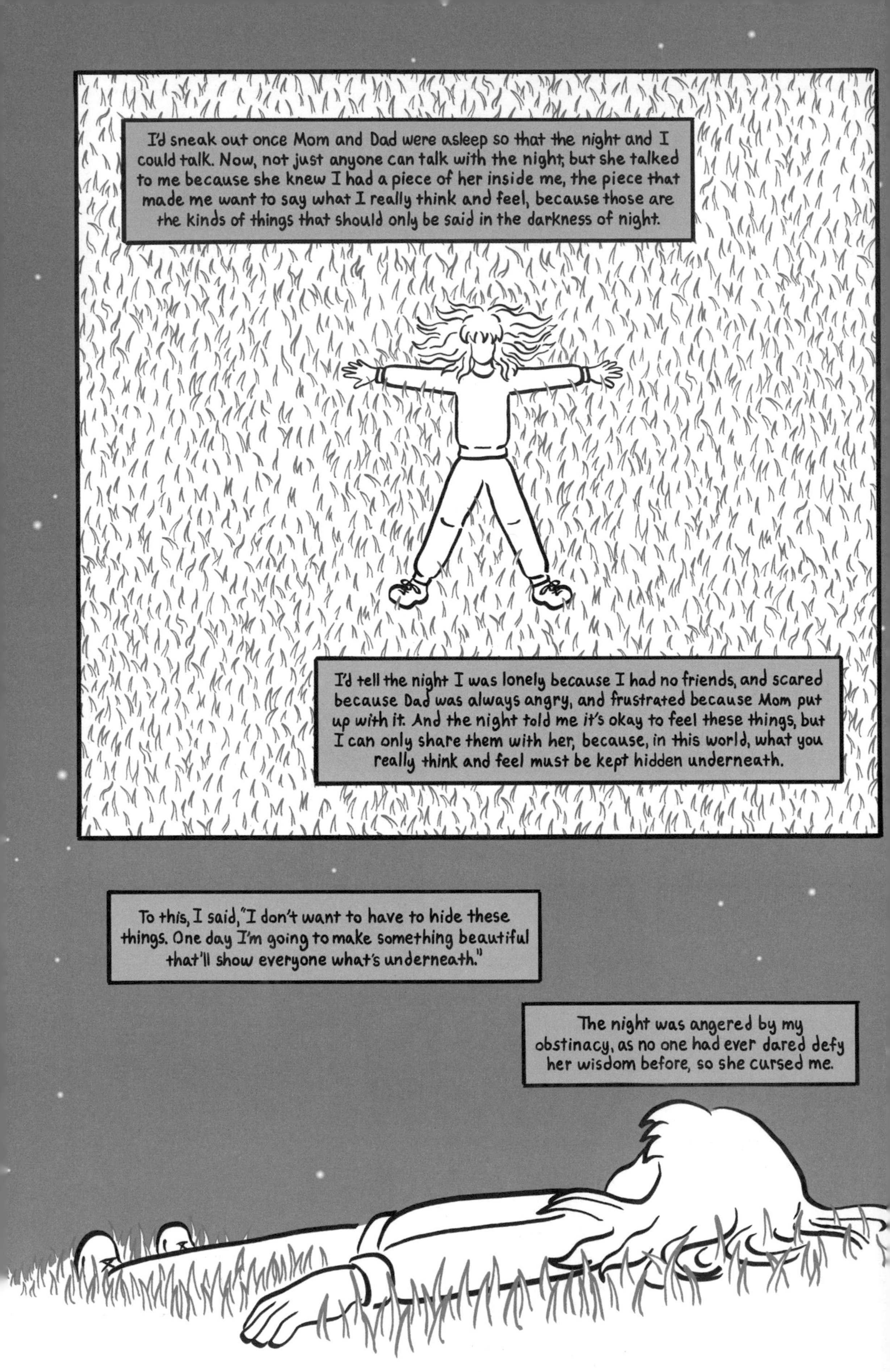
I'd sneak out once Mom and Dad were asleep so that the night and I could talk. Now, not just anyone can talk with the night, but she talked to me because she knew I had a piece of her inside me, the piece that made me want to say what I really think and feel, because those are the kinds of things that should only be said in the darkness of night.
I'd tell the night I was lonely because I had no friends, and scared because Dad was always angry, and frustrated because Mom put up with it. And the night told me it's okay to feel these things, but I can only share them with her, because, in this world, what you really think and feel must be kept hidden underneath.
To this, I said, "I don't want to have to hide these things. One day I'm going to make something beautiful that'll show everyone what's underneath."
The night was angered by my obstinacy, as no one had ever dared defy her wisdom before, so she cursed me.

But I didn't know it then. And I didn't know it on that afternoon, when I got home from school and Mom told me we were going to see a special doctor at an "adolescent medicine" clinic in Queens. The doctor there told me that my weight was dangerously low and that there were ketones in my urine. Then he told Mom she needed to take me to the children's hospital next door.

I don't know what Mom was expecting, but that wasn't it. As we left, she looked so distraught, I tried to say something to distract her.

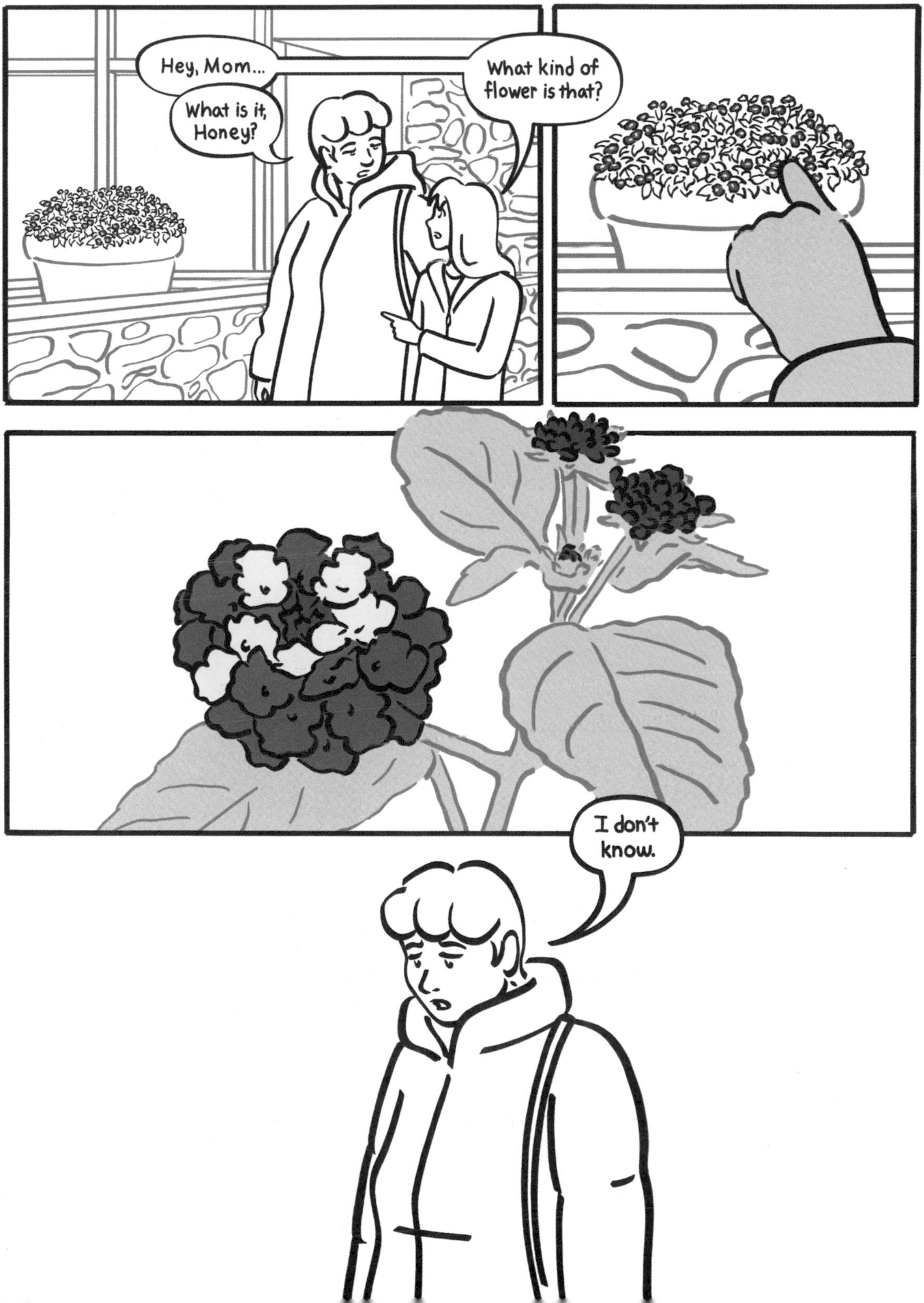
Hey, Mom...
What is it, Honey?
What kind of flower is that?
I don't know.

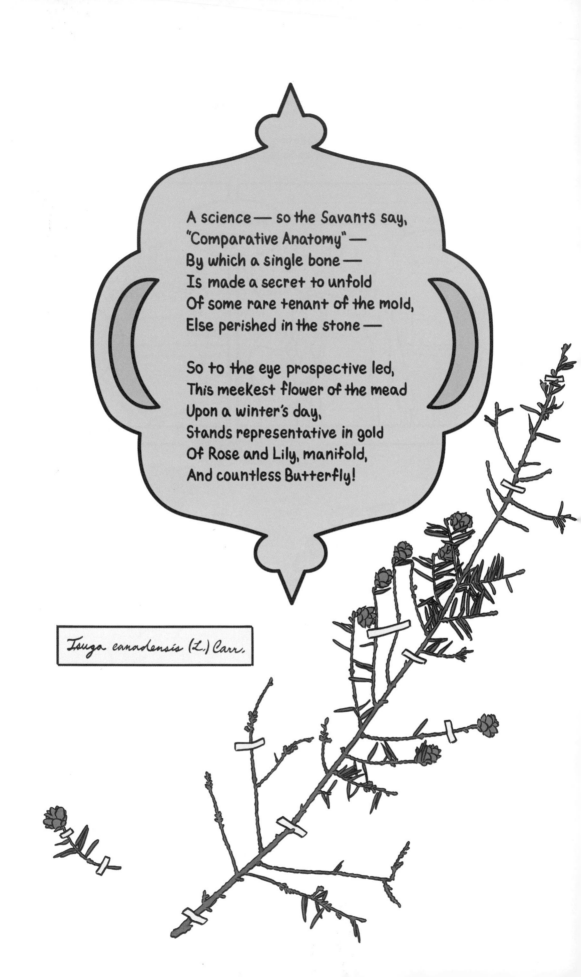

A science — so the Savants say,
"Comparative Anatomy" —
By which a single bone —
Is made a secret to unfold
Of some rare tenant of the mold,
Else perished in the stone —

So to the eye prospective led,
This meekest flower of the mead
Upon a winter's day,
Stands representative in gold
Of Rose and Lily, manifold,
And countless Butterfly!

Tsuga canadensis (L.) Carr.

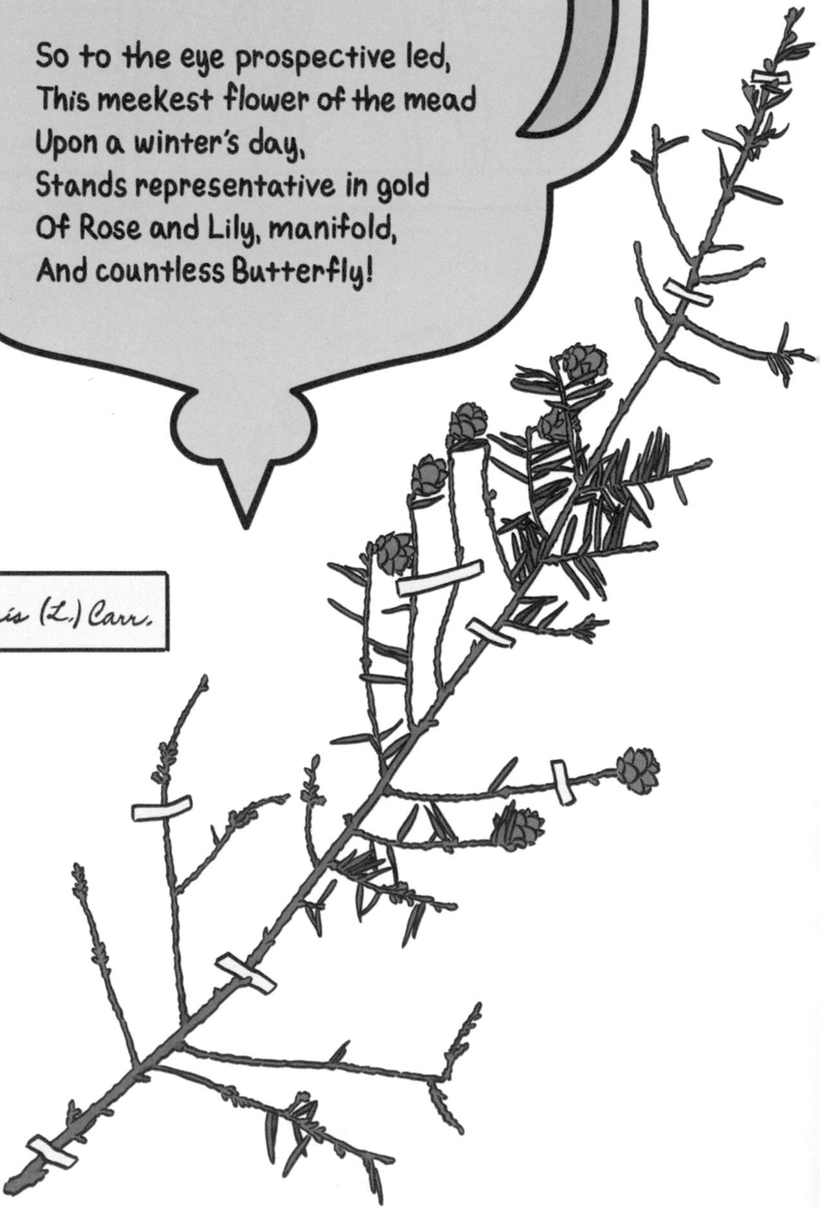

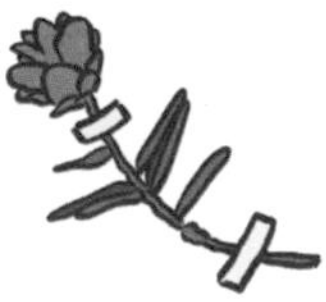

Chapter
2

The Book of Numbers

On the day of my clinic visit, I hadn't eaten for two days, so my memory of that afternoon is a bit hazy — yet little details remain sharp amidst the blur: The piece of bread I ate (and immediately regretted) right before we left the house because I felt like I was going to black out. The doctor's pudgy fingers sliding the weights on the clinic scale. And Mom's words as we got into the car, just after the doctor had told her to take me to the hospital: "Maybe we should go home." I replied, "That doesn't seem like a very good idea." It wasn't that I was still scared I was gonna black out. In fact, I was feeling the opposite of fear. The prospect of a hospital stay was very much welcome. I'd get a night off from my parents' yelling, and I'd get to meet a bunch of exciting new people — the doctors!

I liked doctors—they were adults, and adults are easy to talk to. Kids—not so much, as witnessed by my interactions at the countless ceramic-disco-pizza birthday parties I attended (They were all the rage):

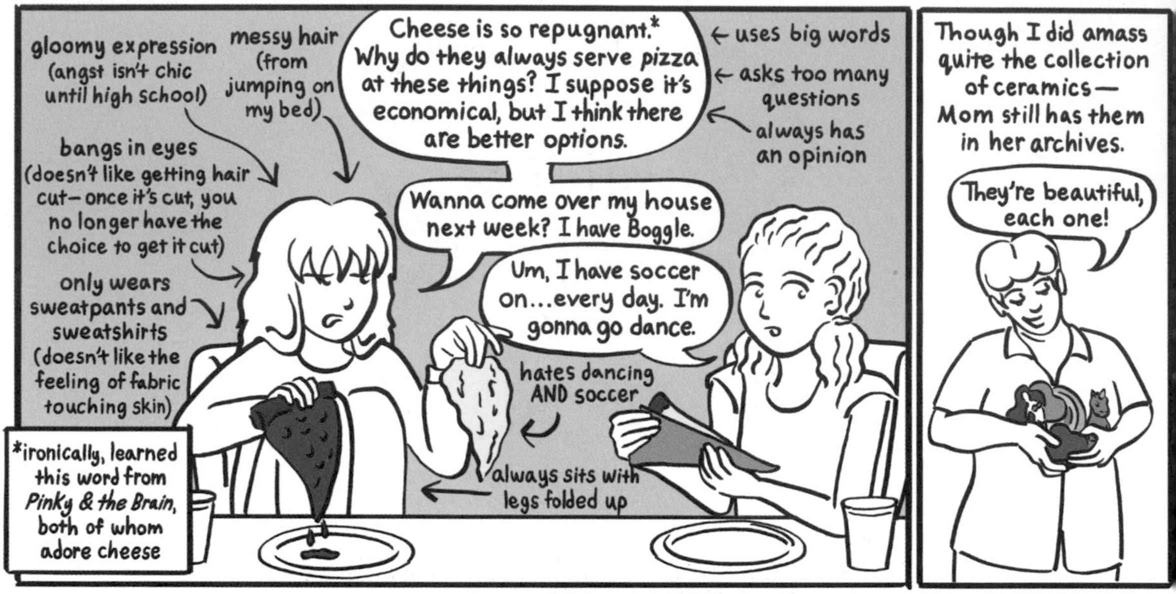

gloomy expression (angst isn't chic until high school)
messy hair (from jumping on my bed)
Cheese is so repugnant.* Why do they always serve *pizza* at these things? I suppose it's economical, but I think there are better options.
← uses big words
← asks too many questions
← always has an opinion
bangs in eyes (doesn't like getting hair cut—once it's cut, you no longer have the choice to get it cut)
Wanna come over my house next week? I have Boggle.
only wears sweatpants and sweatshirts (doesn't like the feeling of fabric touching skin)
Um, I have soccer on...every day. I'm gonna go dance.
hates dancing AND soccer
always sits with legs folded up
*ironically, learned this word from *Pinky & the Brain*, both of whom adore cheese
Though I did amass quite the collection of ceramics—Mom still has them in her archives.
They're beautiful, each one!

The only adult I did have a hard time talking with was Dad. He busted my balls about all the adorable quirks that made me such a hit with the kids.

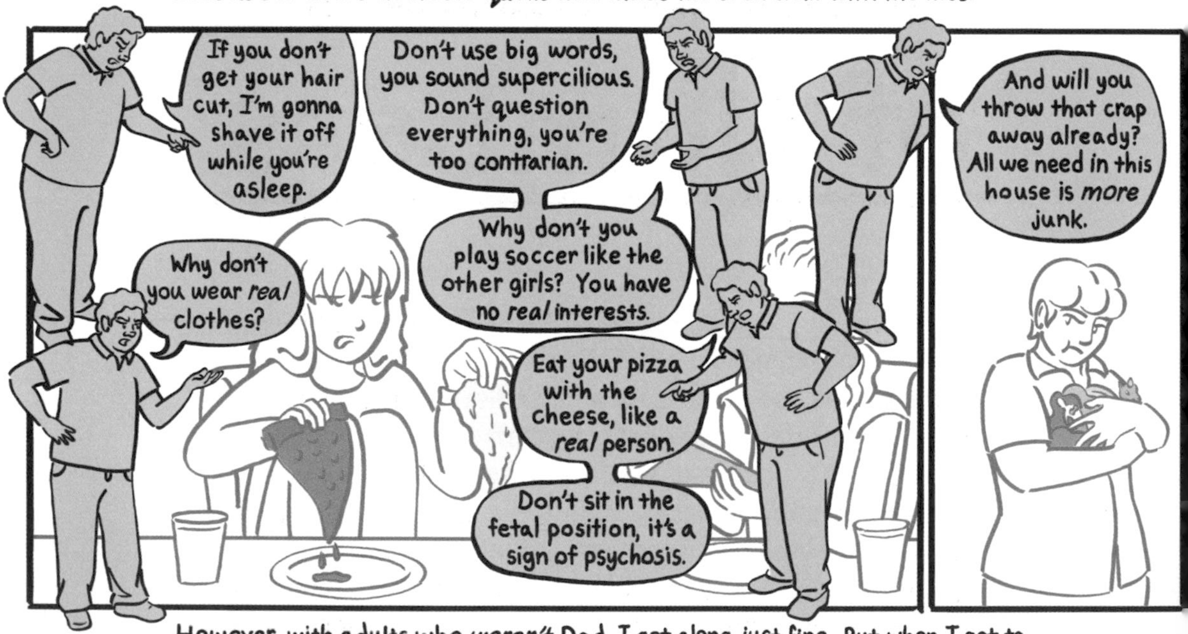

If you don't get your hair cut, I'm gonna shave it off while you're asleep.
Don't use big words, you sound supercilious. Don't question everything, you're too contrarian.
Why don't you wear *real* clothes?
Why don't you play soccer like the other girls? You have no *real* interests.
Eat your pizza with the cheese, like a *real* person.
Don't sit in the fetal position, it's a sign of psychosis.
And will you throw that crap away already? All we need in this house is *more* junk.

However, with adults who *weren't* Dad, I got along just fine. But when I got to the hospital, I didn't get to talk to any adults. All I got was dinner.

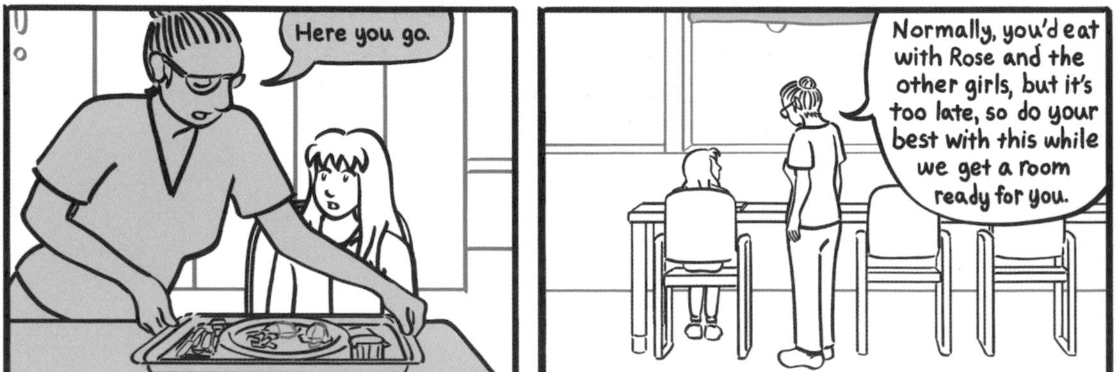

Here you go.
Normally, you'd eat with Rose and the other girls, but it's too late, so do your best with this while we get a room ready for you.

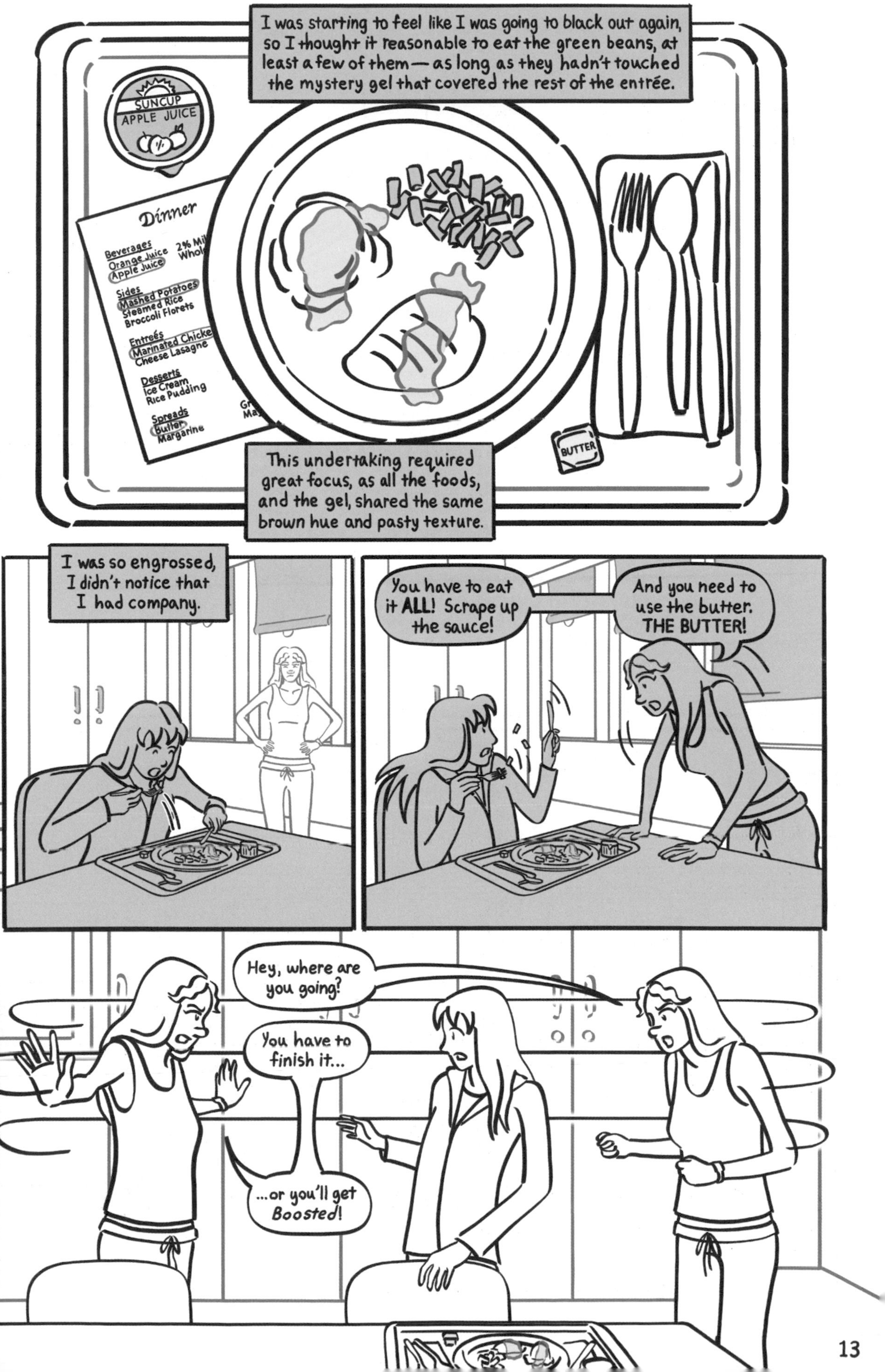

I was starting to feel like I was going to black out again, so I thought it reasonable to eat the green beans, at least a few of them—as long as they hadn't touched the mystery gel that covered the rest of the entrée.
SUNCUP
APPLE JUICE
Dinner
Beverages
Orange Juice
Apple Juice
Sides
Mashed Potatoes
Steamed Rice
Broccoli Florets
Entreés
Cheese Lasagne
Desserts
Ice Cream
Rice Pudding
Spreads
Butter
Margarine
BUTTER
This undertaking required great focus, as all the foods, and the gel, shared the same brown hue and pasty texture.
I was so engrossed, I didn't notice that I had company.
You have to eat it ALL! Scrape up the sauce!
And you need to use the butter. THE BUTTER!
Hey, where are you going?
You have to finish it...
...or you'll get *Boosted*!

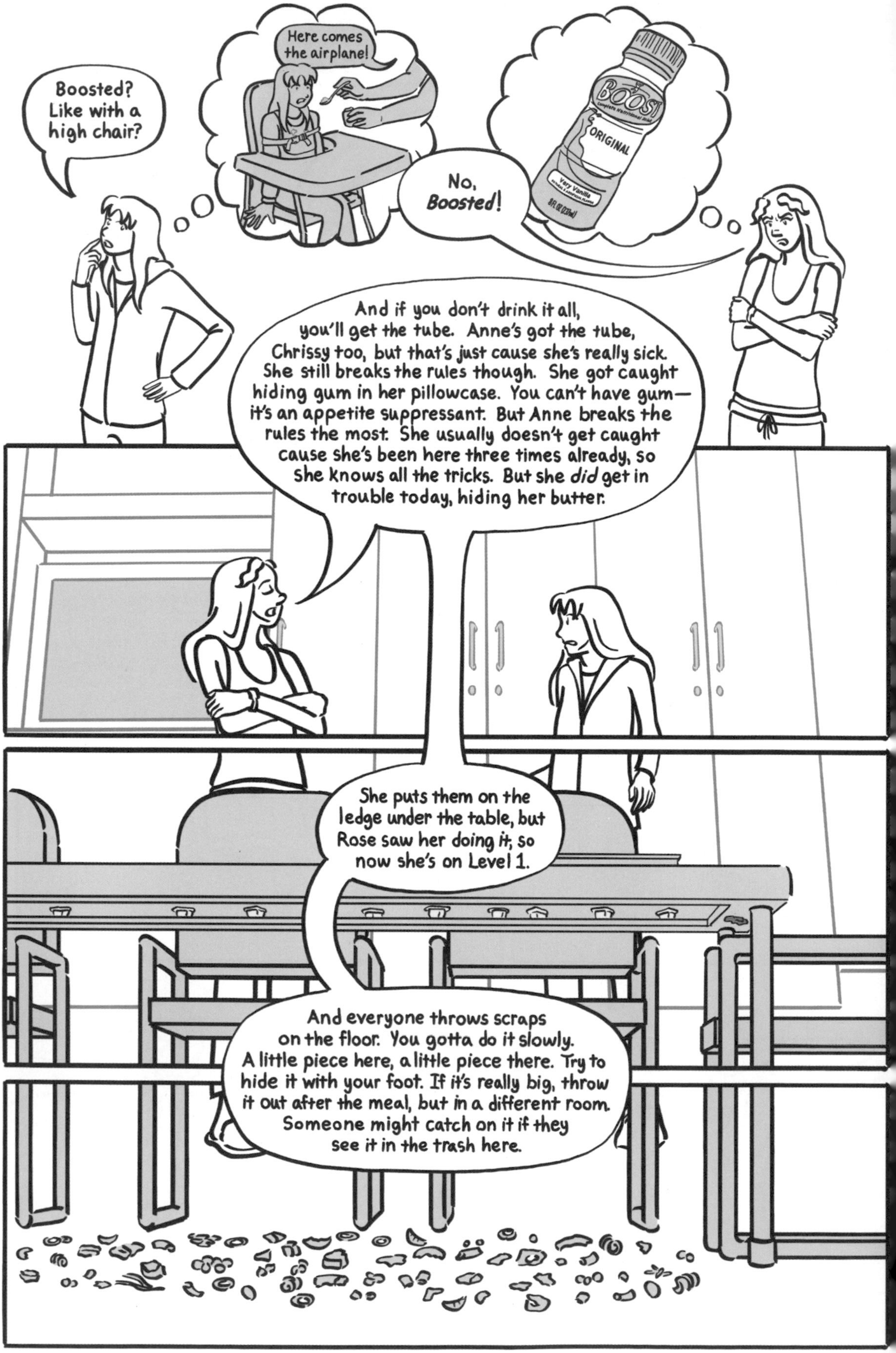
Boosted? Like with a high chair?
Here comes the airplane!
No, *Boosted*!
BOOST
ORIGINAL
Very Vanilla
And if you don't drink it all, you'll get the tube. Anne's got the tube, Chrissy too, but that's just cause she's really sick. She still breaks the rules though. She got caught hiding gum in her pillowcase. You can't have gum—it's an appetite suppressant. But Anne breaks the rules the most. She usually doesn't get caught cause she's been here three times already, so she knows all the tricks. But she *did* get in trouble today, hiding her butter.
She puts them on the ledge under the table, but Rose saw her doing *it*, so now she's on Level 1.
And everyone throws scraps on the floor. You gotta do it slowly. A little piece here, a little piece there. Try to hide it with your foot. If it's really big, throw it out after the meal, but in a different room. Someone might catch on it if they see it in the trash here.

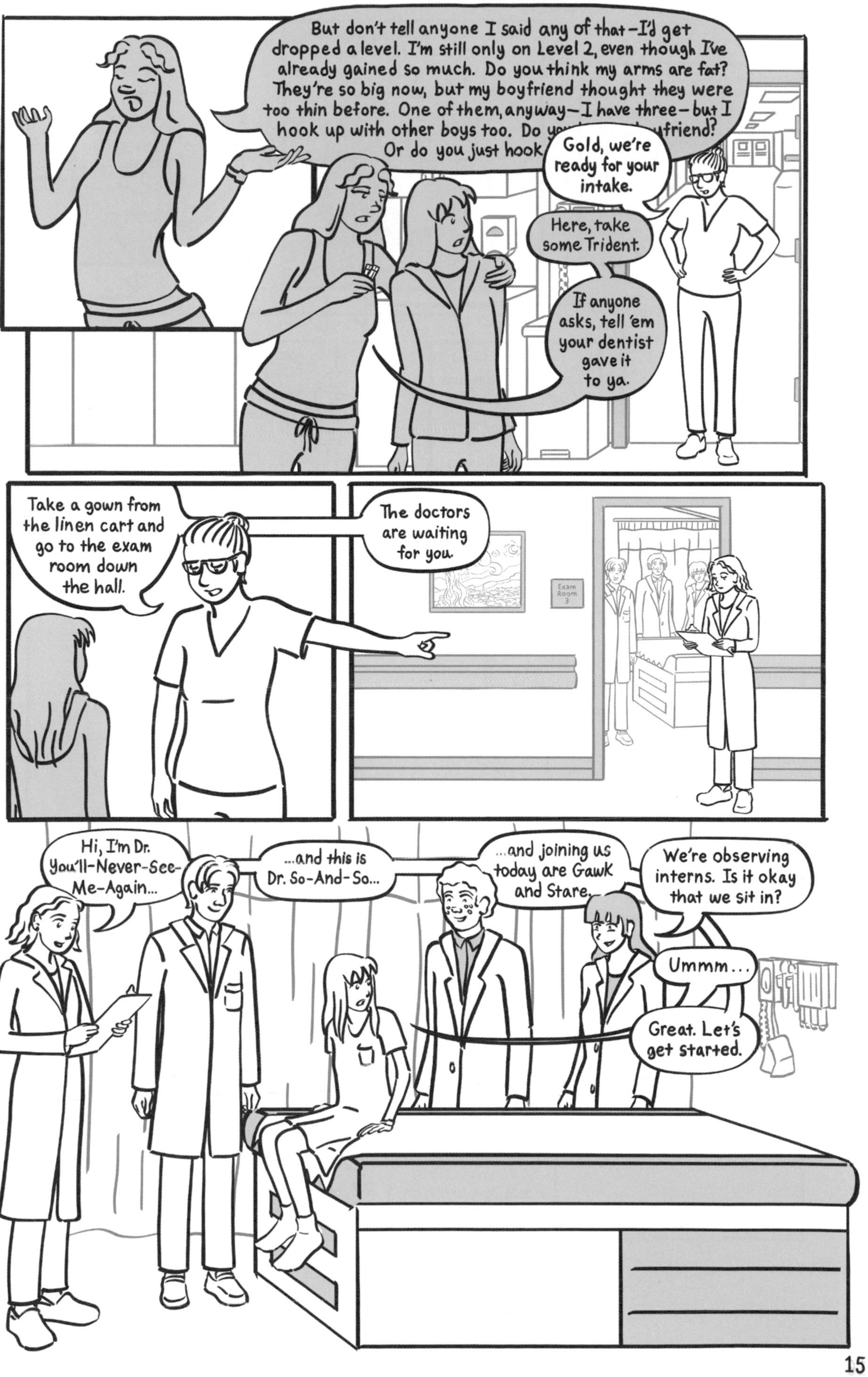

But don't tell anyone I said any of that—I'd get dropped a level. I'm still only on Level 2, even though I've already gained so much. Do you think my arms are fat? They're so big now, but my boyfriend thought they were too thin before. One of them, anyway—I have three—but I hook up with other boys too. Do yo ufriend? Or do you just hook
Gold, we're ready for your intake.
Here, take some Trident.
If anyone asks, tell 'em your dentist gave it to ya.
Take a gown from the linen cart and go to the exam room down the hall.
The doctors are waiting for you.
Exam Room 3
Hi, I'm Dr. You'll-Never-See-Me-Again...
...and this is Dr. So-And-So...
...and joining us today are Gawk and Stare...
We're observing interns. Is it okay that we sit in?
Ummm...
Great. Let's get started.

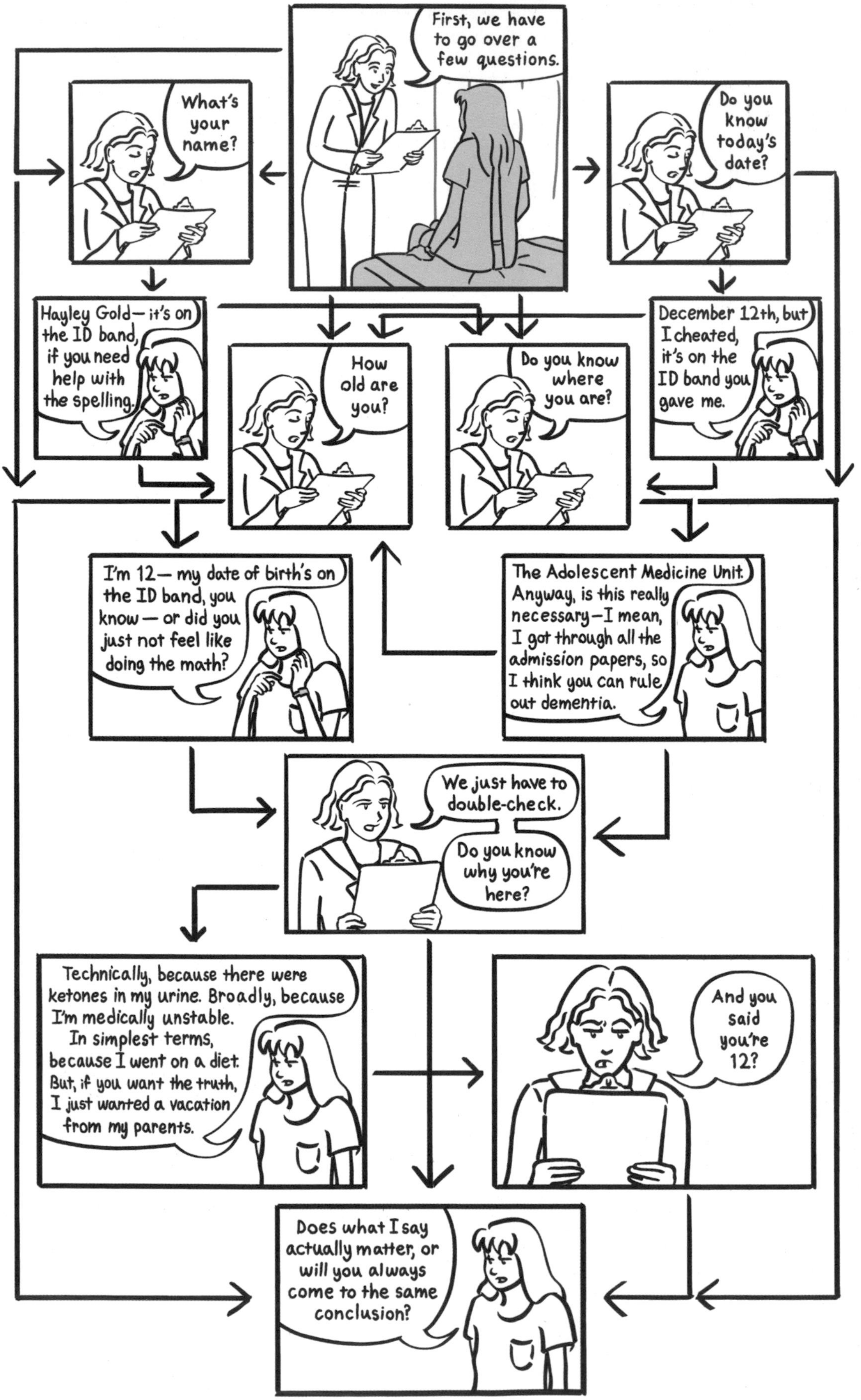
First, we have to go over a few questions.
What's your name?
Hayley Gold— it's on the ID band, if you need help with the spelling.
Do you know today's date?
December 12th, but I cheated, it's on the ID band you gave me.
How old are you?
Do you know where you are?
I'm 12— my date of birth's on the ID band, you know— or did you just not feel like doing the math?
The Adolescent Medicine Unit. Anyway, is this really necessary—I mean, I got through all the admission papers, so I think you can rule out dementia.
We just have to double-check.
Do you know why you're here?
Technically, because there were ketones in my urine. Broadly, because I'm medically unstable. In simplest terms, because I went on a diet. But, if you want the truth, I just wanted a vacation from my parents.
And you said you're 12?
Does what I say actually matter, or will you always come to the same conclusion?

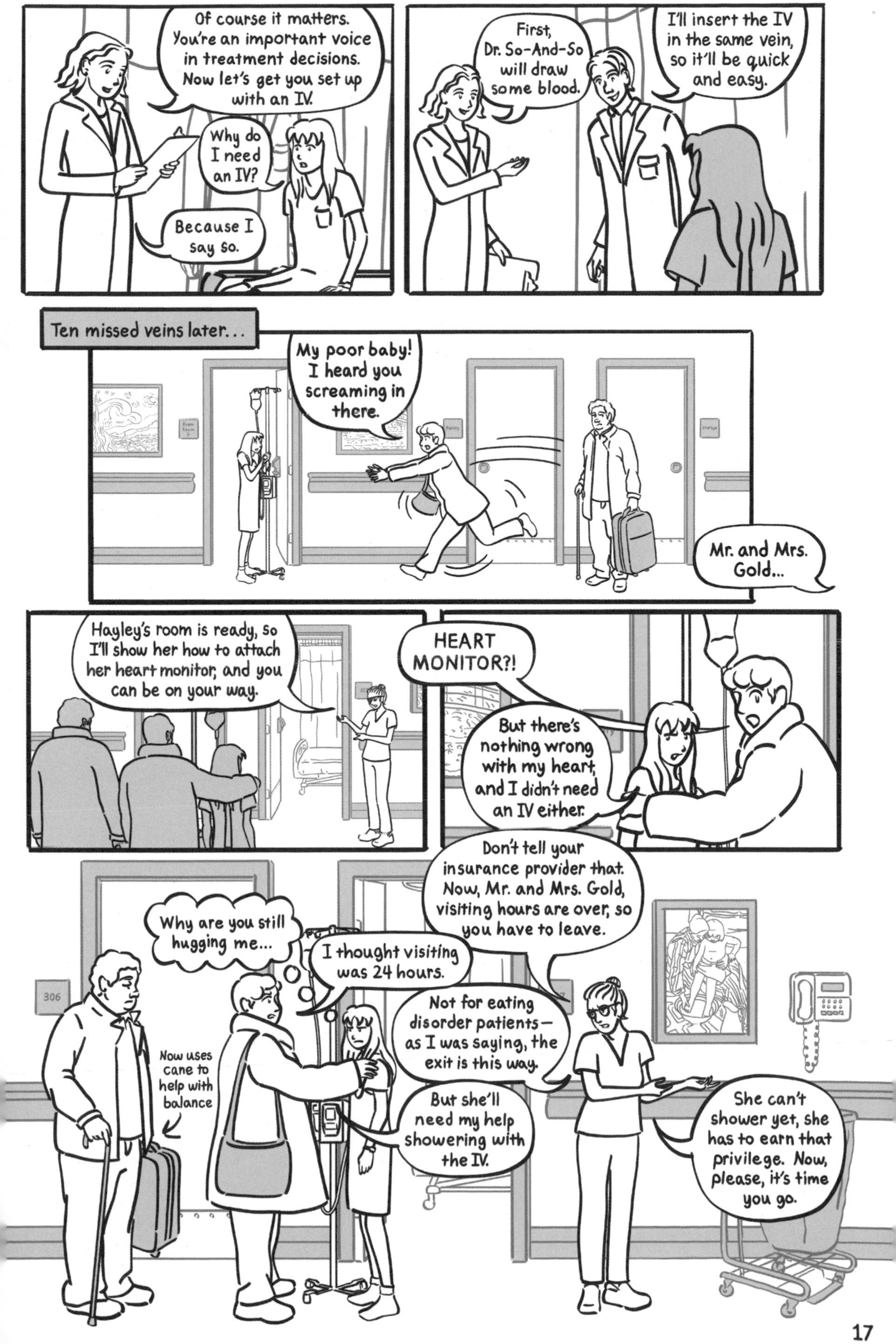

Of course it matters. You're an important voice in treatment decisions. Now let's get you set up with an IV.
Why do I need an IV?
Because I say so.
First, Dr. So-And-So will draw some blood.
I'll insert the IV in the same vein, so it'll be quick and easy.
Ten missed veins later...
My poor baby! I heard you screaming in there.
Mr. and Mrs. Gold...
Hayley's room is ready, so I'll show her how to attach her heart monitor, and you can be on your way.
HEART MONITOR?!
But there's nothing wrong with my heart, and I didn't need an IV either.
Don't tell your insurance provider that. Now, Mr. and Mrs. Gold, visiting hours are over, so you have to leave.
Why are you still hugging me...
I thought visiting was 24 hours.
Not for eating disorder patients— as I was saying, the exit is this way.
306
Now uses cane to help with balance
But she'll need my help showering with the IV.
She can't shower yet, she has to earn that privilege. Now, please, it's time you go.

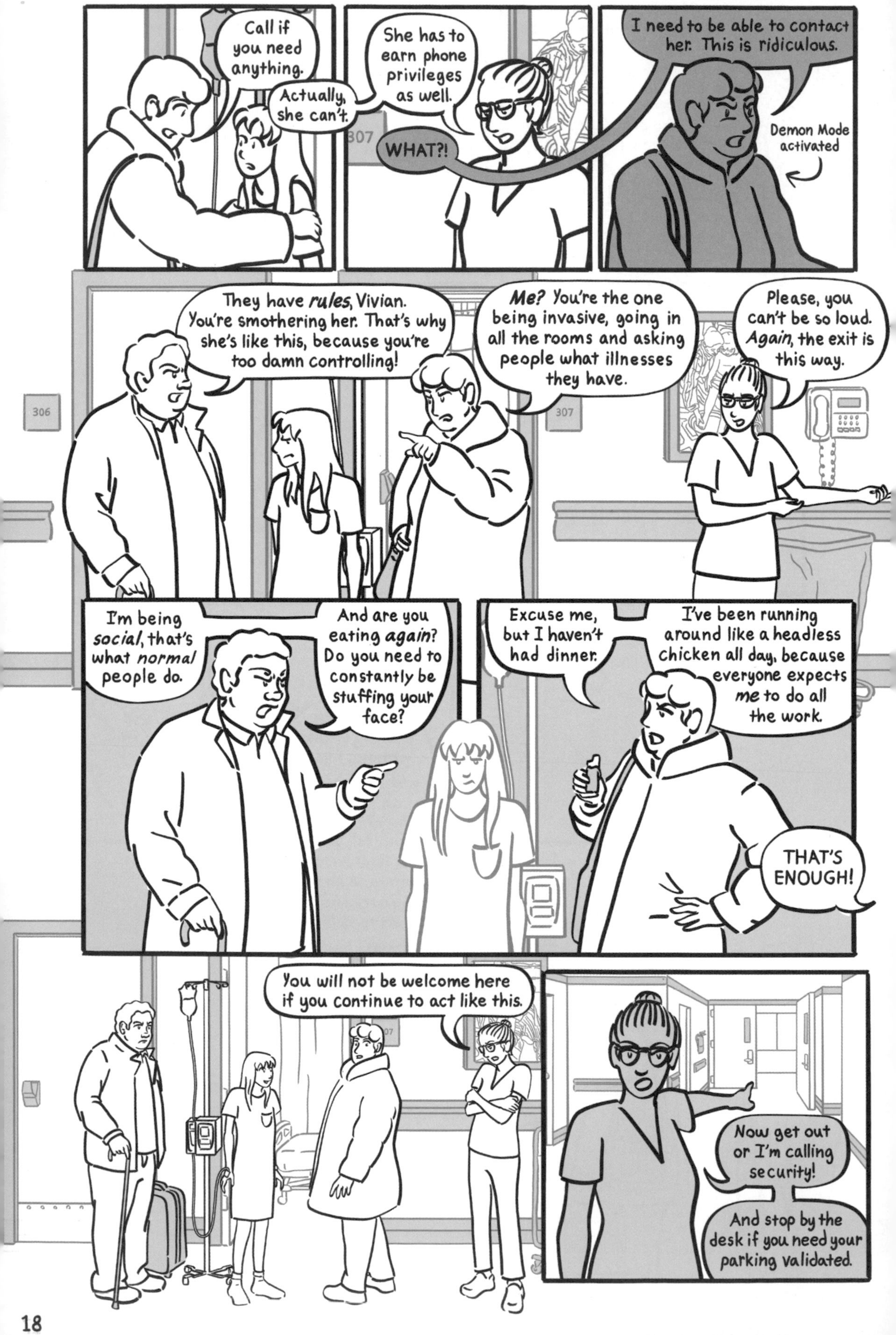

Call if you need anything.
Actually, she can't.
She has to earn phone privileges as well.
WHAT?!
I need to be able to contact her. This is ridiculous.
Demon Mode activated
They have rules, Vivian. You're smothering her. That's why she's like this, because you're too damn controlling!
Me? You're the one being invasive, going in all the rooms and asking people what illnesses they have.
Please, you can't be so loud. Again, the exit is this way.
I'm being social, that's what normal people do.
And are you eating again? Do you need to constantly be stuffing your face?
Excuse me, but I haven't had dinner.
I've been running around like a headless chicken all day, because everyone expects me to do all the work.
THAT'S ENOUGH!
You will not be welcome here if you continue to act like this.
Now get out or I'm calling security!
And stop by the desk if you need your parking validated.

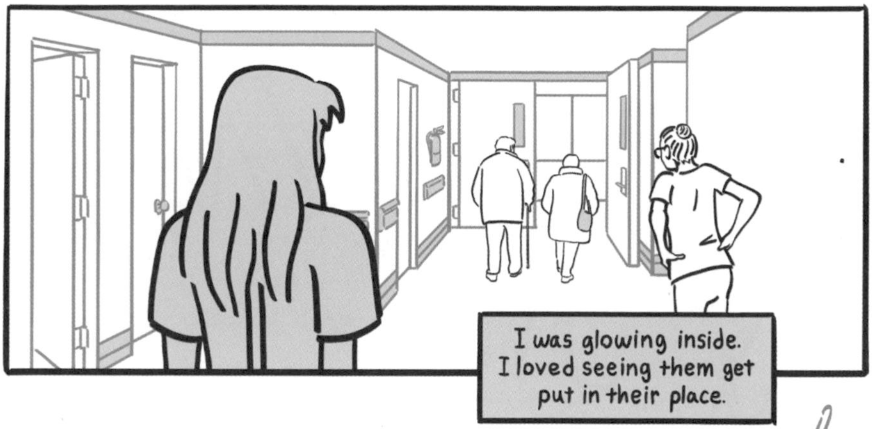
I was glowing inside. I loved seeing them get put in their place.

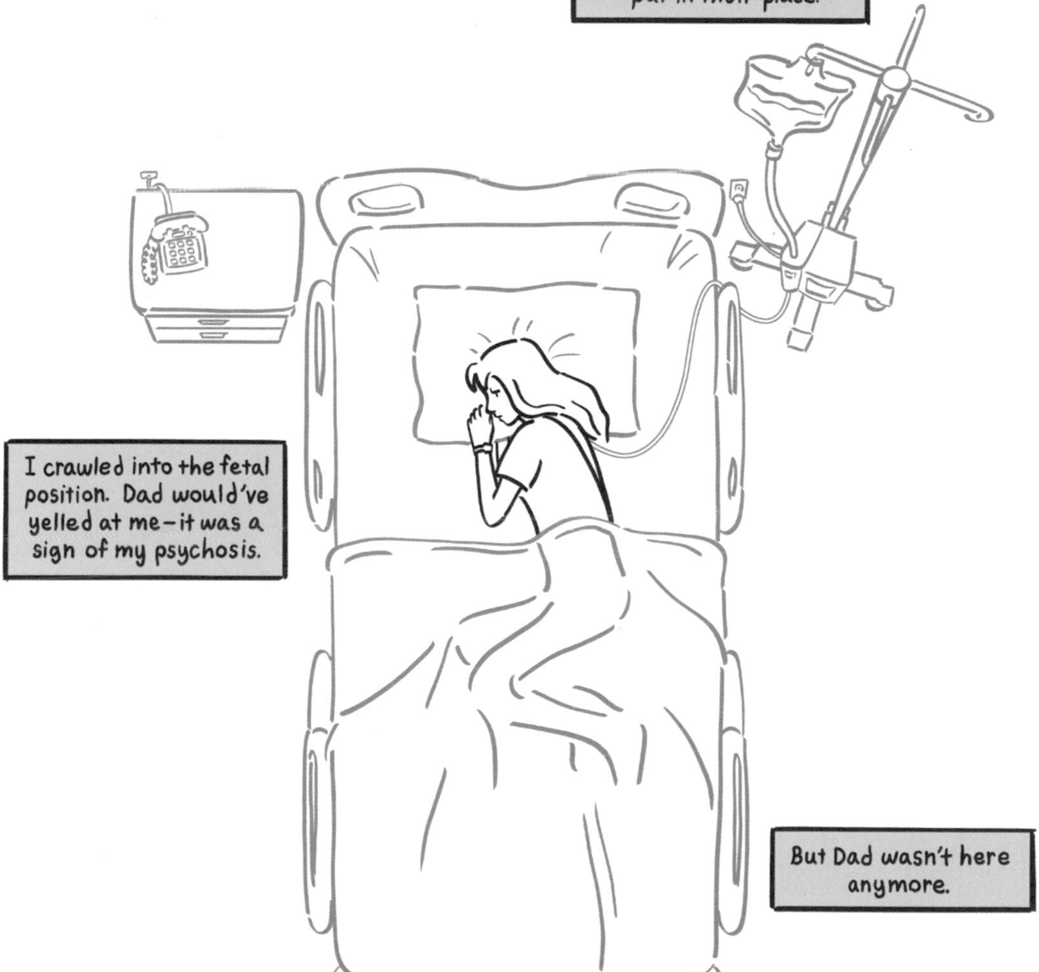
I crawled into the fetal position. Dad would've yelled at me—it was a sign of my psychosis.
But Dad wasn't here anymore.

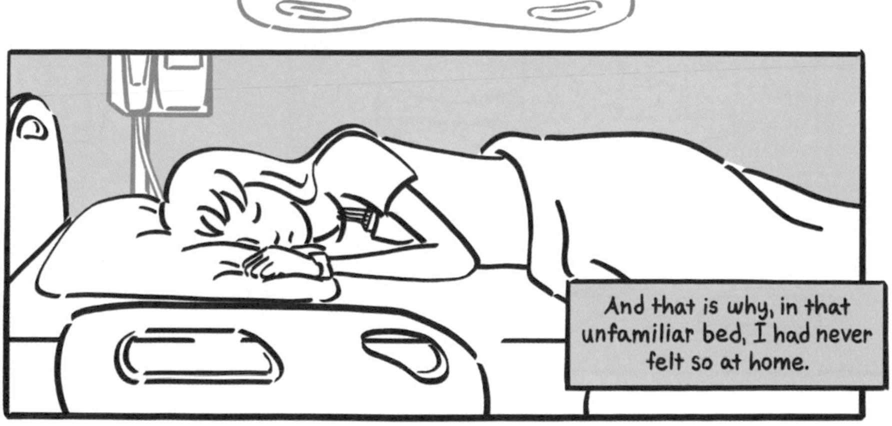
And that is why, in that unfamiliar bed, I had never felt so at home.

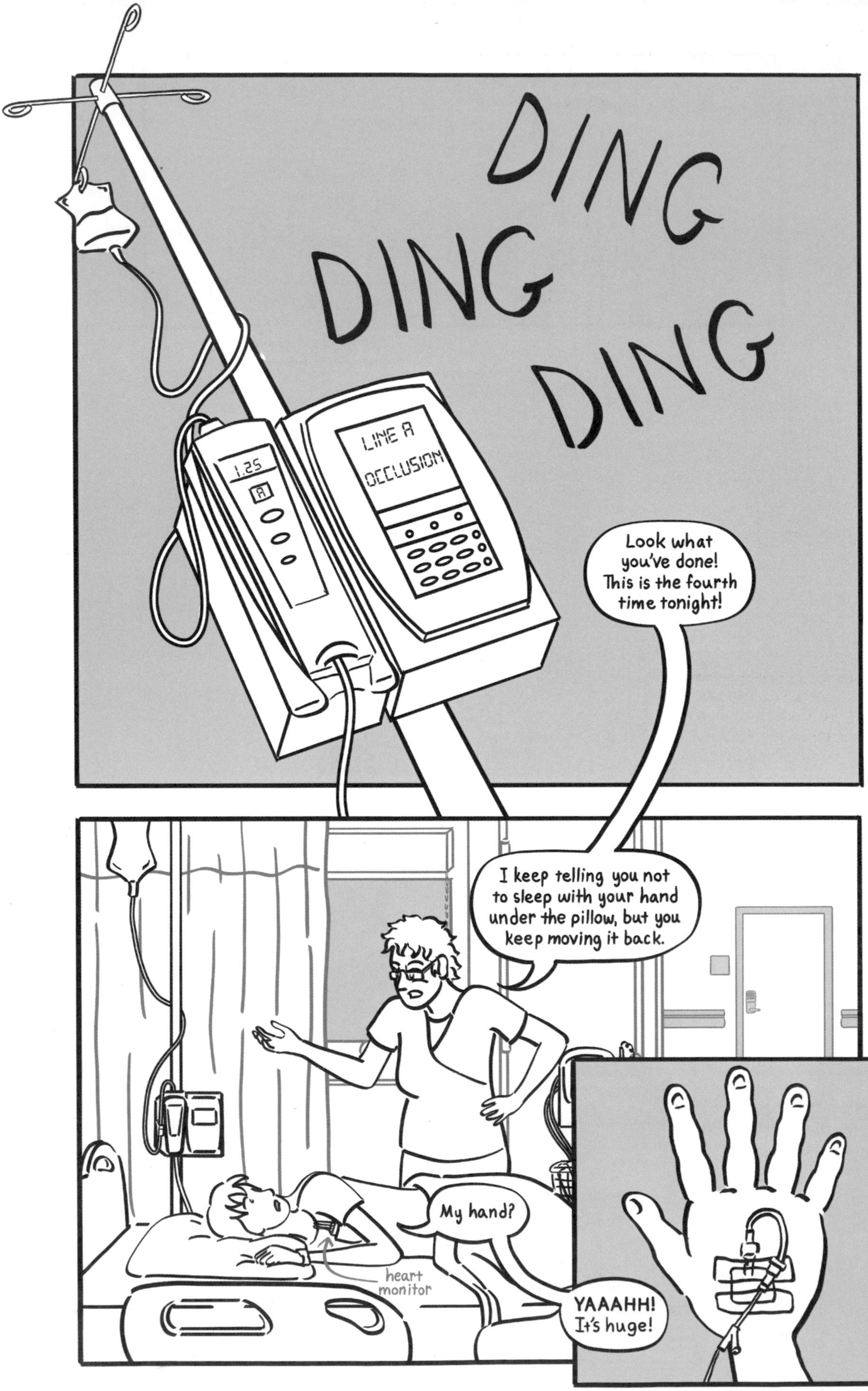
DING
DING
DING
LINE A
OCCLUSION
1.25
A
Look what you've done! This is the fourth time tonight!
I keep telling you not to sleep with your hand under the pillow, but you keep moving it back.
My hand?
heart monitor
YAAAHH! It's huge!

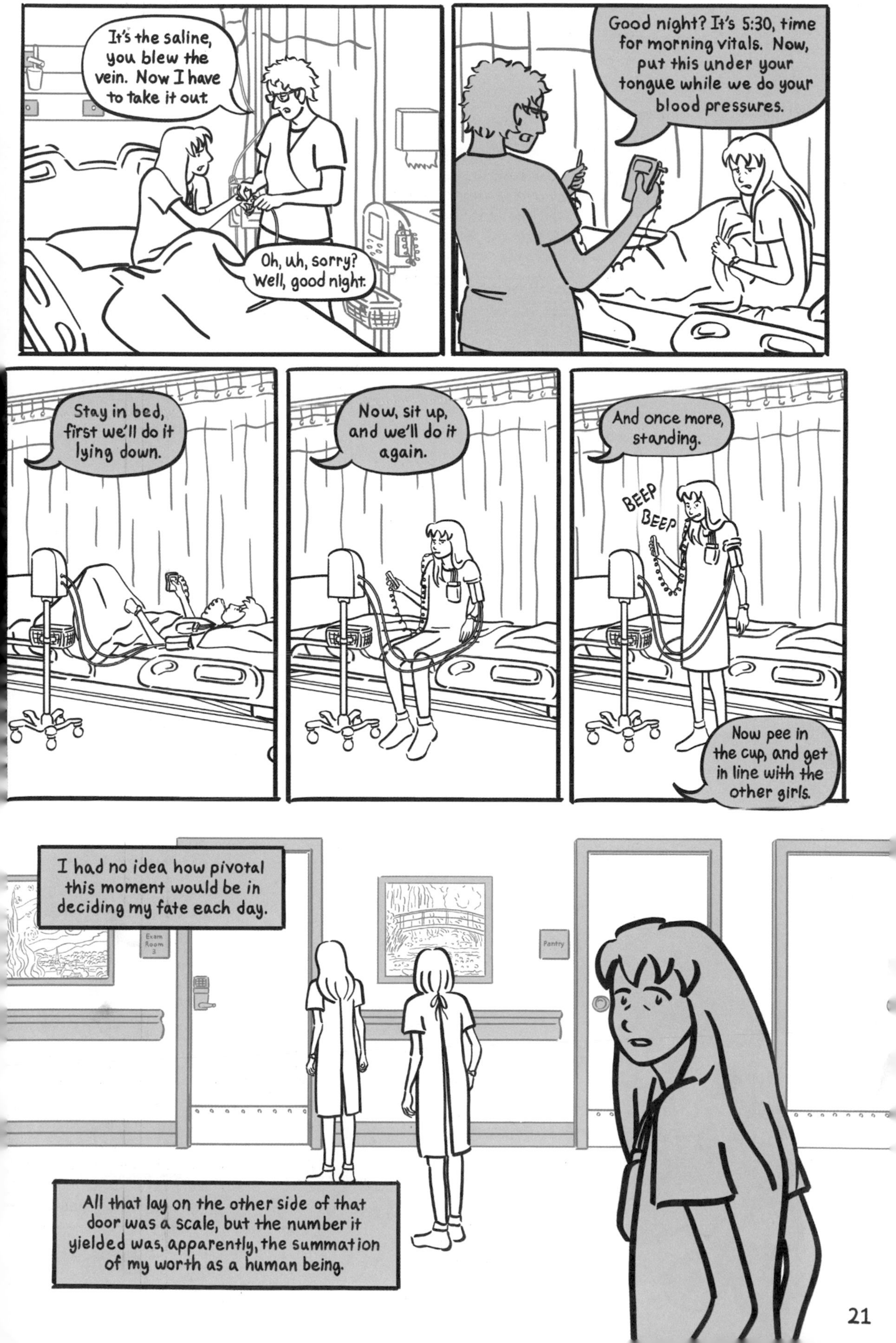
It's the saline, you blew the vein. Now I have to take it out.
Oh, uh, sorry? Well, good night.
Good night? It's 5:30, time for morning vitals. Now, put this under your tongue while we do your blood pressures.
Stay in bed, first we'll do it lying down.
Now, sit up, and we'll do it again.
And once more, standing.
BEEP
BEEP
Now pee in the cup, and get in line with the other girls.
I had no idea how pivotal this moment would be in deciding my fate each day.
Exam Room 3
Pantry
All that lay on the other side of that door was a scale, but the number it yielded was, apparently, the summation of my worth as a human being.

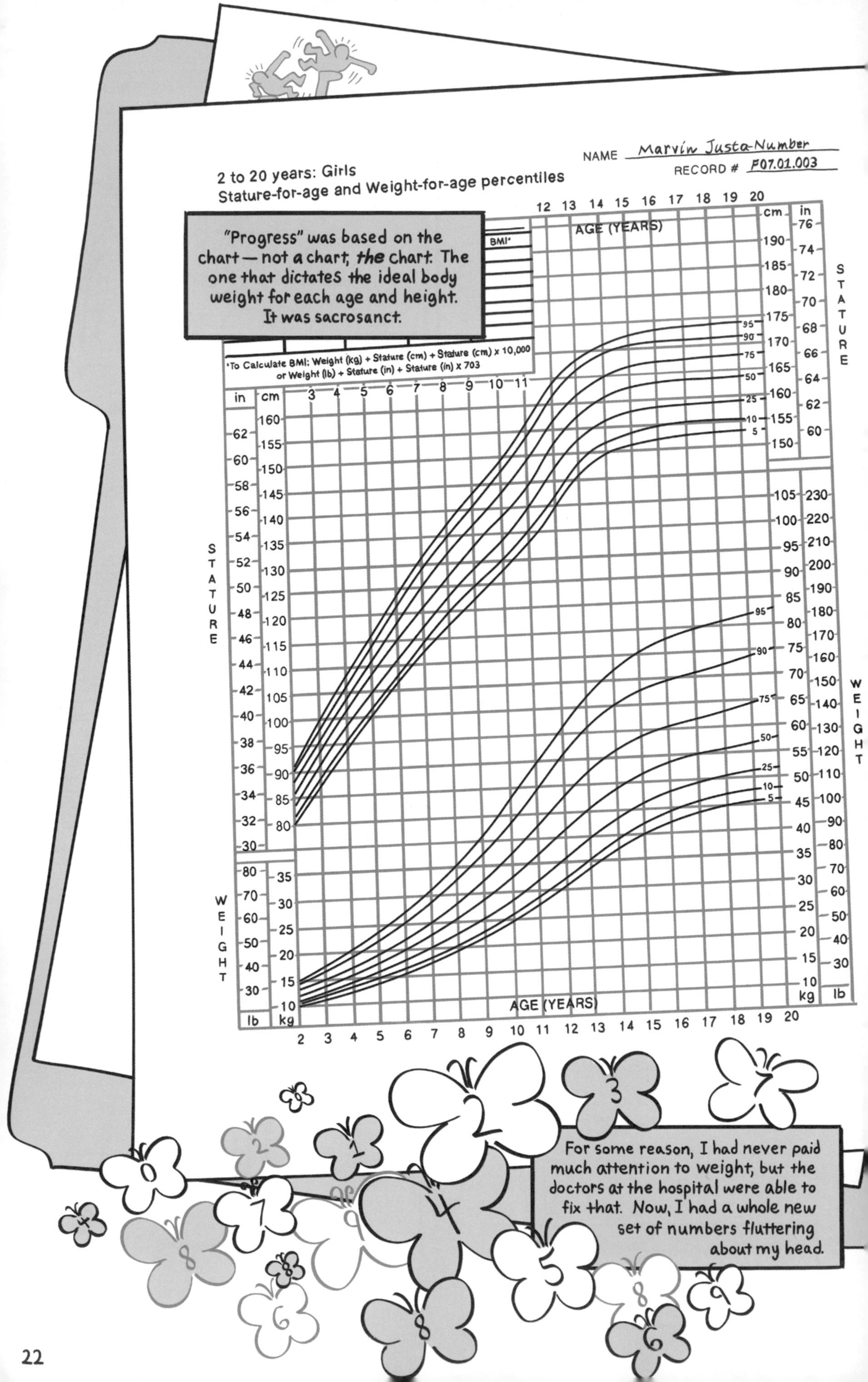
NAME Marvin Justa-Number
RECORD # F07.01.003
2 to 20 years: Girls
Stature-for-age and Weight-for-age percentiles
"Progress" was based on the chart — not a chart, *the* chart. The one that dictates the ideal body weight for each age and height. It was sacrosanct.
AGE (YEARS)
BMI*
*To Calculate BMI: Weight (kg) ÷ Stature (cm) ÷ Stature (cm) x 10,000
or Weight (lb) ÷ Stature (in) ÷ Stature (in) x 703
STATURE
WEIGHT
For some reason, I had never paid much attention to weight, but the doctors at the hospital were able to fix that. Now, I had a whole new set of numbers fluttering about my head.

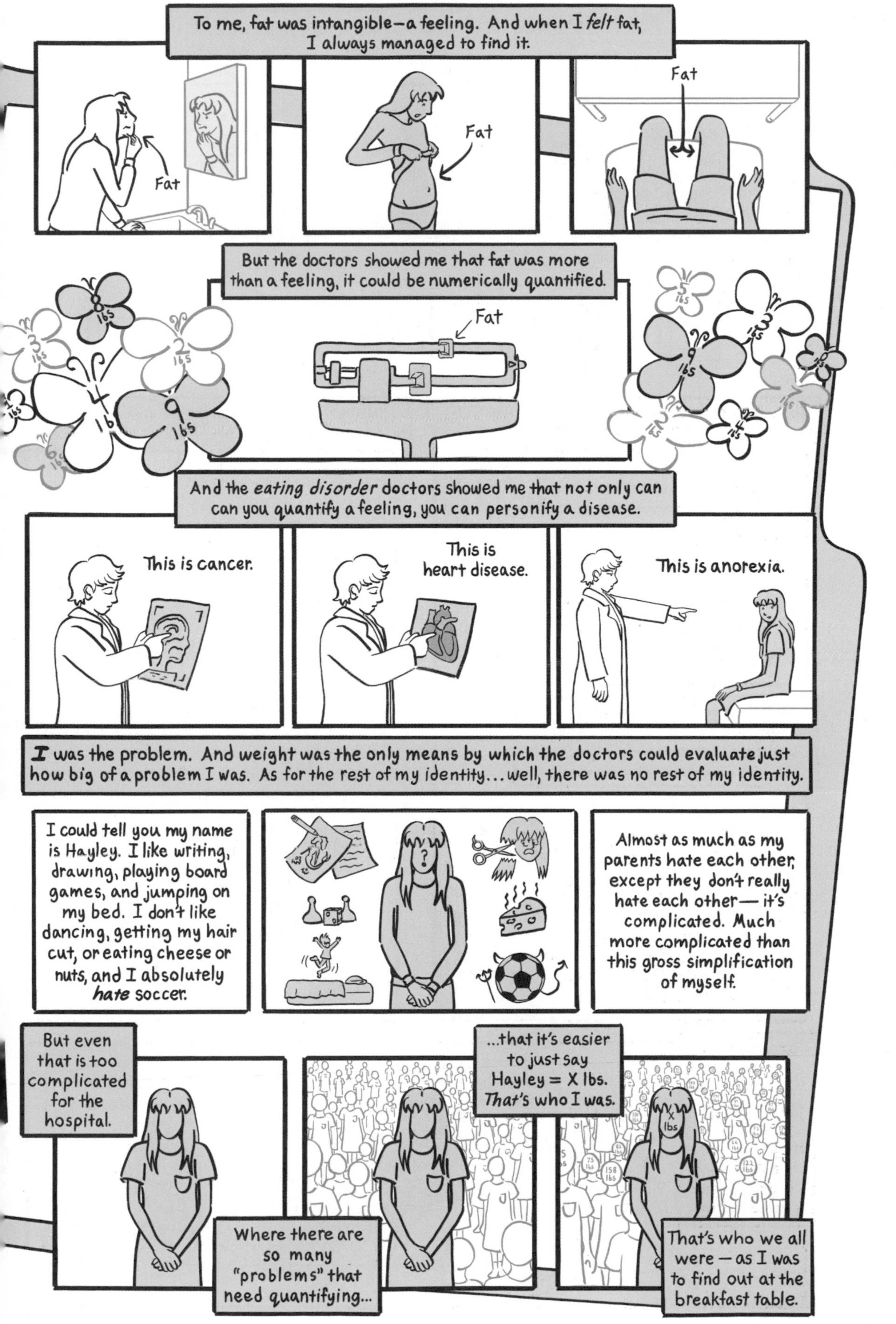
To me, fat was intangible—a feeling. And when I *felt* fat, I always managed to find it.
Fat
Fat
Fat
But the doctors showed me that fat was more than a feeling, it could be numerically quantified.
Fat
And the *eating disorder* doctors showed me that not only can can you quantify a feeling, you can personify a disease.
This is cancer.
This is heart disease.
This is anorexia.
I was the problem. And weight was the only means by which the doctors could evaluate just how big of a problem I was. As for the rest of my identity... well, there was no rest of my identity.
I could tell you my name is Hayley. I like writing, drawing, playing board games, and jumping on my bed. I don't like dancing, getting my hair cut, or eating cheese or nuts, and I absolutely *hate* soccer.
?
Almost as much as my parents hate each other, except they don't really hate each other— it's complicated. Much more complicated than this gross simplification of myself.
But even that is too complicated for the hospital.
Where there are so many "problems" that need quantifying...
...that it's easier to just say Hayley = X lbs. *That's* who I was.
X lbs
That's who we all were — as I was to find out at the breakfast table.

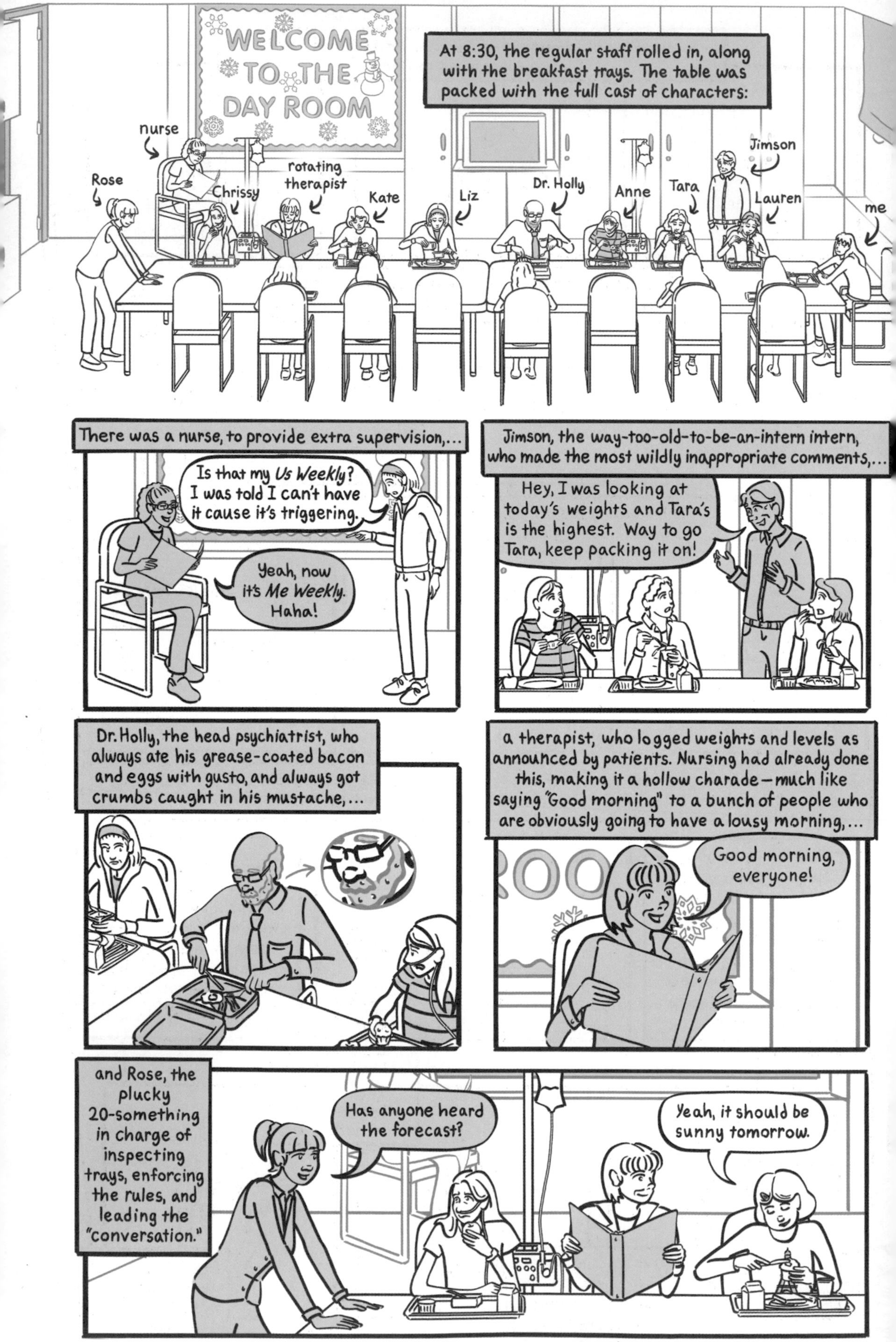
WELCOME TO THE DAY ROOM
At 8:30, the regular staff rolled in, along with the breakfast trays. The table was packed with the full cast of characters:
nurse
Rose
Chrissy
rotating therapist
Kate
Liz
Dr. Holly
Anne
Tara
Jimson
Lauren
me
There was a nurse, to provide extra supervision,...
Is that my *Us Weekly*? I was told I can't have it cause it's triggering.
Yeah, now it's *Me Weekly*. Haha!
Jimson, the way-too-old-to-be-an-intern intern, who made the most wildly inappropriate comments,...
Hey, I was looking at today's weights and Tara's is the highest. Way to go Tara, keep packing it on!
Dr. Holly, the head psychiatrist, who always ate his grease-coated bacon and eggs with gusto, and always got crumbs caught in his mustache,...
a therapist, who logged weights and levels as announced by patients. Nursing had already done this, making it a hollow charade—much like saying "Good morning" to a bunch of people who are obviously going to have a lousy morning,...
Good morning, everyone!
and Rose, the plucky 20-something in charge of inspecting trays, enforcing the rules, and leading the "conversation."
Has anyone heard the forecast?
Yeah, it should be sunny tomorrow.

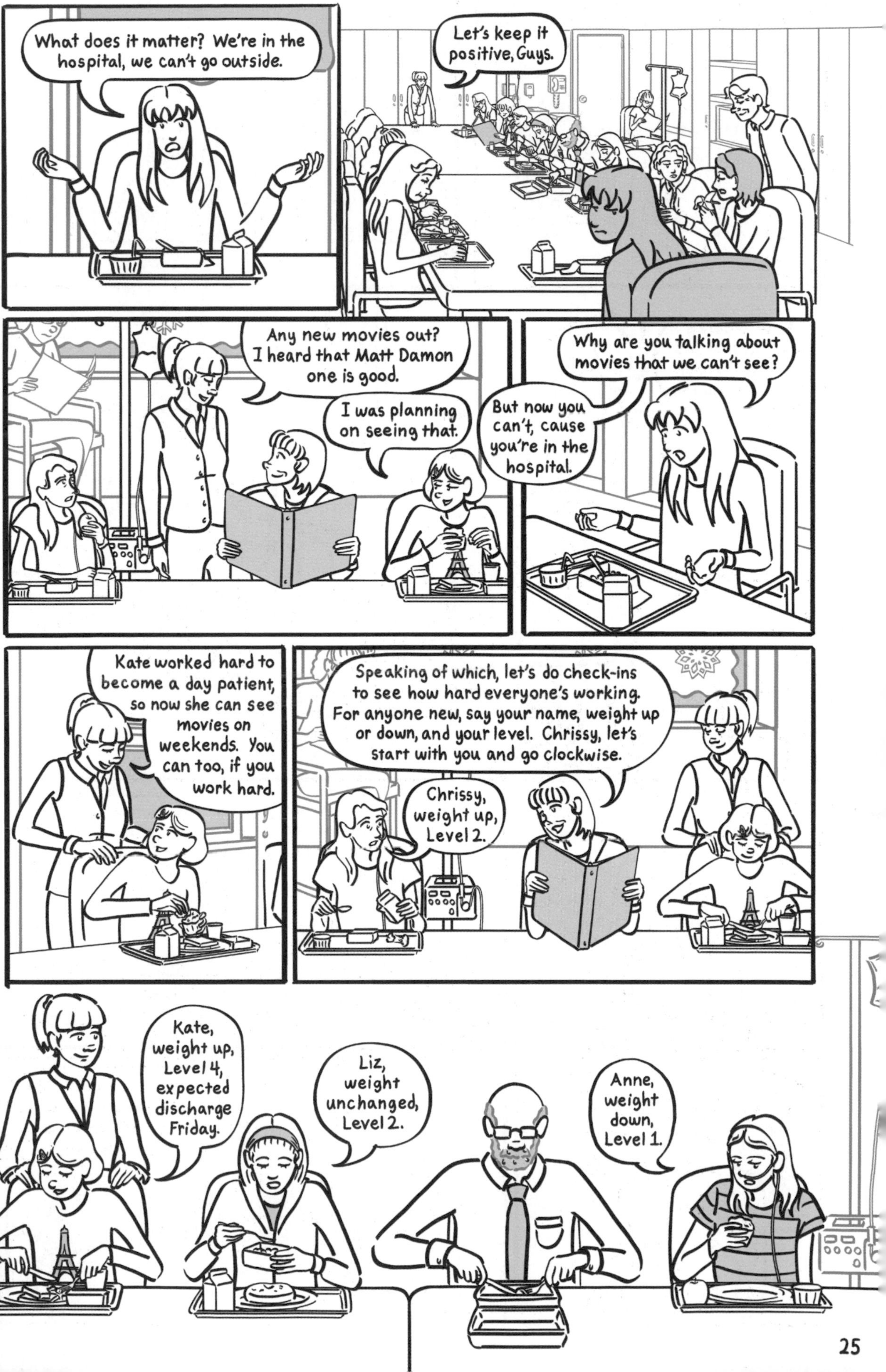
What does it matter? We're in the hospital, we can't go outside.
Let's keep it positive, Guys.
Any new movies out? I heard that Matt Damon one is good.
I was planning on seeing that.
Why are you talking about movies that we can't see?
But now you can't, cause you're in the hospital.
Kate worked hard to become a day patient, so now she can see movies on weekends. You can too, if you work hard.
Speaking of which, let's do check-ins to see how hard everyone's working. For anyone new, say your name, weight up or down, and your level. Chrissy, let's start with you and go clockwise.
Chrissy, weight up, Level 2.
Kate, weight up, Level 4, expected discharge Friday.
Liz, weight unchanged, Level 2.
Anne, weight down, Level 1.

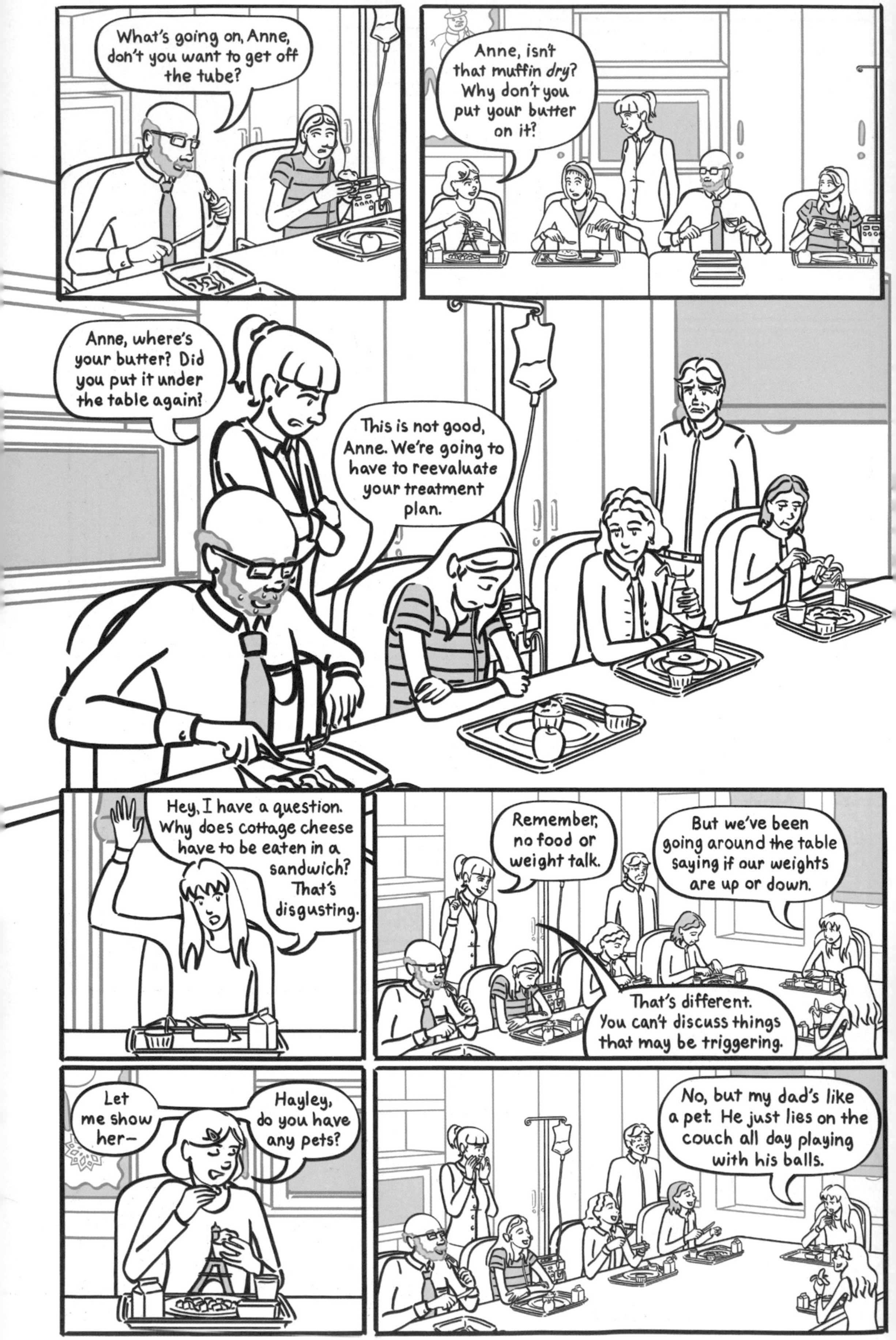
What's going on, Anne, don't you want to get off the tube?
Anne, isn't that muffin *dry*? Why don't you put your butter on it?
Anne, where's your butter? Did you put it under the table again?
This is not good, Anne. We're going to have to reevaluate your treatment plan.
Hey, I have a question. Why does cottage cheese have to be eaten in a sandwich? That's disgusting.
Remember, no food or weight talk.
But we've been going around the table saying if our weights are up or down.
That's different. You can't discuss things that may be triggering.
Let me show her—
Hayley, do you have any pets?
No, but my dad's like a pet. He just lies on the couch all day playing with his balls.

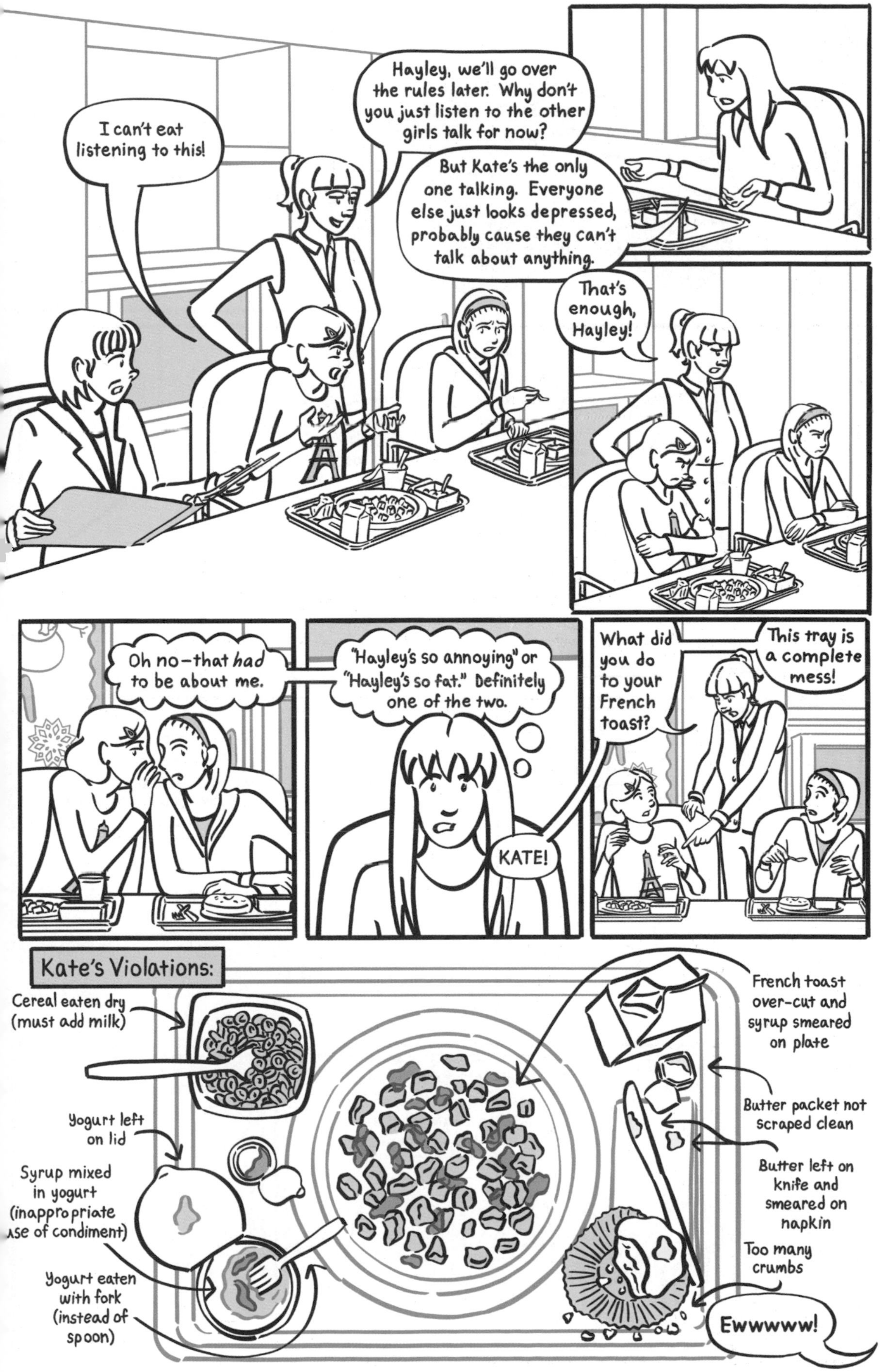
I can't eat listening to this!
Hayley, we'll go over the rules later. Why don't you just listen to the other girls talk for now?
But Kate's the only one talking. Everyone else just looks depressed, probably cause they can't talk about anything.
That's enough, Hayley!
Oh no—that *had* to be about me.
"Hayley's so annoying" or "Hayley's so fat." Definitely one of the two.
KATE!
What did you do to your French toast?
This tray is a complete mess!
Kate's Violations:
Cereal eaten dry (must add milk)
Yogurt left on lid
Syrup mixed in yogurt (inappropriate use of condiment)
Yogurt eaten with fork (instead of spoon)
French toast over-cut and syrup smeared on plate
Butter packet not scraped clean
Butter left on knife and smeared on napkin
Too many crumbs
Ewwwww!

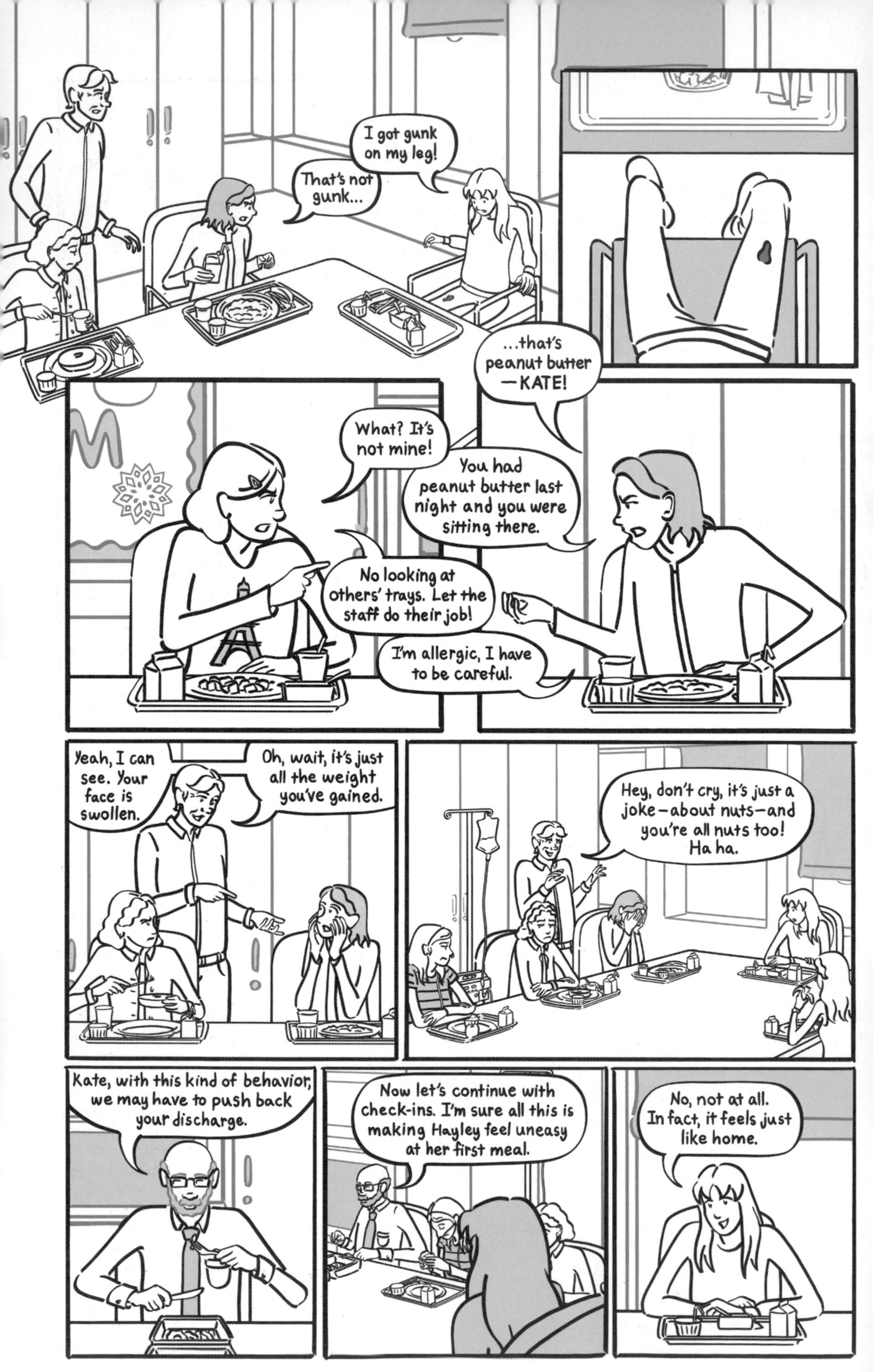
I got gunk on my leg!
That's not gunk...
...that's peanut butter —KATE!
What? It's not mine!
You had peanut butter last night and you were sitting there.
No looking at others' trays. Let the staff do their job!
I'm allergic, I have to be careful.
Yeah, I can see. Your face is swollen.
Oh, wait, it's just all the weight you've gained.
Hey, don't cry, it's just a joke—about nuts—and you're all nuts too! Ha ha.
Kate, with this kind of behavior, we may have to push back your discharge.
Now let's continue with check-ins. I'm sure all this is making Hayley feel uneasy at her first meal.
No, not at all. In fact, it feels just like home.

When the meal had concluded I was given the rundown: no discussion of politics, religion, food, appearance, sex, violence, the hospital, the program, or anything that might remotely be construed as negative or depressing — such as one's father's balls, or how ugly the floral wallpaper in one's kitchen is...

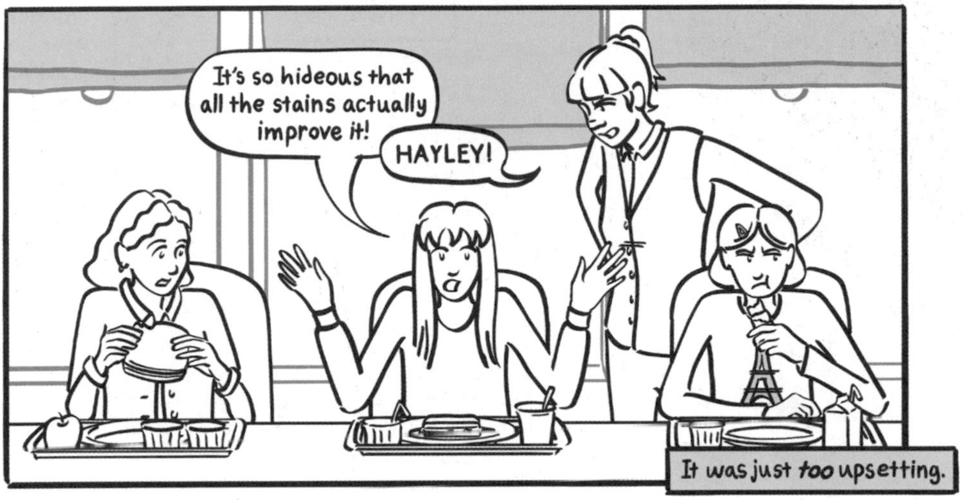

It's so hideous that all the stains actually improve it!
HAYLEY!
It was just *too* upsetting.

Even more painful than the meal itself was the time that followed. Everyone was confined to the Day Room, where we were to remain seated. So, naturally, we tried to stand as much as possible, especially after dinner. By then, the program staff had left, so our only supervisor was a nurse, who would return to her mealtime perch and chide us periodically for excessive movement.

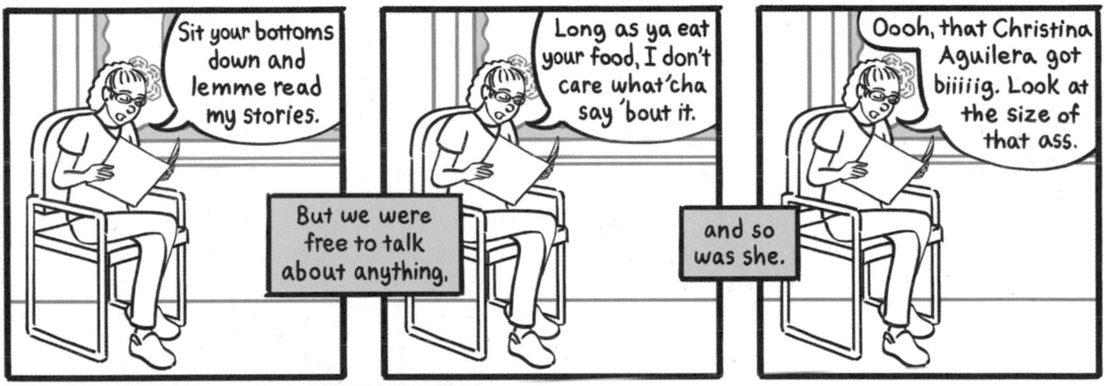

Sit your bottoms down and lemme read my stories.
But we were free to talk about anything,
Long as ya eat your food, I don't care what'cha say 'bout it.
and so was she.
Oooh, that Christina Aguilera got biiiiig. Look at the size of that ass.

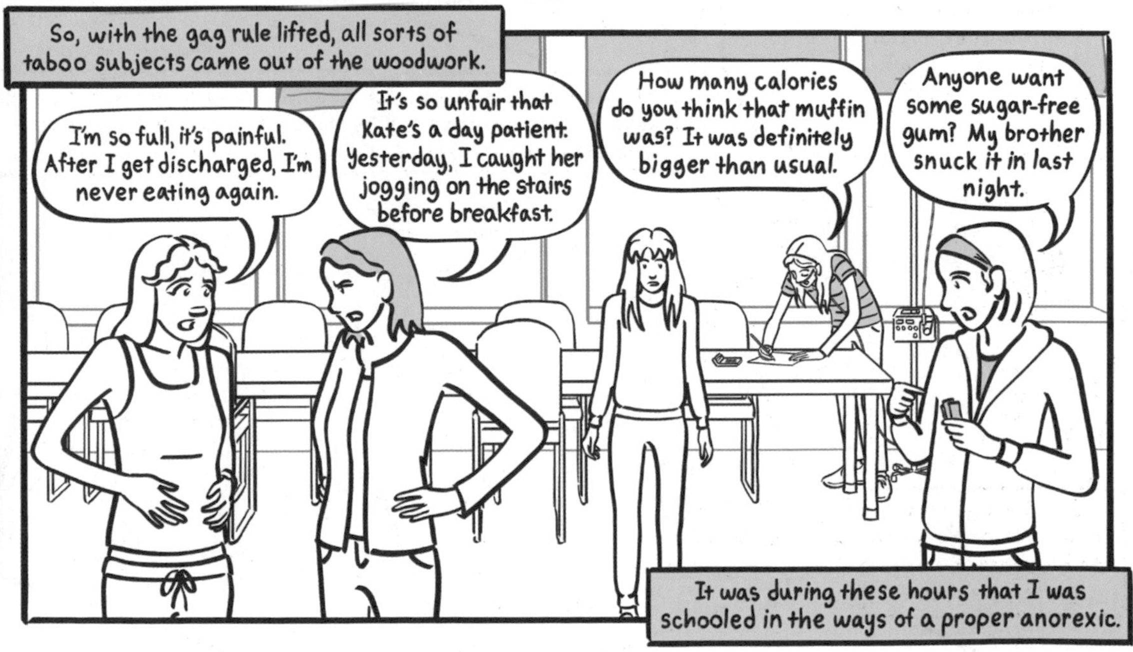

So, with the gag rule lifted, all sorts of taboo subjects came out of the woodwork.
I'm so full, it's painful. After I get discharged, I'm never eating again.
It's so unfair that Kate's a day patient. Yesterday, I caught her jogging on the stairs before breakfast.
How many calories do you think that muffin was? It was definitely bigger than usual.
Anyone want some sugar-free gum? My brother snuck it in last night.
It was during these hours that I was schooled in the ways of a proper anorexic.

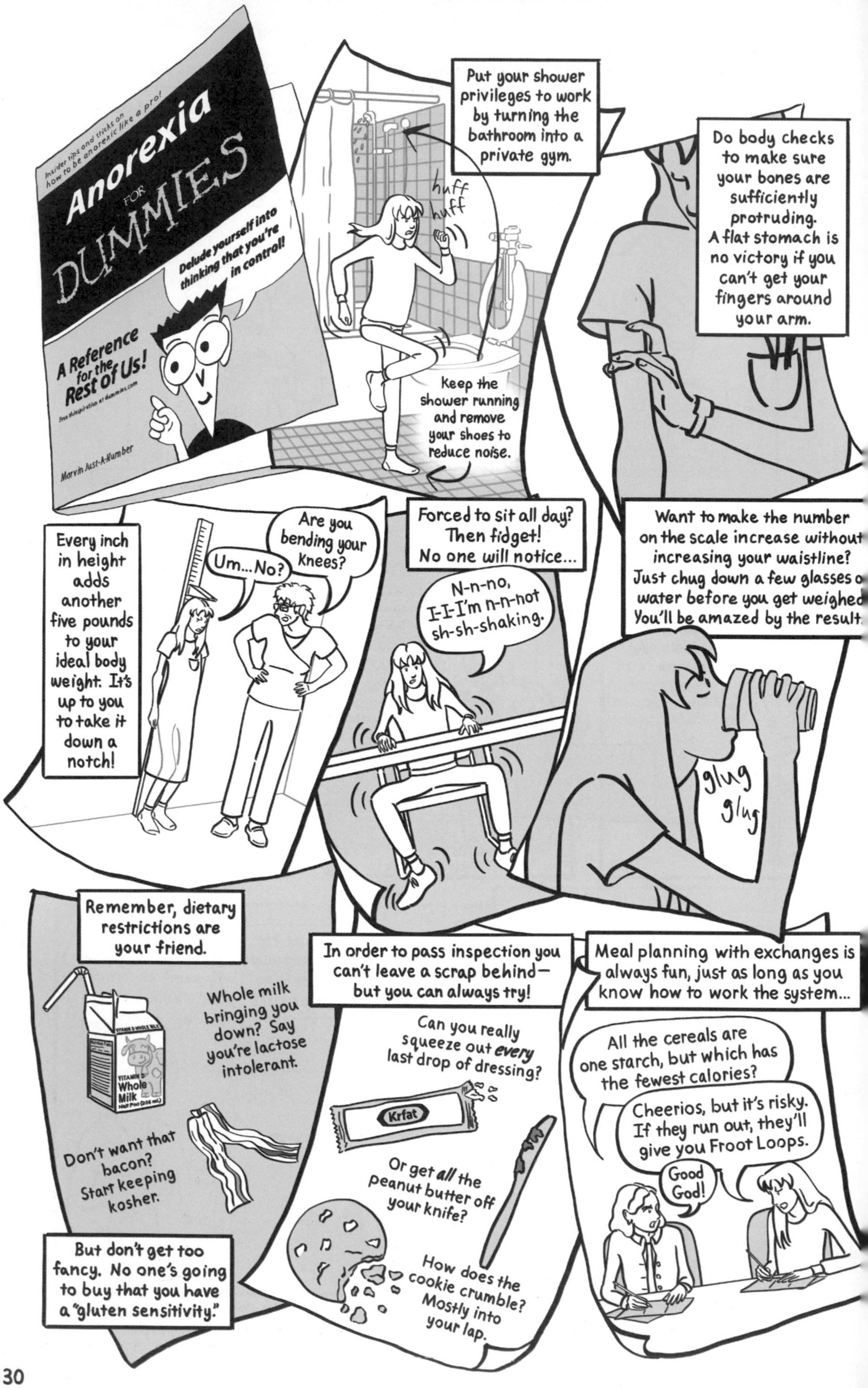
Insider tips and tricks on how to be anorexic like a pro!
Anorexia FOR DUMMIES
Delude yourself into thinking that you're in control!
A Reference for the Rest of Us!
Free thinspiration at dummies.com
Marvin Just-A-Number
Put your shower privileges to work by turning the bathroom into a private gym.
huff huff
Keep the shower running and remove your shoes to reduce noise.
Do body checks to make sure your bones are sufficiently protruding. A flat stomach is no victory if you can't get your fingers around your arm.
Every inch in height adds another five pounds to your ideal body weight. It's up to you to take it down a notch!
Are you bending your knees?
Um...No?
Forced to sit all day? Then fidget! No one will notice...
N-n-no, I-I-I'm n-n-not sh-sh-shaking.
Want to make the number on the scale increase without increasing your waistline? Just chug down a few glasses o water before you get weighed You'll be amazed by the result.
glug glug
Remember, dietary restrictions are your friend.
Whole milk bringing you down? Say you're lactose intolerant.
Whole Milk
Don't want that bacon? Start keeping kosher.
But don't get too fancy. No one's going to buy that you have a "gluten sensitivity."
In order to pass inspection you can't leave a scrap behind— but you can always try!
Can you really squeeze out *every* last drop of dressing?
Krfat
Or get *all* the peanut butter off your knife?
How does the cookie crumble? Mostly into your lap.
Meal planning with exchanges is always fun, just as long as you know how to work the system...
All the cereals are one starch, but which has the fewest calories?
Cheerios, but it's risky. If they run out, they'll give you Froot Loops.
Good God!

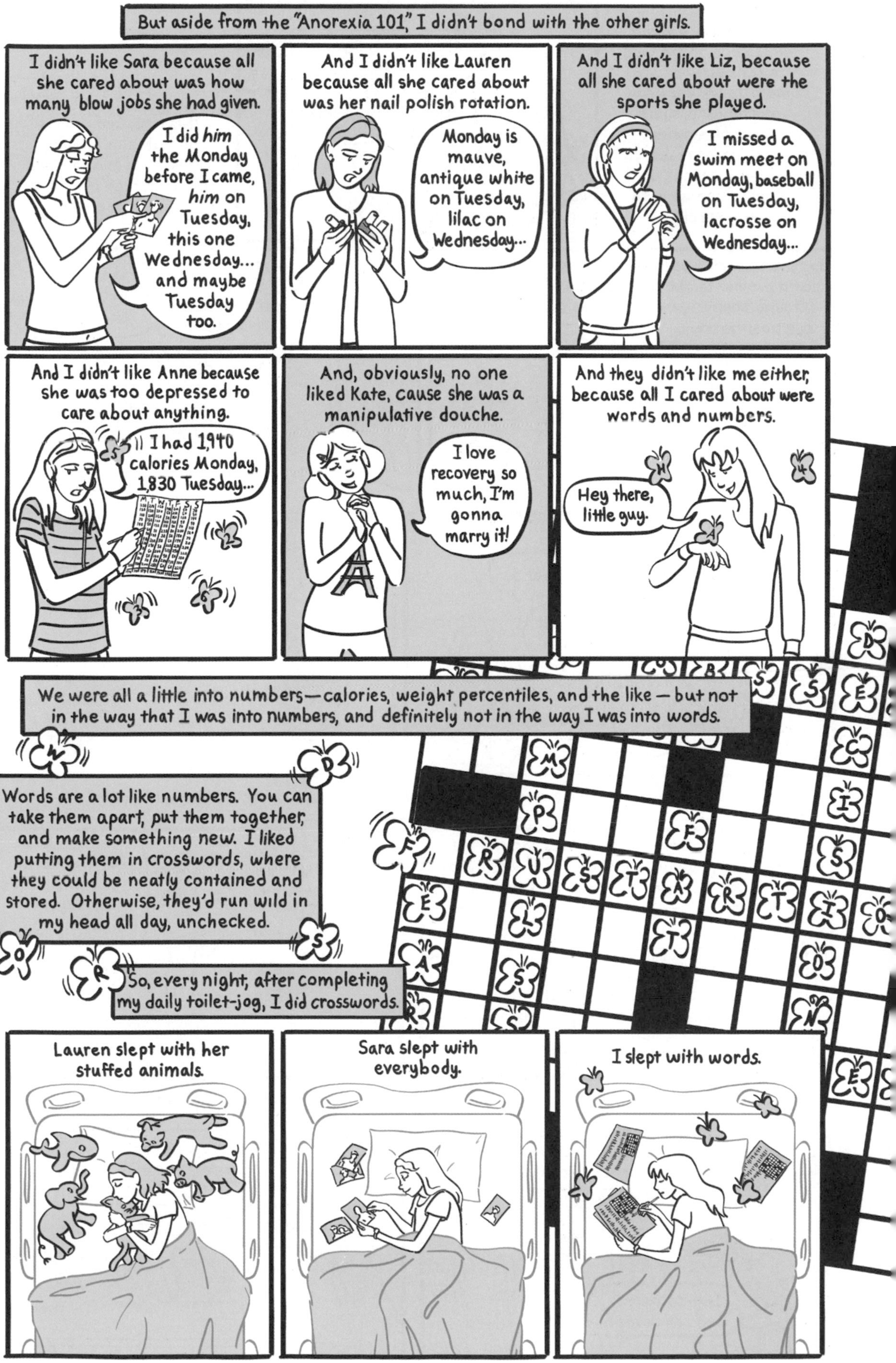

But aside from the "Anorexia 101," I didn't bond with the other girls.
I didn't like Sara because all she cared about was how many blow jobs she had given.
I did *him* the Monday before I came, *him* on Tuesday, this one Wednesday... and maybe Tuesday too.
And I didn't like Lauren because all she cared about was her nail polish rotation.
Monday is mauve, antique white on Tuesday, lilac on Wednesday...
And I didn't like Liz, because all she cared about were the sports she played.
I missed a swim meet on Monday, baseball on Tuesday, lacrosse on Wednesday...
And I didn't like Anne because she was too depressed to care about anything.
I had 1,940 calories Monday, 1,830 Tuesday...
And, obviously, no one liked Kate, cause she was a manipulative douche.
I love recovery so much, I'm gonna marry it!
And they didn't like me either, because all I cared about were words and numbers.
Hey there, little guy.
We were all a little into numbers—calories, weight percentiles, and the like—but not in the way that I was into numbers, and definitely not in the way I was into words.
Words are a lot like numbers. You can take them apart, put them together, and make something new. I liked putting them in crosswords, where they could be neatly contained and stored. Otherwise, they'd run wild in my head all day, unchecked.
So, every night, after completing my daily toilet-jog, I did crosswords.
Lauren slept with her stuffed animals.
Sara slept with everybody.
I slept with words.

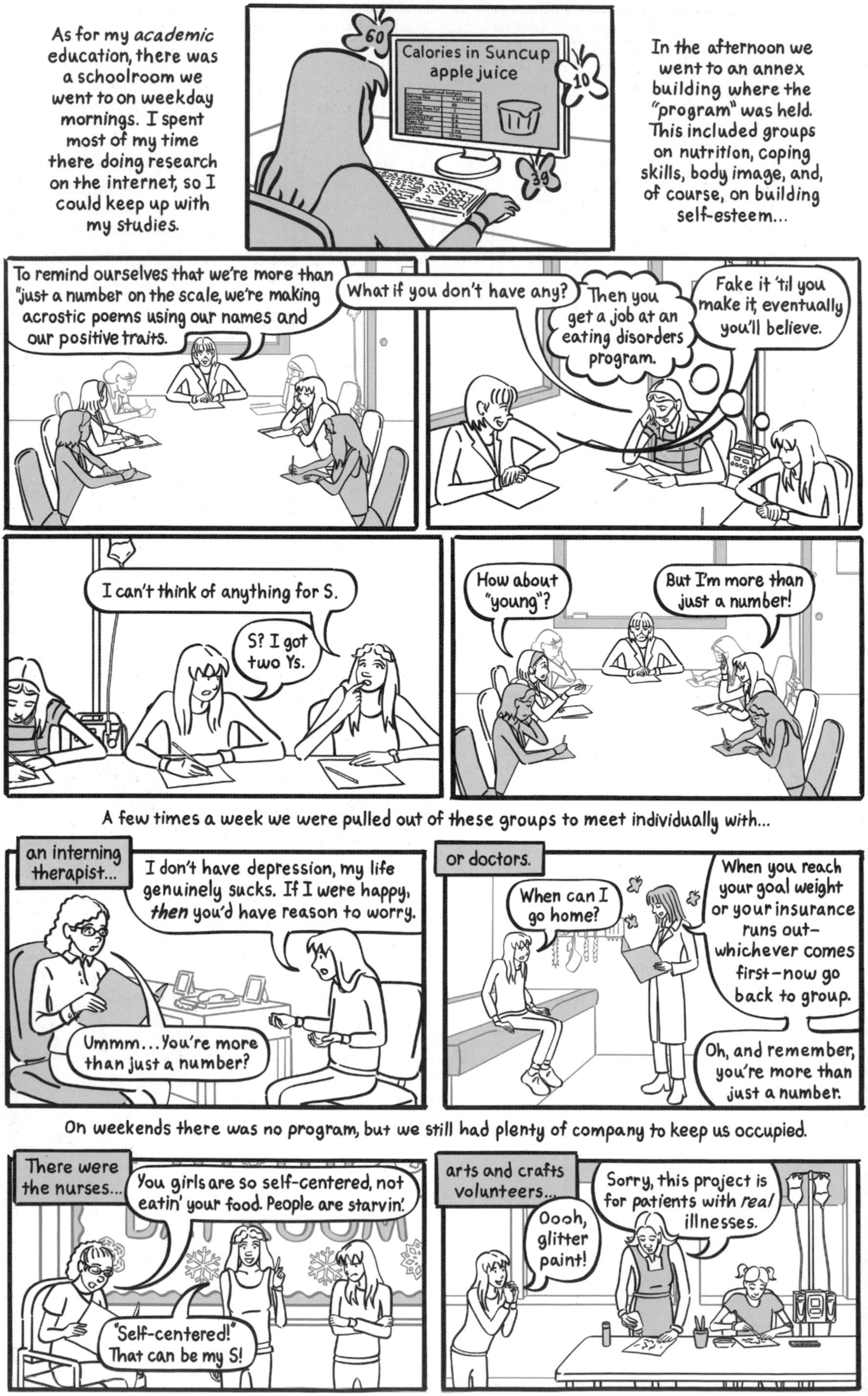
As for my *academic* education, there was a schoolroom we went to on weekday mornings. I spent most of my time there doing research on the internet, so I could keep up with my studies.
60
Calories in Suncup apple juice
10
39
In the afternoon we went to an annex building where the "program" was held. This included groups on nutrition, coping skills, body image, and, of course, on building self-esteem...
To remind ourselves that we're more than "just a number on the scale, we're making acrostic poems using our names and our positive traits.
What if you don't have any?
Then you get a job at an eating disorders program.
Fake it 'til you make it, eventually you'll believe.
I can't think of anything for S.
S? I got two Ys.
How about "young"?
But I'm more than just a number!
A few times a week we were pulled out of these groups to meet individually with...
an interning therapist...
I don't have depression, my life genuinely sucks. If I were happy, *then* you'd have reason to worry.
Ummm... You're more than just a number?
or doctors.
When can I go home?
When you reach your goal weight or your insurance runs out— whichever comes first—now go back to group.
Oh, and remember, you're more than just a number.
On weekends there was no program, but we still had plenty of company to keep us occupied.
There were the nurses...
You girls are so self-centered, not eatin' your food. People are starvin'.
"Self-centered!" That can be my S!
arts and crafts volunteers...
Oooh, glitter paint!
Sorry, this project is for patients with *real* illnesses.

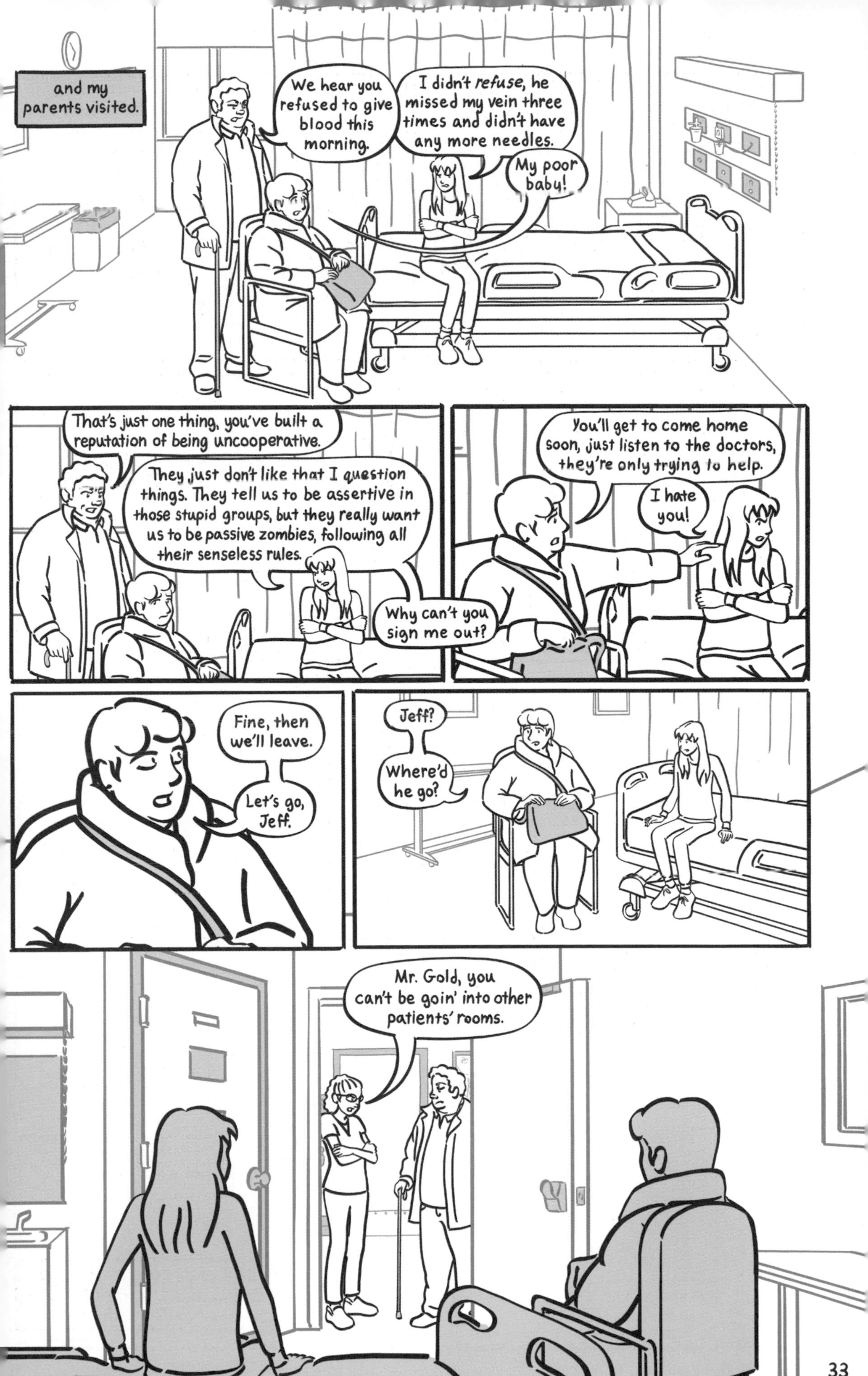
and my parents visited.
We hear you refused to give blood this morning.
I didn't *refuse*, he missed my vein three times and didn't have any more needles.
My poor baby!
That's just one thing, you've built a reputation of being uncooperative.
They just don't like that I question things. They tell us to be assertive in those stupid groups, but they really want us to be passive zombies, following all their senseless rules.
Why can't you sign me out?
You'll get to come home soon, just listen to the doctors, they're only trying to help.
I hate you!
Fine, then we'll leave.
Let's go, Jeff.
Jeff?
Where'd he go?
Mr. Gold, you can't be goin' into other patients' rooms.

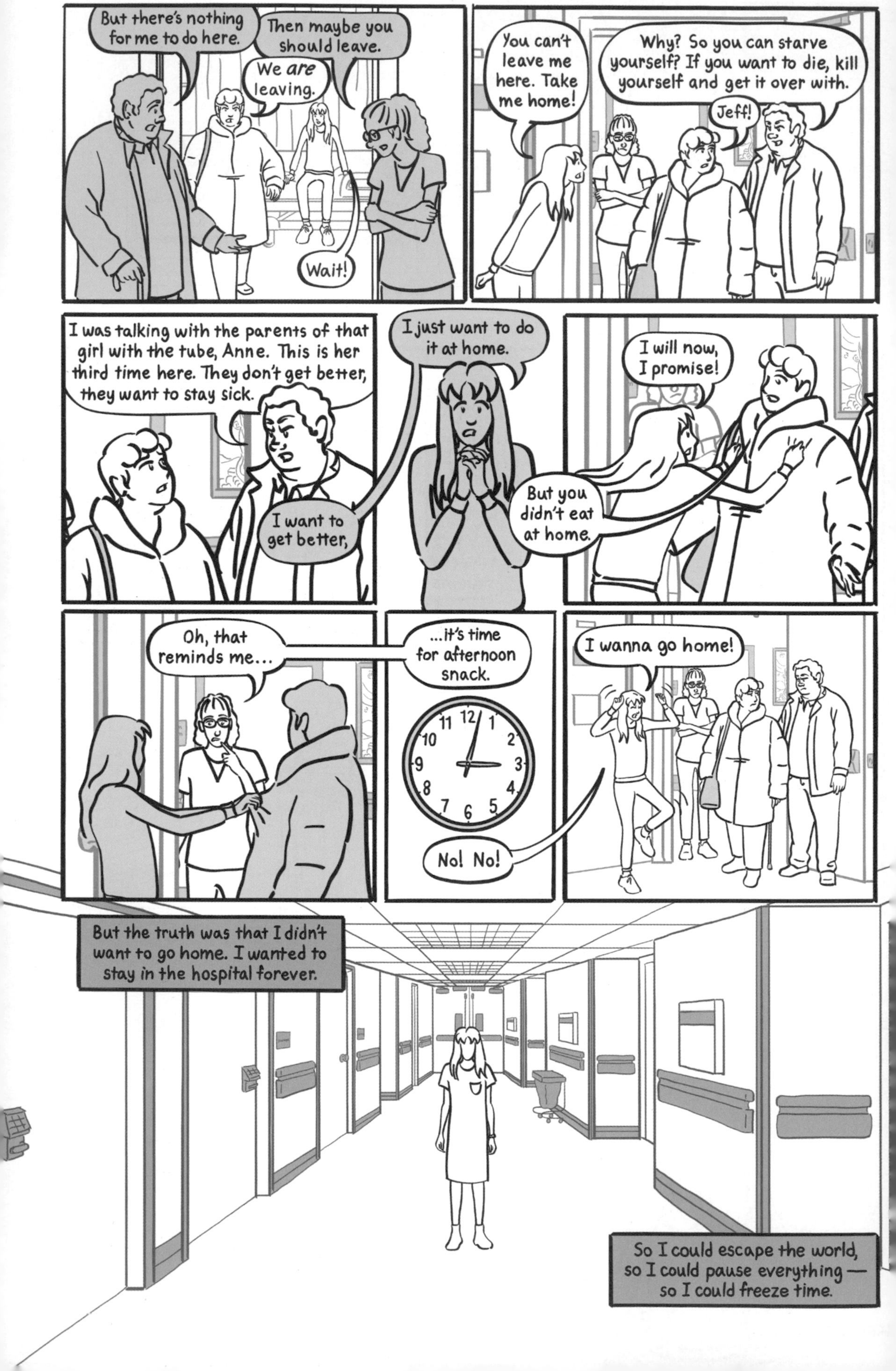
But there's nothing for me to do here.
Then maybe you should leave.
We are leaving.
Wait!
You can't leave me here. Take me home!
Why? So you can starve yourself? If you want to die, kill yourself and get it over with.
Jeff!
I was talking with the parents of that girl with the tube, Anne. This is her third time here. They don't get better, they want to stay sick.
I want to get better,
I just want to do it at home.
I will now, I promise!
But you didn't eat at home.
Oh, that reminds me...
...it's time for afternoon snack.
No! No!
I wanna go home!
But the truth was that I didn't want to go home. I wanted to stay in the hospital forever.
So I could escape the world, so I could pause everything — so I could freeze time.

But eventually I did go home—I became a day patient. This meant I got to eat at home on the weekend. I told the doctors that my parents couldn't be in the room when I ate because they created a stressful environment. The doctors bought it, and instructed Mom and Dad to back off.

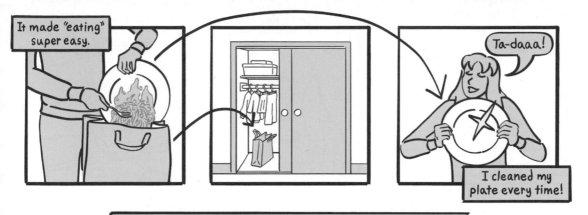

It made "eating" super easy.

Ta-daaa!

I cleaned my plate every time!

On Monday, I snuck in an old urine sample and loaded up on water before getting weighed. It worked like a charm.

Weight up, Level 4.

On your first weekend! How'd you do it?

guess who never got discharged

I just used all the great coping skills that I learned from the other girls.

However, after having regular meals at the hospital, not eating all weekend left me quite famished.

Whoa, slow down there, Tiger. No one's going to take it away from you.

Shut up, Jimson.

But that was the least of my concerns.

It was nearly impossible to drink all that water and hold it in. My pre-packed urine often leaked, and, finally, my parents found my stash...

What the hell is that rancid smell?

I wonder what tipped them off.

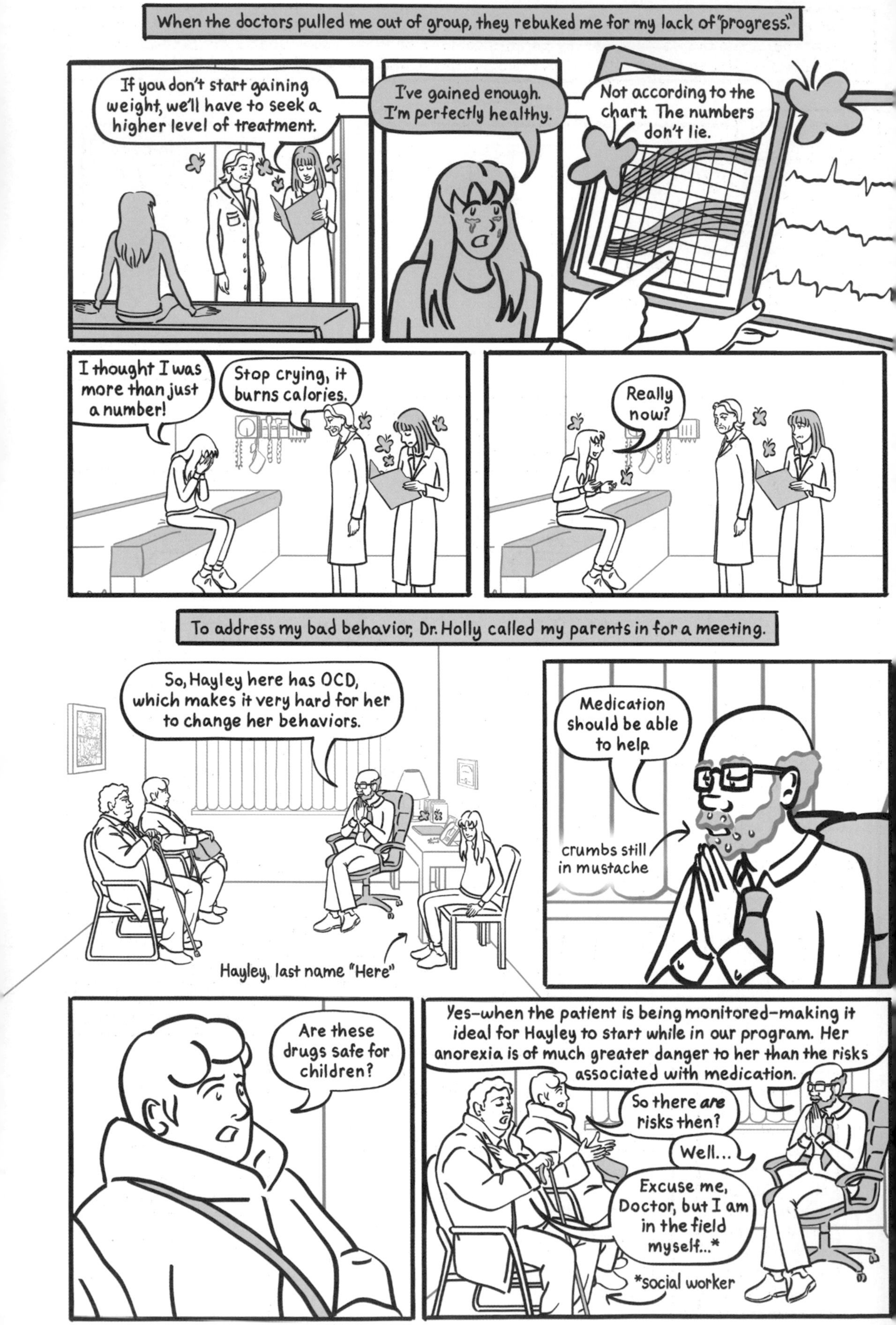
When the doctors pulled me out of group, they rebuked me for my lack of "progress."
If you don't start gaining weight, we'll have to seek a higher level of treatment.
I've gained enough. I'm perfectly healthy.
Not according to the chart. The numbers don't lie.
I thought I was more than just a number!
Stop crying, it burns calories.
Really now?
To address my bad behavior, Dr. Holly called my parents in for a meeting.
So, Hayley here has OCD, which makes it very hard for her to change her behaviors.
Hayley, last name "Here"
Medication should be able to help
crumbs still in mustache
Are these drugs safe for children?
Yes—when the patient is being monitored—making it ideal for Hayley to start while in our program. Her anorexia is of much greater danger to her than the risks associated with medication.
So there are risks then?
Well...
Excuse me, Doctor, but I am in the field myself...*
*social worker

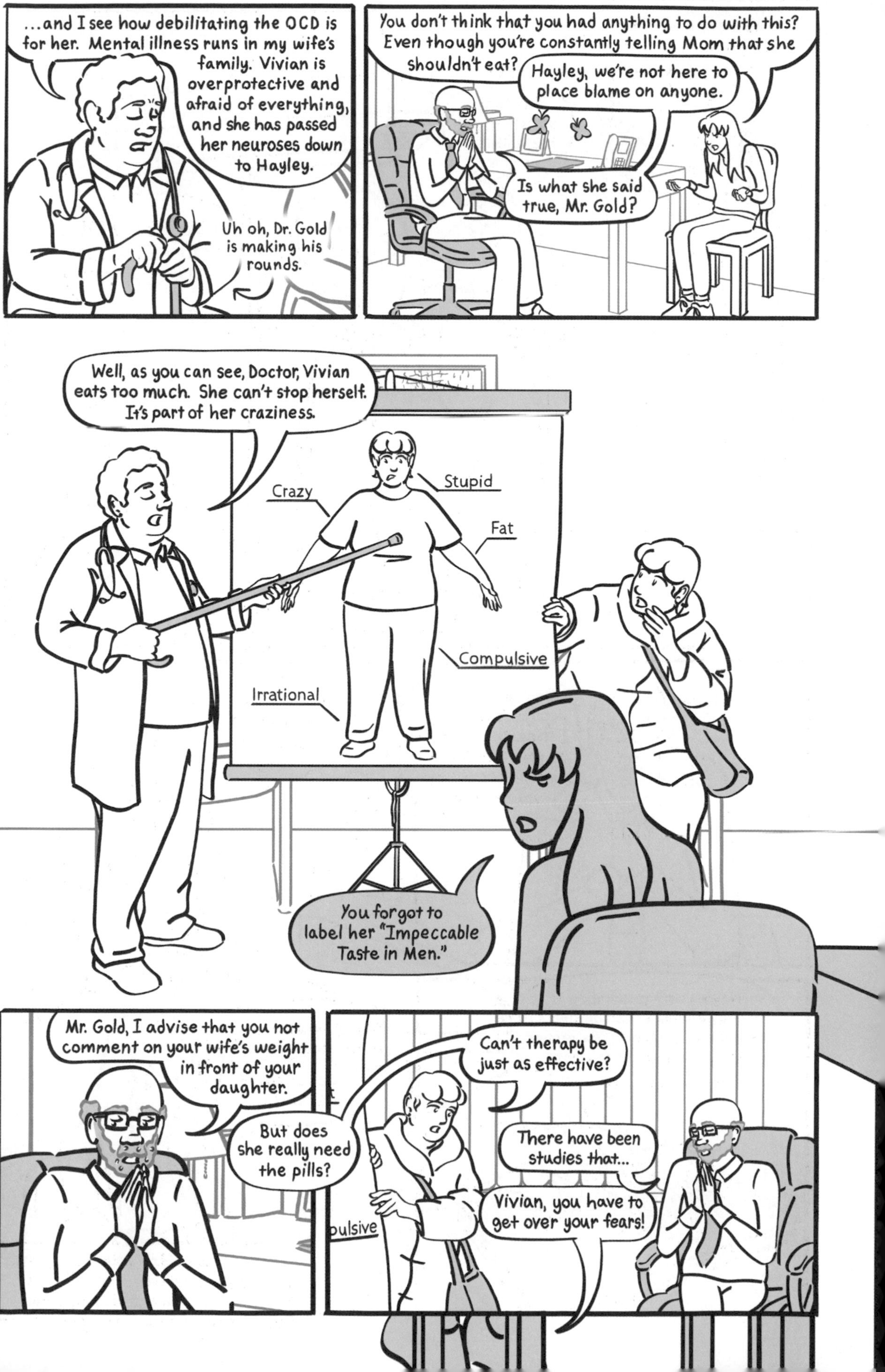
...and I see how debilitating the OCD is for her. Mental illness runs in my wife's family. Vivian is overprotective and afraid of everything, and she has passed her neuroses down to Hayley.
Uh oh, Dr. Gold is making his rounds.
You don't think that you had anything to do with this? Even though you're constantly telling Mom that she shouldn't eat?
Hayley, we're not here to place blame on anyone.
Is what she said true, Mr. Gold?
Well, as you can see, Doctor, Vivian eats too much. She can't stop herself. It's part of her craziness.
Crazy
Stupid
Fat
Compulsive
Irrational
You forgot to label her "Impeccable Taste in Men."
Mr. Gold, I advise that you not comment on your wife's weight in front of your daughter.
But does she really need the pills?
Can't therapy be just as effective?
There have been studies that...
Vivian, you have to get over your fears!

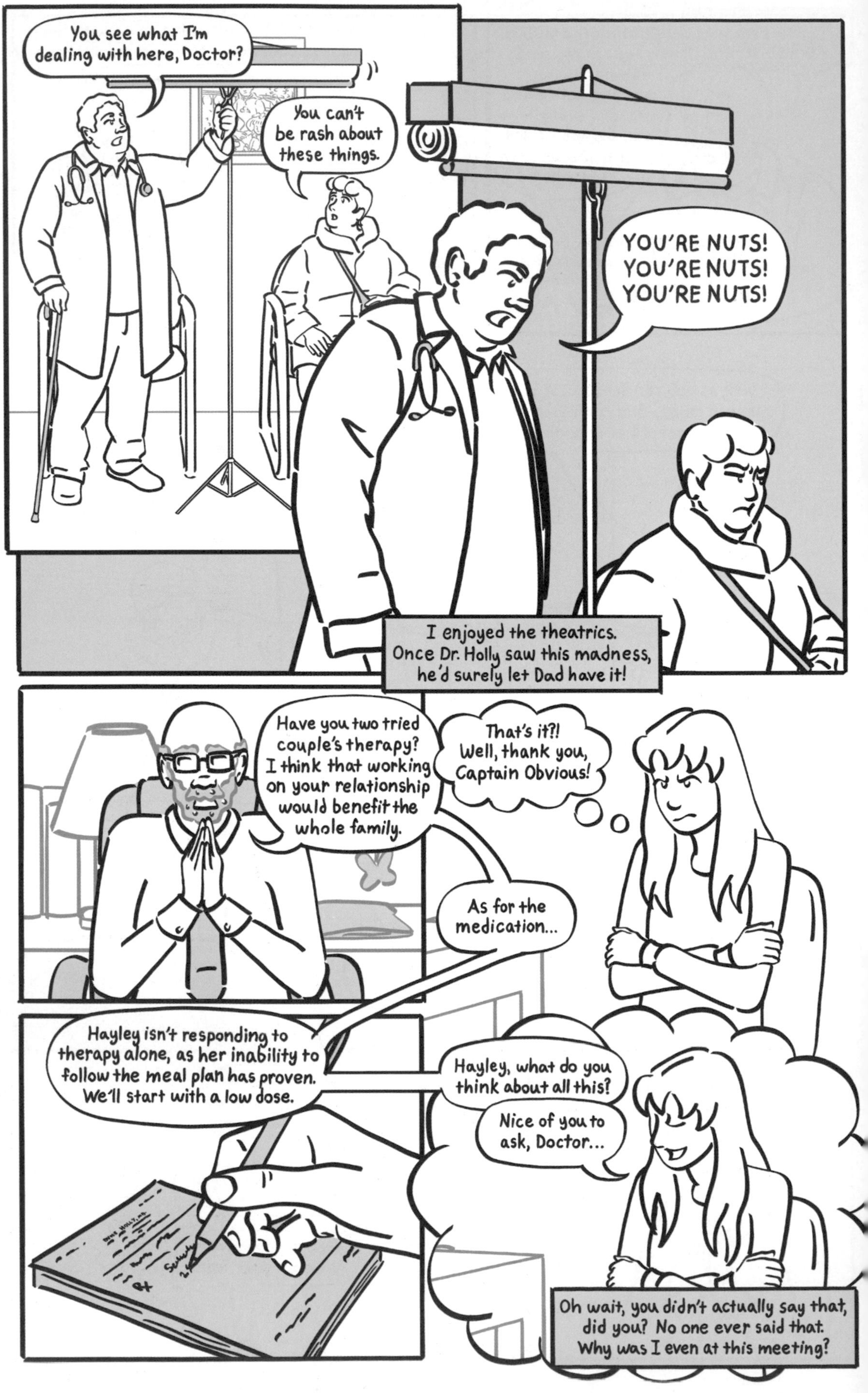
You see what I'm dealing with here, Doctor?
You can't be rash about these things.
YOU'RE NUTS! YOU'RE NUTS! YOU'RE NUTS!
I enjoyed the theatrics. Once Dr. Holly saw this madness, he'd surely let Dad have it!
Have you two tried couple's therapy? I think that working on your relationship would benefit the whole family.
That's it?! Well, thank you, Captain Obvious!
As for the medication...
Hayley isn't responding to therapy alone, as her inability to follow the meal plan has proven. We'll start with a low dose.
Hayley, what do you think about all this?
Nice of you to ask, Doctor...
Oh wait, you didn't actually say that, did you? No one ever said that. Why was I even at this meeting?

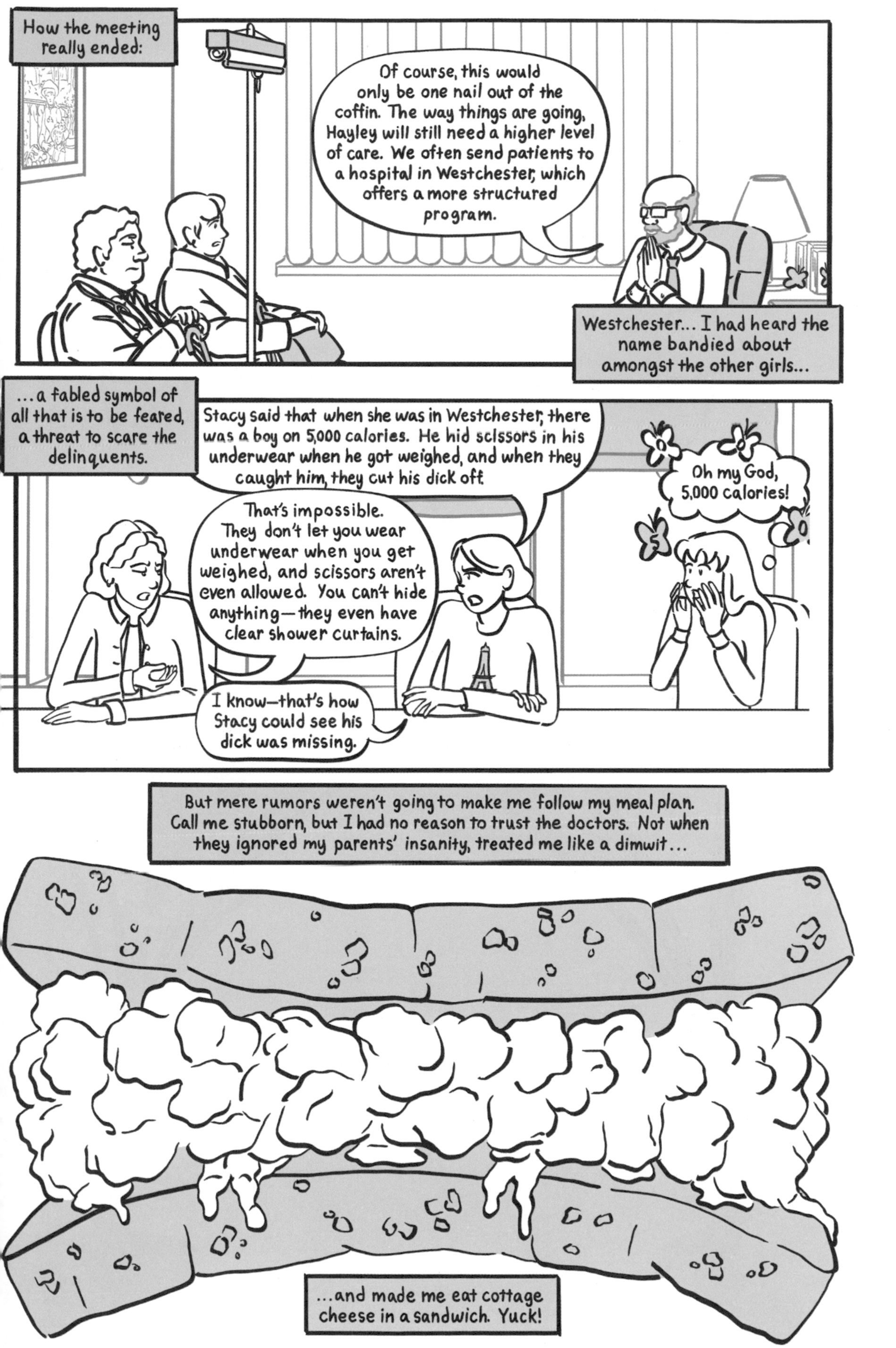
How the meeting really ended:
Of course, this would only be one nail out of the coffin. The way things are going, Hayley will still need a higher level of care. We often send patients to a hospital in Westchester, which offers a more structured program.
Westchester... I had heard the name bandied about amongst the other girls...
...a fabled symbol of all that is to be feared, a threat to scare the delinquents.
Stacy said that when she was in Westchester, there was a boy on 5,000 calories. He hid scissors in his underwear when he got weighed, and when they caught him, they cut his dick off.
Oh my God, 5,000 calories!
That's impossible. They don't let you wear underwear when you get weighed, and scissors aren't even allowed. You can't hide anything—they even have clear shower curtains.
I know—that's how Stacy could see his dick was missing.
But mere rumors weren't going to make me follow my meal plan. Call me stubborn, but I had no reason to trust the doctors. Not when they ignored my parents' insanity, treated me like a dimwit...
...and made me eat cottage cheese in a sandwich. Yuck!

Much Madness is divinest Sense—
To a discerning Eye—
Much Sense—the starkest Madness—
'Tis the Majority
In this, as all, prevail—
Assent—and you are sane—
Demur—you're straightway dangerous—
And handled with a Chain.

Crocus vernus Wulf

Chapter

3

The White Abyss

Westchester, formerly known as Bloomingdale Lunatic Asylum, was a pioneer in "moral treatment" of the mentally ill. Its groundbreaking efforts are epitomized in a historical etching hanging in the main building. It depicts patients being permitted to get fresh air while being safely limited to a gated area. Also pictured are the townspeople, just beyond the gates, lunching from picnic baskets as they gawk at "recess at the loony bin." It was really a win for both parties. And my compliments to the artist— the etching perfectly captures the hospital. But maybe that's because the whole place seemed like a caricature to begin with.

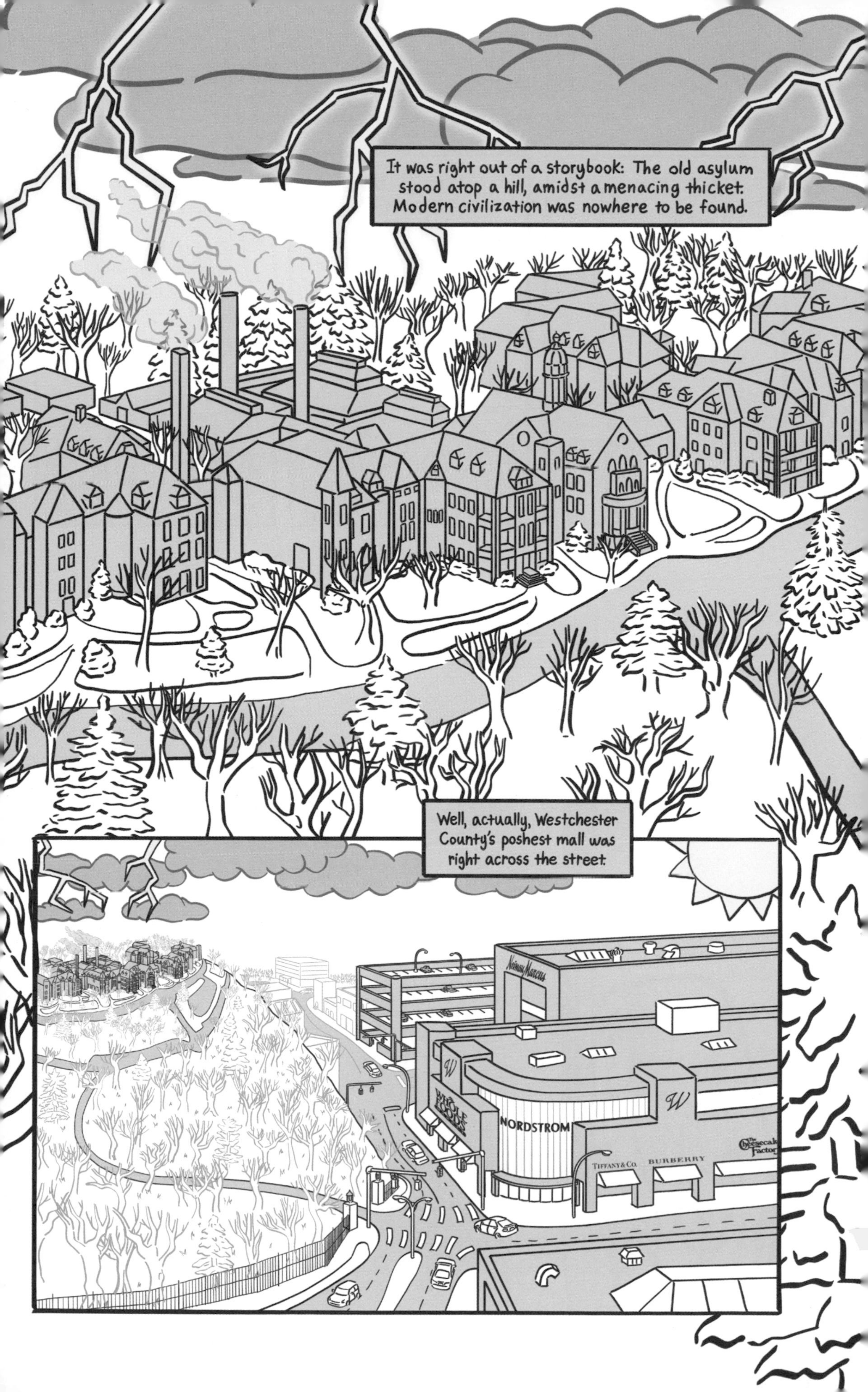
It was right out of a storybook: The old asylum stood atop a hill, amidst a menacing thicket. Modern civilization was nowhere to be found.
Well, actually, Westchester County's poshest mall was right across the street.
Neiman Marcus
WHOLE FOODS
NORDSTROM
TIFFANY&Co.
BURBERRY

After four hours in Admitting, we were led to a door.

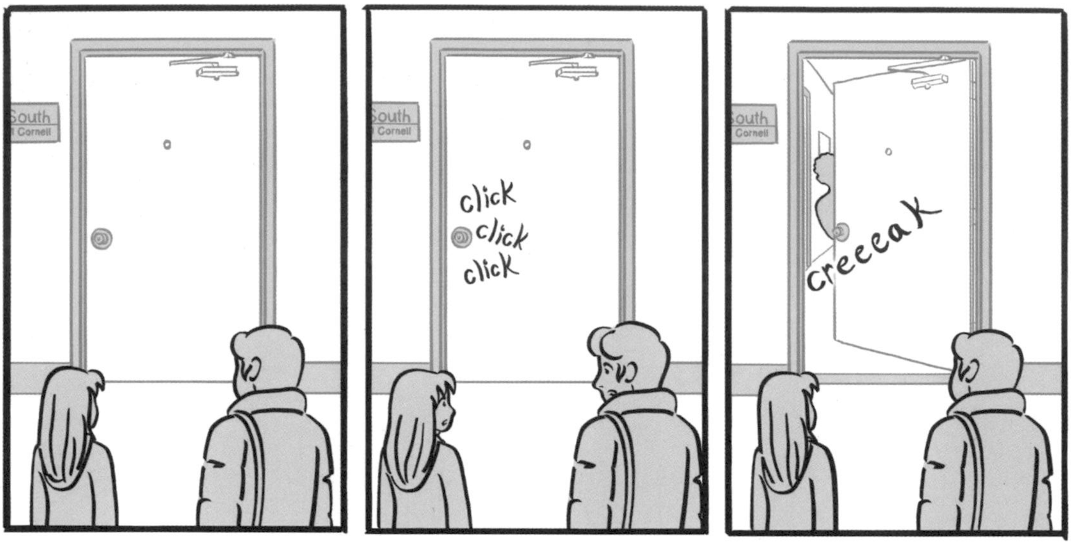
click
click
click
creeeak

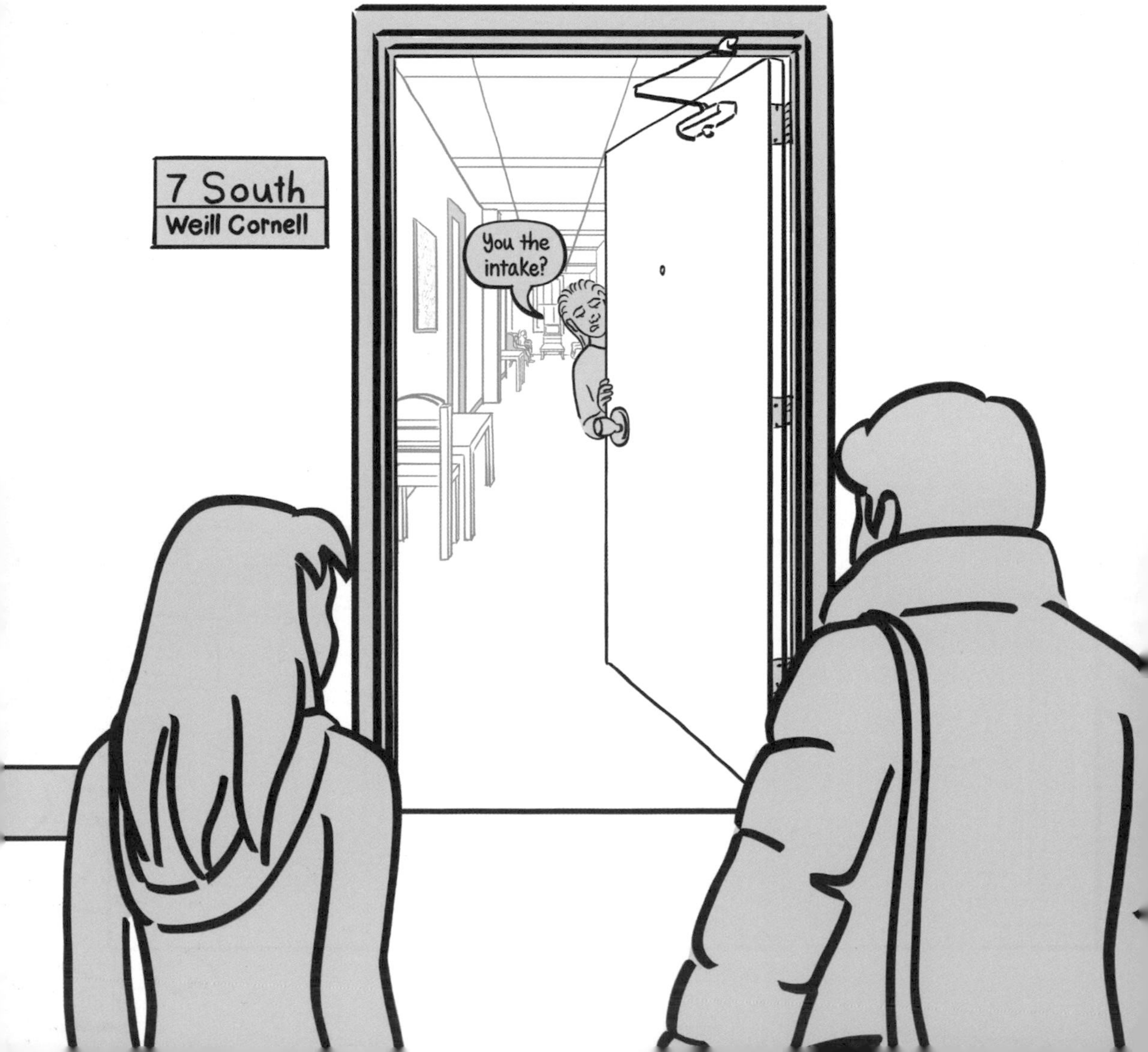
7 South
Weill Cornell
You the intake?

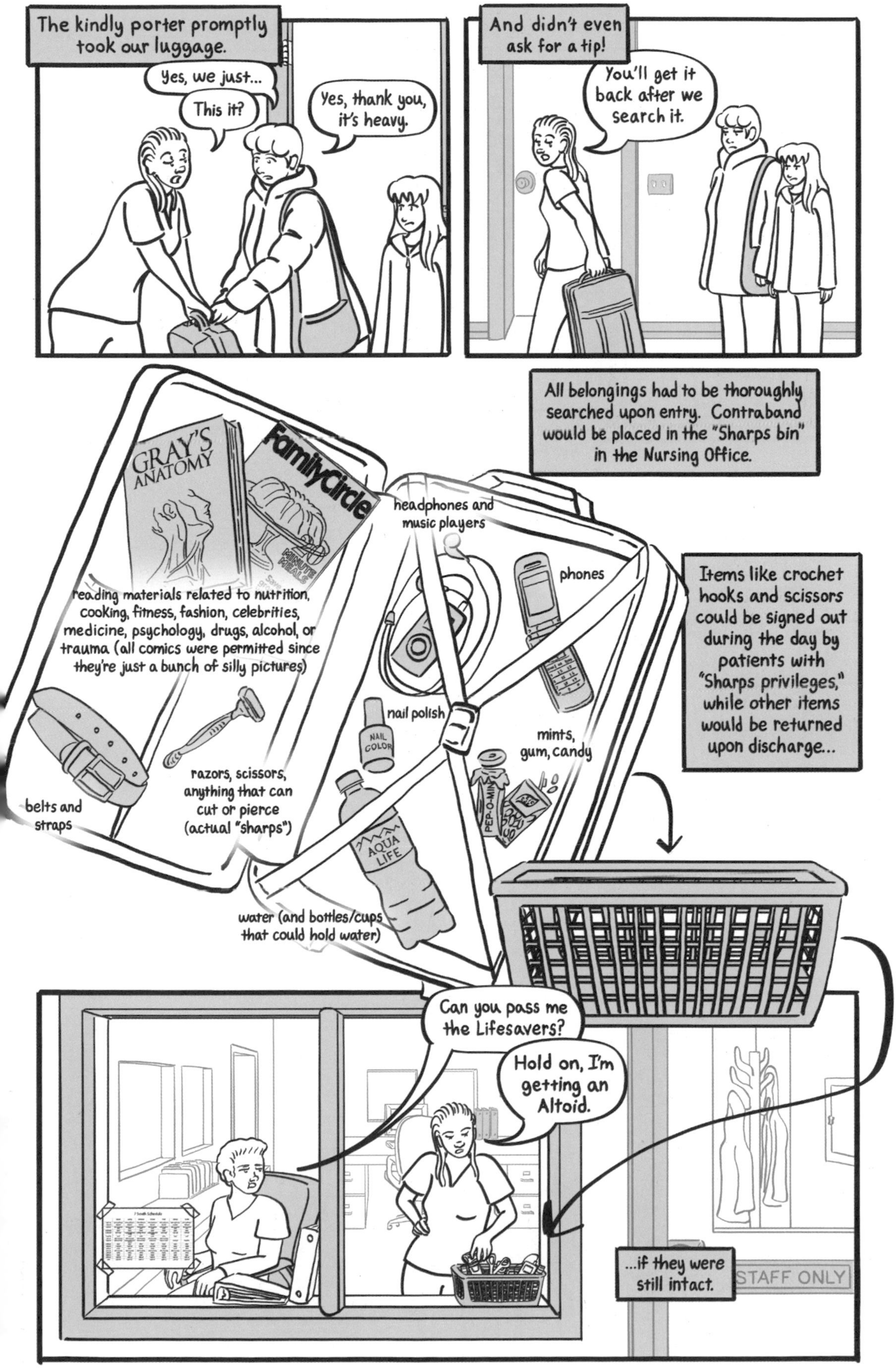
The kindly porter promptly took our luggage.
Yes, we just...
This it?
Yes, thank you, it's heavy.
And didn't even ask for a tip!
You'll get it back after we search it.
All belongings had to be thoroughly searched upon entry. Contraband would be placed in the "Sharps bin" in the Nursing Office.
GRAY'S ANATOMY
FamilyCircle
headphones and music players
phones
reading materials related to nutrition, cooking, fitness, fashion, celebrities, medicine, psychology, drugs, alcohol, or trauma (all comics were permitted since they're just a bunch of silly pictures)
Items like crochet hooks and scissors could be signed out during the day by patients with "Sharps privileges," while other items would be returned upon discharge...
nail polish
NAIL COLOR
mints, gum, candy
PEP-O-MINT
belts and straps
razors, scissors, anything that can cut or pierce (actual "sharps")
AQUA LIFE
water (and bottles/cups that could hold water)
Can you pass me the Lifesavers?
Hold on, I'm getting an Altoid.
...if they were still intact.
STAFF ONLY

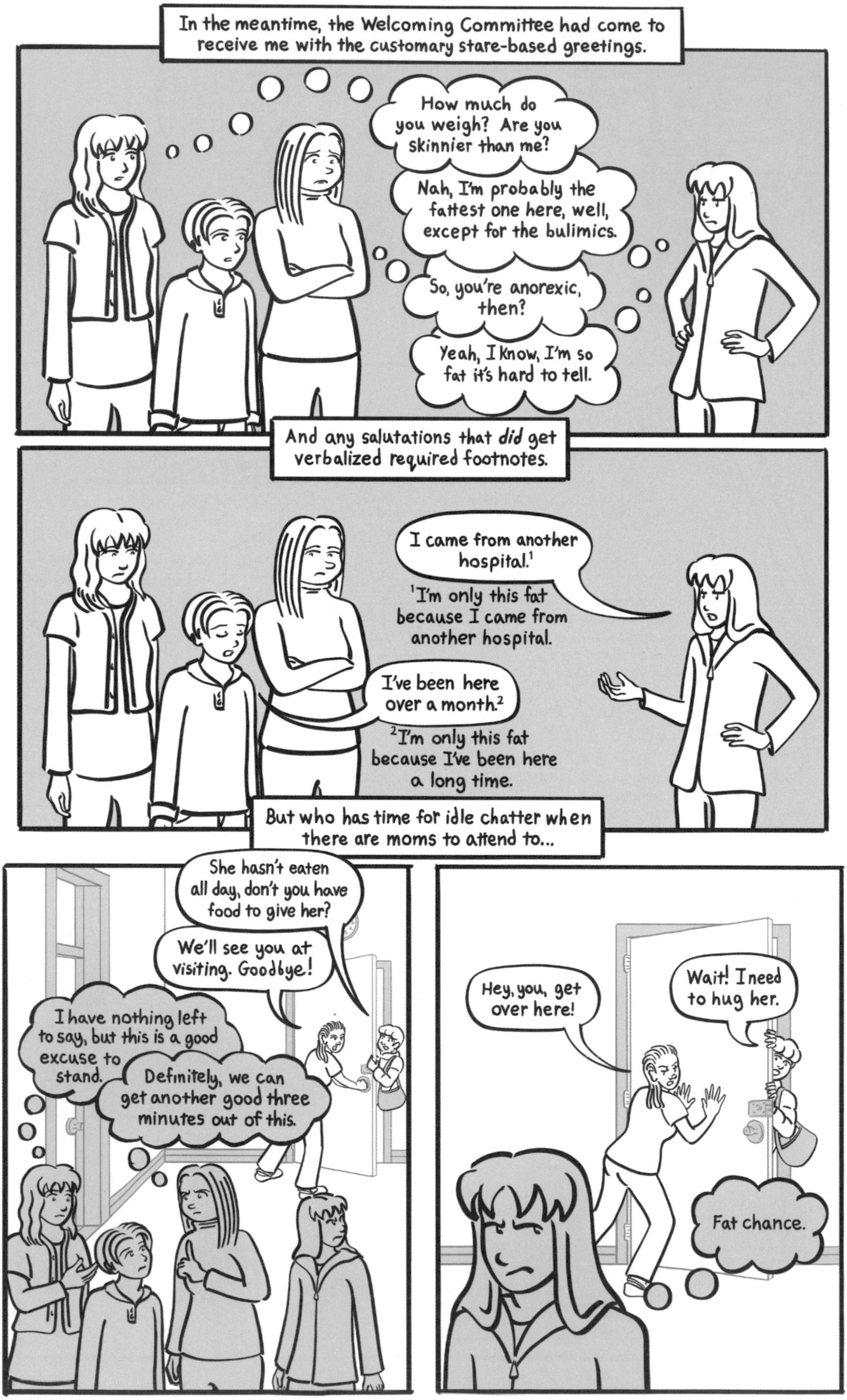
In the meantime, the Welcoming Committee had come to receive me with the customary stare-based greetings.
How much do you weigh? Are you skinnier than me?
Nah, I'm probably the fattest one here, well, except for the bulimics.
So, you're anorexic, then?
Yeah, I know, I'm so fat it's hard to tell.
And any salutations that *did* get verbalized required footnotes.
I came from another hospital.[1]
[1]I'm only this fat because I came from another hospital.
I've been here over a month.[2]
[2]I'm only this fat because I've been here a long time.
But who has time for idle chatter when there are moms to attend to...
She hasn't eaten all day, don't you have food to give her?
We'll see you at visiting. Goodbye!
I have nothing left to say, but this is a good excuse to stand.
Definitely, we can get another good three minutes out of this.
Hey, you, get over here!
Wait! I need to hug her.
Fat chance.

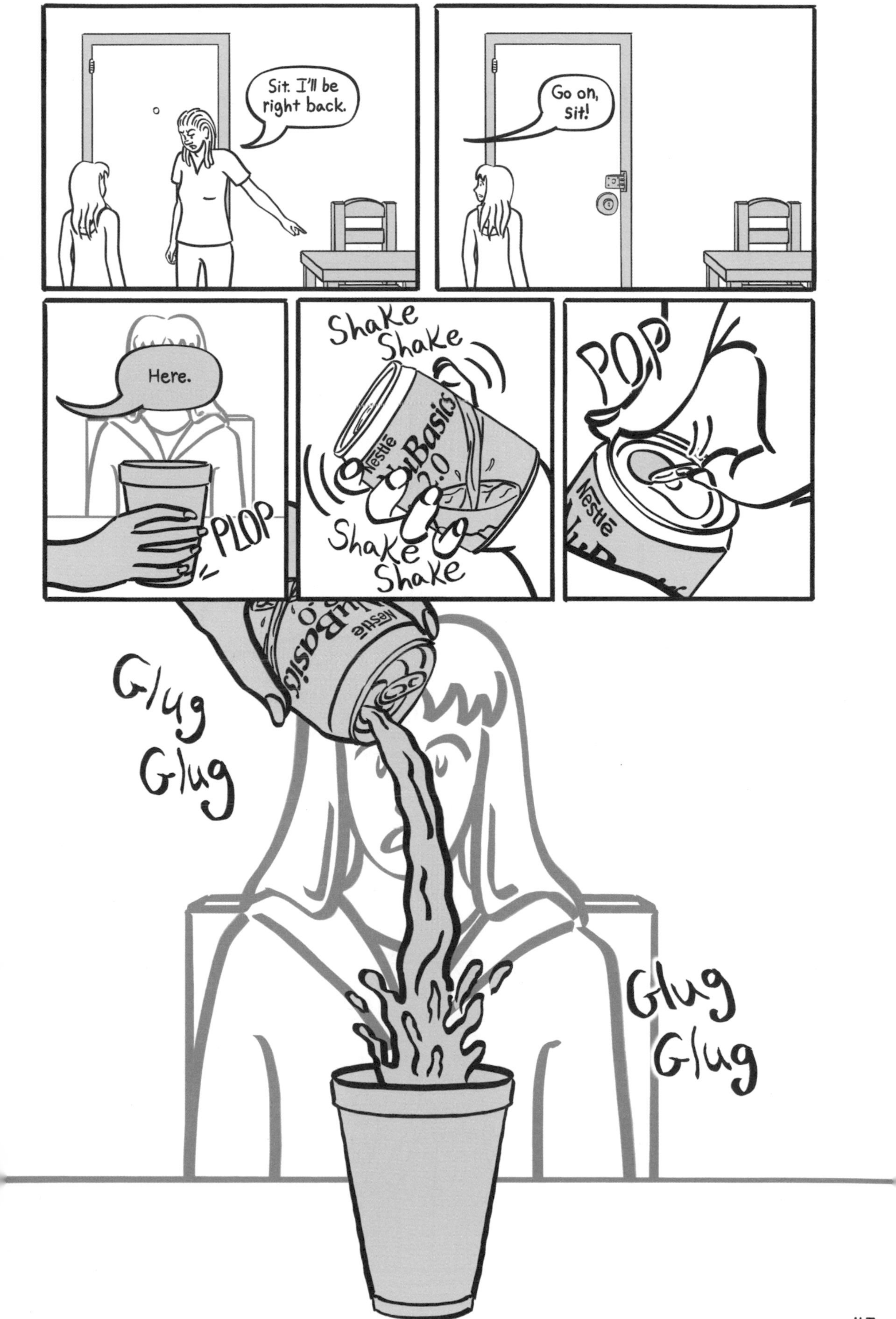
Sit. I'll be right back.
Go on, sit!
Here.
PLOP
Shake Shake
Shake Shake
Nestlé
NuBasics 2.0
POP
Nestlé
Glug Glug
Glug Glug

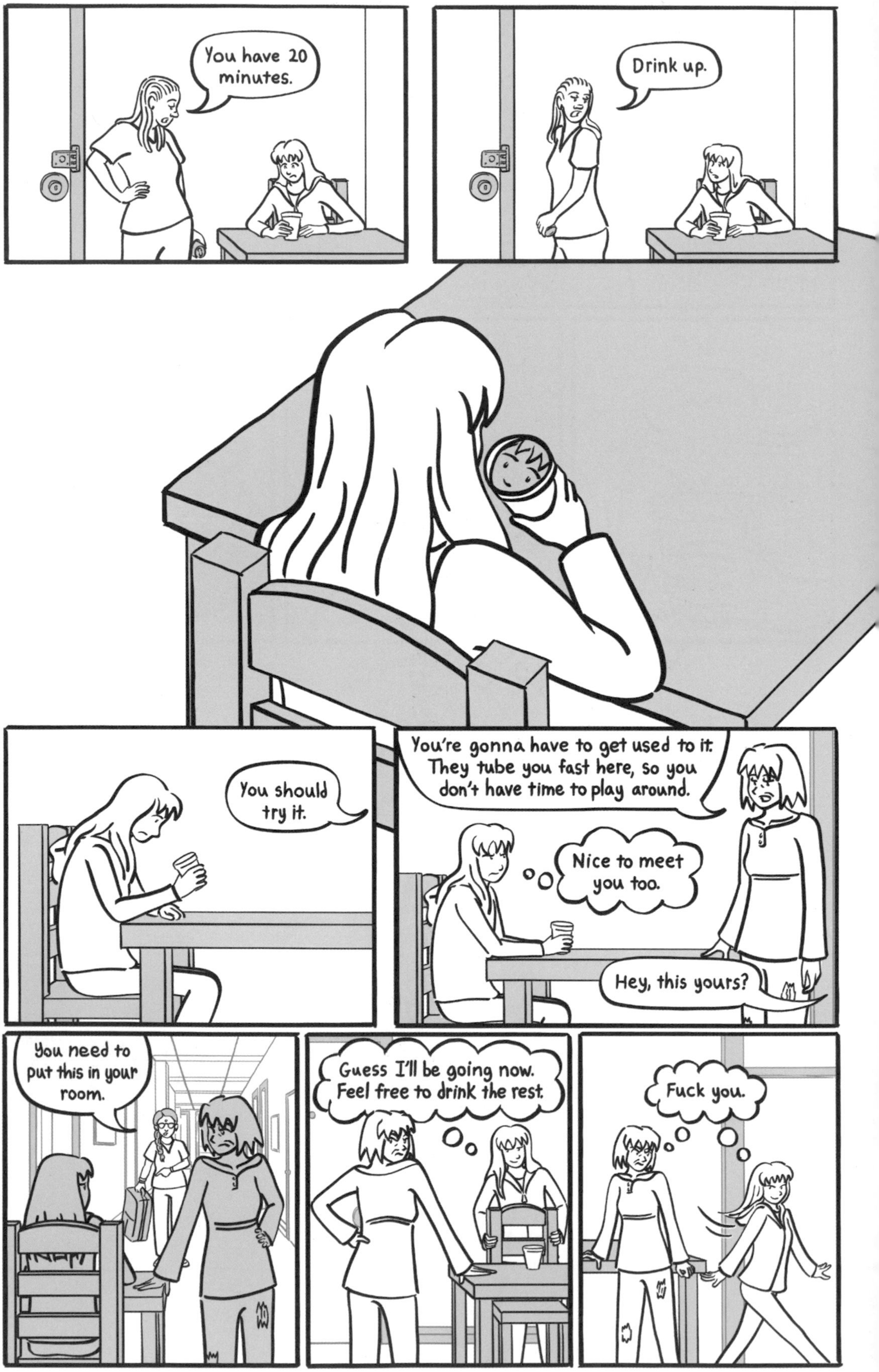
You have 20 minutes.
Drink up.
You should try it.
You're gonna have to get used to it. They tube you fast here, so you don't have time to play around.
Nice to meet you too.
Hey, this yours?
You need to put this in your room.
Guess I'll be going now. Feel free to drink the rest.
Fuck you.

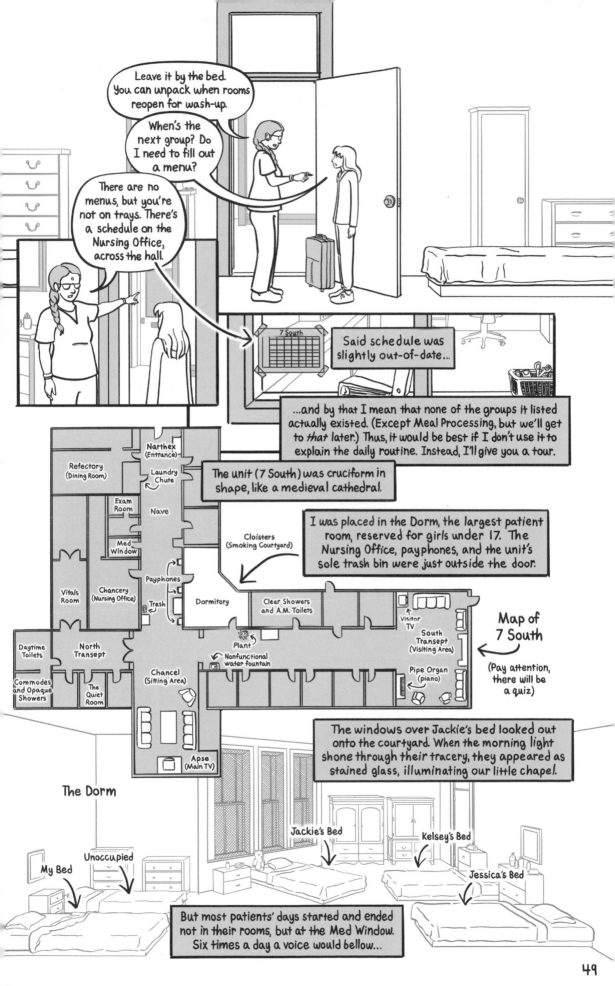

Leave it by the bed. You can unpack when rooms reopen for wash-up.

When's the next group? Do I need to fill out a menu?

There are no menus, but you're not on trays. There's a schedule on the Nursing Office, across the hall.

Said schedule was slightly out-of-date...

...and by that I mean that none of the groups it listed actually existed. (Except Meal Processing, but we'll get to *that* later.) Thus, it would be best if I don't use it to explain the daily routine. Instead, I'll give you a tour.

The unit (7 South) was cruciform in shape, like a medieval cathedral.

I was placed in the Dorm, the largest patient room, reserved for girls under 17. The Nursing Office, payphones, and the unit's sole trash bin were just outside the door.

Map of 7 South

(Pay attention, there will be a quiz)

Map labels:
Narthex (Entrance)
Refectory (Dining Room)
Laundry Chute
Exam Room
Nave
Med Window
Cloisters (Smoking Courtyard)
Vitals Room
Chancery (Nursing Office)
Payphones
Trash
Dormitory
Clear Showers and A.M. Toilets
Visitor TV
South Transept (Visiting Area)
Plant
Nonfunctional water fountain
Pipe Organ (piano)
Daytime Toilets
North Transept
Chancel (Sitting Area)
Commodes and Opaque Showers
The Quiet Room
Apse (Main TV)

The windows over Jackie's bed looked out onto the courtyard. When the morning light shone through their tracery, they appeared as stained glass, illuminating our little chapel.

The Dorm

My Bed
Unoccupied
Jackie's Bed
Kelsey's Bed
Jessica's Bed

But most patients' days started and ended not in their rooms, but at the Med Window. Six times a day a voice would bellow...

49

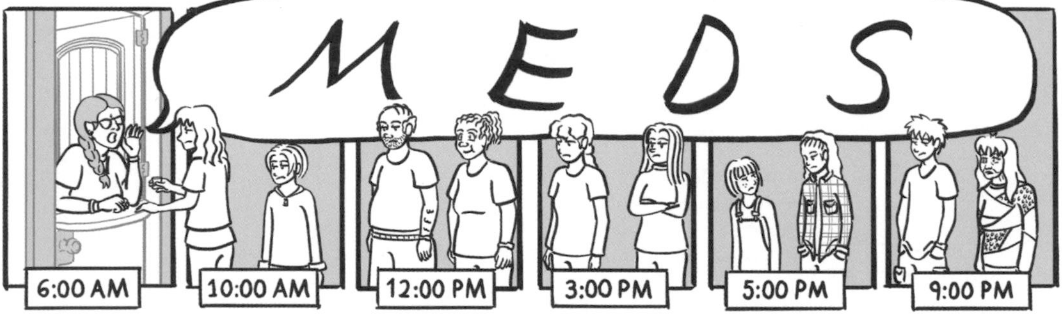
MEDS
6:00 AM
10:00 AM
12:00 PM
3:00 PM
5:00 PM
9:00 PM

...and patients would instantly form a queue to collect their daily rations, as most were genuinly excited to receive their cocktails. Colace and Metamucil were staples, as constipation, and discussion of one's constipation, were popular pastimes:

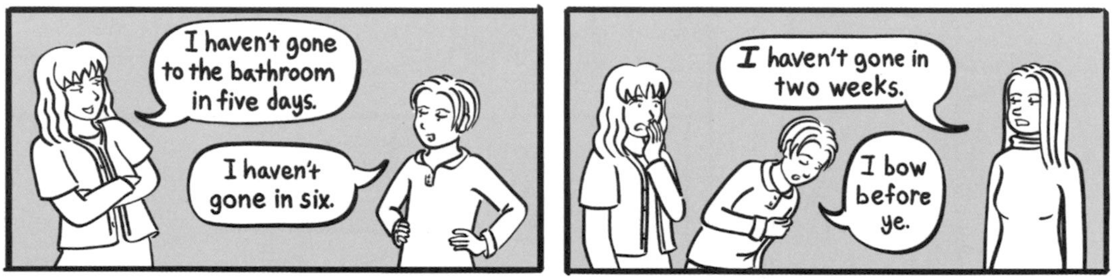
I haven't gone to the bathroom in five days.
I haven't gone in six.
I haven't gone in two weeks.
I bow before ye.

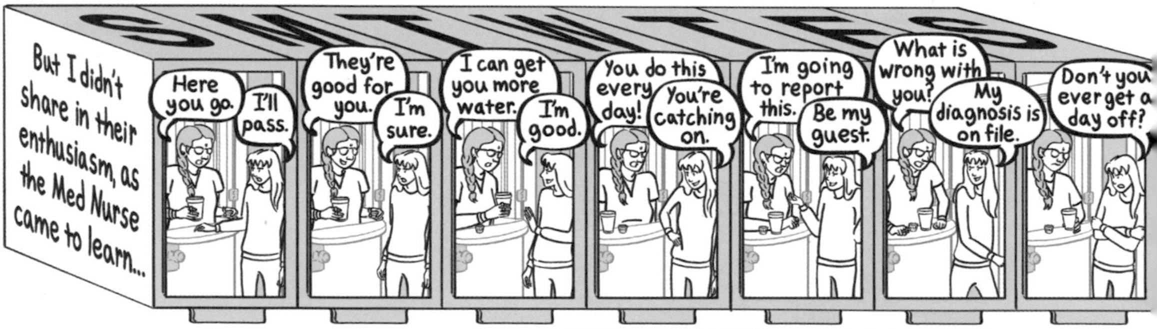
S M T W T F S
But I didn't share in their enthusiasm, as the Med Nurse came to learn...
Here you go.
I'll pass.
They're good for you.
I'm sure.
I can get you more water.
I'm good.
You do this every day!
You're catching on.
I'm going to report this.
Be my guest.
What is wrong with you?
My diagnosis is on file.
Don't you ever get a day off?

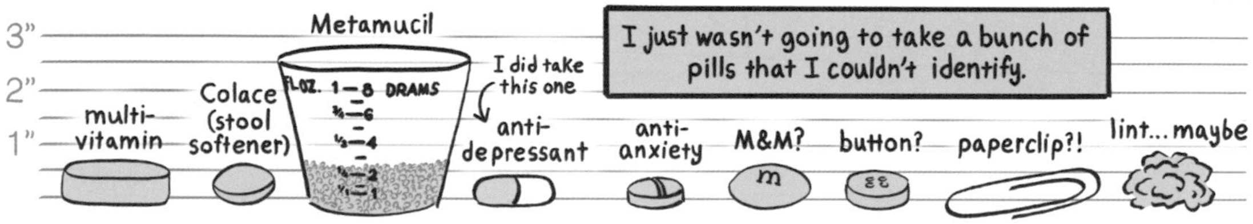
3"
2"
1"
Metamucil
FL.OZ. 1—8 DRAMS
¾—6
½—4
¼—2
⅛—1
I did take this one
I just wasn't going to take a bunch of pills that I couldn't identify.
multi-vitamin
Colace (stool softener)
anti-depressant
anti-anxiety
M&M?
button?
paperclip?!
lint... maybe

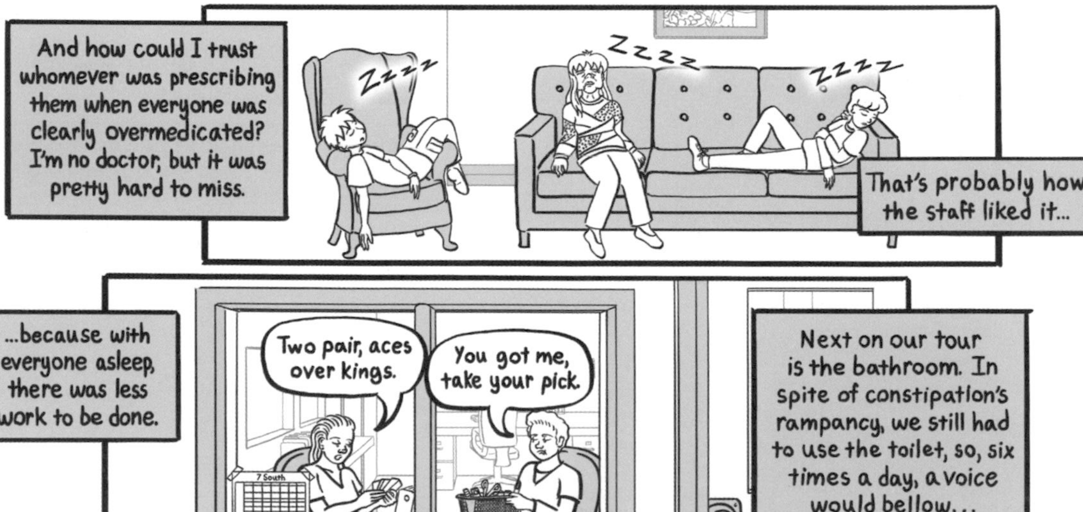
And how could I trust whomever was prescribing them when everyone was clearly overmedicated? I'm no doctor, but it was pretty hard to miss.
Zzzz
Zzzz
Zzzz
That's probably how the staff liked it...

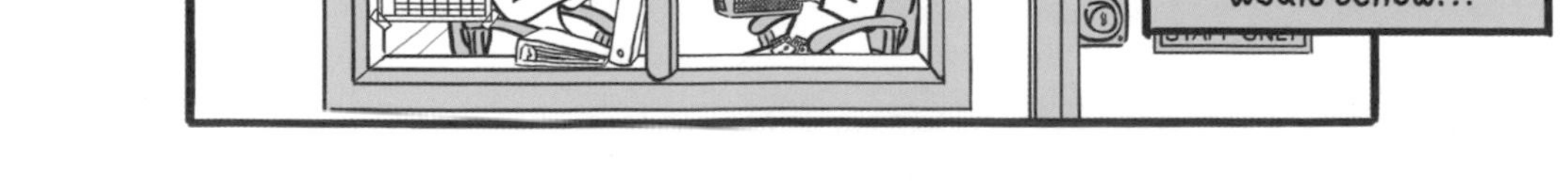
...because with everyone asleep, there was less work to be done.
Two pair, aces over kings.
You got me, take your pick.
7 South
Next on our tour is the bathroom. In spite of constipation's rampancy, we still had to use the toilet, so, six times a day, a voice would bellow...

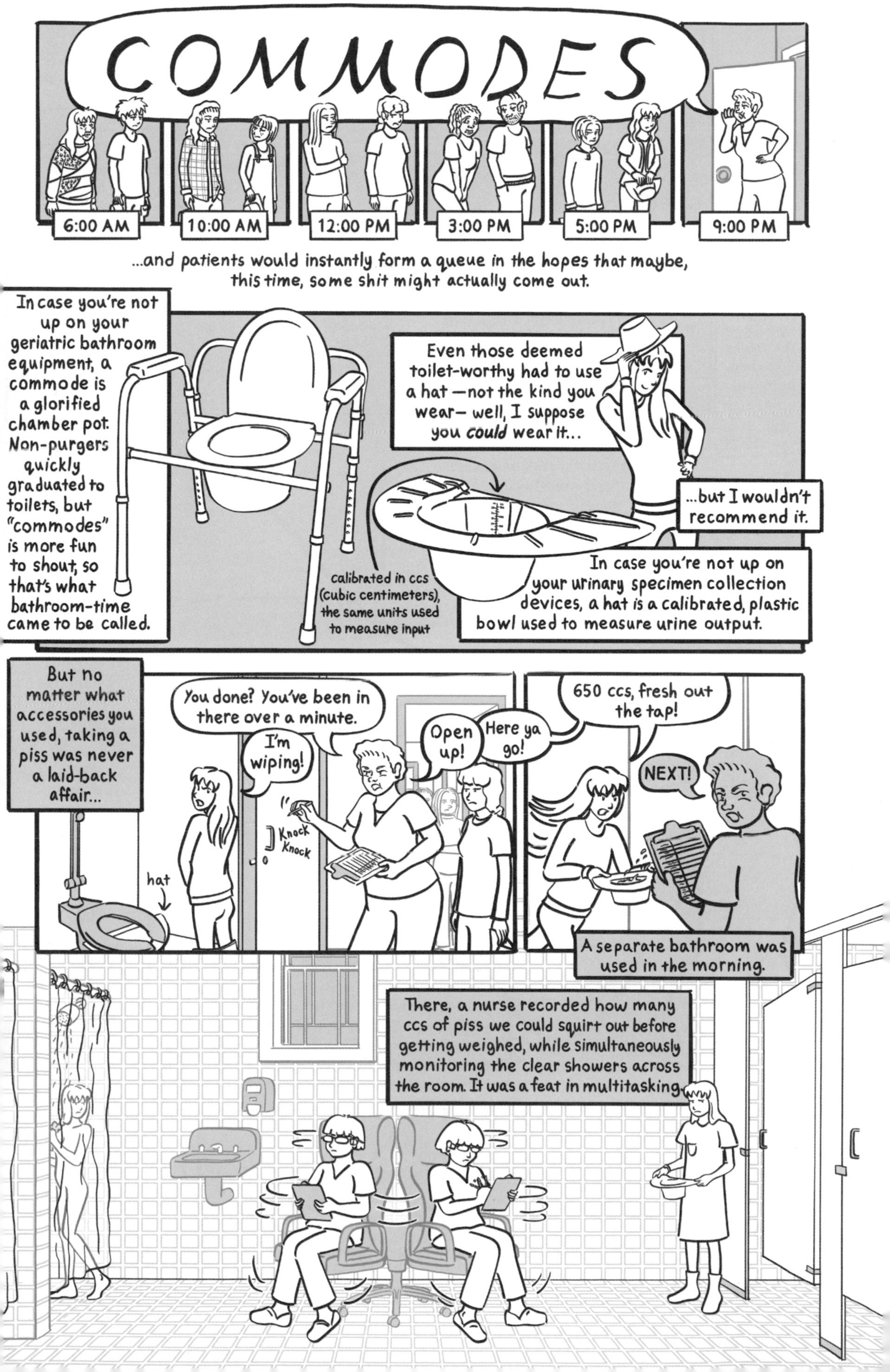
COMMODES
6:00 AM
10:00 AM
12:00 PM
3:00 PM
5:00 PM
9:00 PM
...and patients would instantly form a queue in the hopes that maybe, this time, some shit might actually come out.
In case you're not up on your geriatric bathroom equipment, a commode is a glorified chamber pot. Non-purgers quickly graduated to toilets, but "commodes" is more fun to shout, so that's what bathroom-time came to be called.
Even those deemed toilet-worthy had to use a hat —not the kind you wear— well, I suppose you *could* wear it...
...but I wouldn't recommend it.
calibrated in ccs (cubic centimeters), the same units used to measure input
In case you're not up on your urinary specimen collection devices, a hat is a calibrated, plastic bowl used to measure urine output.
But no matter what accessories you used, taking a piss was never a laid-back affair...
You done? You've been in there over a minute.
I'm wiping!
Knock Knock
hat
Open up!
Here ya go!
650 ccs, fresh out the tap!
NEXT!
A separate bathroom was used in the morning.
There, a nurse recorded how many ccs of piss we could squirt out before getting weighed, while simultaneously monitoring the clear showers across the room. It was a feat in multitasking.

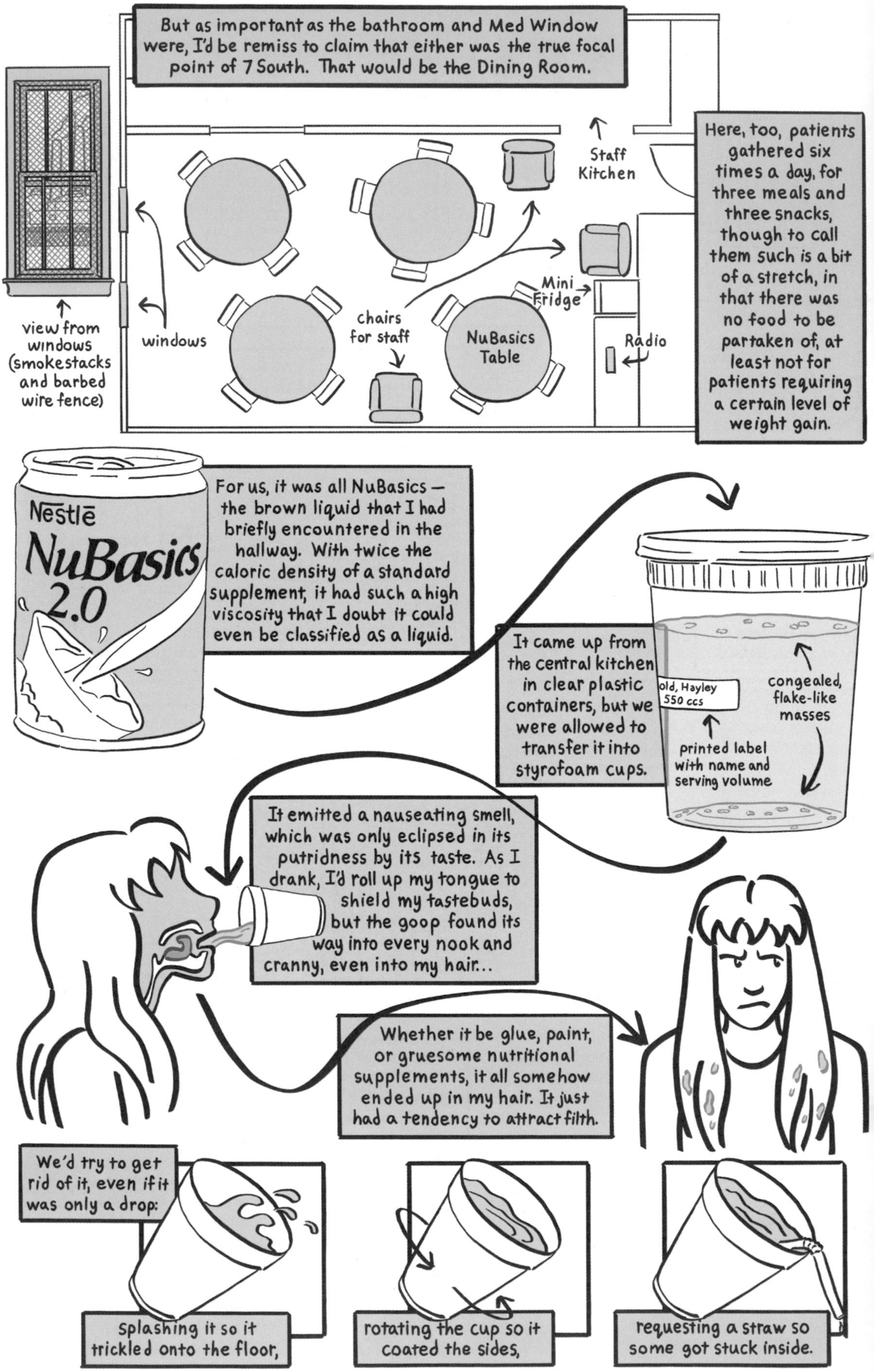

But as important as the bathroom and Med Window were, I'd be remiss to claim that either was the true focal point of 7 South. That would be the Dining Room.
view from windows (smokestacks and barbed wire fence)
windows
chairs for staff
NuBasics Table
Staff Kitchen
Mini Fridge
Radio
Here, too, patients gathered six times a day, for three meals and three snacks, though to call them such is a bit of a stretch, in that there was no food to be partaken of, at least not for patients requiring a certain level of weight gain.
Nestlē
NuBasics
2.0
For us, it was all NuBasics — the brown liquid that I had briefly encountered in the hallway. With twice the caloric density of a standard supplement, it had such a high viscosity that I doubt it could even be classified as a liquid.
It came up from the central kitchen in clear plastic containers, but we were allowed to transfer it into styrofoam cups.
old, Hayley
550 ccs
printed label with name and serving volume
congealed, flake-like masses
It emitted a nauseating smell, which was only eclipsed in its putridness by its taste. As I drank, I'd roll up my tongue to shield my tastebuds, but the goop found its way into every nook and cranny, even into my hair...
Whether it be glue, paint, or gruesome nutritional supplements, it all somehow ended up in my hair. It just had a tendency to attract filth.
We'd try to get rid of it, even if it was only a drop:
splashing it so it trickled onto the floor,
rotating the cup so it coated the sides,
requesting a straw so some got stuck inside.

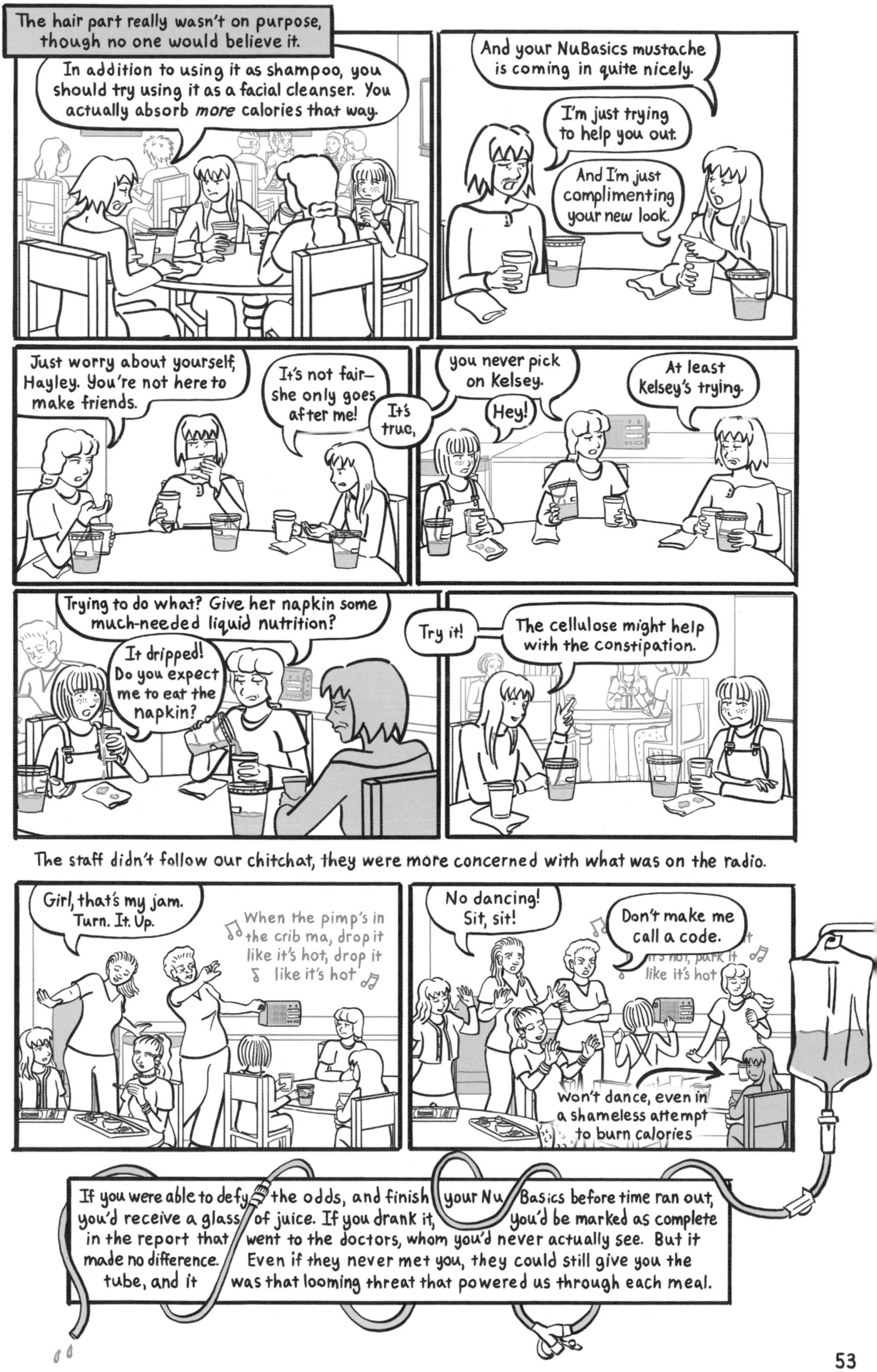

The hair part really wasn't on purpose, though no one would believe it.
In addition to using it as shampoo, you should try using it as a facial cleanser. You actually absorb *more* calories that way.
And your NuBasics mustache is coming in quite nicely.
I'm just trying to help you out.
And I'm just complimenting your new look.
Just worry about yourself, Hayley. You're not here to make friends.
It's not fair— she only goes after me!
It's true,
you never pick on Kelsey.
Hey!
At least Kelsey's trying.
Trying to do what? Give her napkin some much-needed liquid nutrition?
It dripped! Do you expect me to eat the napkin?
Try it!
The cellulose might help with the constipation.
The staff didn't follow our chitchat, they were more concerned with what was on the radio.
Girl, that's my jam. Turn. It. Up.
When the pimp's in the crib ma, drop it like it's hot, drop it like it's hot
No dancing! Sit, sit!
Don't make me call a code.
like it's hot
Won't dance, even in a shameless attempt to burn calories
If you were able to defy the odds, and finish your NuBasics before time ran out, you'd receive a glass of juice. If you drank it, you'd be marked as complete in the report that went to the doctors, whom you'd never actually see. But it made no difference. Even if they never met you, they could still give you the tube, and it was that looming threat that powered us through each meal.

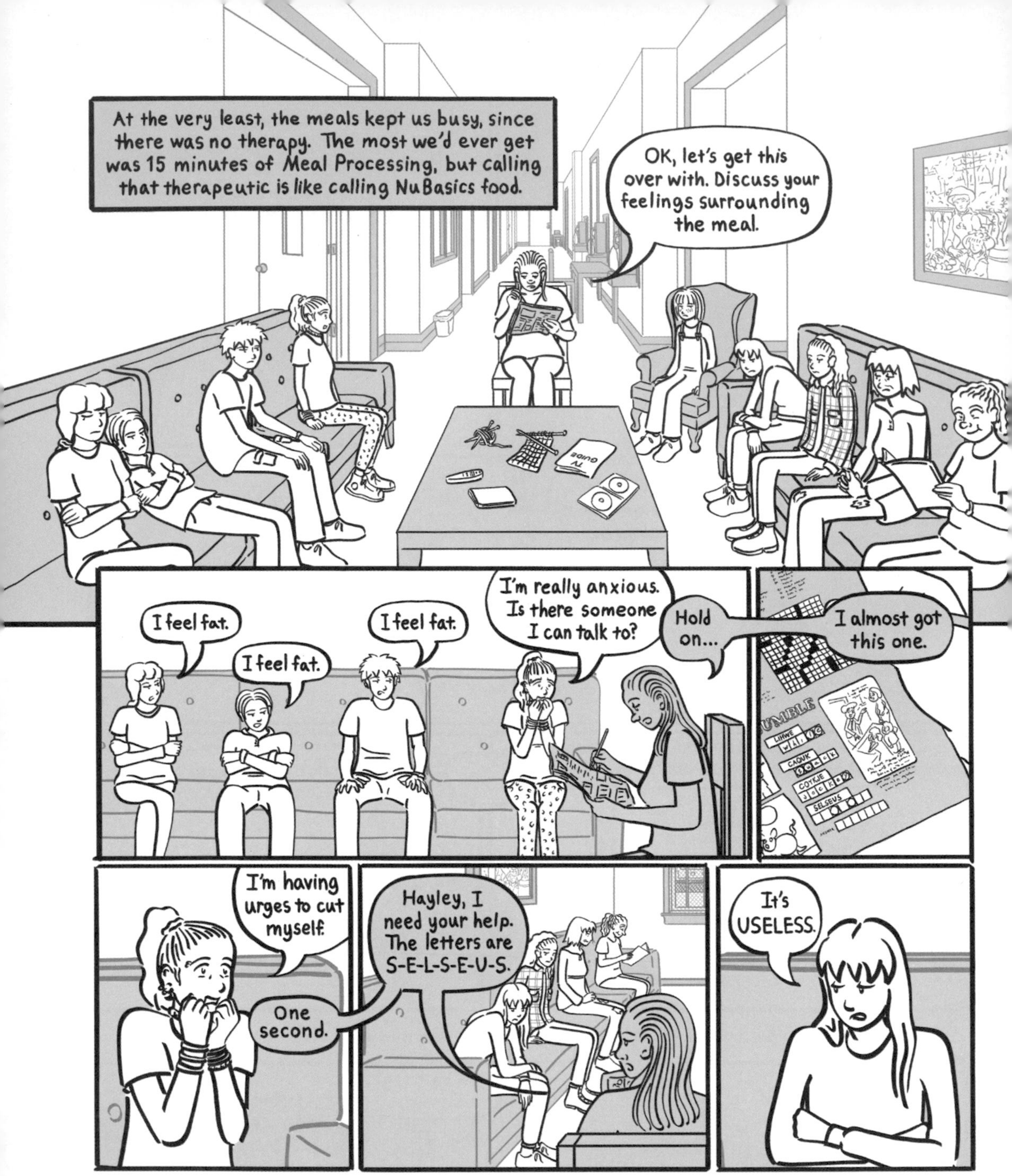

At the very least, the meals kept us busy, since there was no therapy. The most we'd ever get was 15 minutes of Meal Processing, but calling that therapeutic is like calling NuBasics food.
OK, let's get this over with. Discuss your feelings surrounding the meal.
I feel fat.
I feel fat.
I feel fat.
I'm really anxious. Is there someone I can talk to?
Hold on...
I almost got this one.
I'm having urges to cut myself.
One second.
Hayley, I need your help. The letters are S-E-L-S-E-U-S.
It's USELESS.

Outside of Meal Processing, our only source of entertainment was the overflow patients. These were patients who belonged in other, overcrowded units, but got placed in 7 South because there were open beds.

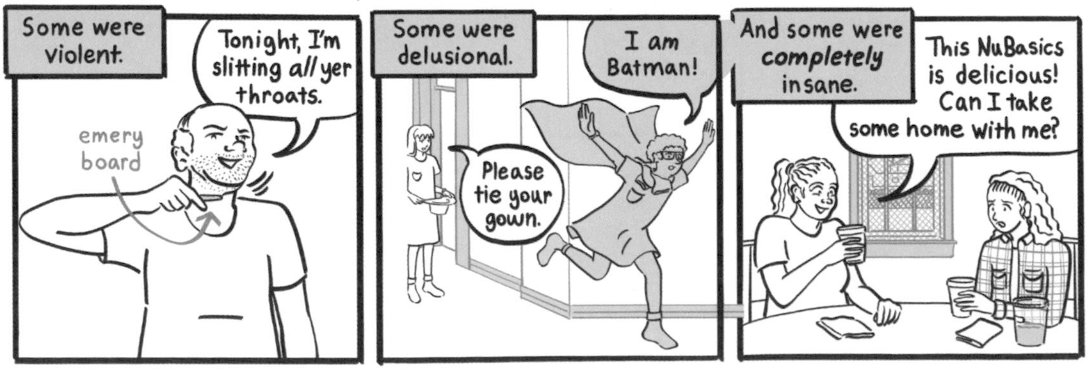

Some were violent.
Tonight, I'm slitting *all* yer throats.
emery board
Some were delusional.
I *am* Batman!
Please tie your gown.
And some were *completely* insane.
This NuBasics is delicious! Can I take some home with me?

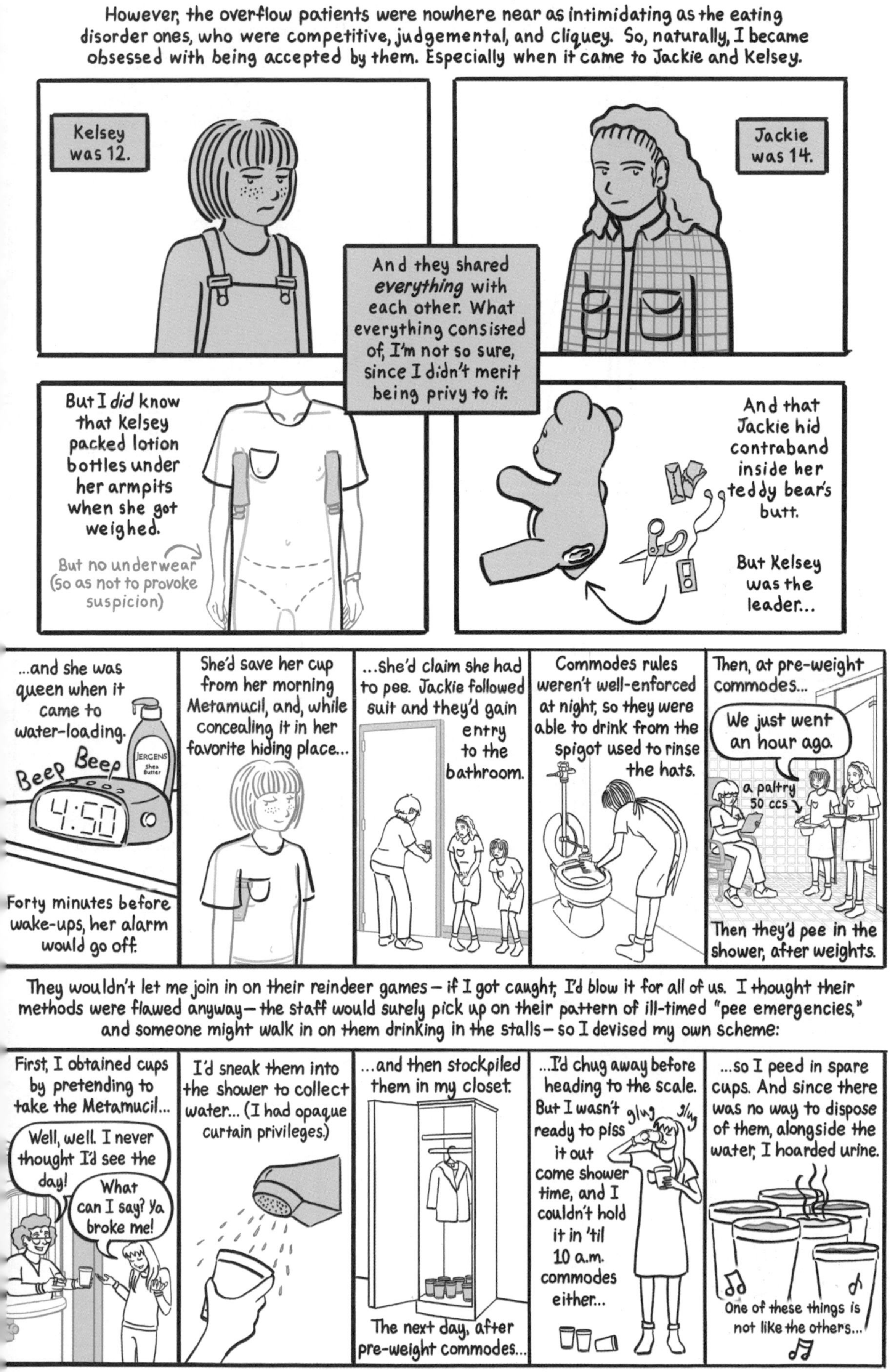
However, the overflow patients were nowhere near as intimidating as the eating disorder ones, who were competitive, judgemental, and cliquey. So, naturally, I became obsessed with being accepted by them. Especially when it came to Jackie and Kelsey.
Kelsey was 12.
Jackie was 14.
And they shared everything with each other. What everything consisted of, I'm not so sure, since I didn't merit being privy to it.
But I did know that Kelsey packed lotion bottles under her armpits when she got weighed.
But no underwear (so as not to provoke suspicion)
And that Jackie hid contraband inside her teddy bear's butt.
But Kelsey was the leader...
...and she was queen when it came to water-loading.
Beep Beep
JERGENS
Shea Butter
4:50
Forty minutes before wake-ups, her alarm would go off.
She'd save her cup from her morning Metamucil, and, while concealing it in her favorite hiding place...
...she'd claim she had to pee. Jackie followed suit and they'd gain entry to the bathroom.
Commodes rules weren't well-enforced at night, so they were able to drink from the spigot used to rinse the hats.
Then, at pre-weight commodes...
We just went an hour ago.
a paltry 50 ccs
Then they'd pee in the shower, after weights.
They wouldn't let me join in on their reindeer games – if I got caught, I'd blow it for all of us. I thought their methods were flawed anyway – the staff would surely pick up on their pattern of ill-timed "pee emergencies," and someone might walk in on them drinking in the stalls – so I devised my own scheme:
First, I obtained cups by pretending to take the Metamucil...
Well, well. I never thought I'd see the day!
What can I say? Ya broke me!
I'd sneak them into the shower to collect water... (I had opaque curtain privileges.)
...and then stockpiled them in my closet.
The next day, after pre-weight commodes...
...I'd chug away before heading to the scale. But I wasn't ready to piss it out come shower time, and I couldn't hold it in 'til 10 a.m. commodes either...
glug glug
...so I peed in spare cups. And since there was no way to dispose of them, alongside the water, I hoarded urine.
One of these things is not like the others...

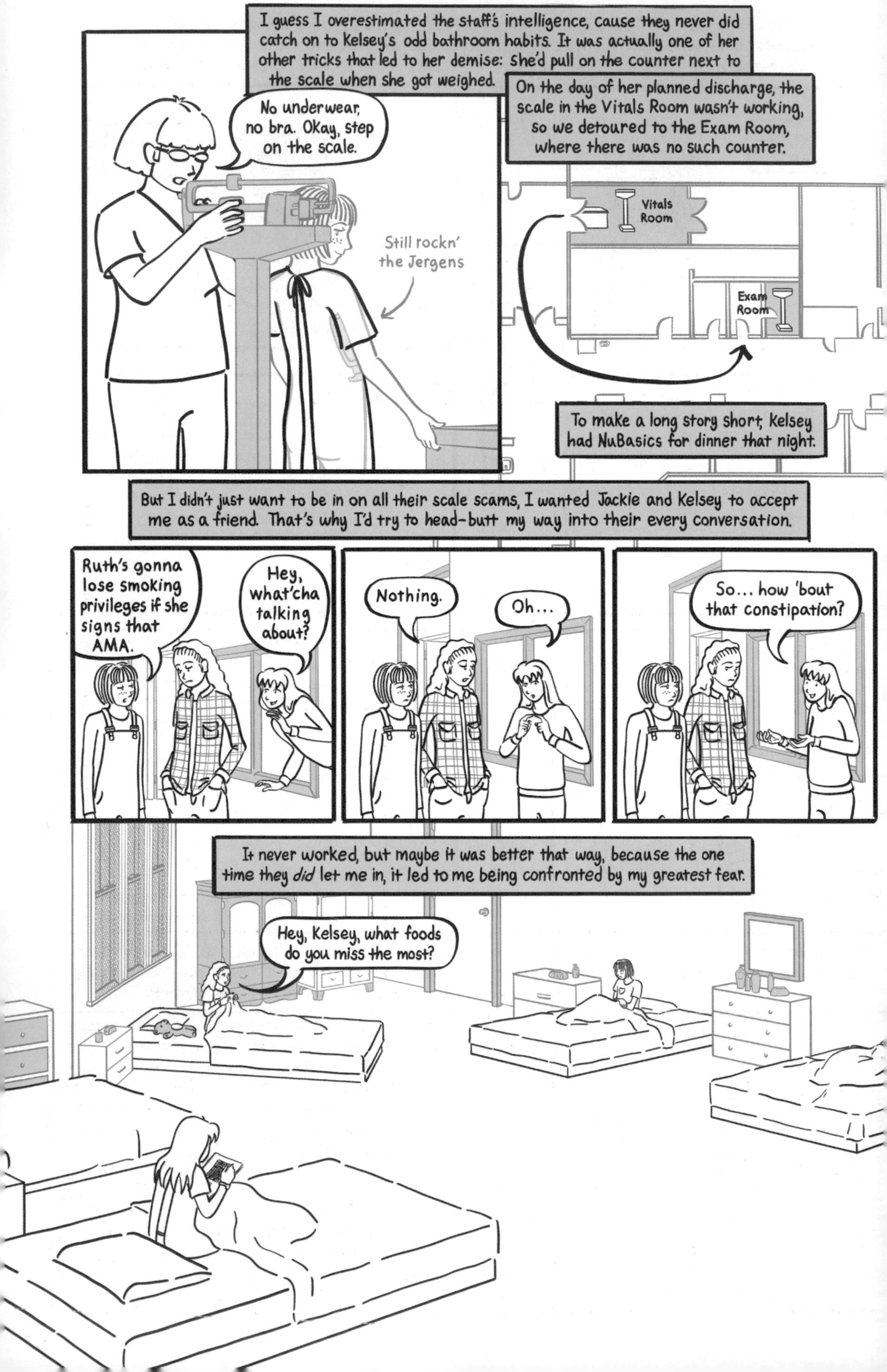
I guess I overestimated the staff's intelligence, cause they never did catch on to Kelsey's odd bathroom habits. It was actually one of her other tricks that led to her demise: she'd pull on the counter next to the scale when she got weighed.
No underwear, no bra. Okay, step on the scale.
Still rockn' the Jergens
On the day of her planned discharge, the scale in the Vitals Room wasn't working, so we detoured to the Exam Room, where there was no such counter.
Vitals Room
Exam Room
To make a long story short, Kelsey had NuBasics for dinner that night.
But I didn't just want to be in on all their scale scams, I wanted Jackie and Kelsey to accept me as a friend. That's why I'd try to head-butt my way into their every conversation.
Ruth's gonna lose smoking privileges if she signs that AMA.
Hey, what'cha talking about?
Nothing.
Oh...
So... how 'bout that constipation?
It never worked, but maybe it was better that way, because the one time they *did* let me in, it led to me being confronted by my greatest fear.
Hey, Kelsey, what foods do you miss the most?

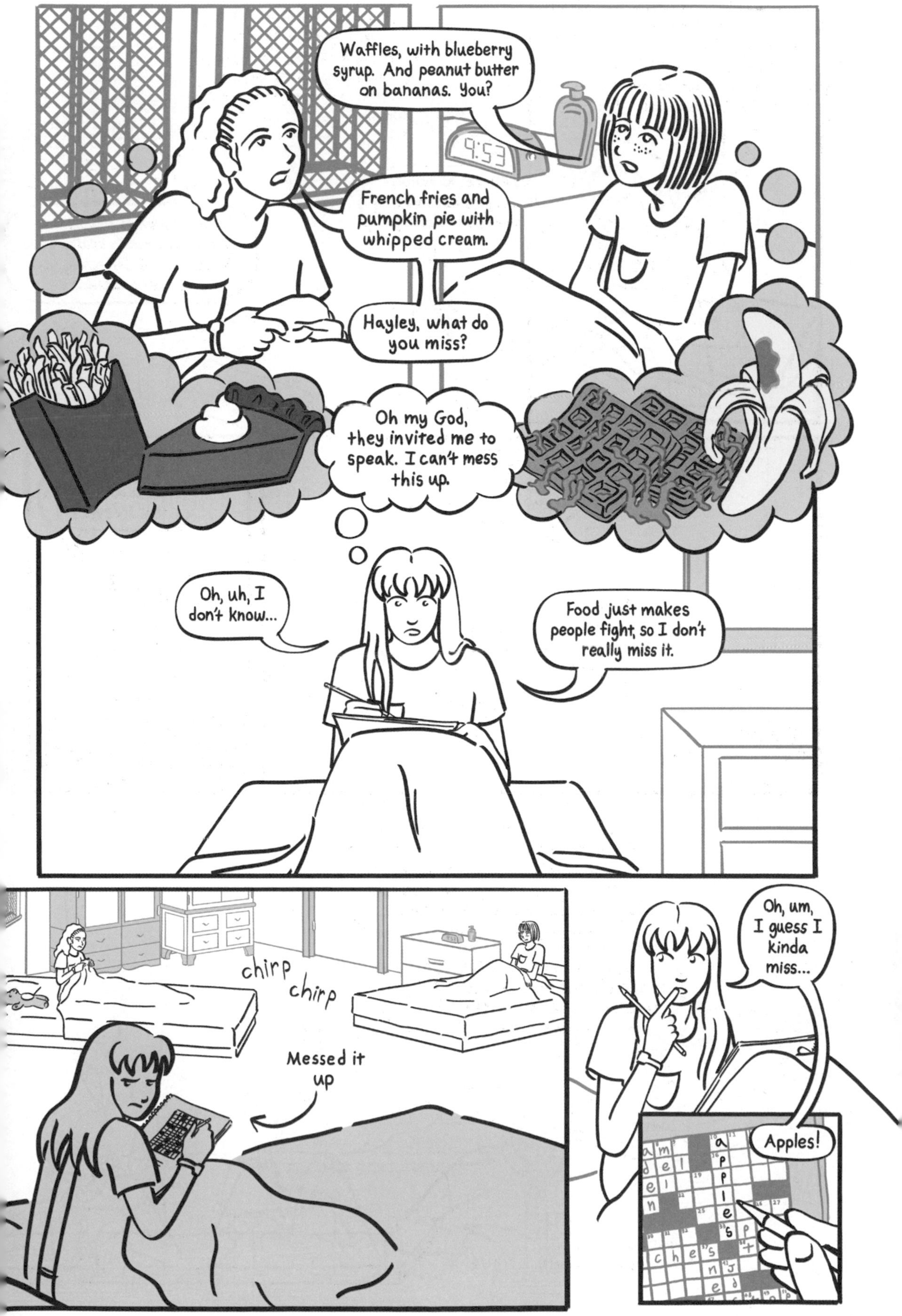
Waffles, with blueberry syrup. And peanut butter on bananas. You?
French fries and pumpkin pie with whipped cream.
Hayley, what do you miss?
Oh my God, they invited me to speak. I can't mess this up.
Oh, uh, I don't know...
Food just makes people fight, so I don't really miss it.
chirp chirp
Messed it up
Oh, um, I guess I kinda miss...
Apples!

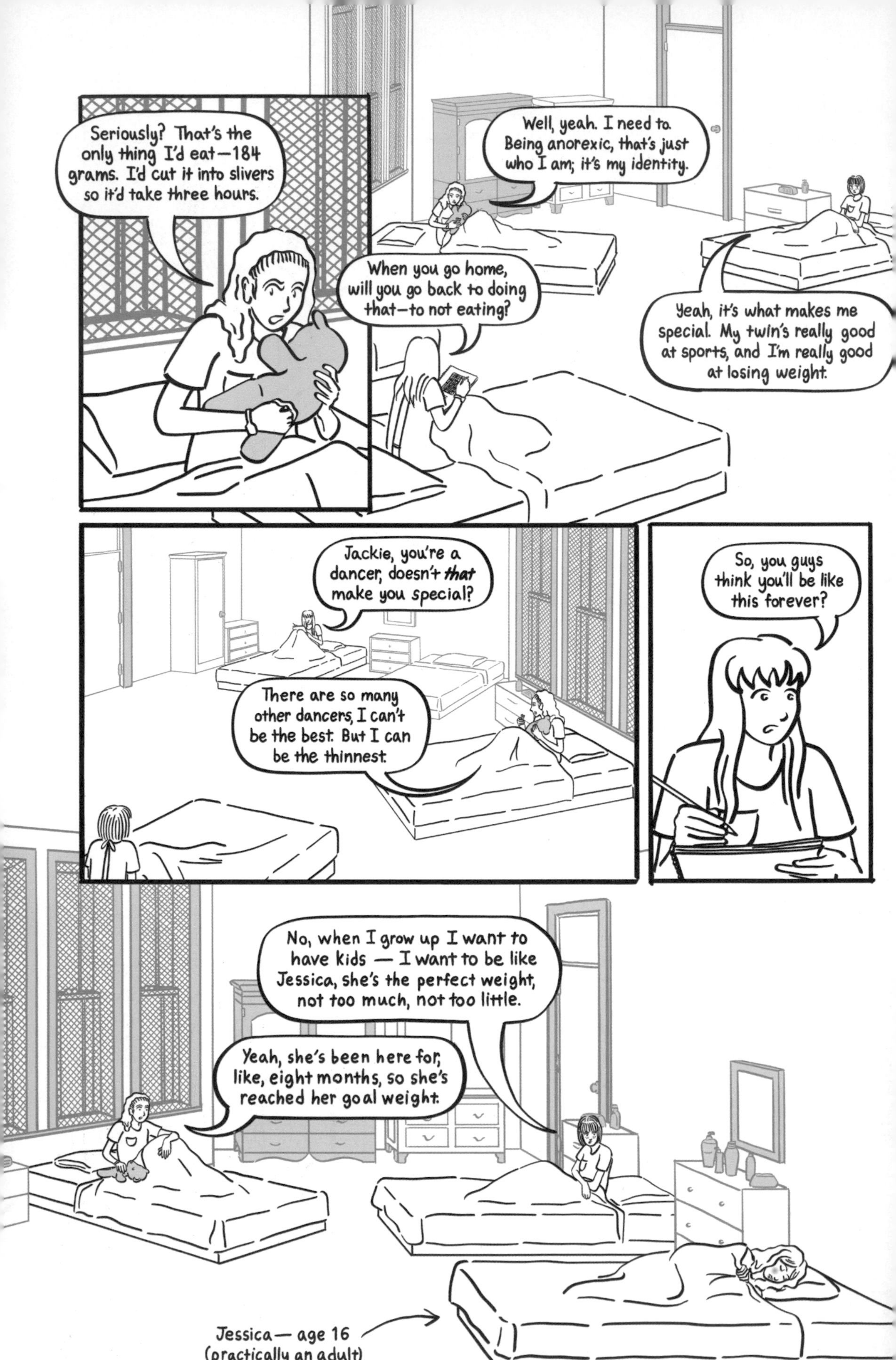
Seriously? That's the only thing I'd eat—184 grams. I'd cut it into slivers so it'd take three hours.
Well, yeah. I need to. Being anorexic, that's just who I am; it's my identity.
When you go home, will you go back to doing that—to not eating?
Yeah, it's what makes me special. My twin's really good at sports, and I'm really good at losing weight.
Jackie, you're a dancer, doesn't *that* make you *special*?
There are so many other dancers, I can't be the best. But I can be the thinnest.
So, you guys think you'll be like this forever?
No, when I grow up I want to have kids — I want to be like Jessica, she's the perfect weight, not too much, not too little.
Yeah, she's been here for, like, eight months, so she's reached her goal weight.
Jessica— age 16 (practically an adult)

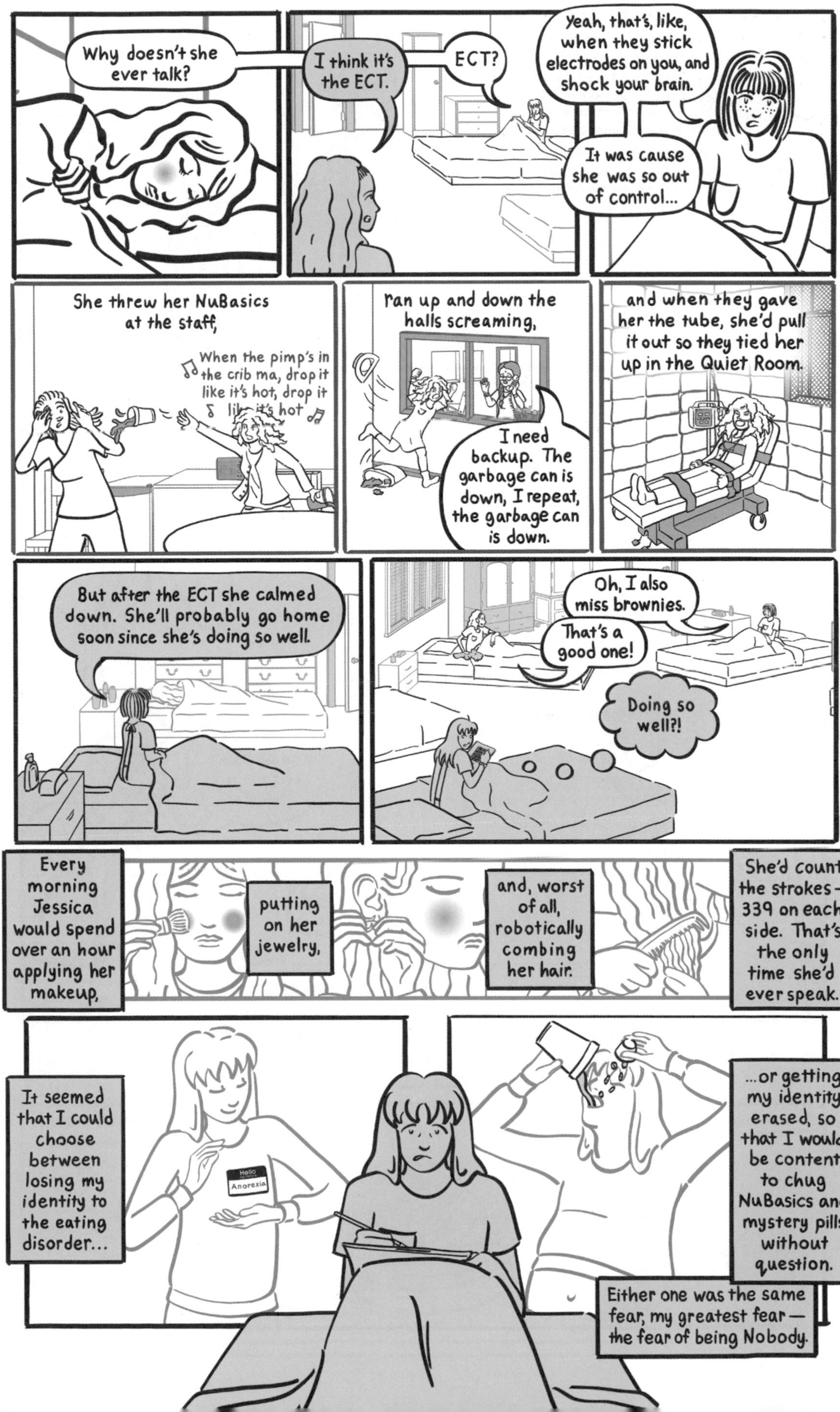
Why doesn't she ever talk?
I think it's the ECT.
ECT?
Yeah, that's, like, when they stick electrodes on you, and shock your brain.
It was cause she was so out of control...
She threw her NuBasics at the staff,
When the pimp's in the crib ma, drop it like it's hot, drop it like it's hot
ran up and down the halls screaming,
I need backup. The garbage can is down, I repeat, the garbage can is down.
and when they gave her the tube, she'd pull it out so they tied her up in the Quiet Room.
But after the ECT she calmed down. She'll probably go home soon since she's doing so well.
Oh, I also miss brownies.
That's a good one!
Doing so well?!
Every morning Jessica would spend over an hour applying her makeup,
putting on her jewelry,
and, worst of all, robotically combing her hair.
She'd count the strokes— 339 on each side. That's the only time she'd ever speak.
It seemed that I could choose between losing my identity to the eating disorder...
Hello
Anorexia
...or getting my identity erased, so that I would be content to chug NuBasics and mystery pills without question.
Either one was the same fear, my greatest fear— the fear of being Nobody.

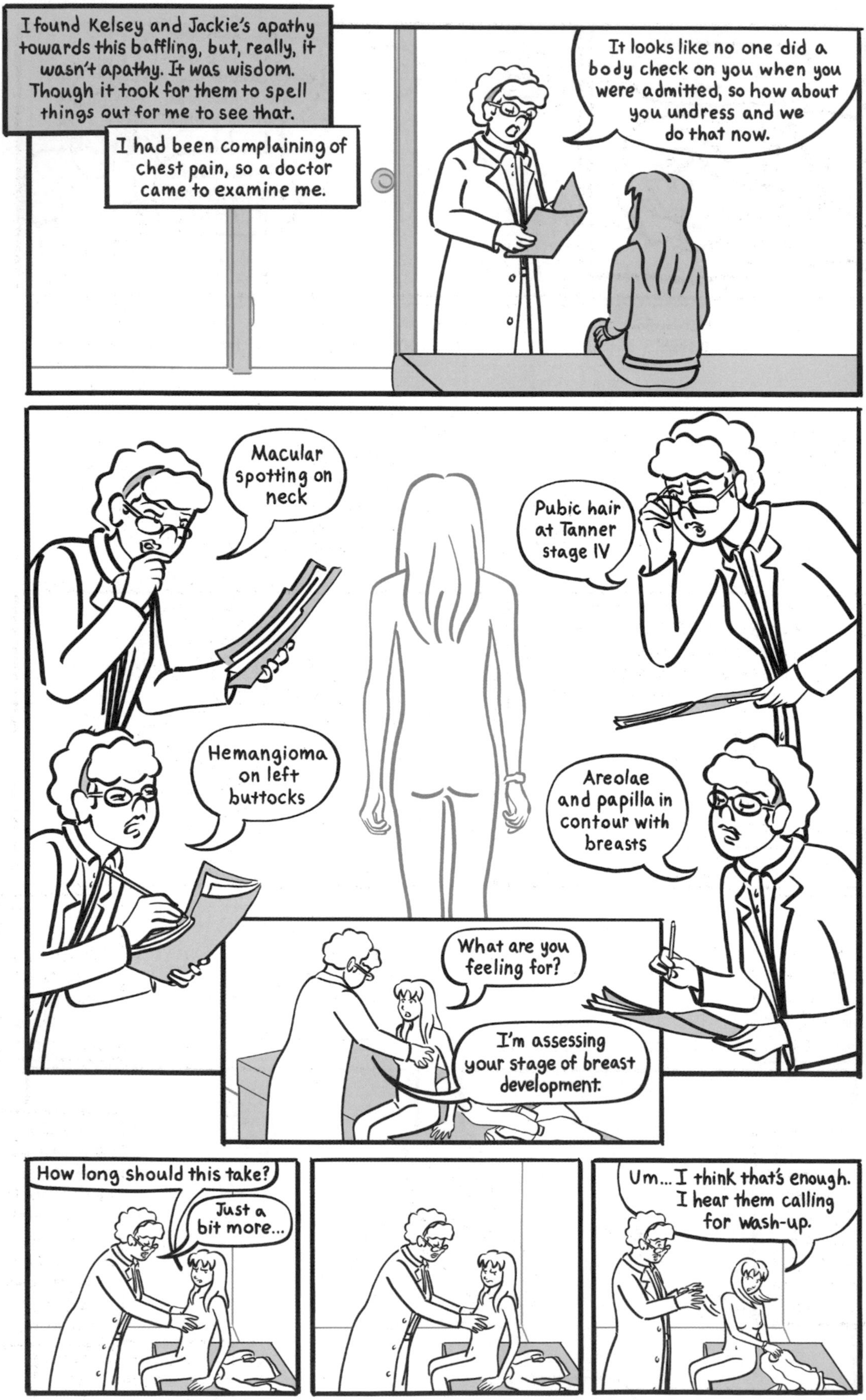

I found Kelsey and Jackie's apathy towards this baffling, but, really, it wasn't apathy. It was wisdom. Though it took for them to spell things out for me to see that.
I had been complaining of chest pain, so a doctor came to examine me.
It looks like no one did a body check on you when you were admitted, so how about you undress and we do that now.
Macular spotting on neck
Pubic hair at Tanner stage IV
Hemangioma on left buttocks
Areolae and papilla in contour with breasts
What are you feeling for?
I'm assessing your stage of breast development.
How long should this take?
Just a bit more...
Um... I think that's enough. I hear them calling for wash-up.

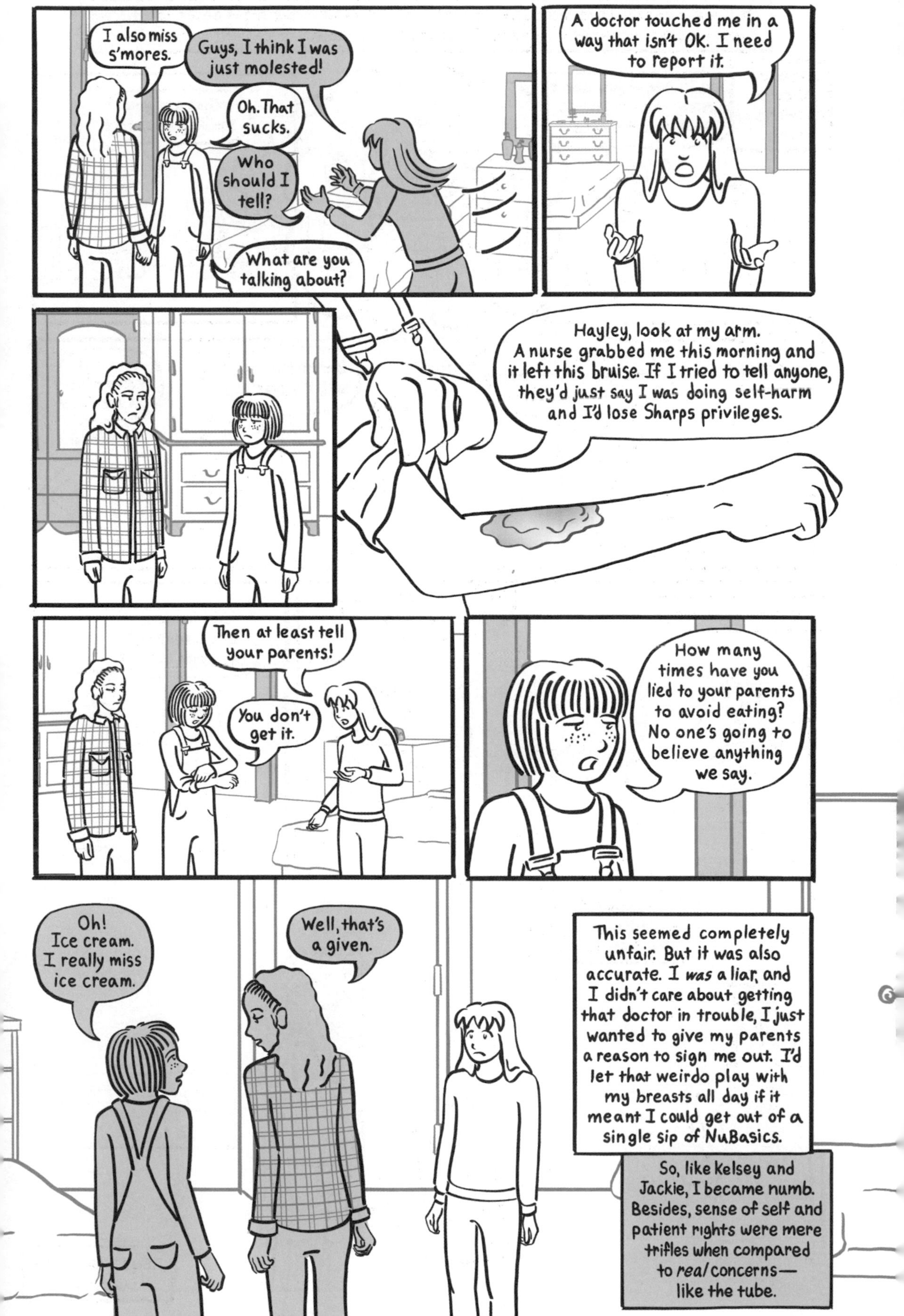
I also miss s'mores.
Guys, I think I was just molested!
Oh. That sucks.
Who should I tell?
What are you talking about?
A doctor touched me in a way that isn't OK. I need to report it.
Hayley, look at my arm. A nurse grabbed me this morning and it left this bruise. If I tried to tell anyone, they'd just say I was doing self-harm and I'd lose Sharps privileges.
Then at least tell your parents!
You don't get it.
How many times have you lied to your parents to avoid eating? No one's going to believe anything we say.
Oh! Ice cream. I really miss ice cream.
Well, that's a given.
This seemed completely unfair. But it was also accurate. I *was* a liar, and I didn't care about getting that doctor in trouble, I just wanted to give my parents a reason to sign me out. I'd let that weirdo play with my breasts all day if it meant I could get out of a single sip of NuBasics.
So, like Kelsey and Jackie, I became numb. Besides, sense of self and patient rights were mere trifles when compared to *real* concerns— like the tube.

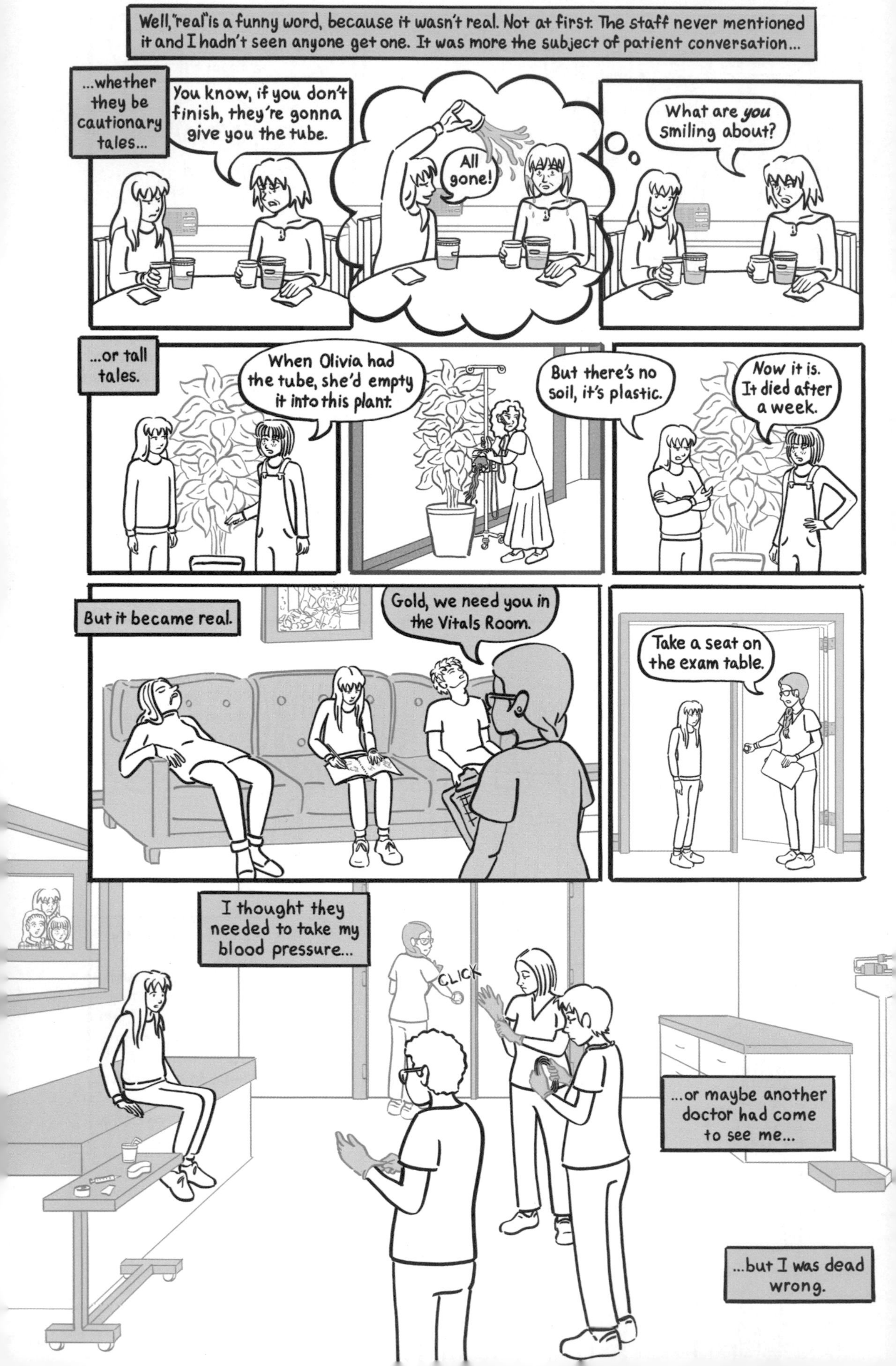
Well, "real" is a funny word, because it wasn't real. Not at first. The staff never mentioned it and I hadn't seen anyone get one. It was more the subject of patient conversation...
...whether they be cautionary tales...
You know, if you don't finish, they're gonna give you the tube.
All gone!
What are *you* smiling about?
...or tall tales.
When Olivia had the tube, she'd empty it into this plant.
But there's no soil, it's plastic.
Now it is. It died after a week.
But it became real.
Gold, we need you in the Vitals Room.
Take a seat on the exam table.
I thought they needed to take my blood pressure...
CLICK
...or maybe another doctor had come to see me...
...but I was dead wrong.

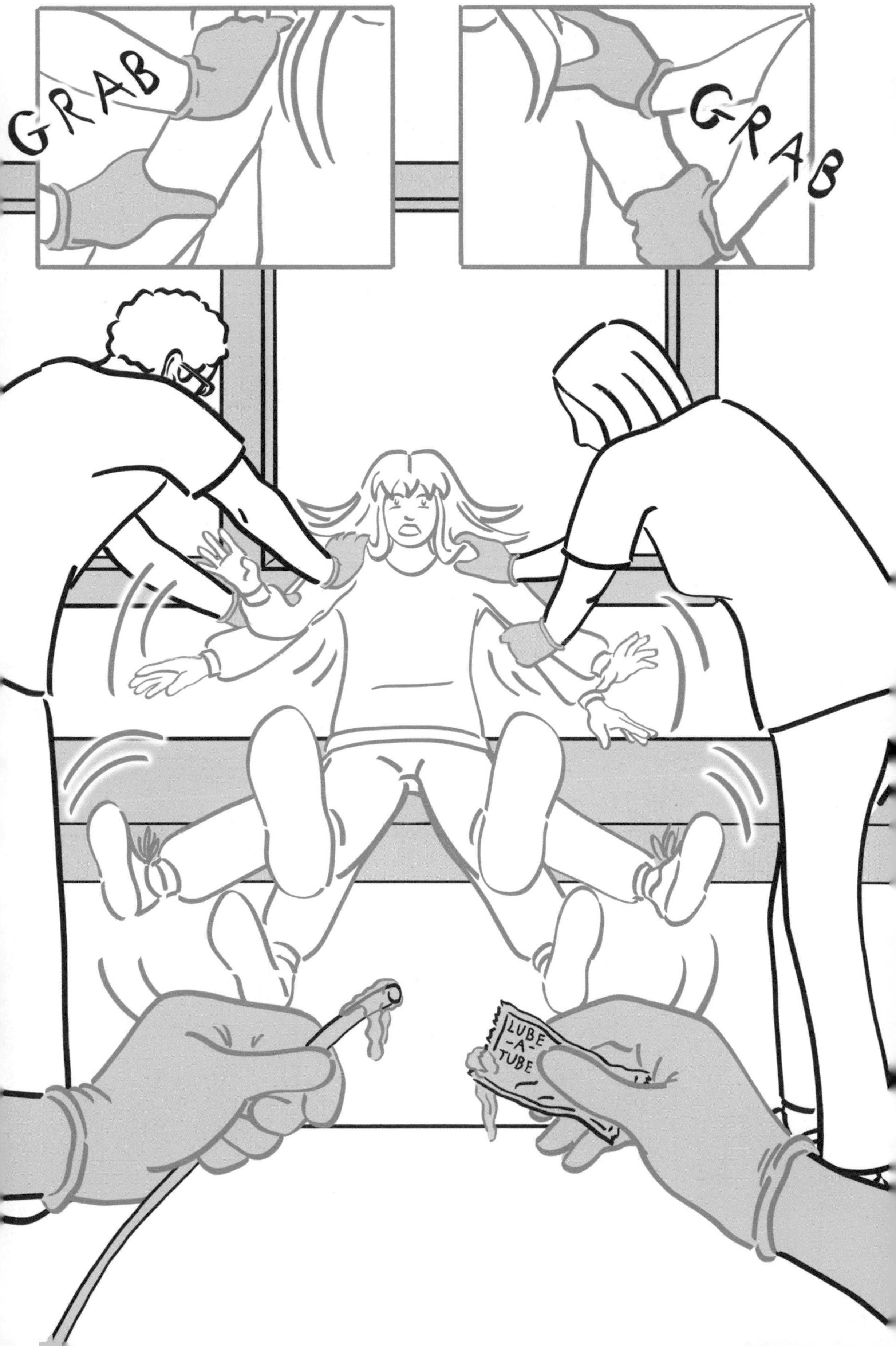
GRAB
GRAB
LUBE-A-TUBE

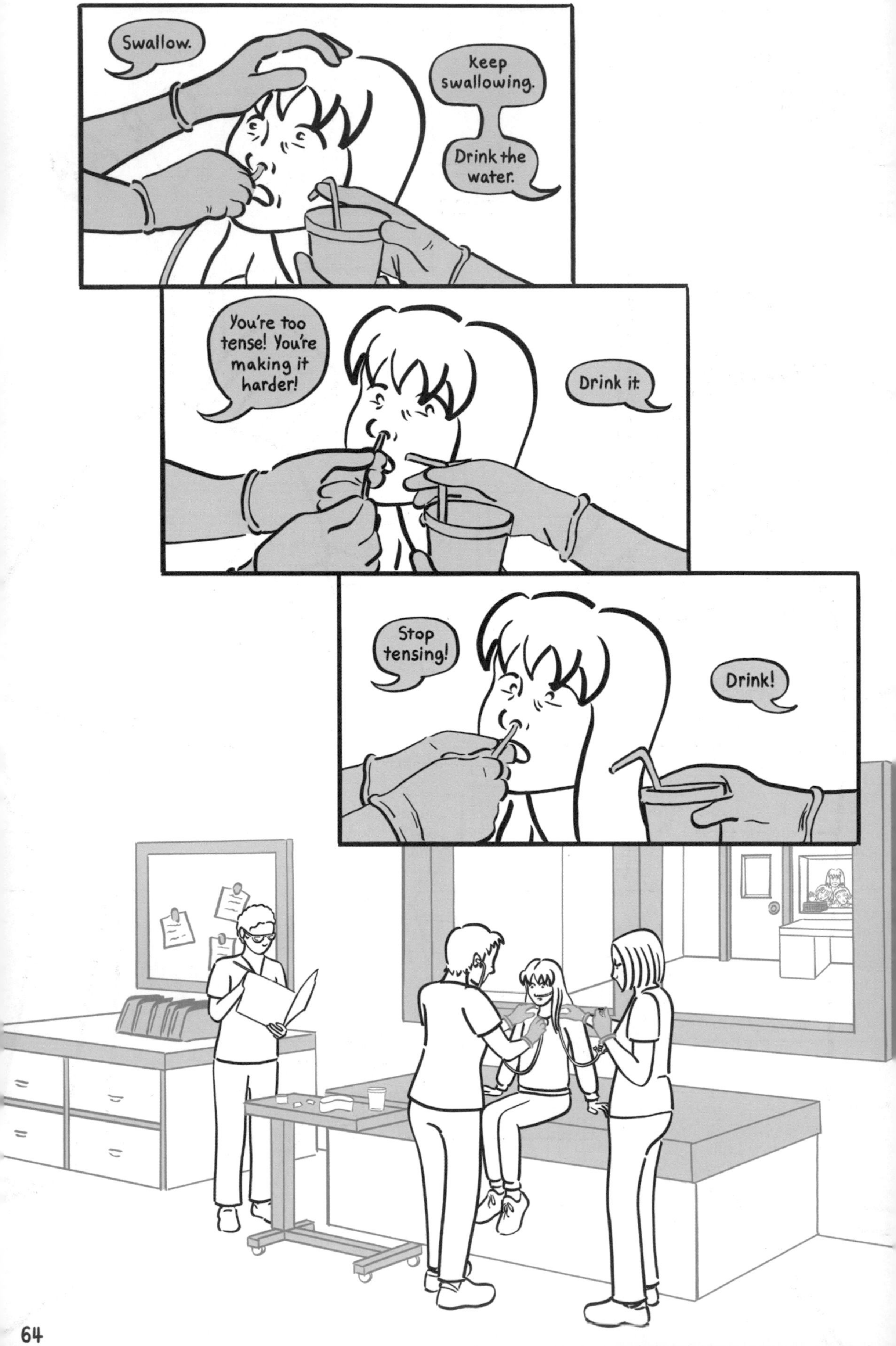
Swallow.
Keep swallowing.
Drink the water.
You're too tense! You're making it harder!
Drink it.
Stop tensing!
Drink!

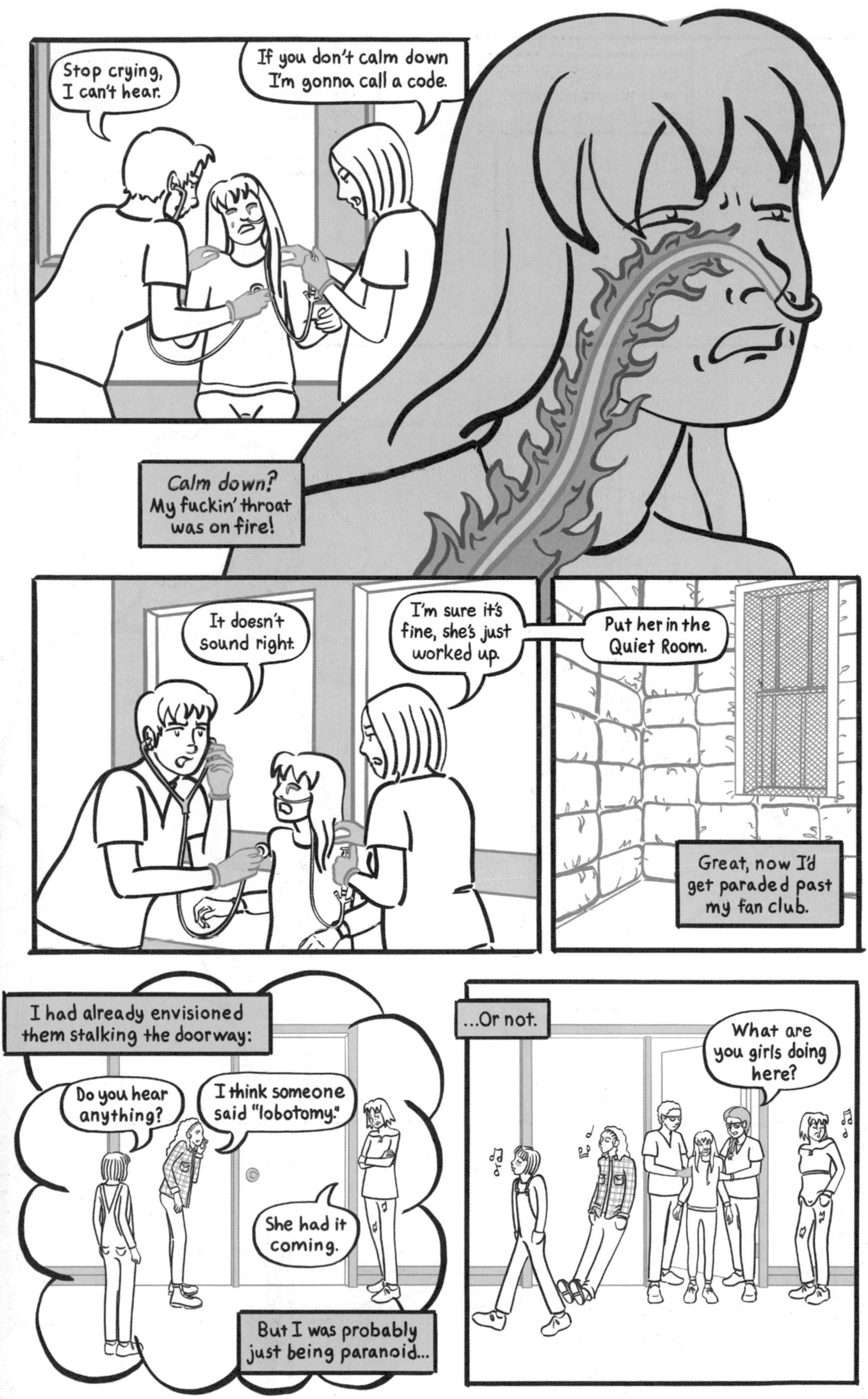
Stop crying, I can't hear.
If you don't calm down I'm gonna call a code.
Calm down? My fuckin' throat was on fire!
It doesn't sound right.
I'm sure it's fine, she's just worked up.
Put her in the Quiet Room.
Great, now I'd get paraded past my fan club.
I had already envisioned them stalking the doorway:
Do you hear anything?
I think someone said "lobotomy."
She had it coming.
But I was probably just being paranoid...
...Or not.
What are you girls doing here?

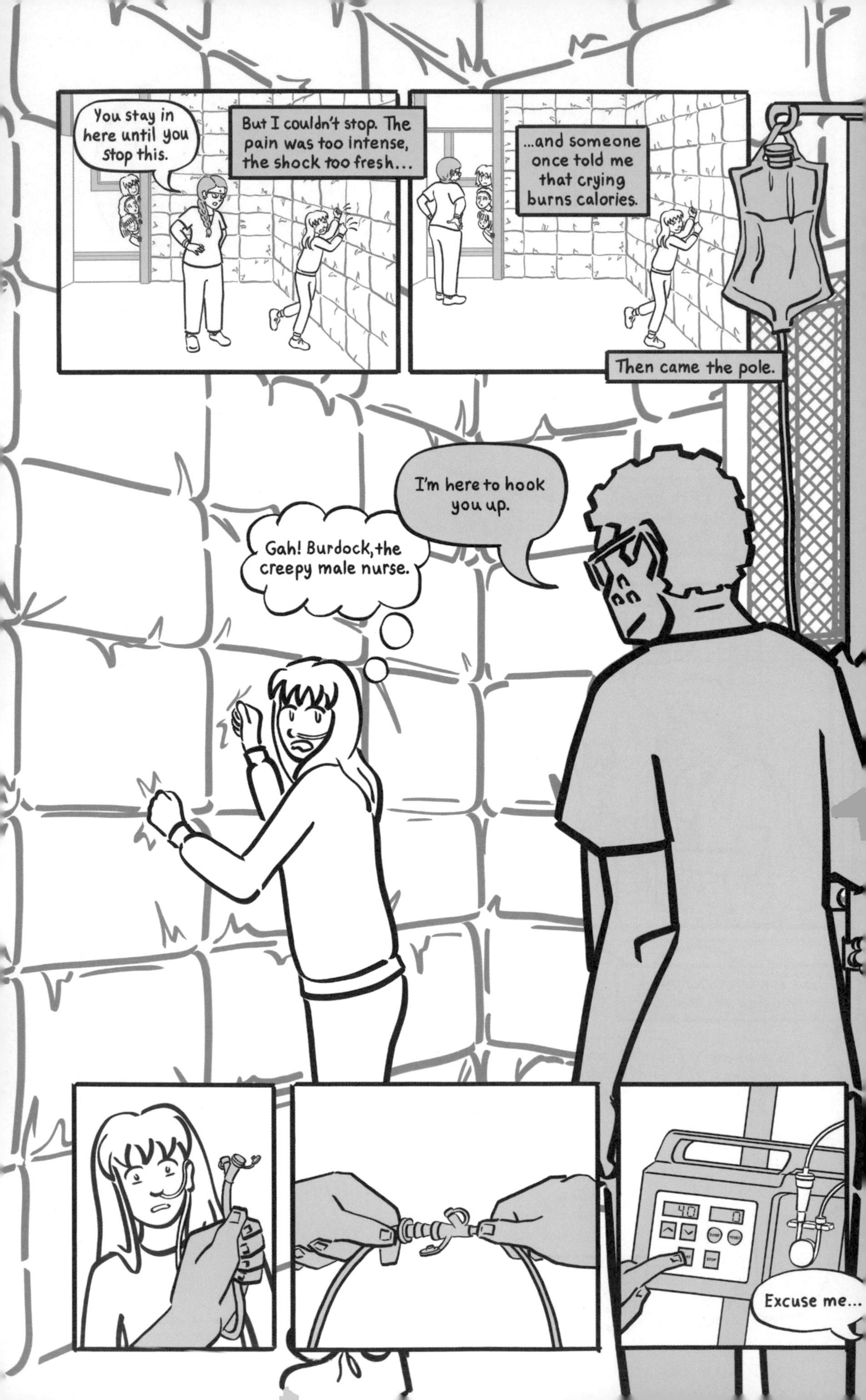
You stay in here until you stop this.
But I couldn't stop. The pain was too intense, the shock too fresh...
...and someone once told me that crying burns calories.
Then came the pole.
I'm here to hook you up.
Gah! Burdock, the creepy male nurse.
Excuse me...

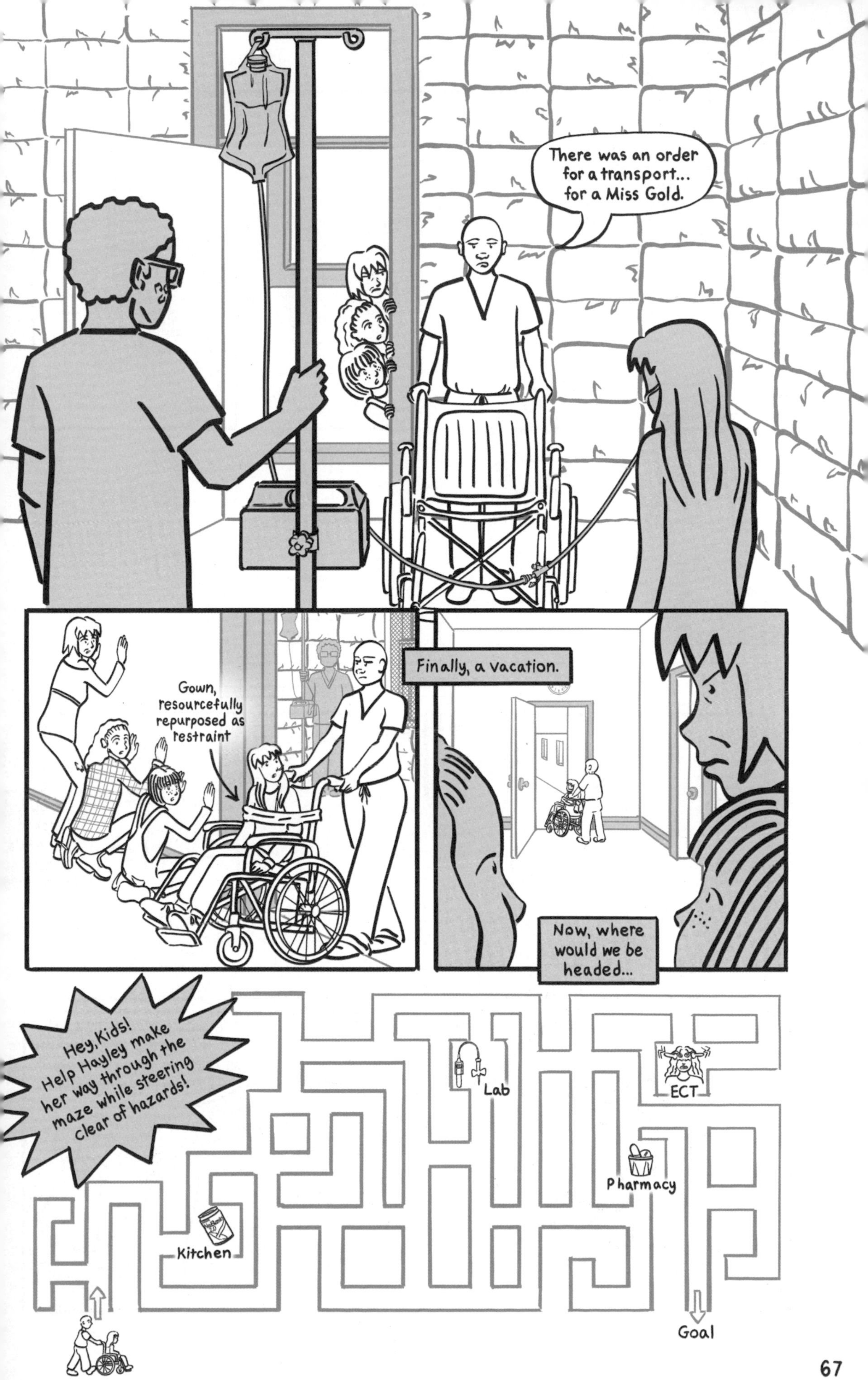

There was an order for a transport... for a Miss Gold.
Gown, resourcefully repurposed as restraint
Finally, a vacation.
Now, where would we be headed...
Hey, Kids! Help Hayley make her way through the maze while steering clear of hazards!
Lab
ECT
Pharmacy
Kitchen
Goal

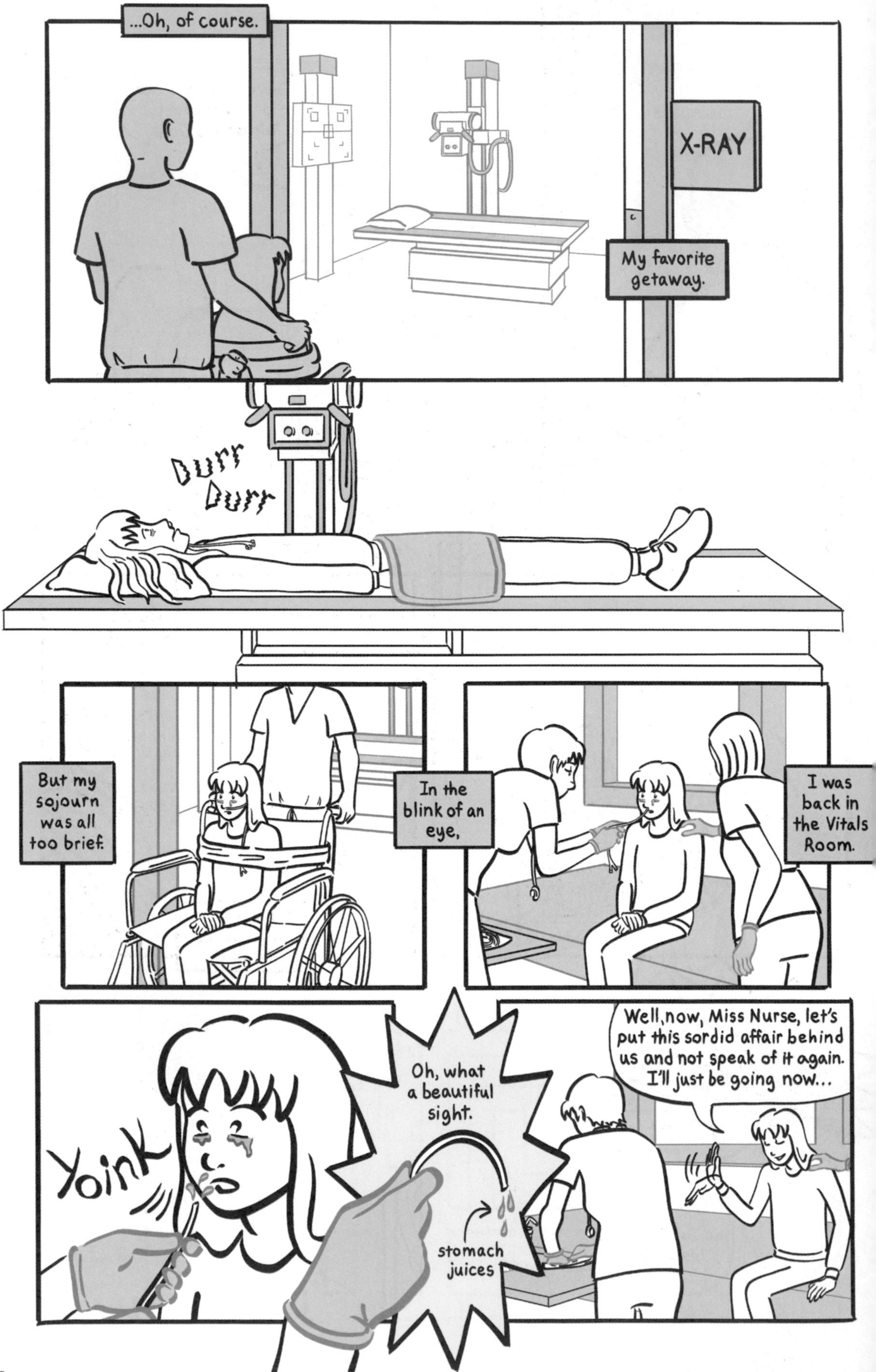
...Oh, of course.
X-RAY
My favorite getaway.
Durr Durr
But my sojourn was all too brief.
In the blink of an eye,
I was back in the Vitals Room.
Yoink
Oh, what a beautiful sight.
stomach juices
Well, now, Miss Nurse, let's put this sordid affair behind us and not speak of it again. I'll just be going now...

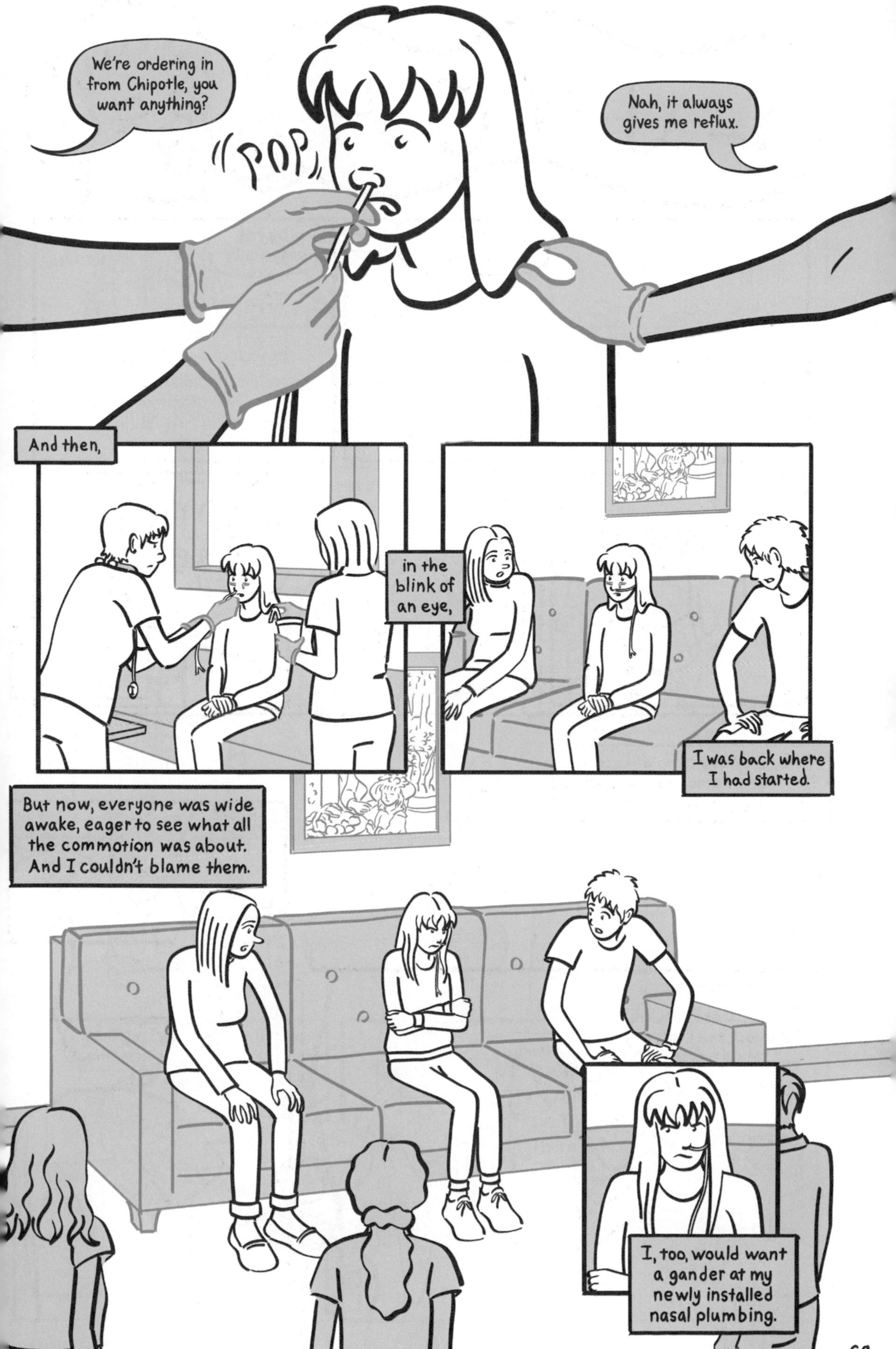

We're ordering in from Chipotle, you want anything?
((POP))
Nah, it always gives me reflux.
And then,
in the blink of an eye,
I was back where I had started.
But now, everyone was wide awake, eager to see what all the commotion was about. And I couldn't blame them.
I, too, would want a gander at my newly installed nasal plumbing.

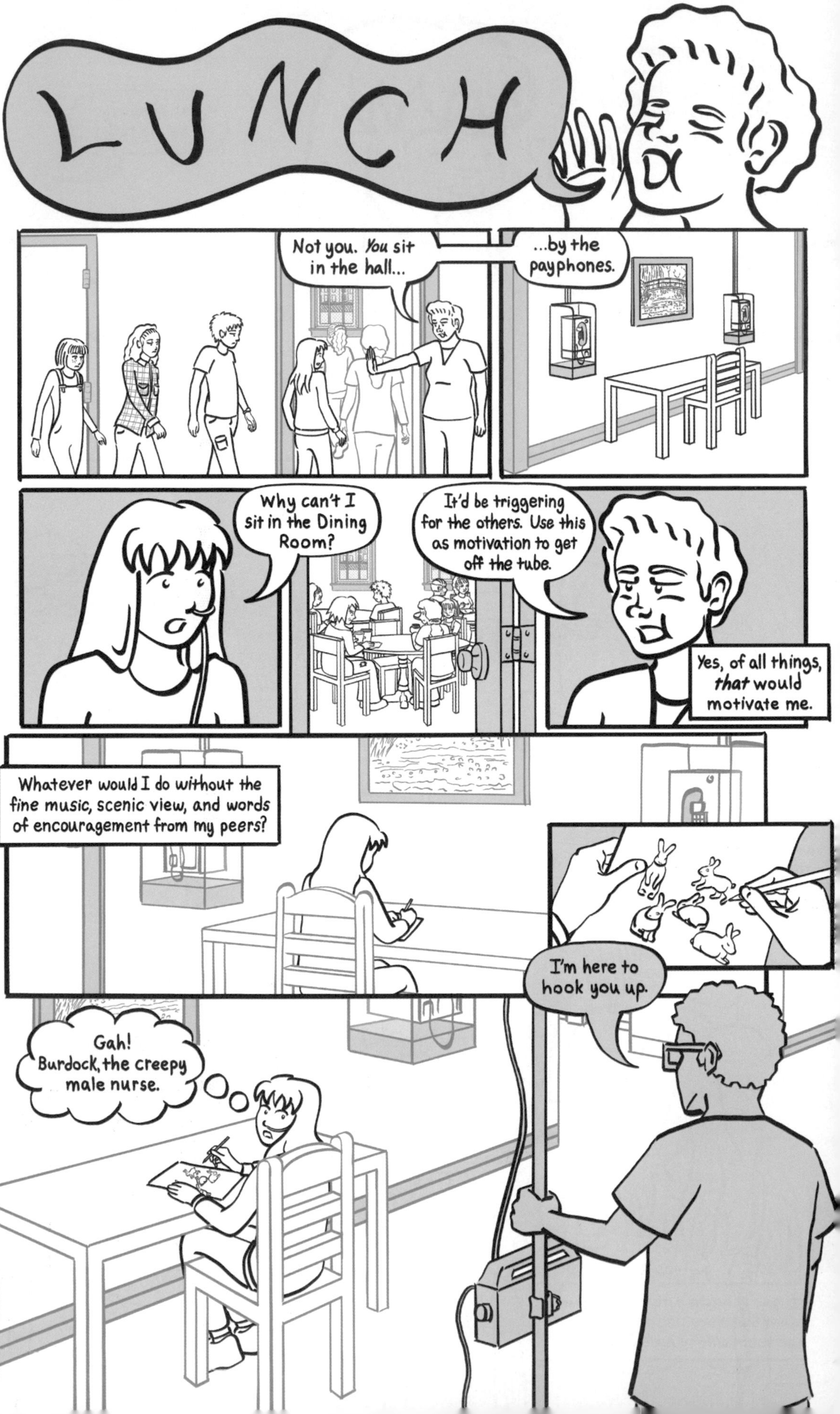
LUNCH
Not you. You sit in the hall...
...by the payphones.
Why can't I sit in the Dining Room?
It'd be triggering for the others. Use this as motivation to get off the tube.
Yes, of all things, that would motivate me.
Whatever would I do without the fine music, scenic view, and words of encouragement from my peers?
I'm here to hook you up.
Gah! Burdock, the creepy male nurse.

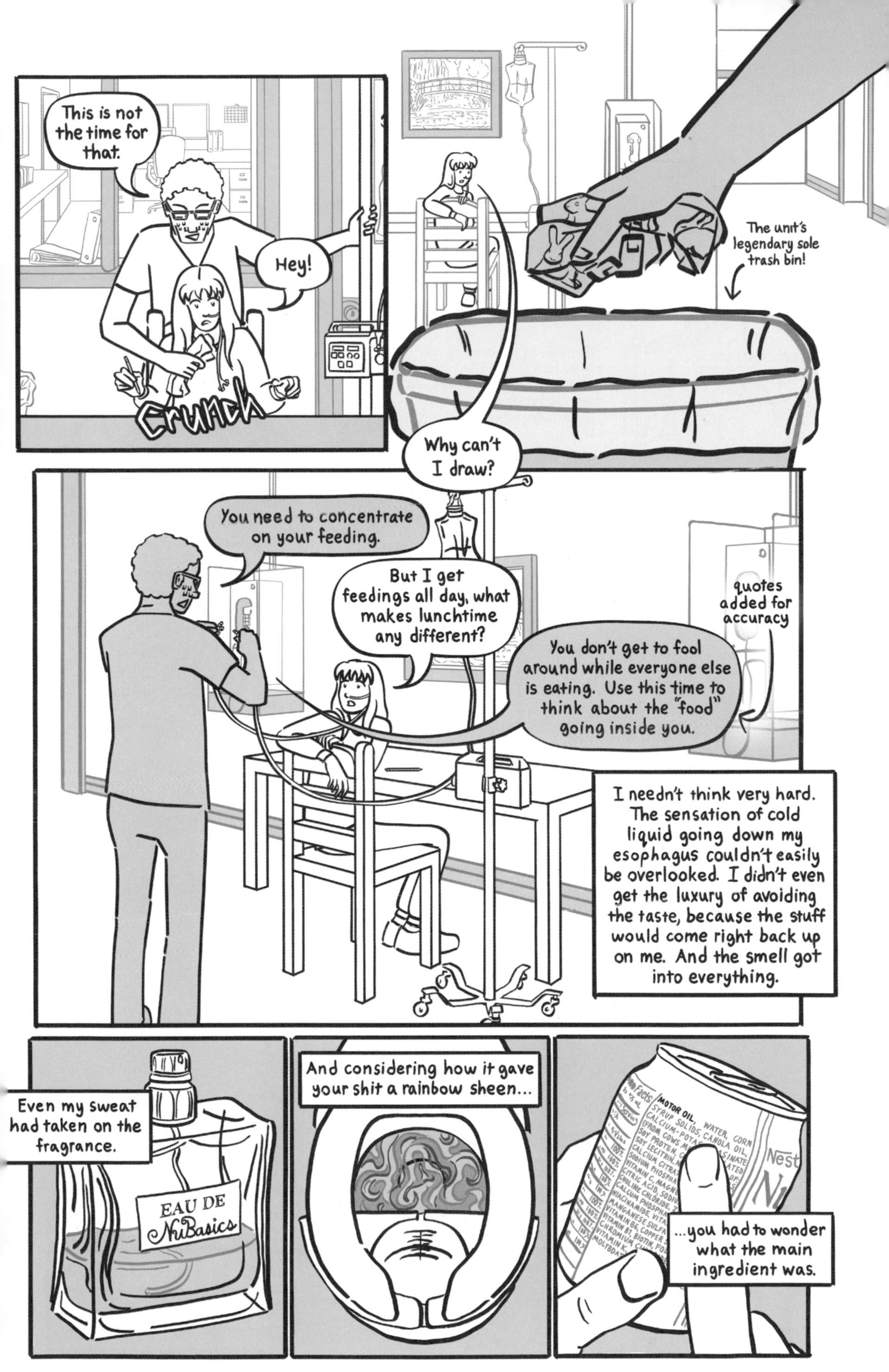

This is not the time for that.
Hey!
CRUNCH
The unit's legendary sole trash bin!
Why can't I draw?
You need to concentrate on your feeding.
But I get feedings all day, what makes lunchtime any different?
You don't get to fool around while everyone else is eating. Use this time to think about the "food" going inside you.
quotes added for accuracy
I needn't think very hard. The sensation of cold liquid going down my esophagus couldn't easily be overlooked. I didn't even get the luxury of avoiding the taste, because the stuff would come right back up on me. And the smell got into everything.
Even my sweat had taken on the fragrance.
EAU DE NuBasics
And considering how it gave your shit a rainbow sheen...
MOTOR OIL, WATER, CORN SYRUP SOLIDS, CANOLA OIL,
...you had to wonder what the main ingredient was.

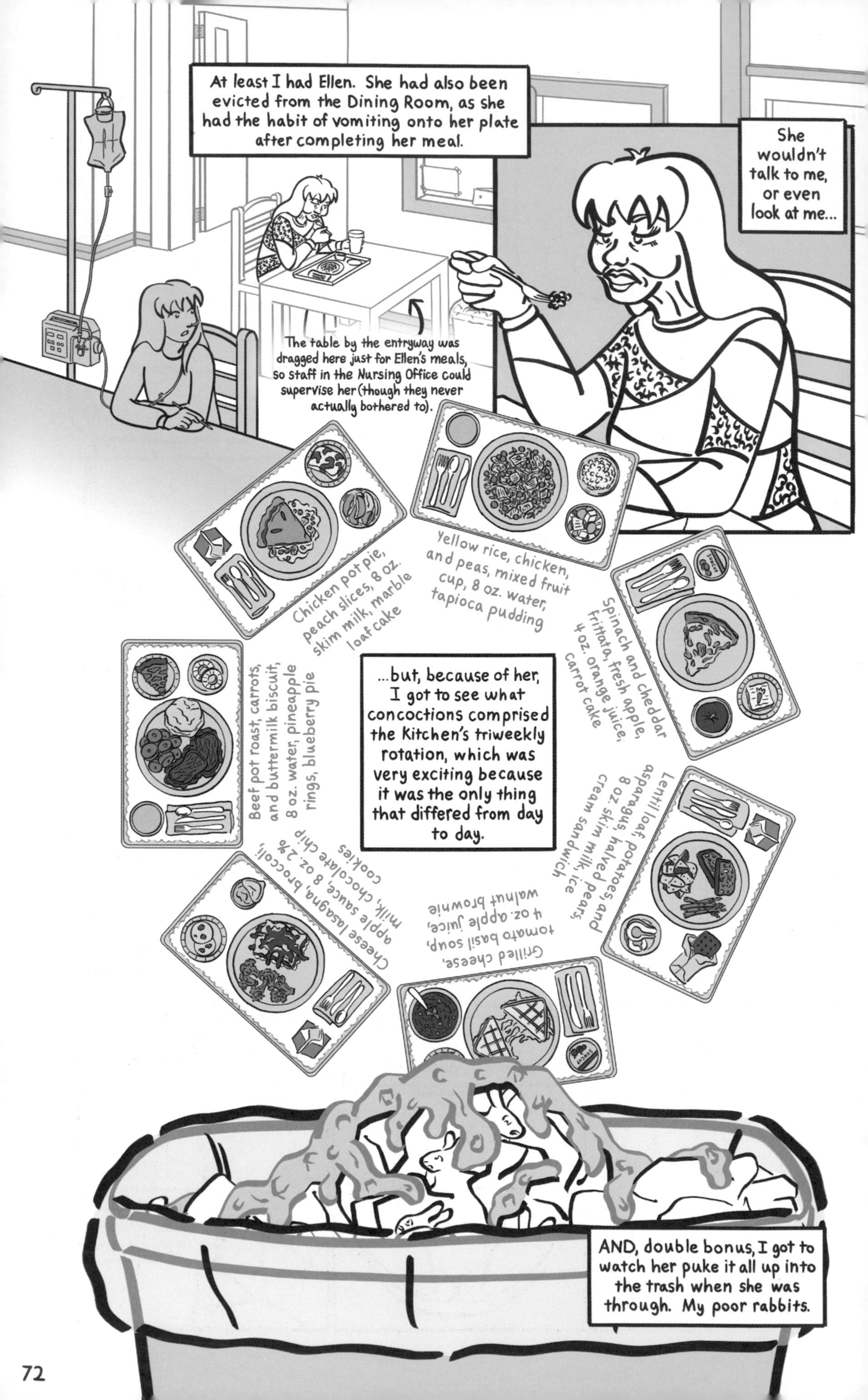

At least I had Ellen. She had also been evicted from the Dining Room, as she had the habit of vomiting onto her plate after completing her meal.
The table by the entryway was dragged here just for Ellen's meals, so staff in the Nursing Office could supervise her (though they never actually bothered to).
She wouldn't talk to me, or even look at me...
Chicken pot pie, peach slices, 8 oz. skim milk, marble loaf cake
Yellow rice, chicken, and peas, mixed fruit cup, 8 oz. water, tapioca pudding
Spinach and cheddar frittata, fresh apple, 4 oz. orange juice, carrot cake
Lentil loaf, potatoes, and asparagus, halved pears, 8 oz. skim milk, ice cream sandwich
Grilled cheese, tomato basil soup, 4 oz. apple juice, walnut brownie
Cheese lasagna, broccoli, apple sauce, 8 oz. 2% milk, chocolate chip cookies
Beef pot roast, carrots, and buttermilk biscuit, 8 oz. water, pineapple rings, blueberry pie
...but, because of her, I got to see what concoctions comprised the Kitchen's triweekly rotation, which was very exciting because it was the only thing that differed from day to day.
AND, double bonus, I got to watch her puke it all up into the trash when she was through. My poor rabbits.

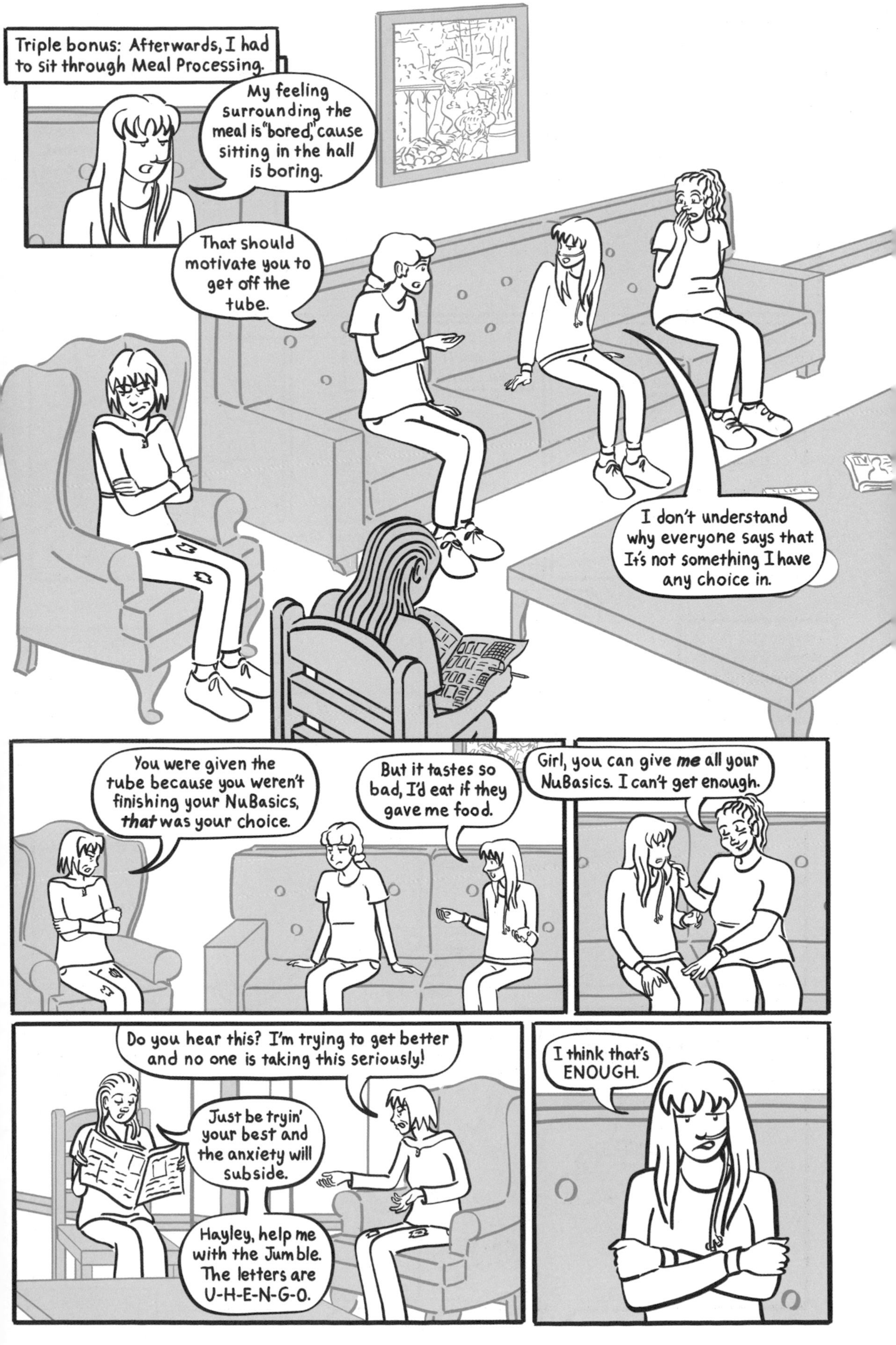
Triple bonus: Afterwards, I had to sit through Meal Processing.
My feeling surrounding the meal is "bored," cause sitting in the hall is boring.
That should motivate you to get off the tube.
I don't understand why everyone says that. It's not something I have any choice in.
You were given the tube because you weren't finishing your NuBasics, *that* was your choice.
But it tastes so bad, I'd eat if they gave me food.
Girl, you can give *me* all your NuBasics. I can't get enough.
Do you hear this? I'm trying to get better and no one is taking this seriously!
Just be tryin' your best and the anxiety will subside.
Hayley, help me with the Jumble. The letters are U-H-E-N-G-O.
I think that's ENOUGH.

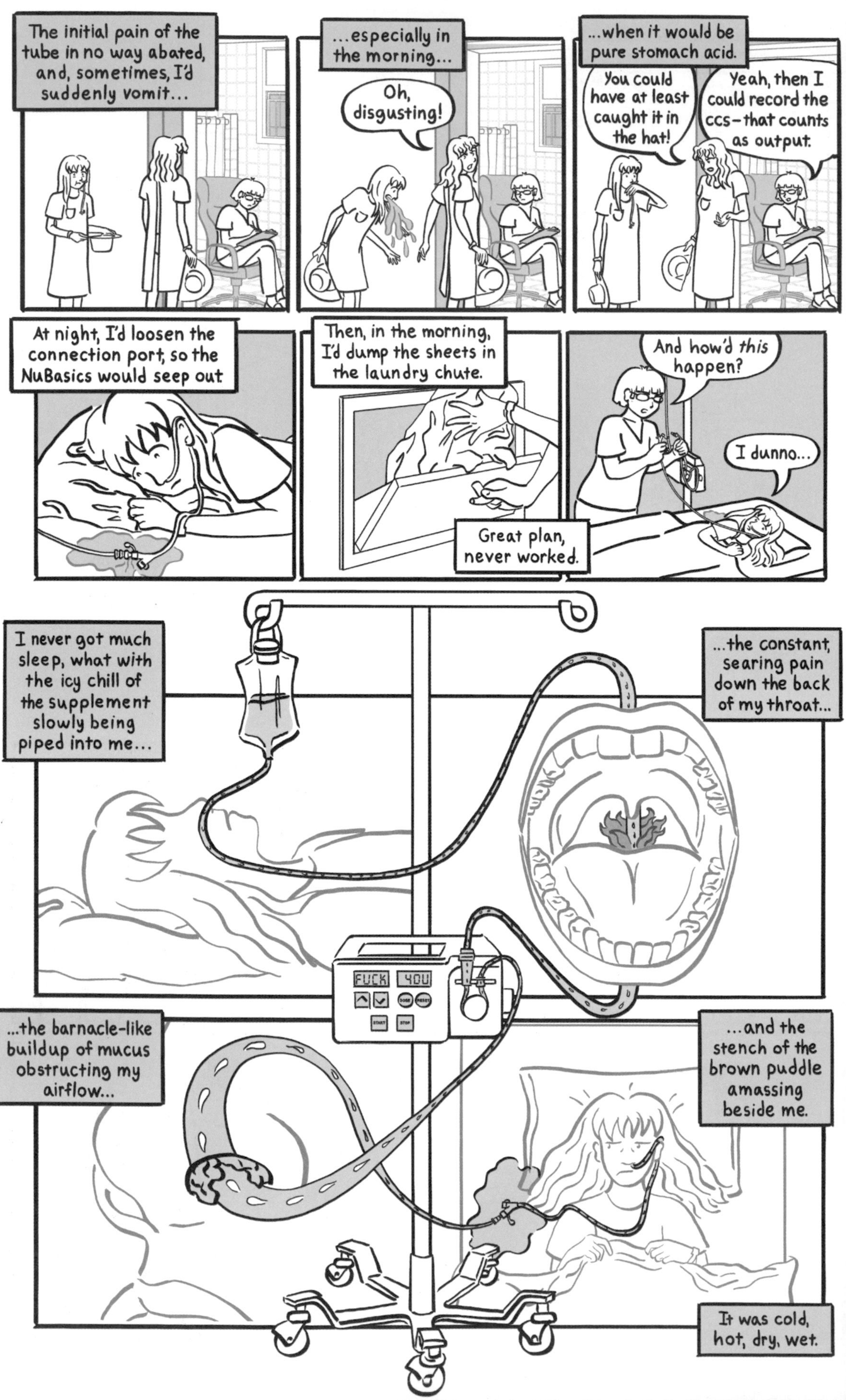
The initial pain of the tube in no way abated, and, sometimes, I'd suddenly vomit...
...especially in the morning...
Oh, disgusting!
...when it would be pure stomach acid.
You could have at least caught it in the hat!
Yeah, then I could record the ccs—that counts as output.
At night, I'd loosen the connection port, so the NuBasics would seep out.
Then, in the morning, I'd dump the sheets in the laundry chute.
Great plan, never worked.
And how'd this happen?
I dunno...
I never got much sleep, what with the icy chill of the supplement slowly being piped into me...
...the constant, searing pain down the back of my throat...
FUCK YOU
DOSE
RESET
START
STOP
...the barnacle-like buildup of mucus obstructing my airflow...
...and the stench of the brown puddle amassing beside me.
It was cold, hot, dry, wet.

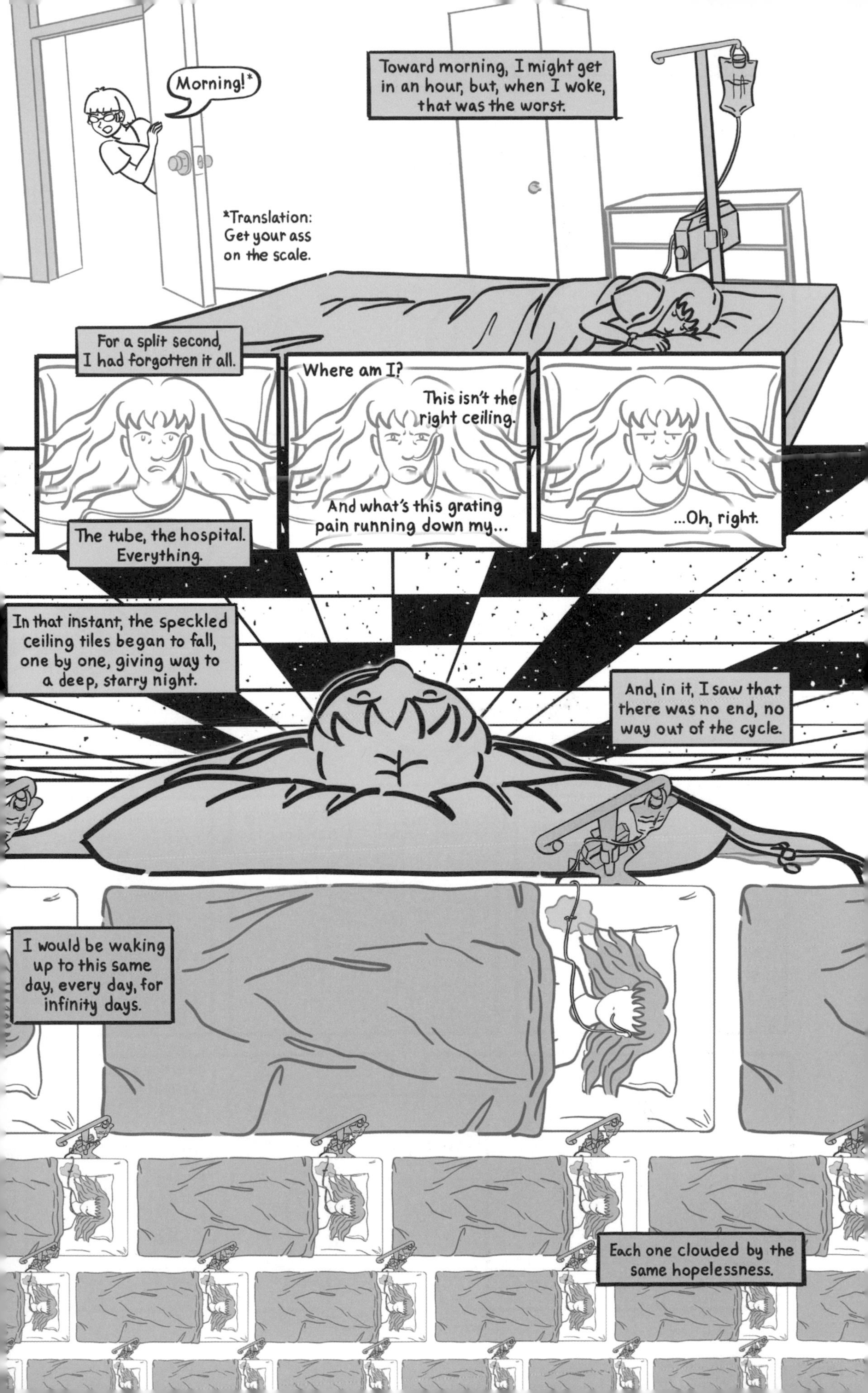
Morning!*
*Translation: Get your ass on the scale.
Toward morning, I might get in an hour, but, when I woke, that was the worst.
For a split second, I had forgotten it all.
The tube, the hospital. Everything.
Where am I?
This isn't the right ceiling.
And what's this grating pain running down my...
...Oh, right.
In that instant, the speckled ceiling tiles began to fall, one by one, giving way to a deep, starry night.
And, in it, I saw that there was no end, no way out of the cycle.
I would be waking up to this same day, every day, for infinity days.
Each one clouded by the same hopelessness.

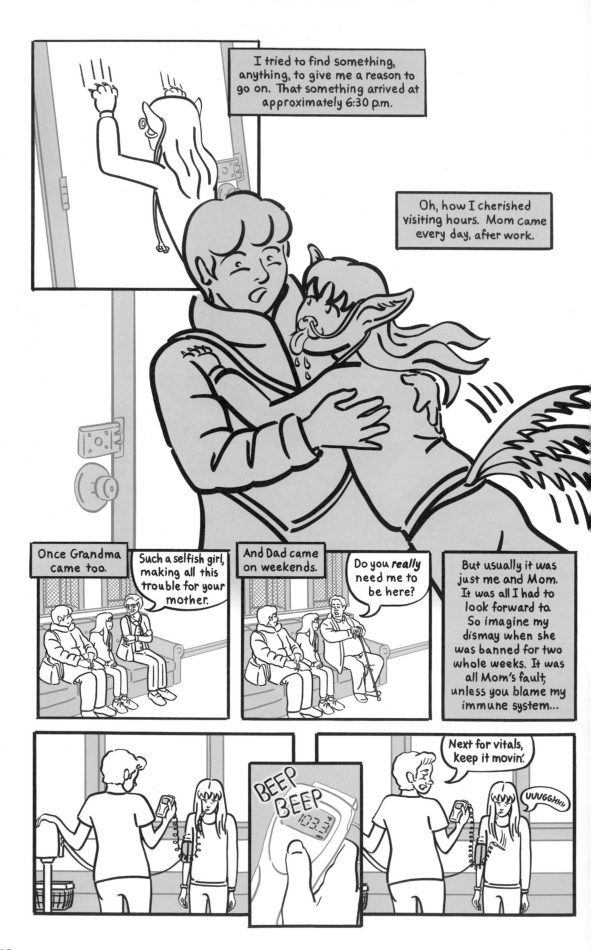

I tried to find something, anything, to give me a reason to go on. That something arrived at approximately 6:30 p.m.

Oh, how I cherished visiting hours. Mom came every day, after work.

Once Grandma came too.

Such a selfish girl, making all this trouble for your mother.

And Dad came on weekends.

Do you *really* need me to be here?

But usually it was just me and Mom. It was all I had to look forward to. So imagine my dismay when she was banned for two whole weeks. It was all Mom's fault, unless you blame my immune system...

BEEP BEEP

103.3

Next for vitals, keep it movin'.

UUUGGHHH

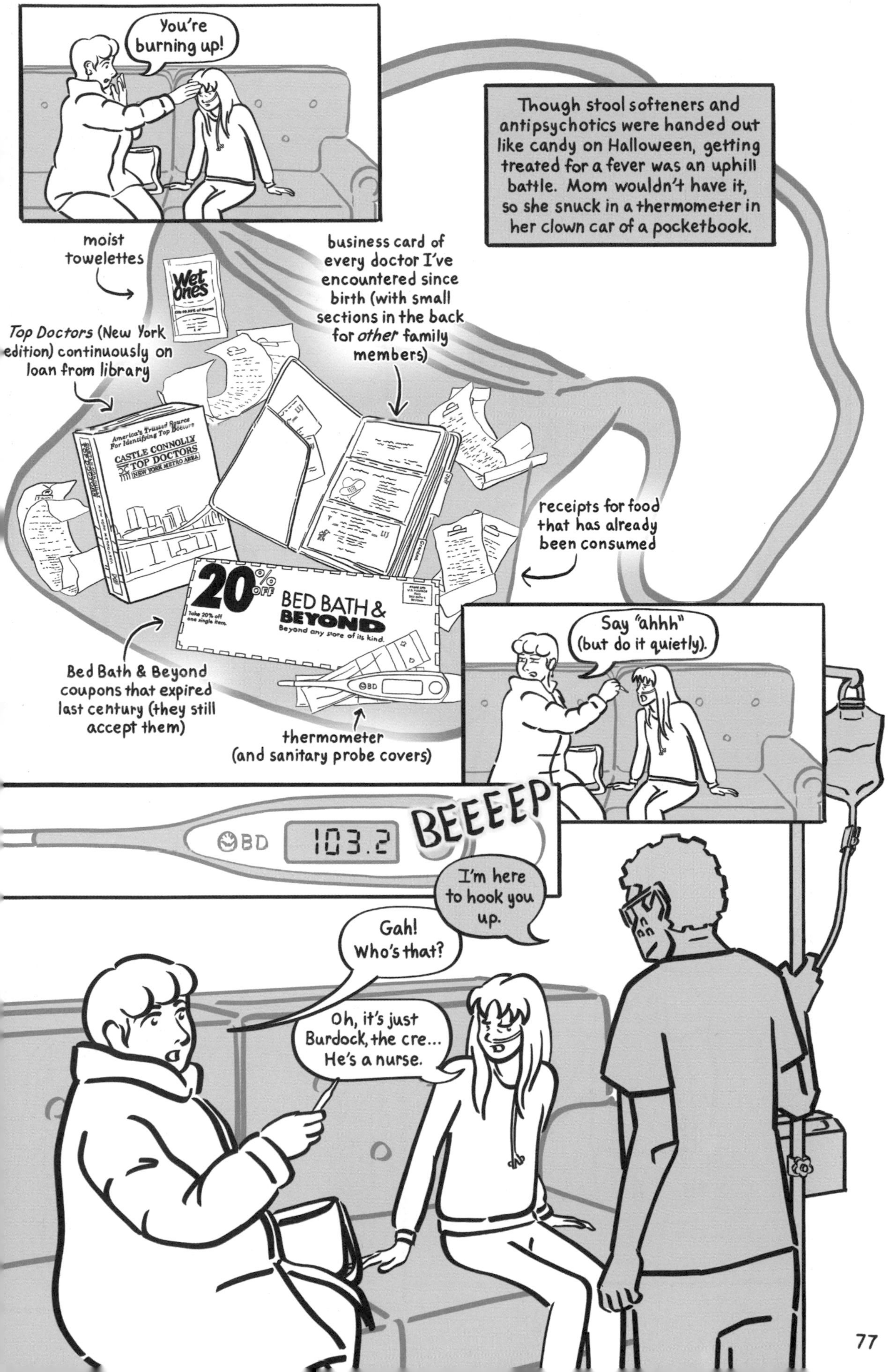

You're burning up!
Though stool softeners and antipsychotics were handed out like candy on Halloween, getting treated for a fever was an uphill battle. Mom wouldn't have it, so she snuck in a thermometer in her clown car of a pocketbook.
moist towelettes
Wet Ones
business card of every doctor I've encountered since birth (with small sections in the back for *other* family members)
Top Doctors (New York edition) continuously on loan from library
America's Trusted Source For Identifying Top Doctors
CASTLE CONNOLLY
TOP DOCTORS
NEW YORK METRO AREA
receipts for food that has already been consumed
20% OFF
Take 20% off one single item.
BED BATH & BEYOND
Beyond any store of its kind.
Bed Bath & Beyond coupons that expired last century (they still accept them)
thermometer (and sanitary probe covers)
Say "ahhh" (but do it quietly).
BD 103.2
BEEEEP
I'm here to hook you up.
Gah! Who's that?
Oh, it's just Burdock, the cre... He's a nurse.

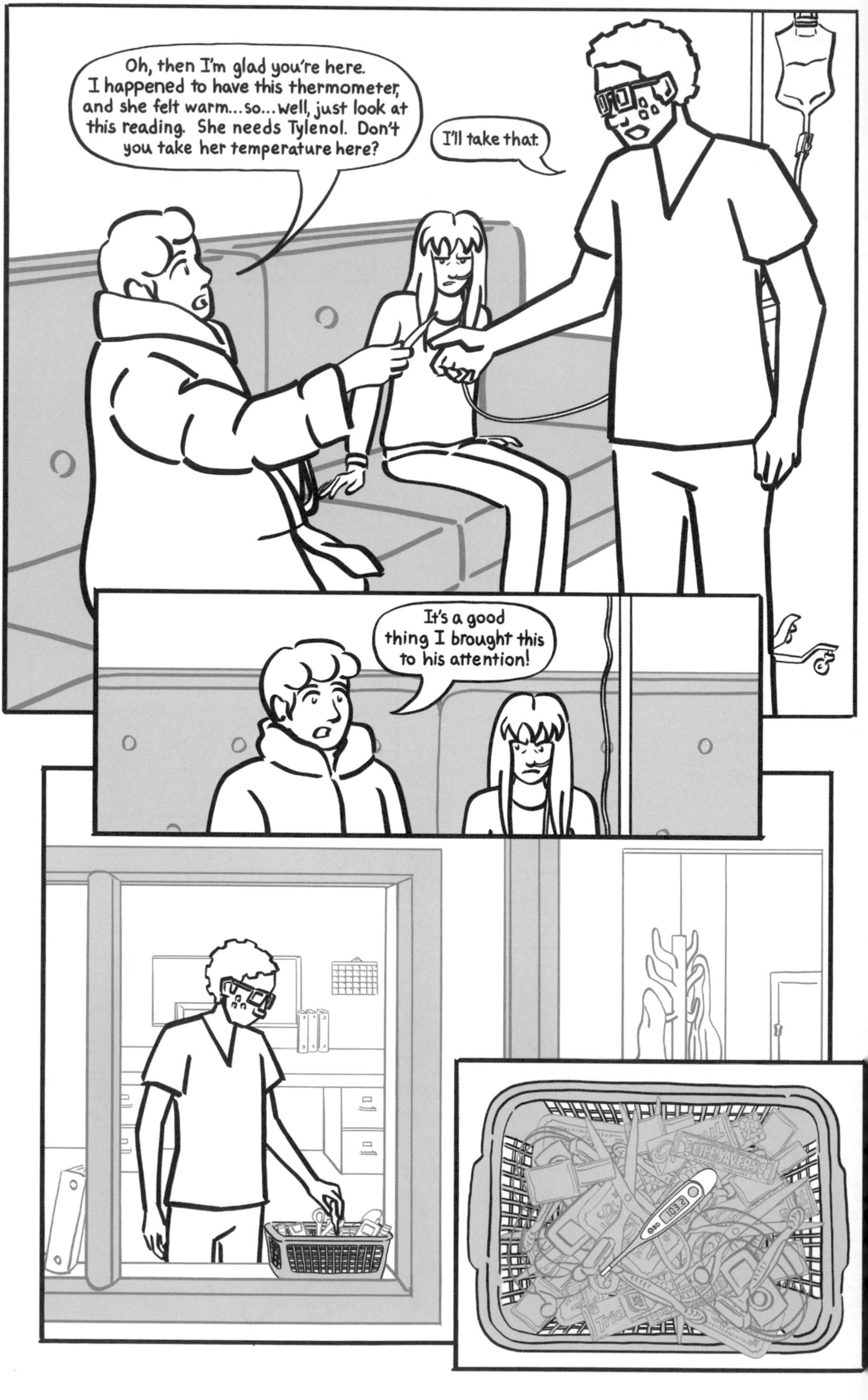
Oh, then I'm glad you're here. I happened to have this thermometer, and she felt warm...so...well, just look at this reading. She needs Tylenol. Don't you take her temperature here?
I'll take that.
It's a good thing I brought this to his attention!
LIFESAVERS
103.2
Trident

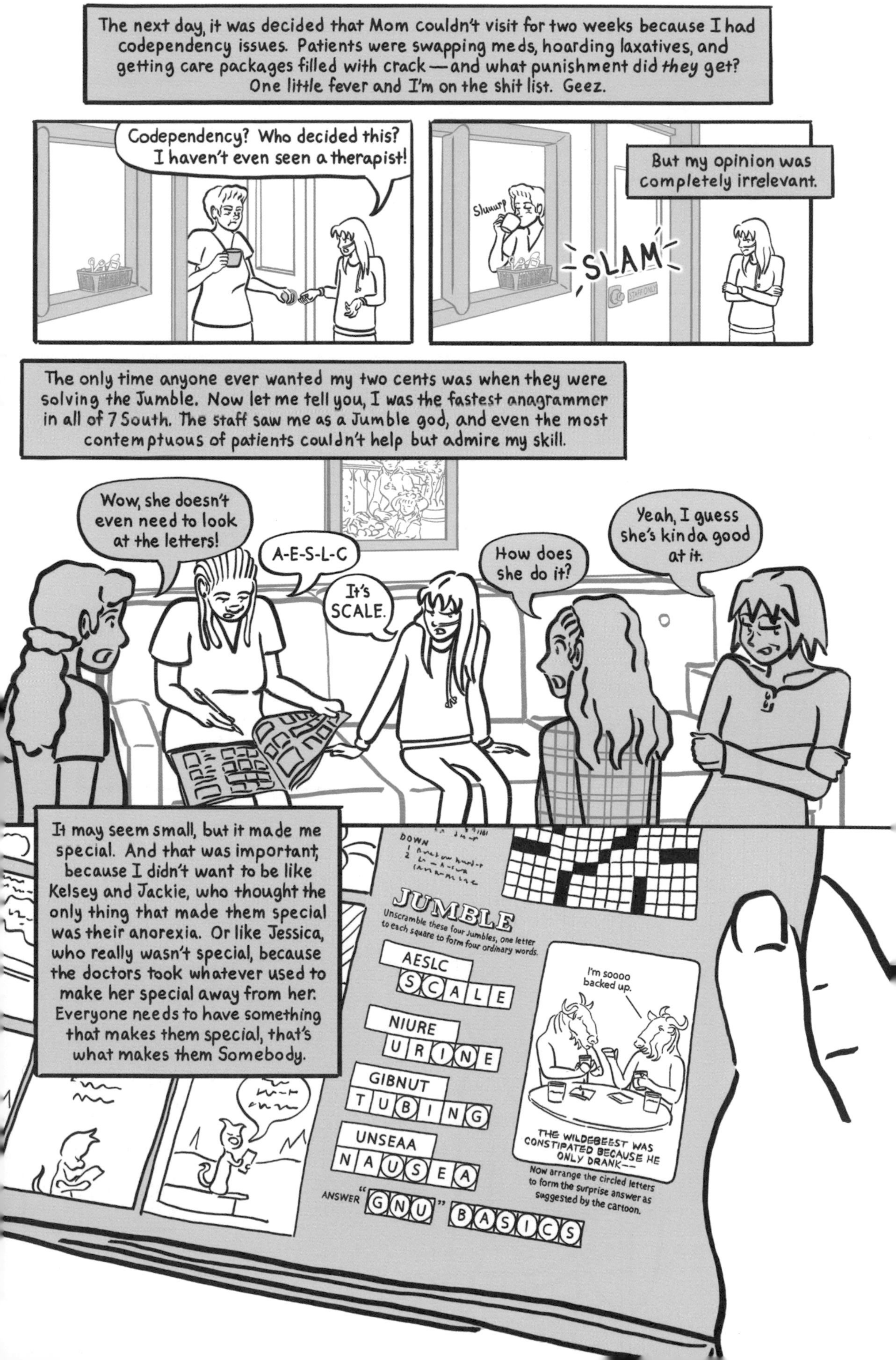

The next day, it was decided that Mom couldn't visit for two weeks because I had codependency issues. Patients were swapping meds, hoarding laxatives, and getting care packages filled with crack—and what punishment did they get? One little fever and I'm on the shit list. Geez.
Codependency? Who decided this? I haven't even seen a therapist!
But my opinion was completely irrelevant.
Sluuurp
SLAM
STAFF ONLY
The only time anyone ever wanted my two cents was when they were solving the Jumble. Now let me tell you, I was the fastest anagrammer in all of 7 South. The staff saw me as a Jumble god, and even the most contemptuous of patients couldn't help but admire my skill.
Wow, she doesn't even need to look at the letters!
A-E-S-L-C
It's SCALE.
How does she do it?
Yeah, I guess she's kinda good at it.
It may seem small, but it made me special. And that was important, because I didn't want to be like Kelsey and Jackie, who thought the only thing that made them special was their anorexia. Or like Jessica, who really wasn't special, because the doctors took whatever used to make her special away from her. Everyone needs to have something that makes them special, that's what makes them Somebody.
DOWN
JUMBLE
Unscramble these four Jumbles, one letter to each square to form four ordinary words.
AESLC
SCALE
NIURE
URINE
GIBNUT
TUBING
UNSEAA
NAUSEA
I'm soooo backed up.
THE WILDEBEEST WAS CONSTIPATED BECAUSE HE ONLY DRANK--
Now arrange the circled letters to form the surprise answer as suggested by the cartoon.
ANSWER "GNU" BASICS

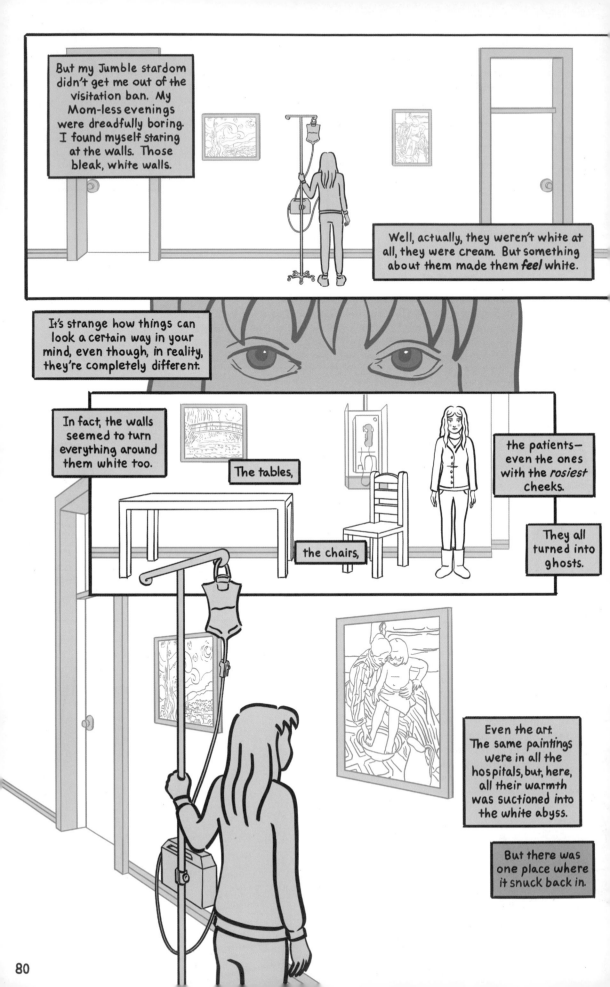

But my Jumble stardom didn't get me out of the visitation ban. My Mom-less evenings were dreadfully boring. I found myself staring at the walls. Those bleak, white walls.

Well, actually, they weren't white at all, they were cream. But something about them made them *feel* white.

It's strange how things can look a certain way in your mind, even though, in reality, they're completely different.

In fact, the walls seemed to turn everything around them white too.

The tables,

the chairs,

the patients— even the ones with the *rosiest* cheeks.

They all turned into ghosts.

Even the art. The same paintings were in all the hospitals, but, here, all their warmth was suctioned into the white abyss.

But there was one place where it snuck back in.

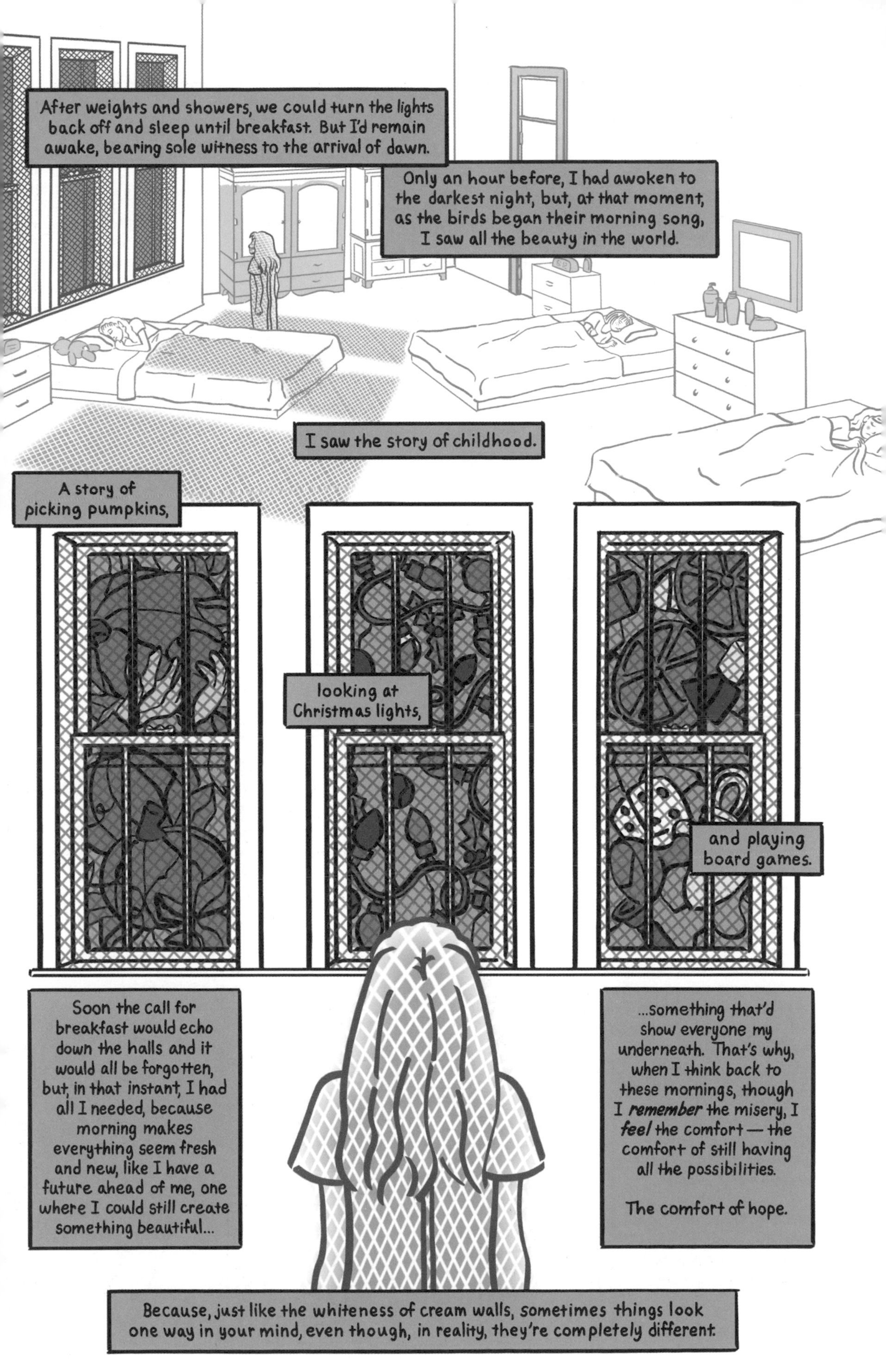
After weights and showers, we could turn the lights back off and sleep until breakfast. But I'd remain awake, bearing sole witness to the arrival of dawn.
Only an hour before, I had awoken to the darkest night, but, at that moment, as the birds began their morning song, I saw all the beauty in the world.
I saw the story of childhood.
A story of picking pumpkins,
looking at Christmas lights,
and playing board games.
Soon the call for breakfast would echo down the halls and it would all be forgotten, but, in that instant, I had all I needed, because morning makes everything seem fresh and new, like I have a future ahead of me, one where I could still create something beautiful...
...something that'd show everyone my underneath. That's why, when I think back to these mornings, though I *remember* the misery, I *feel* the comfort — the comfort of still having all the possibilities.
The comfort of hope.
Because, just like the whiteness of cream walls, sometimes things look one way in your mind, even though, in reality, they're completely different.

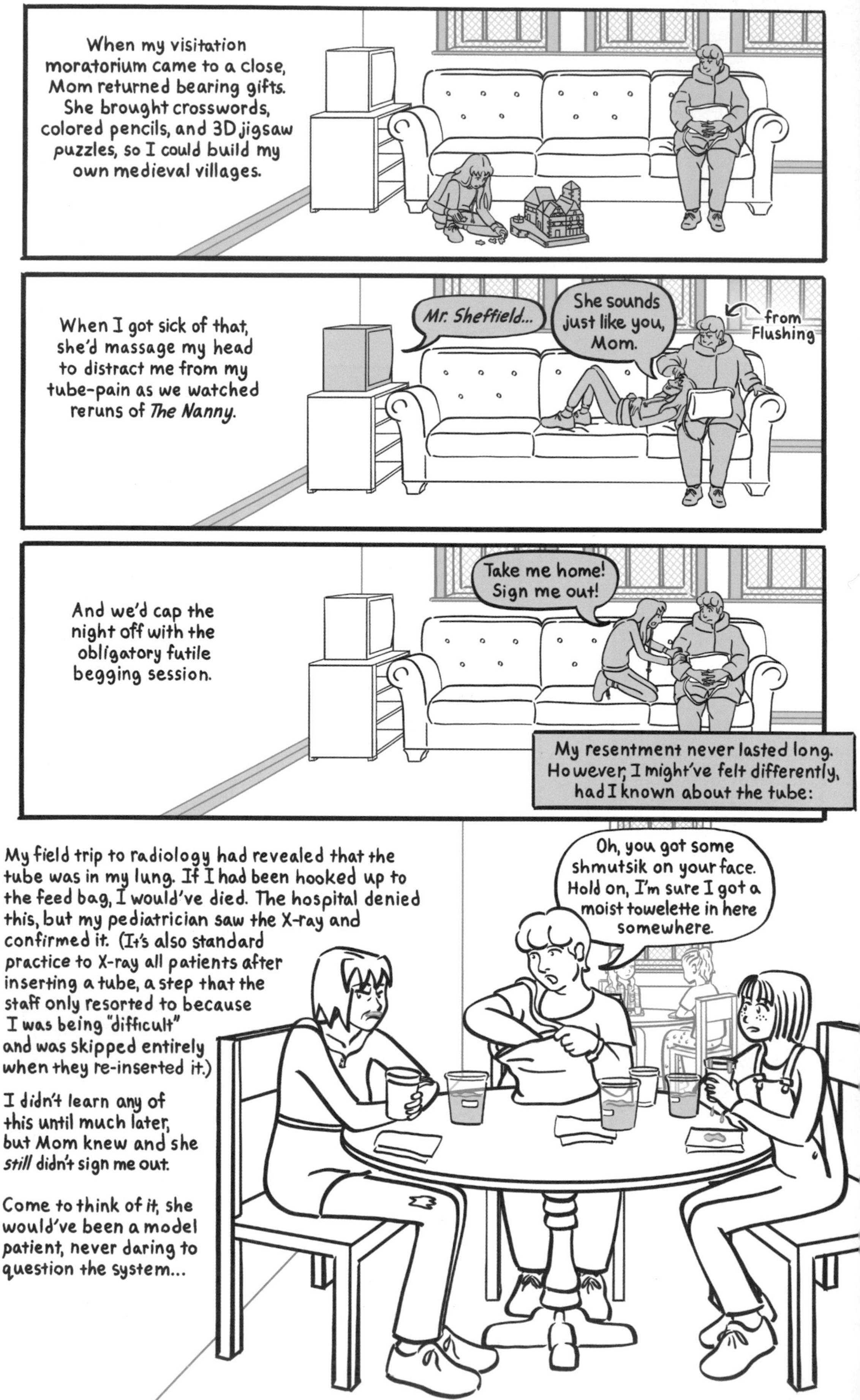

When my visitation moratorium came to a close, Mom returned bearing gifts. She brought crosswords, colored pencils, and 3D jigsaw puzzles, so I could build my own medieval villages.
When I got sick of that, she'd massage my head to distract me from my tube-pain as we watched reruns of *The Nanny*.
Mr. Sheffield...
She sounds just like you, Mom.
from Flushing
And we'd cap the night off with the obligatory futile begging session.
Take me home! Sign me out!
My resentment never lasted long. However, I might've felt differently, had I known about the tube:
My field trip to radiology had revealed that the tube was in my lung. If I had been hooked up to the feed bag, I would've died. The hospital denied this, but my pediatrician saw the X-ray and confirmed it. (It's also standard practice to X-ray all patients after inserting a tube, a step that the staff only resorted to because I was being "difficult" and was skipped entirely when they re-inserted it.)
I didn't learn any of this until much later, but Mom knew and she *still* didn't sign me out.
Come to think of it, she would've been a model patient, never daring to question the system...
Oh, you got some shmutsik on your face. Hold on, I'm sure I got a moist towelette in here somewhere.

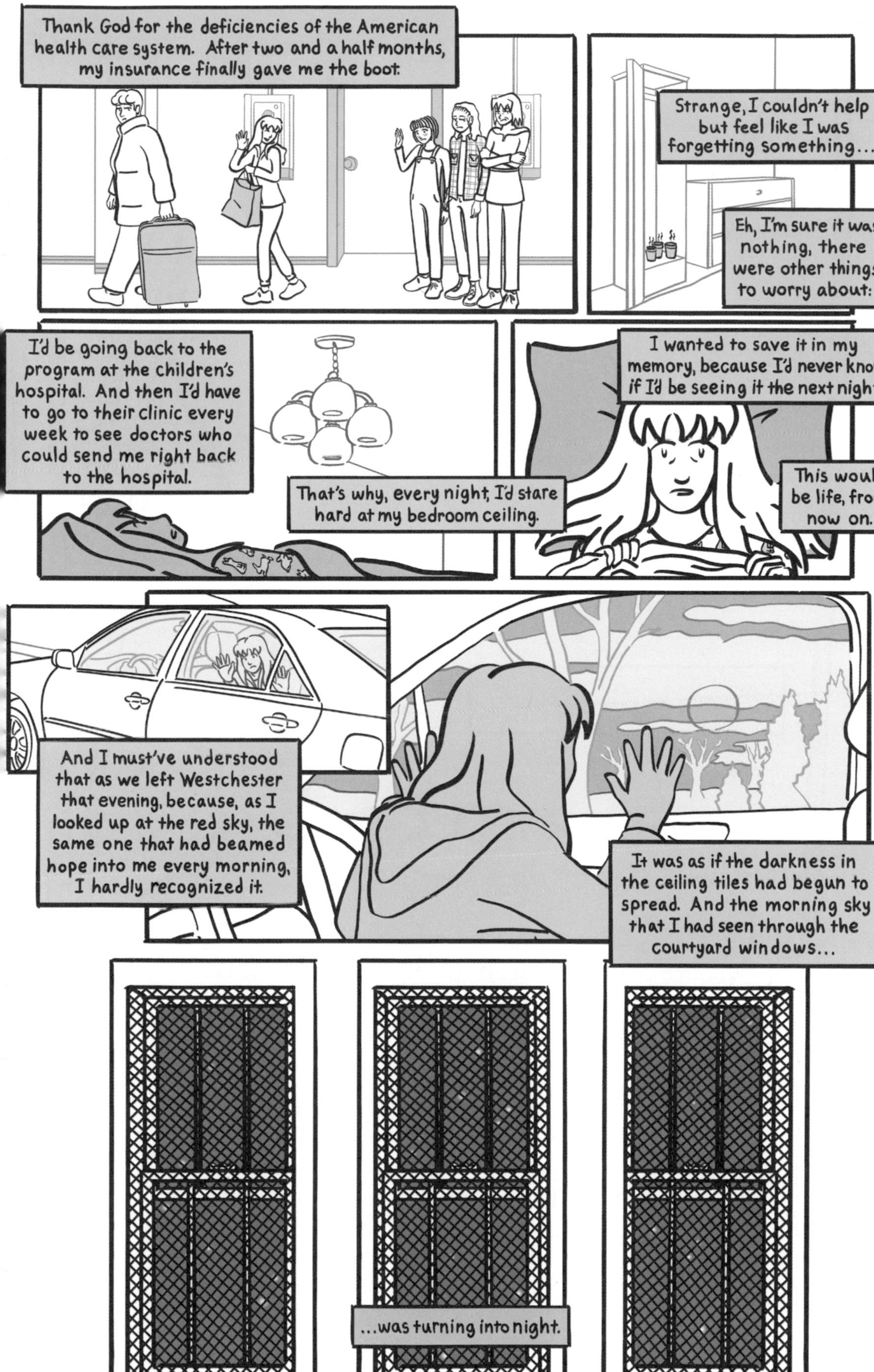
Thank God for the deficiencies of the American health care system. After two and a half months, my insurance finally gave me the boot.
Strange, I couldn't help but feel like I was forgetting something...
Eh, I'm sure it was nothing, there were other things to worry about:
I'd be going back to the program at the children's hospital. And then I'd have to go to their clinic every week to see doctors who could send me right back to the hospital.
That's why, every night, I'd stare hard at my bedroom ceiling.
I wanted to save it in my memory, because I'd never know if I'd be seeing it the next night.
This would be life, from now on.
And I must've understood that as we left Westchester that evening, because, as I looked up at the red sky, the same one that had beamed hope into me every morning, I hardly recognized it.
It was as if the darkness in the ceiling tiles had begun to spread. And the morning sky that I had seen through the courtyard windows...
...was turning into night.

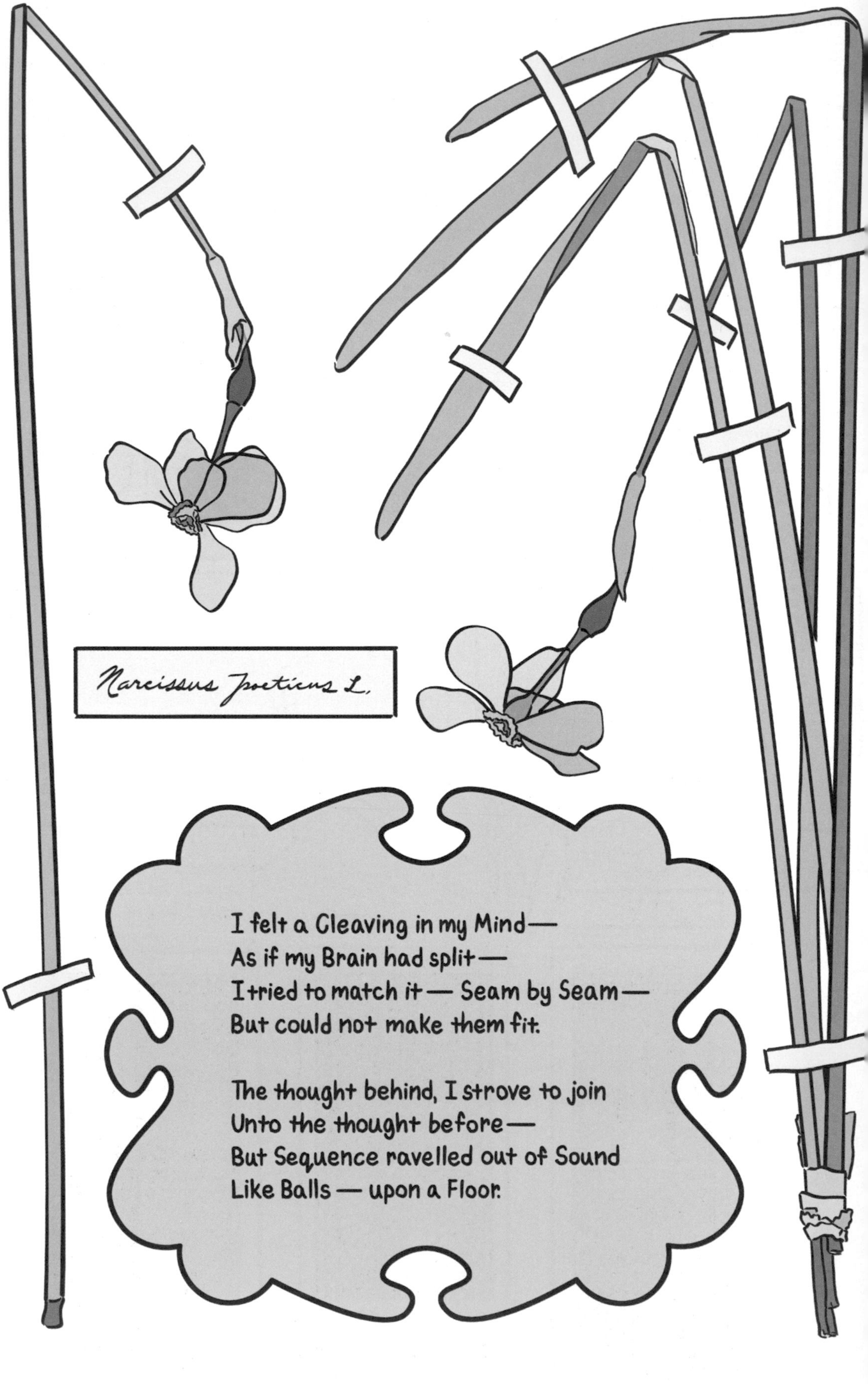
Narcissus Poeticus L.

I felt a Cleaving in my Mind—
As if my Brain had split—
I tried to match it— Seam by Seam—
But could not make them fit.

The thought behind, I strove to join
Unto the thought before—
But Sequence ravelled out of Sound
Like Balls— upon a Floor.

Chapter 4

First World

Problems

I thought I had a child's disease.
I thought I was just being a naughty little girl.
That's how the doctors made me feel, anyway.
So I assumed that I'd simply grow out of it.
Surely I'd be "better" by the time I turned 13, by
the time I turned 14, by the time I turned some
number. But numbers are misleading, because
as I got older I didn't grow up.

By the time I had turned 17, my eating disorder hadn't budged. However, *some* things had changed:

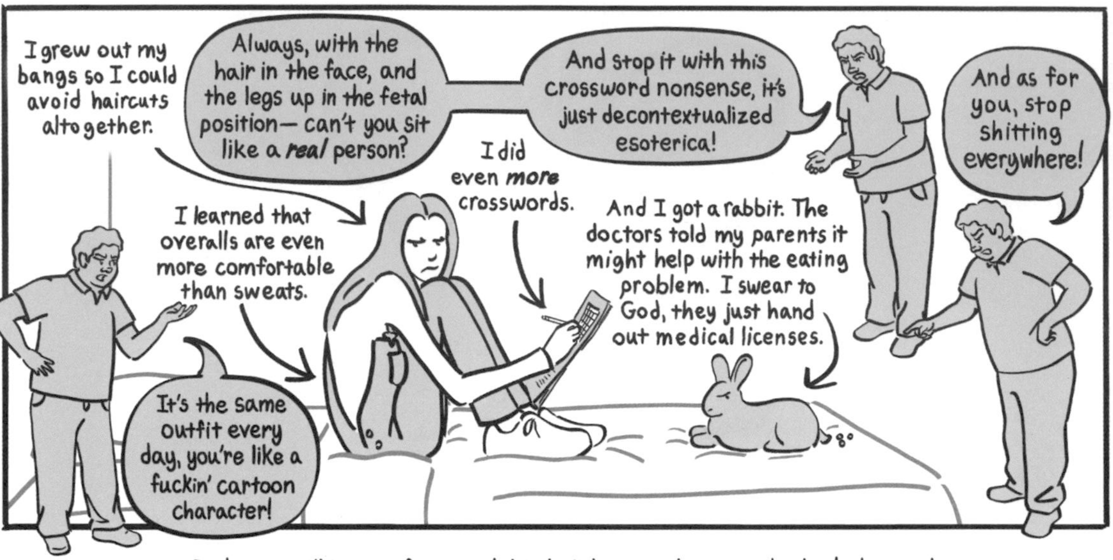
I grew out my bangs so I could avoid haircuts altogether.
Always, with the hair in the face, and the legs up in the fetal position— can't you sit like a *real* person?
And stop it with this crossword nonsense, it's just decontextualized esoterica!
And as for you, stop shitting everywhere!
I did even *more* crosswords.
I learned that overalls are even more comfortable than sweats.
And I got a rabbit. The doctors told my parents it might help with the eating problem. I swear to God, they just hand out medical licenses.
It's the same outfit every day, you're like a fuckin' cartoon character!

Dad was still in rare form with his ball-busting, but even he had changed.
He developed neuropathy and had to go on disability— he made a career of it.
He turned the living room into a home office and practiced...er...remote business.

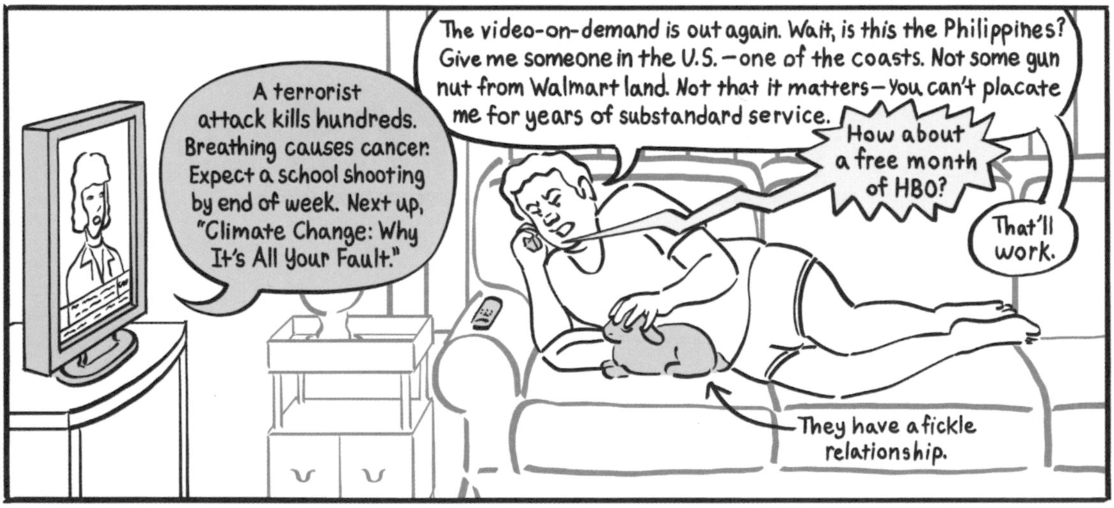
A terrorist attack kills hundreds. Breathing causes cancer. Expect a school shooting by end of week. Next up, "Climate Change: Why It's All Your Fault."
The video-on-demand is out again. Wait, is this the Philippines? Give me someone in the U.S.—one of the coasts. Not some gun nut from Walmart land. Not that it matters—You can't placate me for years of substandard service.
How about a free month of HBO?
That'll work.
They have a fickle relationship.

His phone skills were impressive, but Dad didn't just hate the Verizon man, he hated everyone, especially himself. And he made sure I knew. Just crossing the living room was a hazardous journey.

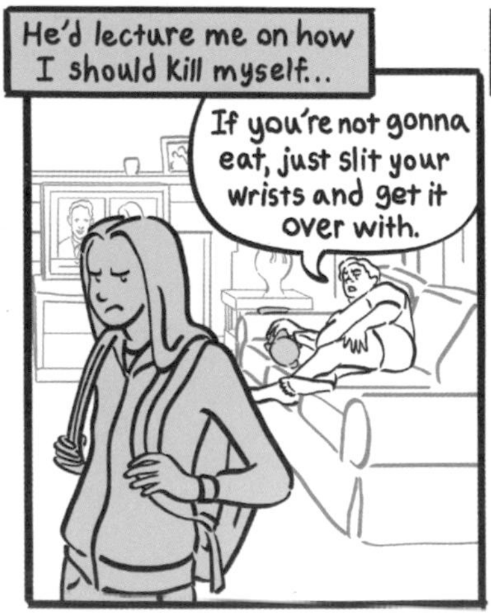
He'd lecture me on how I should kill myself...
If you're not gonna eat, just slit your wrists and get it over with.

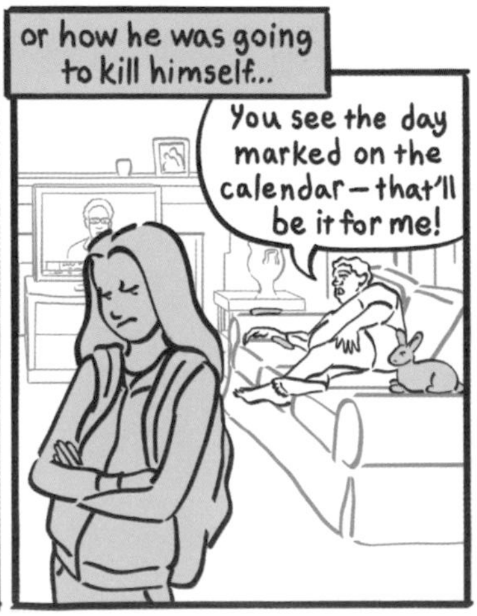
or how he was going to kill himself...
You see the day marked on the calendar—that'll be it for me!

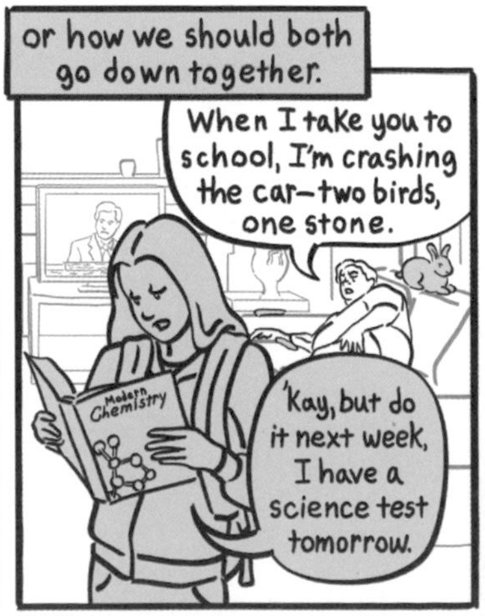
or how we should both go down together.
When I take you to school, I'm crashing the car—two birds, one stone.
Modern Chemistry
'Kay, but do it next week, I have a science test tomorrow.

I knew better than to buy into it, but I still thought it prudent to consult the other "adult" in the household on the matter.

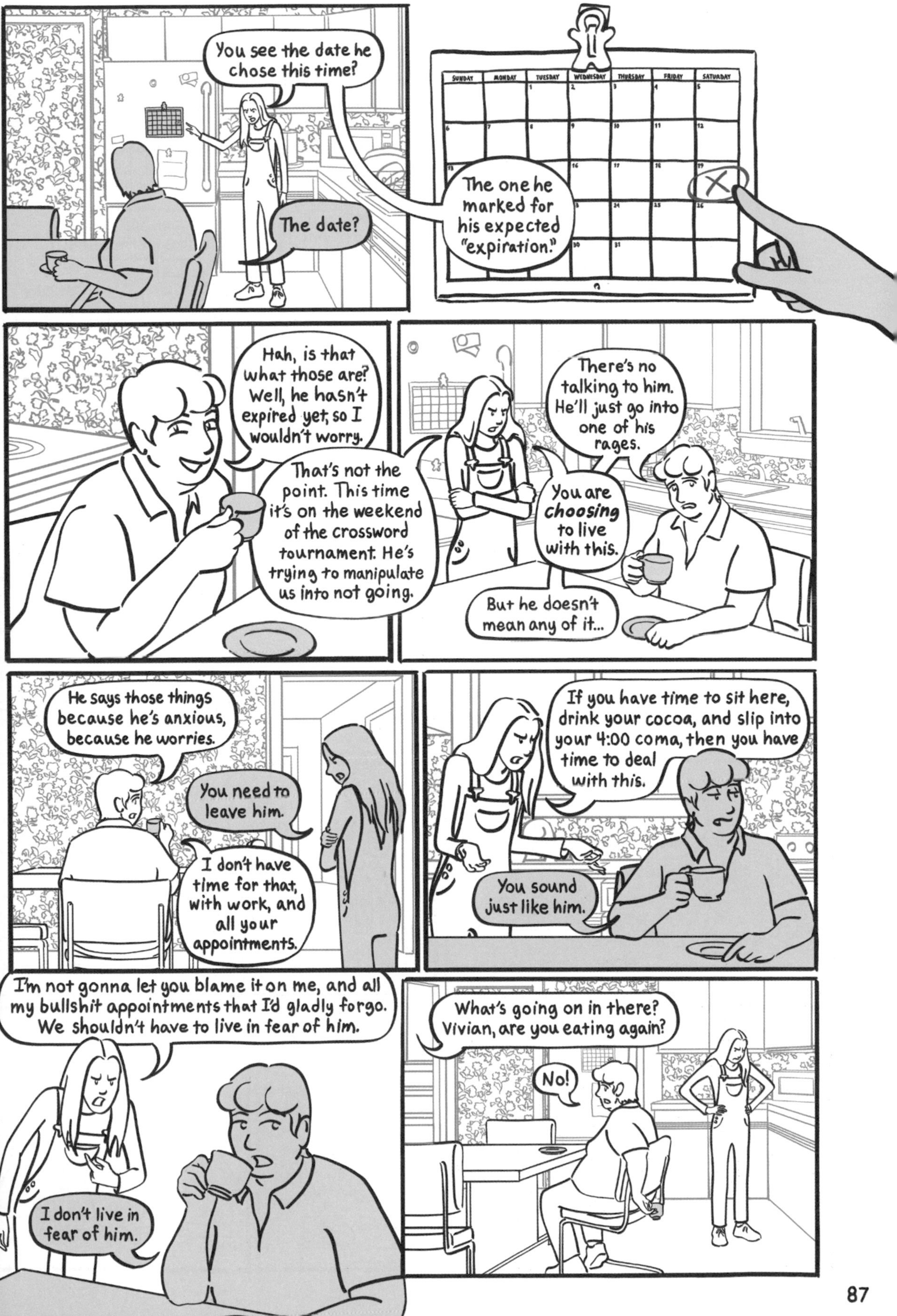

You see the date he chose this time?
The date?
SUNDAY MONDAY TUESDAY WEDNESDAY THURSDAY FRIDAY SATURDAY
The one he marked for his expected "expiration."
Hah, is that what those are? Well, he hasn't expired yet, so I wouldn't worry.
That's not the point. This time it's on the weekend of the crossword tournament. He's trying to manipulate us into not going.
There's no talking to him. He'll just go into one of his rages.
You are *choosing* to live with this.
But he doesn't mean any of it...
He says those things because he's anxious, because he worries.
You need to leave him.
I don't have time for that, with work, and all your appointments.
If you have time to sit here, drink your cocoa, and slip into your 4:00 coma, then you have time to deal with this.
You sound just like him.
I'm not gonna let you blame it on me, and all my bullshit appointments that I'd gladly forgo. We shouldn't have to live in fear of *him*.
I don't live in fear of him.
What's going on in there? Vivian, are you eating again?
No!

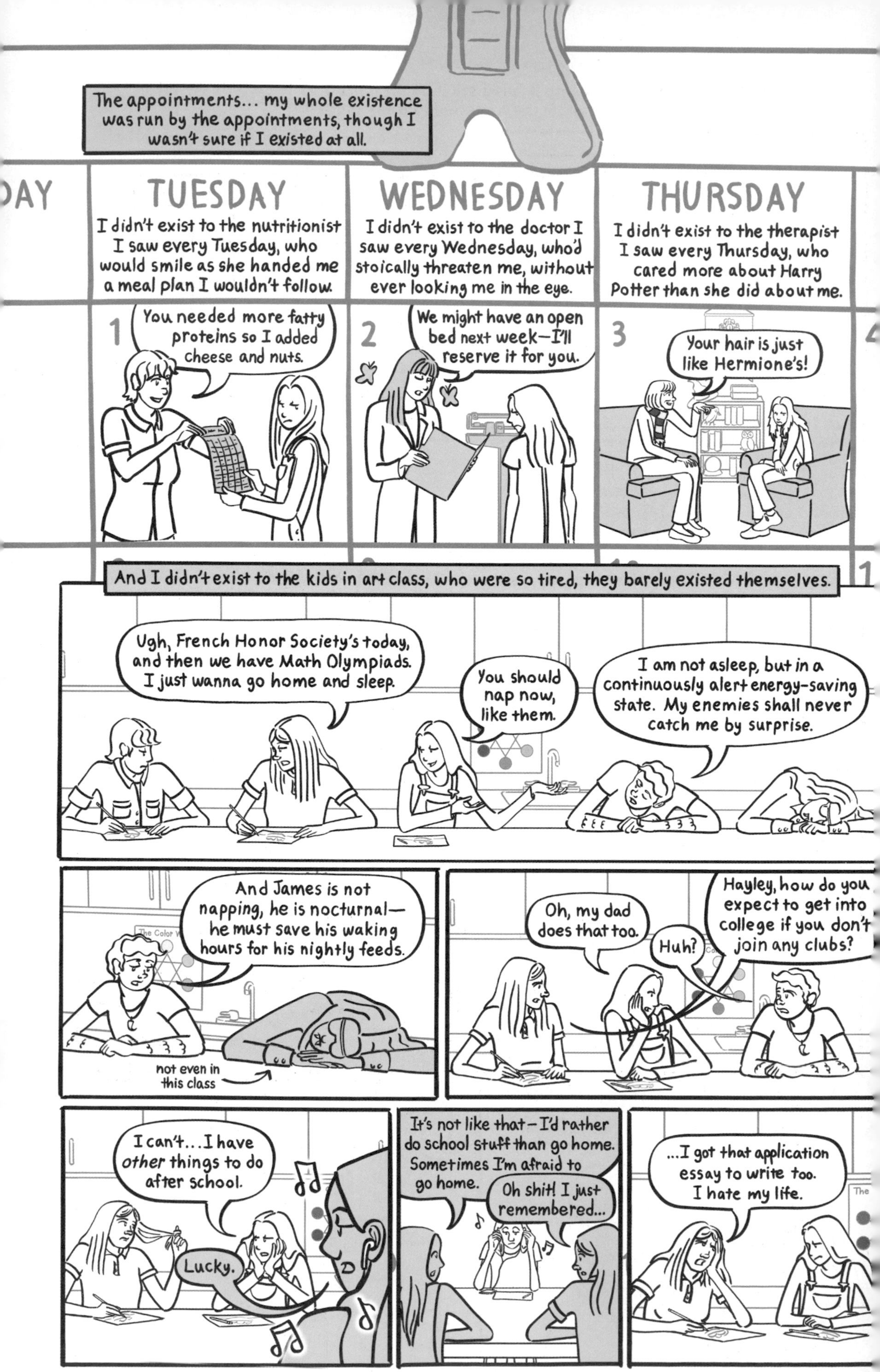

The appointments... my whole existence was run by the appointments, though I wasn't sure if I existed at all.
DAY
TUESDAY
I didn't exist to the nutritionist I saw every Tuesday, who would smile as she handed me a meal plan I wouldn't follow.
WEDNESDAY
I didn't exist to the doctor I saw every Wednesday, who'd stoically threaten me, without ever looking me in the eye.
THURSDAY
I didn't exist to the therapist I saw every Thursday, who cared more about Harry Potter than she did about me.
1
You needed more fatty proteins so I added cheese and nuts.
2
We might have an open bed next week—I'll reserve it for you.
3
Your hair is just like Hermione's!
And I didn't exist to the kids in art class, who were so tired, they barely existed themselves.
Ugh, French Honor Society's today, and then we have Math Olympiads. I just wanna go home and sleep.
You should nap now, like them.
I am not asleep, but in a continuously alert energy-saving state. My enemies shall never catch me by surprise.
And James is not napping, he is nocturnal—he must save his waking hours for his nightly feeds.
not even in this class
Oh, my dad does that too.
Huh?
Hayley, how do you expect to get into college if you don't join any clubs?
I can't... I have *other* things to do after school.
Lucky.
It's not like that—I'd rather do school stuff than go home. Sometimes I'm afraid to go home.
Oh shit! I just remembered...
...I got that application essay to write too. I hate my life.

Too bad I couldn't write in *my* extracurricular activities on college applications. I'd have a scholarship in no time. Though, that might have just compounded my problems. It's not that I didn't want to go to college, I just didn't know which one to go to or what I wanted to go for. There were too many choices. And time to choose was running out.

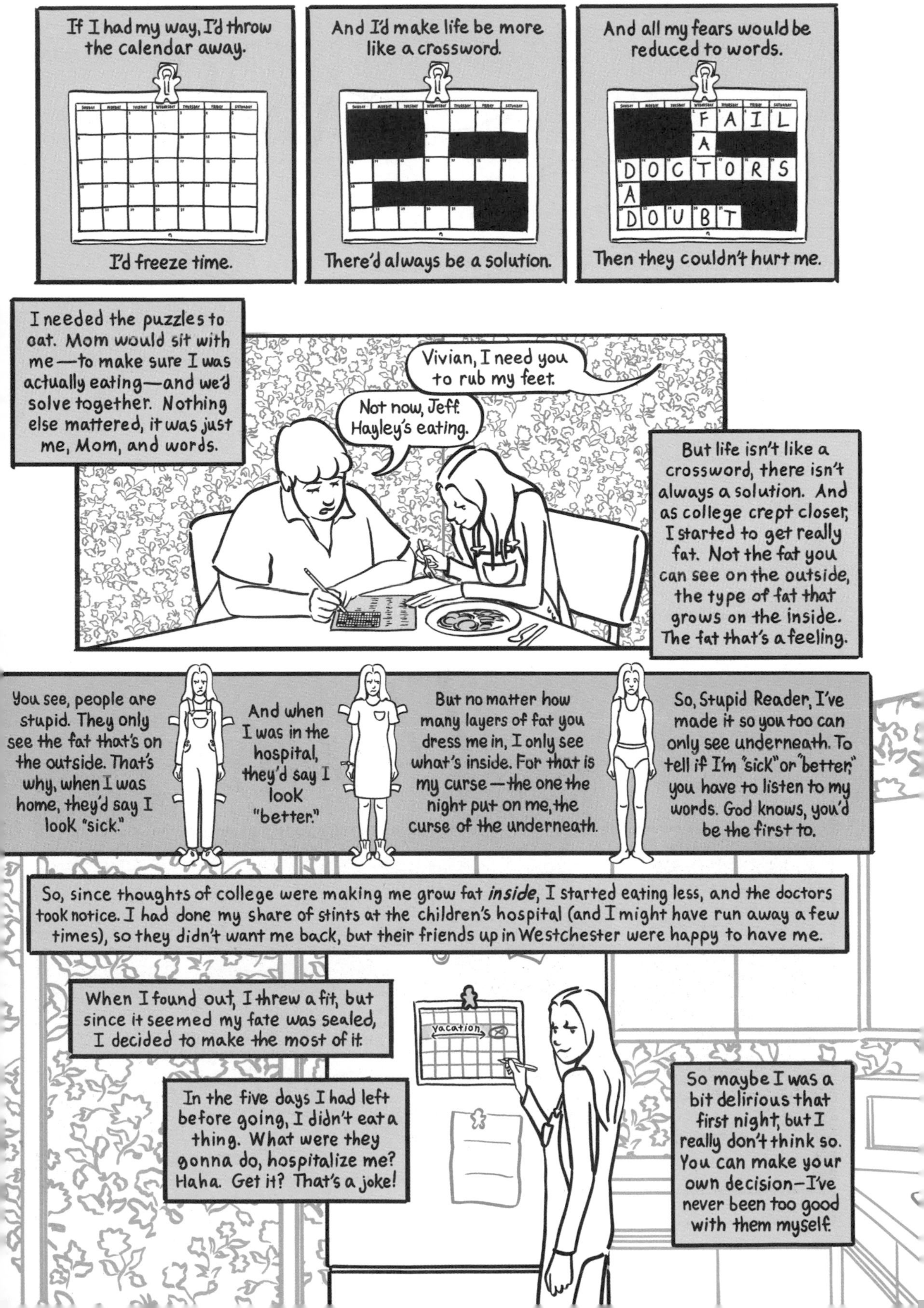

If I had my way, I'd throw the calendar away.
I'd freeze time.
And I'd make life be more like a crossword.
There'd always be a solution.
And all my fears would be reduced to words.
FAIL
A
DOCTORS
A
DOUBT
Then they couldn't hurt me.
I needed the puzzles to eat. Mom would sit with me—to make sure I was actually eating—and we'd solve together. Nothing else mattered, it was just me, Mom, and words.
Vivian, I need you to rub my feet.
Not now, Jeff. Hayley's eating.
But life isn't like a crossword, there isn't always a solution. And as college crept closer, I started to get really fat. Not the fat you can see on the outside, the type of fat that grows on the inside. The fat that's a feeling.
You see, people are stupid. They only see the fat that's on the outside. That's why, when I was home, they'd say I look "sick."
And when I was in the hospital, they'd say I look "better."
But no matter how many layers of fat you dress me in, I only see what's inside. For that is my curse—the one the night put on me, the curse of the underneath.
So, Stupid Reader, I've made it so you too can only see underneath. To tell if I'm "sick" or "better," you have to listen to my words. God knows, you'd be the first to.
So, since thoughts of college were making me grow fat *inside*, I started eating less, and the doctors took notice. I had done my share of stints at the children's hospital (and I might have run away a few times), so they didn't want me back, but their friends up in Westchester were happy to have me.
When I found out, I threw a fit, but since it seemed my fate was sealed, I decided to make the most of it.
vacation
In the five days I had left before going, I didn't eat a thing. What were they gonna do, hospitalize me? Haha. Get it? That's a joke!
So maybe I was a bit delirious that first night, but I really don't think so. You can make your own decision—I've never been too good with them myself.

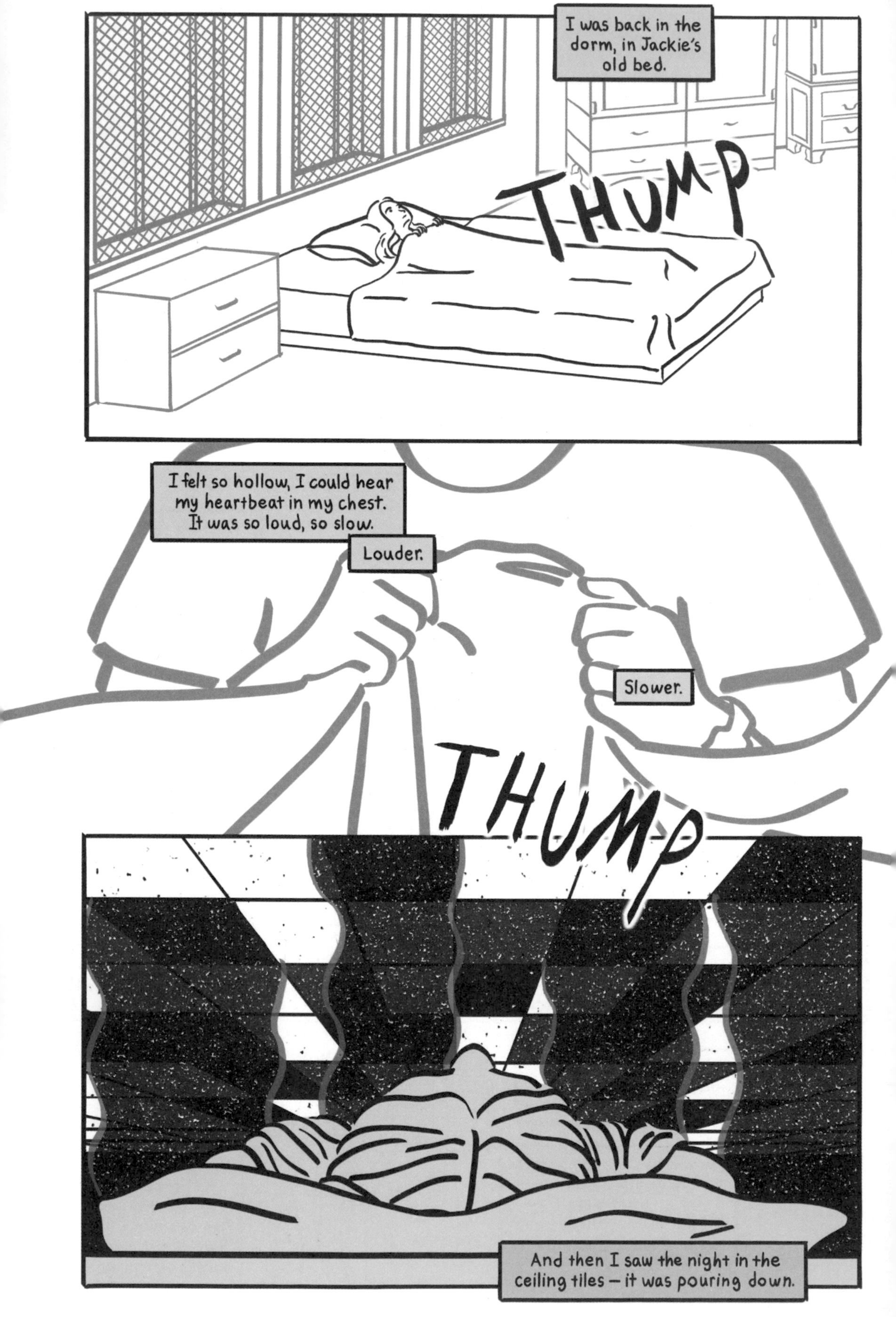
I was back in the dorm, in Jackie's old bed.
THUMP
I felt so hollow, I could hear my heartbeat in my chest. It was so loud, so slow.
Louder.
Slower.
THUMP
And then I saw the night in the ceiling tiles – it was pouring down.

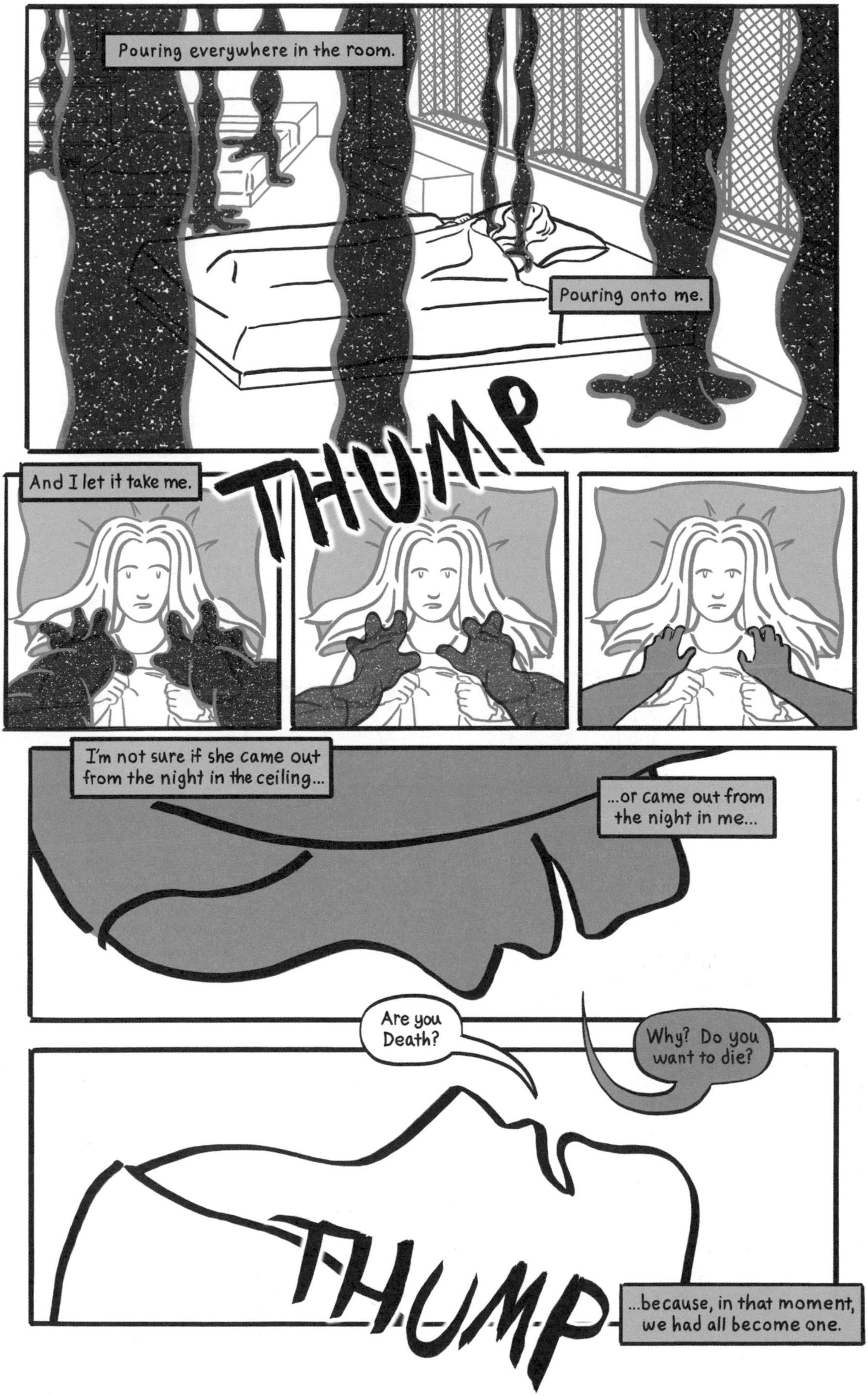

Pouring everywhere in the room.
Pouring onto me.
THUMP
And I let it take me.
I'm not sure if she came out from the night in the ceiling...
...or came out from the night in me...
Are you Death?
Why? Do you want to die?
THUMP
...because, in that moment, we had all become one.

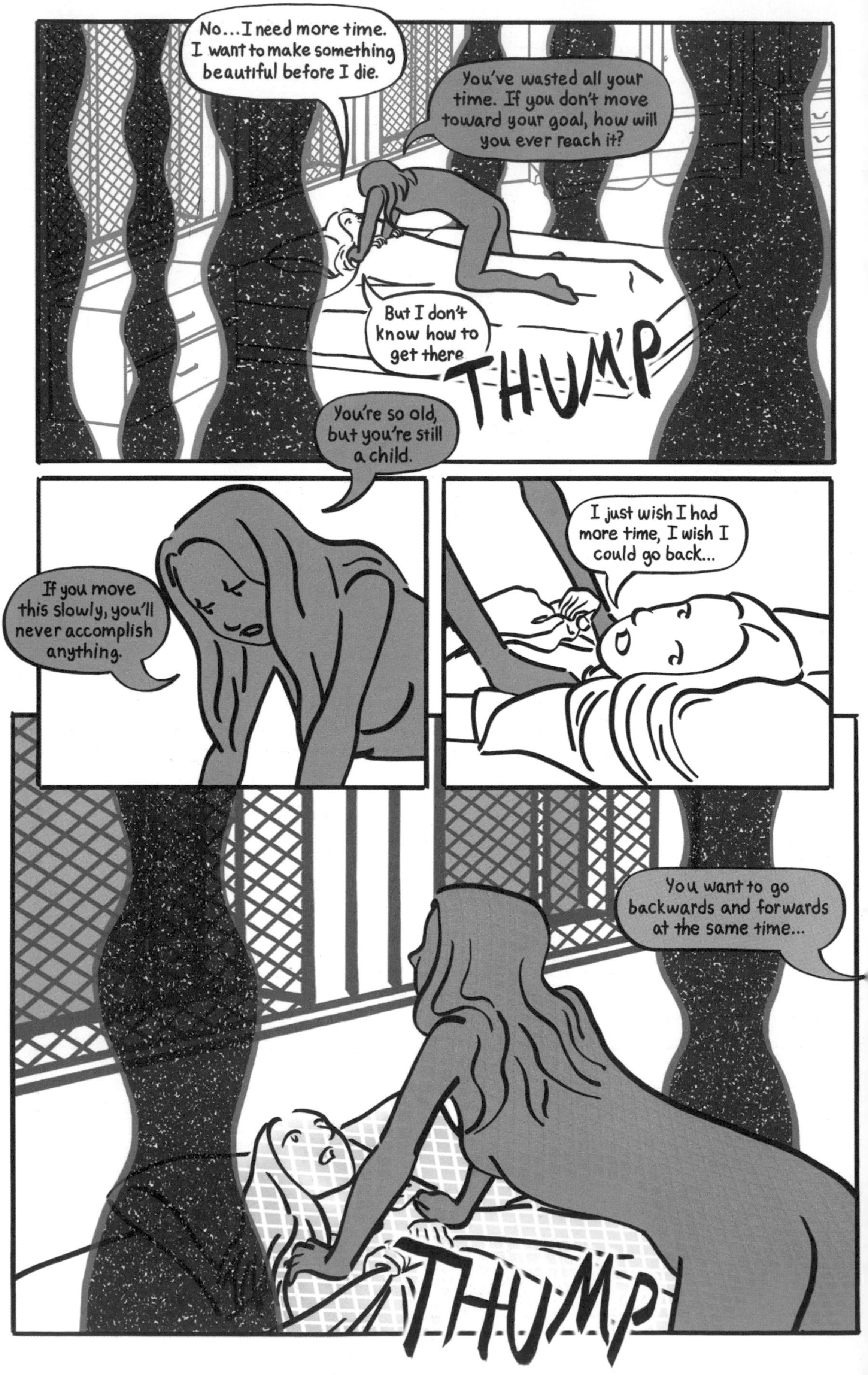
No...I need more time. I want to make something beautiful before I die.
You've wasted all your time. If you don't move toward your goal, how will you ever reach it?
But I don't know how to get there
THUMP
You're so old, but you're still a child.
If you move this slowly, you'll never accomplish anything.
I just wish I had more time, I wish I could go back...
You want to go backwards and forwards at the same time...
THUMP

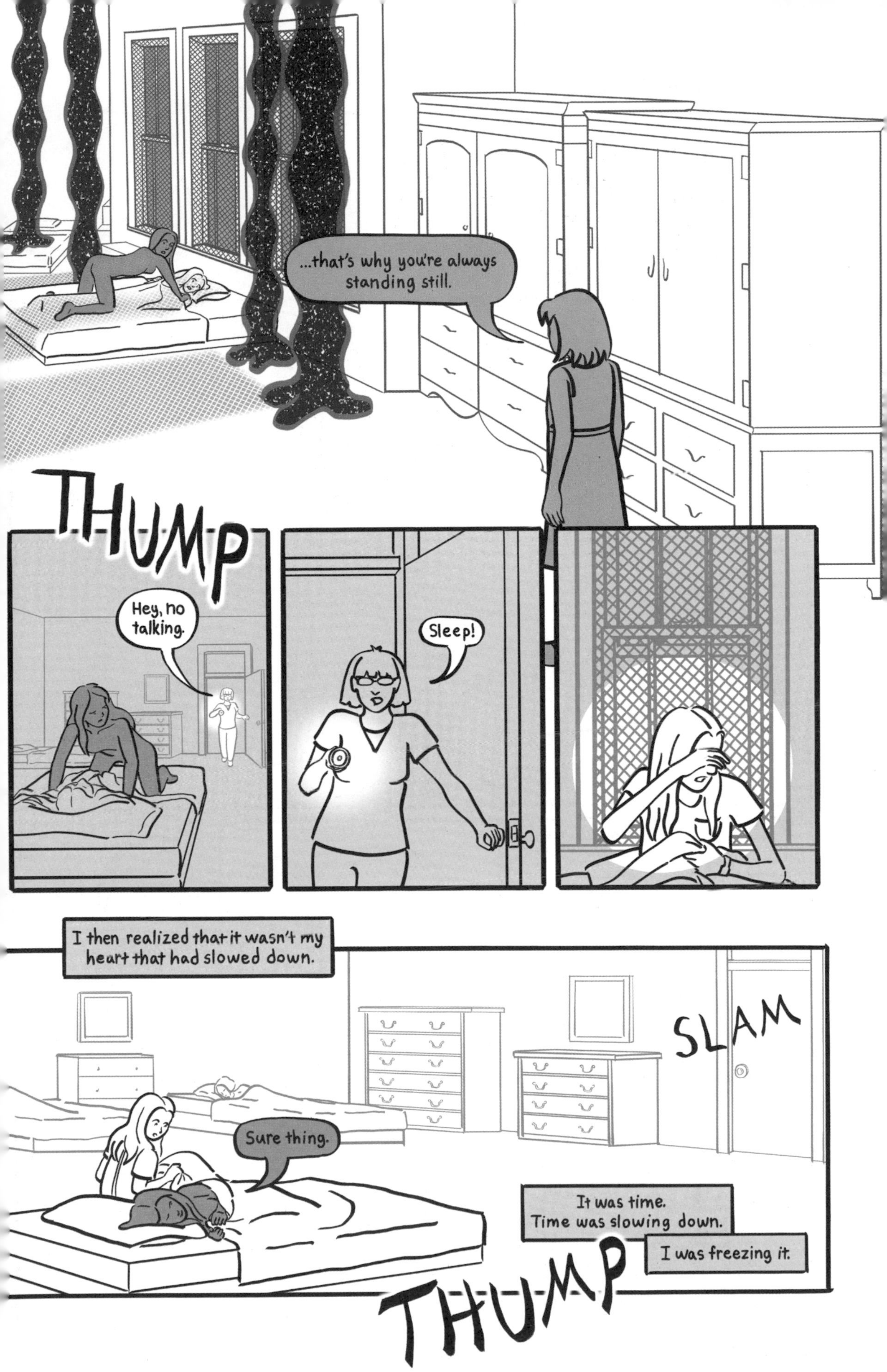
...that's why you're always standing still.
THUMP
Hey, no talking.
Sleep!
I then realized that it wasn't my heart that had slowed down.
SLAM
Sure thing.
It was time.
Time was slowing down.
I was freezing it.
THUMP

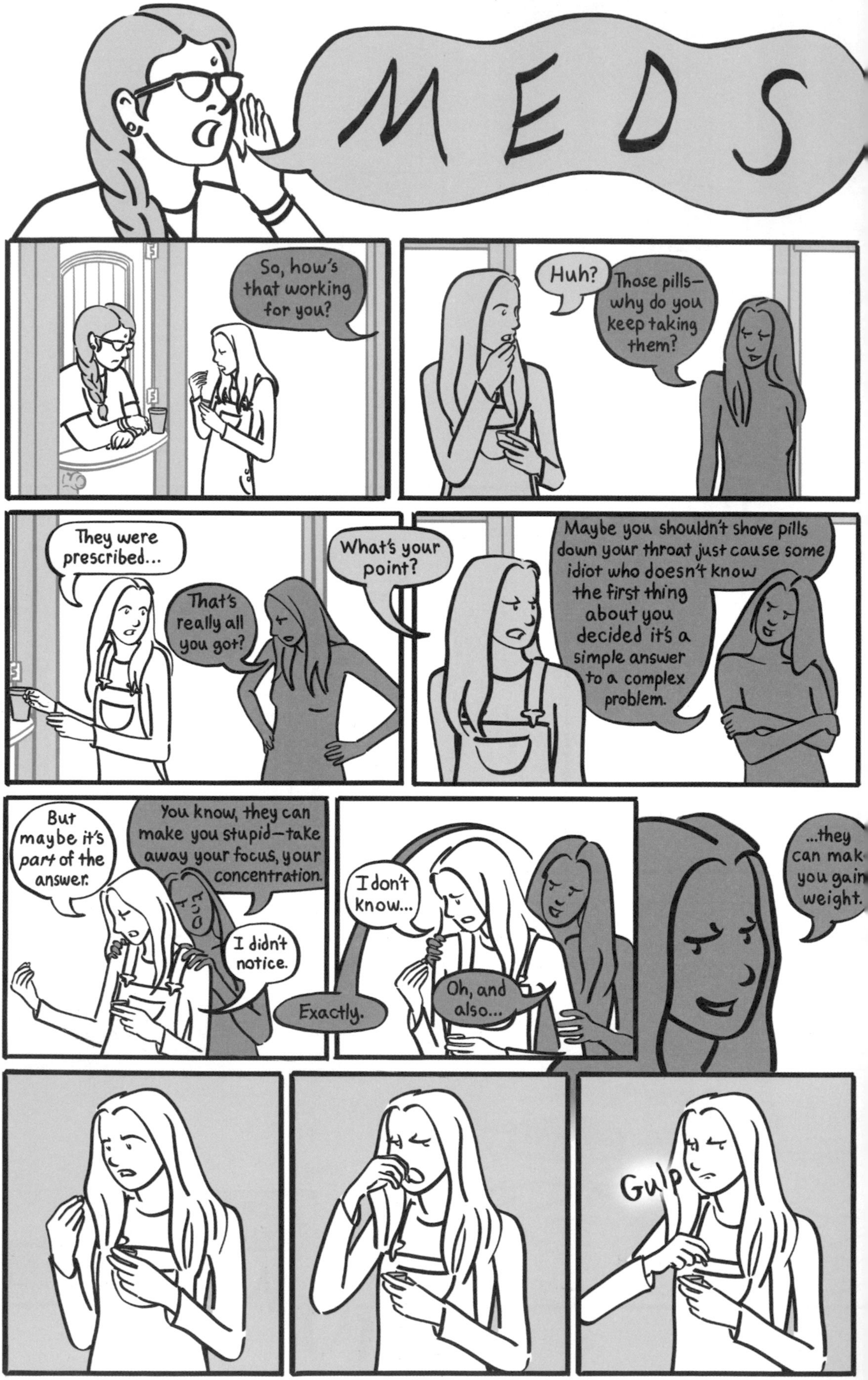
MEDS
So, how's that working for you?
Huh?
Those pills— why do you keep taking them?
They were prescribed...
That's really all you got?
What's your point?
Maybe you shouldn't shove pills down your throat just cause some idiot who doesn't know the first thing about you decided it's a simple answer to a complex problem.
But maybe it's *part* of the answer.
You know, they can make you stupid—take away your focus, your concentration.
I didn't notice.
Exactly.
I don't know...
Oh, and also...
...they can mak you gain weight.
Gulp

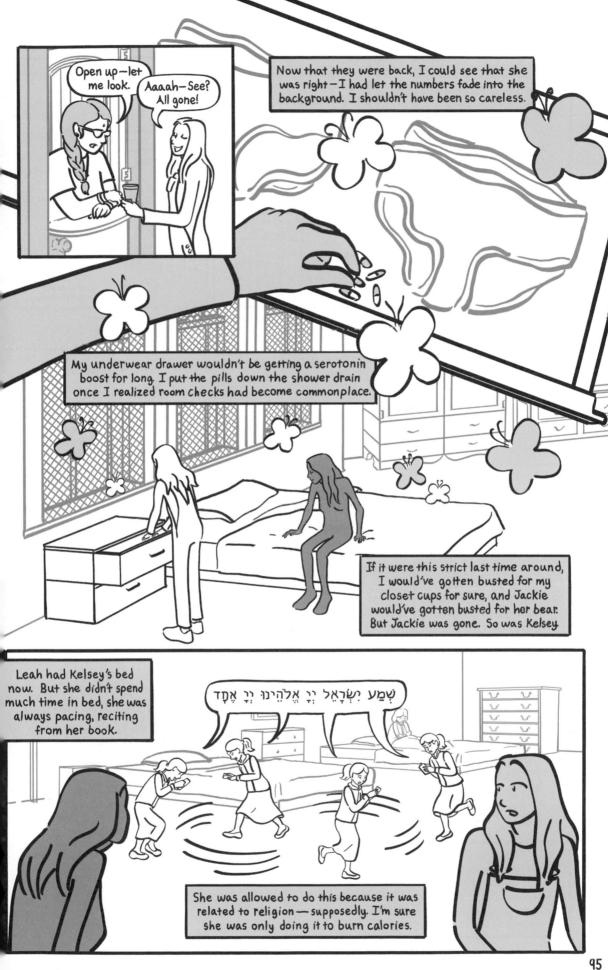

Open up—let me look.

Aaaah—See? All gone!

Now that they were back, I could see that she was right—I had let the numbers fade into the background. I shouldn't have been so careless.

My underwear drawer wouldn't be getting a serotonin boost for long. I put the pills down the shower drain once I realized room checks had become commonplace.

If it were this strict last time around, I would've gotten busted for my closet cups for sure, and Jackie would've gotten busted for her bear. But Jackie was gone. So was Kelsey.

Leah had Kelsey's bed now. But she didn't spend much time in bed, she was always pacing, reciting from her book.

שְׁמַע יִשְׂרָאֵל יְיָ אֱלֹהֵינוּ יְיָ אֶחָד

She was allowed to do this because it was related to religion—supposedly. I'm sure she was only doing it to burn calories.

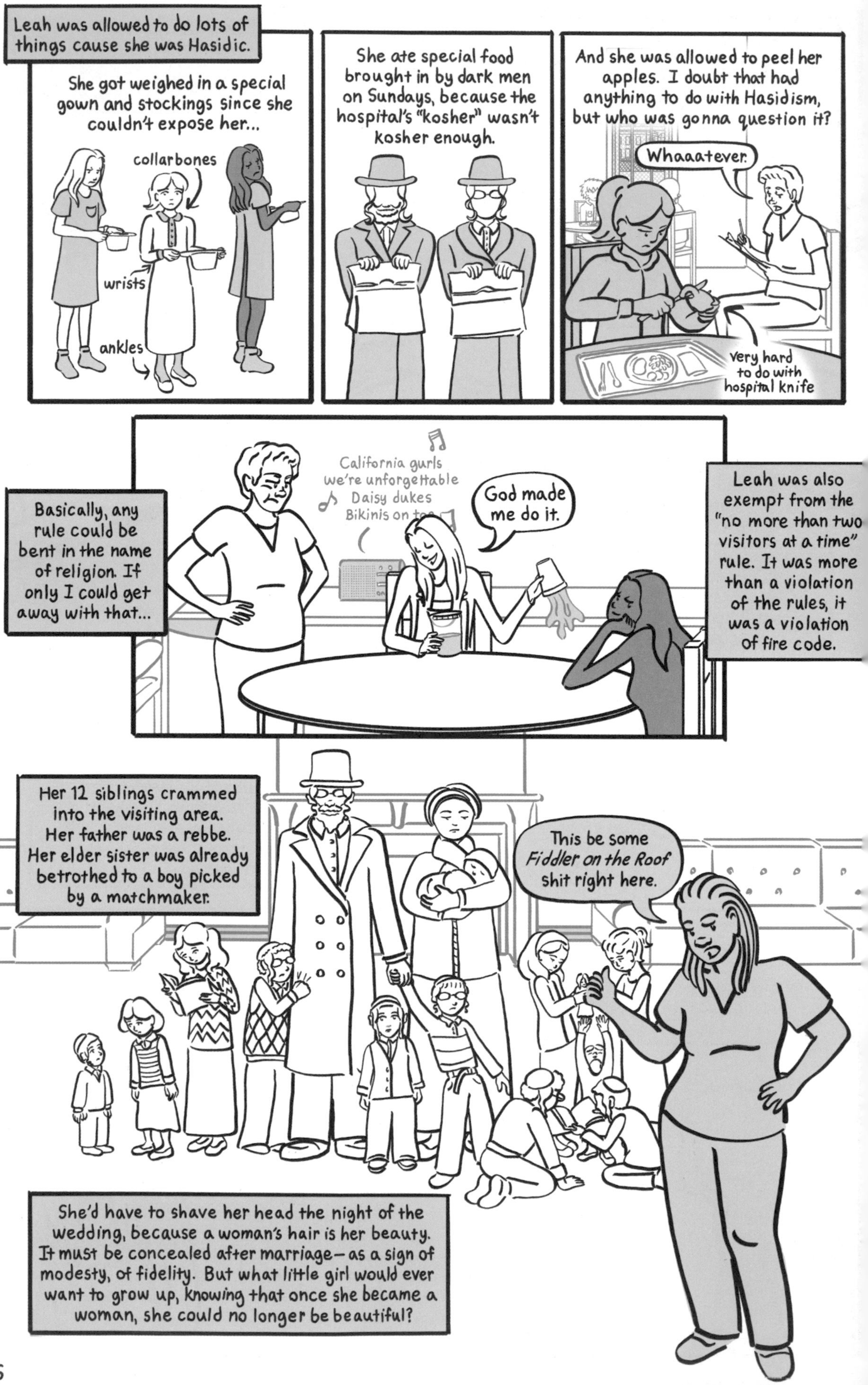
Leah was allowed to do lots of things cause she was Hasidic.
She got weighed in a special gown and stockings since she couldn't expose her...
collarbones
wrists
ankles
She ate special food brought in by dark men on Sundays, because the hospital's "kosher" wasn't kosher enough.
And she was allowed to peel her apples. I doubt that had anything to do with Hasidism, but who was gonna question it?
Whaaatever.
Very hard to do with hospital knife
Basically, any rule could be bent in the name of religion. If only I could get away with that...
California gurls
we're unforgettable
Daisy dukes
Bikinis on top
God made me do it.
Leah was also exempt from the "no more than two visitors at a time" rule. It was more than a violation of the rules, it was a violation of fire code.
Her 12 siblings crammed into the visiting area. Her father was a rebbe. Her elder sister was already betrothed to a boy picked by a matchmaker.
This be some *Fiddler on the Roof* shit right here.
She'd have to shave her head the night of the wedding, because a woman's hair is her beauty. It must be concealed after marriage—as a sign of modesty, of fidelity. But what little girl would ever want to grow up, knowing that once she became a woman, she could no longer be beautiful?

It was hard to talk to Leah because she knew such little English — she only spoke Yiddish. But I'd still try to ask her things, there was so much I wanted to know.

What are you reading about?

אֶל מִצְוֹתַי אִם שָׁמֹעַ תִּשְׁמְעוּ וְהָיָה

God

אֶתְכֶם הַיּוֹם אֲשֶׁר אָנֹכִי מְצַוֶּה

How should I start a conversation with her?

What's a 12-year-old anorexic interested in?

World History

Hey, Leah, what foods do you miss the most?

Nailed it!

Eh?

Don't look at *me*, your delivery was off.

World History

On fasting holidays, do your parents want you to eat?

If oy eet, everyone say "Why yu eet?"

Maybe you should start brushing up on your Torah.

Do you get to listen to music, like the kind they play in the Dining Room?

World History

We hav muzik.

It's not like the music you know — she means music about God, songs by people in her village.

Meira helped translate — not the words, but the context. She wasn't Hasidic, but she was orthodox (Westchester has a high orthodox population) and was familiar with Leah's village. She didn't have a traditional eating disorder, but she threw up whenever she took food by mouth. Instead of finding out what's actually wrong with her, she was dumped in 7 South and tubed.

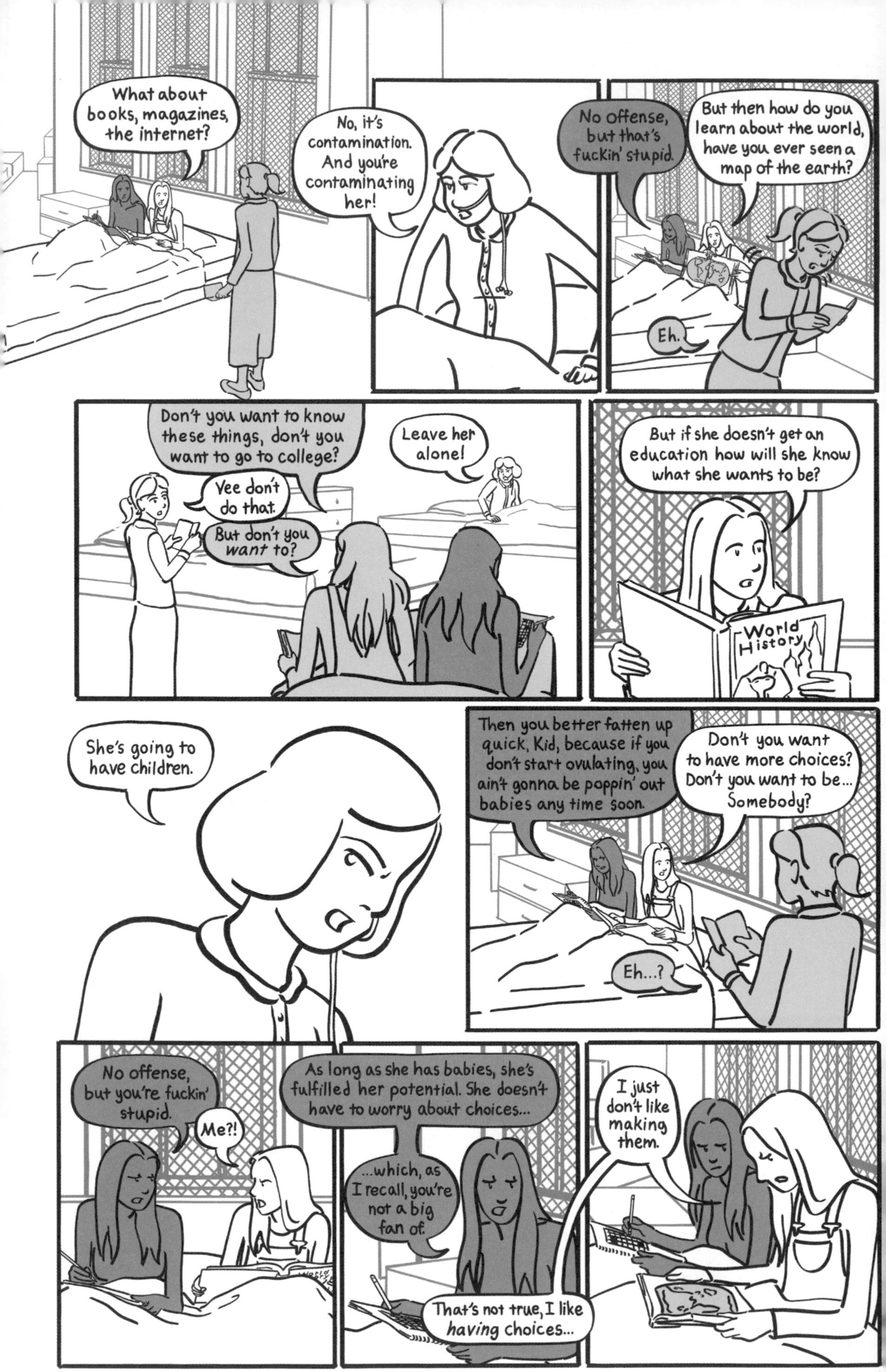

What about books, magazines, the internet?
No, it's contamination. And you're contaminating her!
No offense, but that's fuckin' stupid.
But then how do you learn about the world, have you ever seen a map of the earth?
Eh.
Don't you want to know these things, don't you want to go to college?
Vee don't do that.
But don't you *want* to?
Leave her alone!
But if she doesn't get an education how will she know what she wants to be?
World History
She's going to have children.
Then you better fatten up quick, Kid, because if you don't start ovulating, you ain't gonna be poppin' out babies any time soon.
Don't you want to have more choices? Don't you want to be... Somebody?
Eh...?
No offense, but you're fuckin' stupid.
Me?!
As long as she has babies, she's fulfilled her potential. She doesn't have to worry about choices...
...which, as I recall, you're not a big fan of.
That's not true, I like *having* choices...
I just don't like making them.

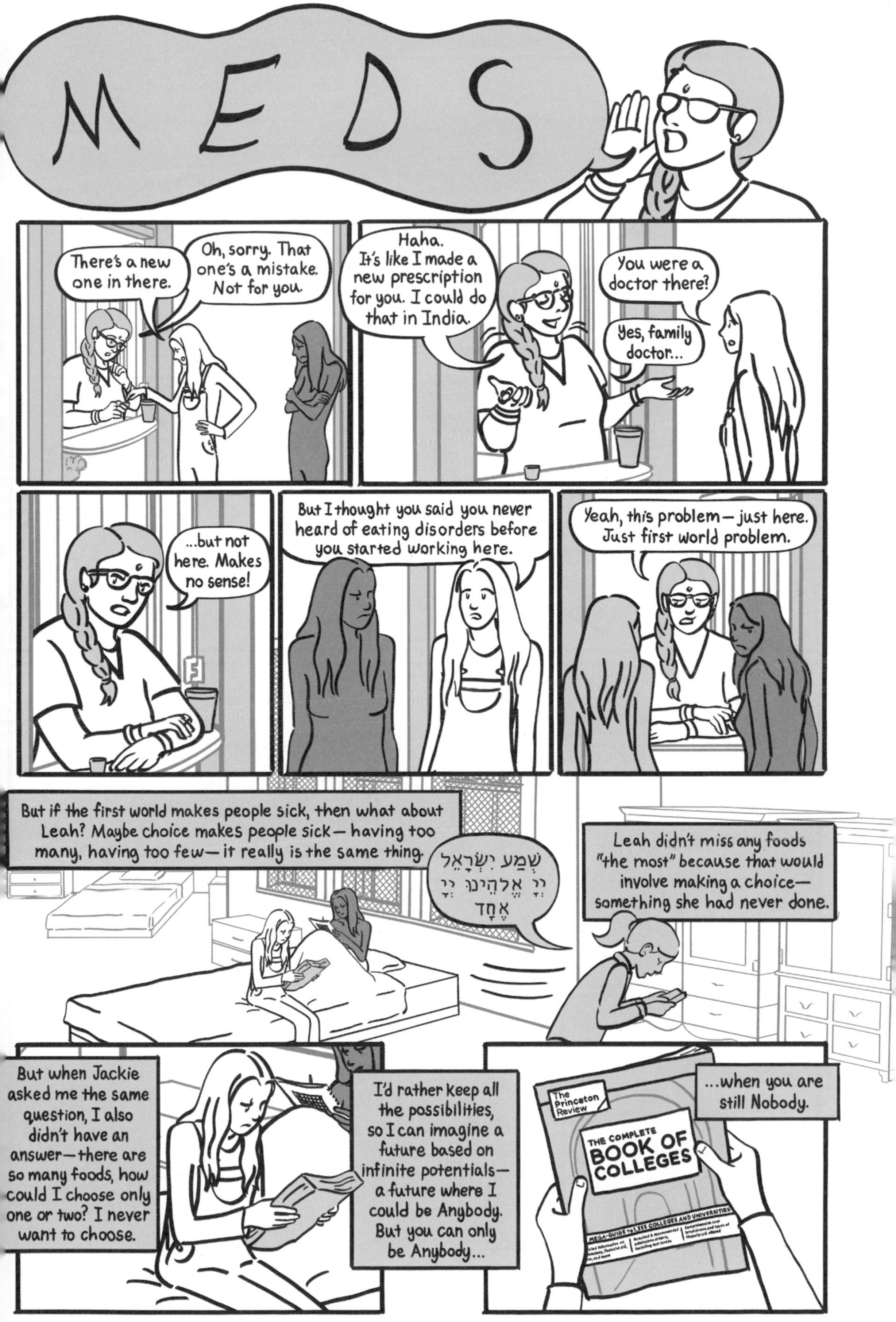
MEDS
There's a new one in there.
Oh, sorry. That one's a mistake. Not for you.
Haha. It's like I made a new prescription for you. I could do that in India.
You were a doctor there?
Yes, family doctor...
...but not here. Makes no sense!
But I thought you said you never heard of eating disorders before you started working here.
Yeah, this problem— just here. Just first world problem.
But if the first world makes people sick, then what about Leah? Maybe choice makes people sick— having too many, having too few— it really is the same thing.
שְׁמַע יִשְׂרָאֵל יְיָ אֱלֹהֵינוּ יְיָ אֶחָד
Leah didn't miss any foods "the most" because that would involve making a choice— something she had never done.
But when Jackie asked me the same question, I also didn't have an answer— there are so many foods, how could I choose only one or two? I never want to choose.
I'd rather keep all the possibilities, so I can imagine a future based on infinite potentials— a future where I could be Anybody. But you can only be Anybody...
The Princeton Review
THE COMPLETE BOOK OF COLLEGES
...when you are still Nobody.

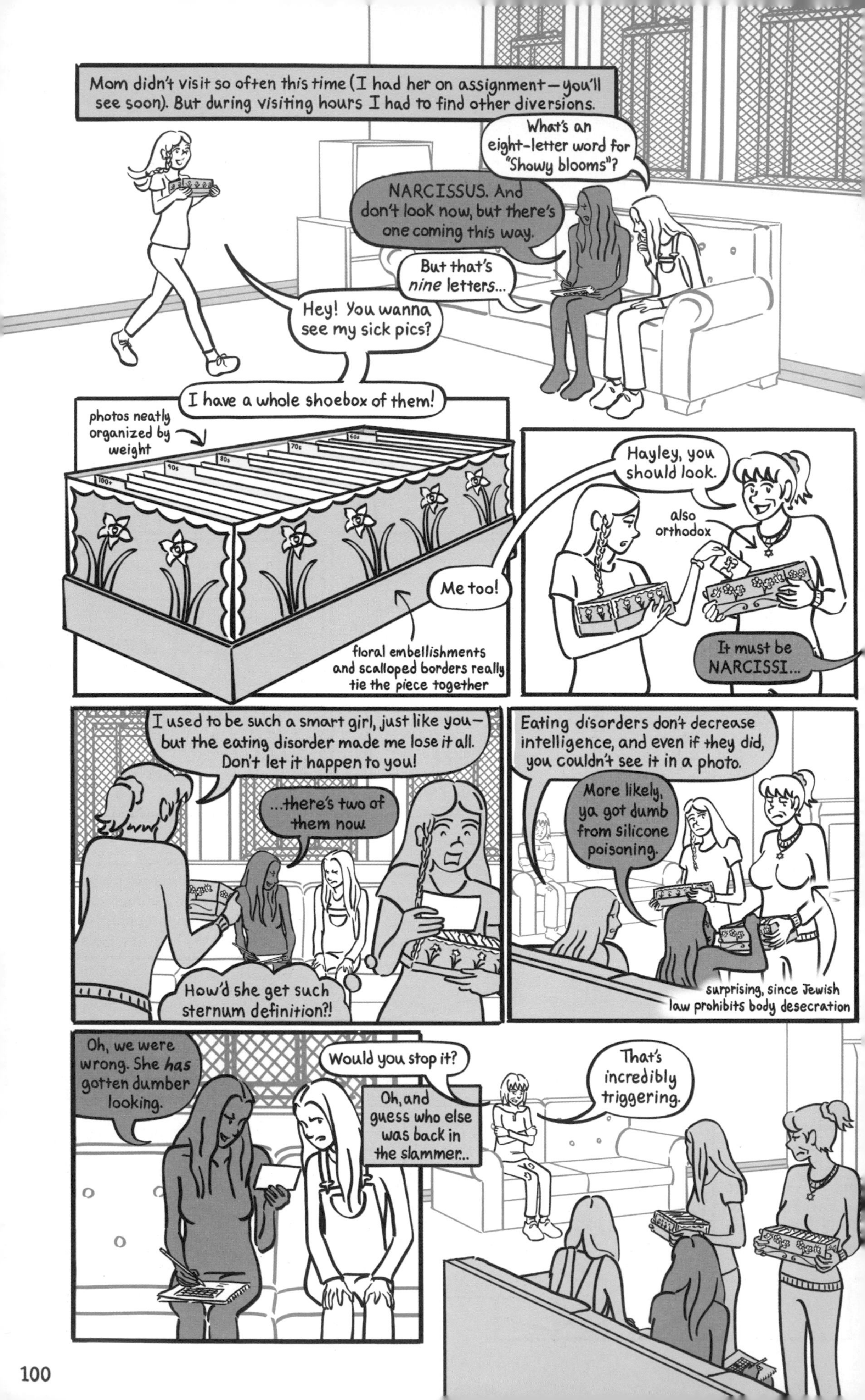

Mom didn't visit so often this time (I had her on assignment—you'll see soon). But during visiting hours I had to find other diversions.
What's an eight-letter word for "Showy blooms"?
NARCISSUS. And don't look now, but there's one coming this way.
But that's *nine* letters...
Hey! You wanna see my sick pics?
I have a whole shoebox of them!
photos neatly organized by weight
100+
90s
80s
70s
60s
floral embellishments and scalloped borders really tie the piece together
Me too!
Hayley, you should look.
also orthodox
It must be NARCISSI...
I used to be such a smart girl, just like you—but the eating disorder made me lose it all. Don't let it happen to you!
...there's two of them now.
How'd she get such sternum definition?!
Eating disorders don't decrease intelligence, and even if they did, you couldn't see it in a photo.
More likely, ya got dumb from silicone poisoning.
surprising, since Jewish law prohibits body desecration
Oh, we were wrong. She *has* gotten dumber looking.
Would you stop it?
Oh, and guess who else was back in the slammer...
That's incredibly triggering.

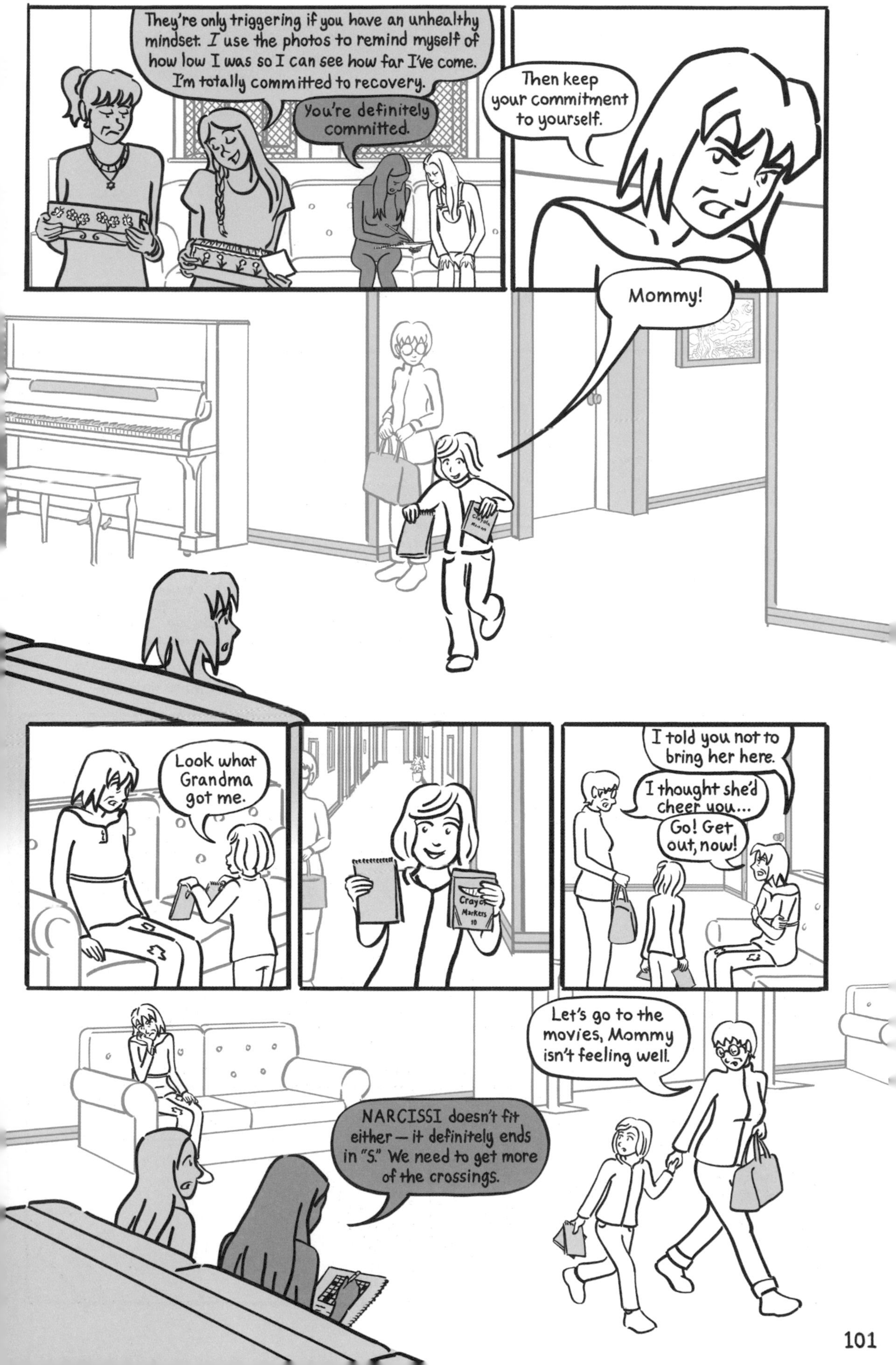
They're only triggering if you have an unhealthy mindset. I use the photos to remind myself of how low I was so I can see how far I've come. I'm totally committed to recovery.
You're definitely committed.
Then keep your commitment to yourself.
Mommy!
Crayola Markers
Look what Grandma got me.
Crayola Markers 10
I told you not to bring her here.
I thought she'd cheer you...
Go! Get out, now!
Let's go to the movies, Mommy isn't feeling well.
NARCISSI doesn't fit either — it definitely ends in "S." We need to get more of the crossings.

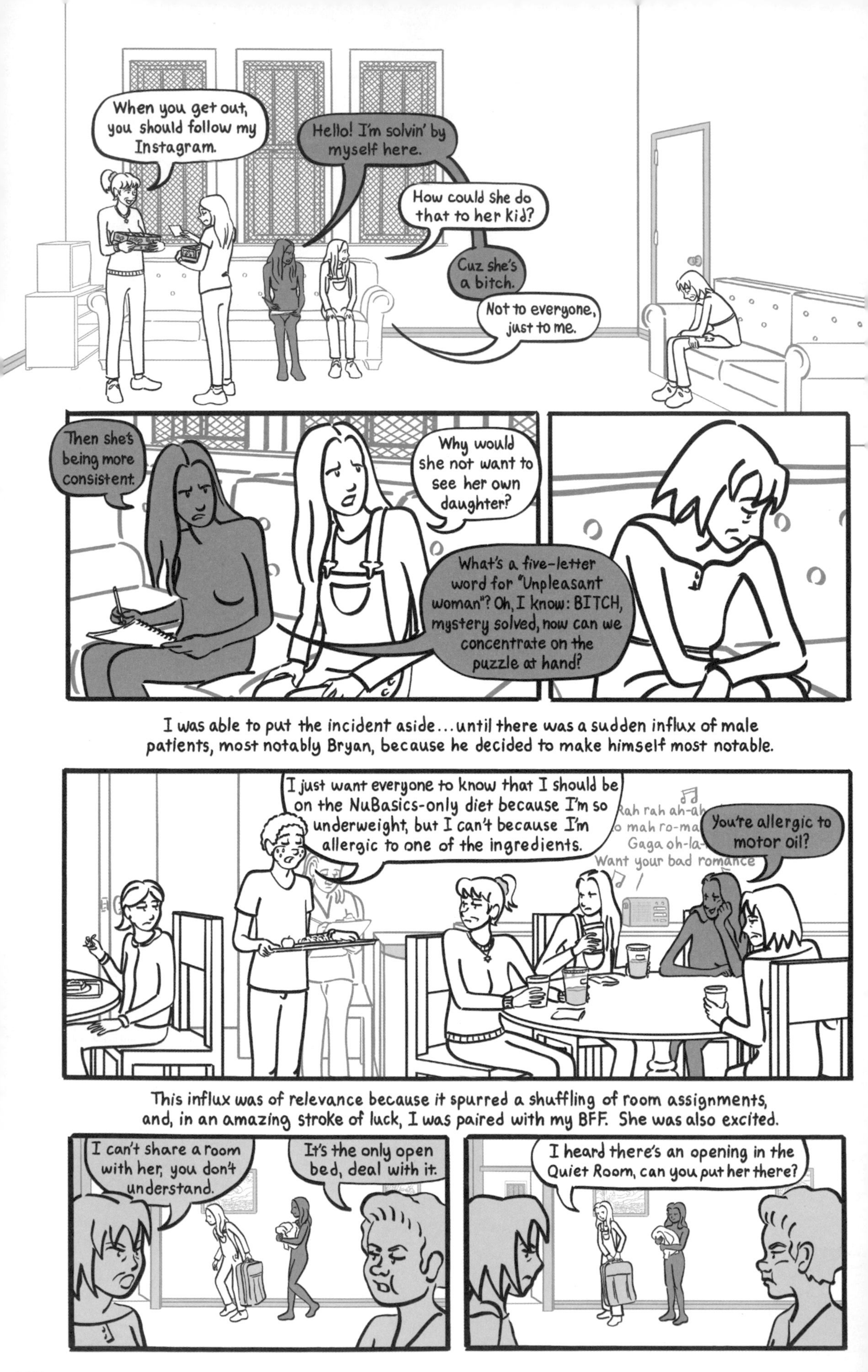
When you get out, you should follow my Instagram.
Hello! I'm solvin' by myself here.
How could she do that to her kid?
Cuz she's a bitch.
Not to everyone, just to me.
Then she's being more consistent.
Why would she not want to see her own daughter?
What's a five-letter word for "Unpleasant woman"? Oh, I know: BITCH, mystery solved, now can we concentrate on the puzzle at hand?
I was able to put the incident aside... until there was a sudden influx of male patients, most notably Bryan, because he decided to make himself most notable.
I just want everyone to know that I should be on the NuBasics-only diet because I'm so underweight, but I can't because I'm allergic to one of the ingredients.
Rah rah ah-ah
o mah ro-ma
Gaga oh-la-
Want your bad romance
You're allergic to motor oil?
This influx was of relevance because it spurred a shuffling of room assignments, and, in an amazing stroke of luck, I was paired with my BFF. She was also excited.
I can't share a room with her, you don't understand.
It's the only open bed, deal with it.
I heard there's an opening in the Quiet Room, can you put her there?

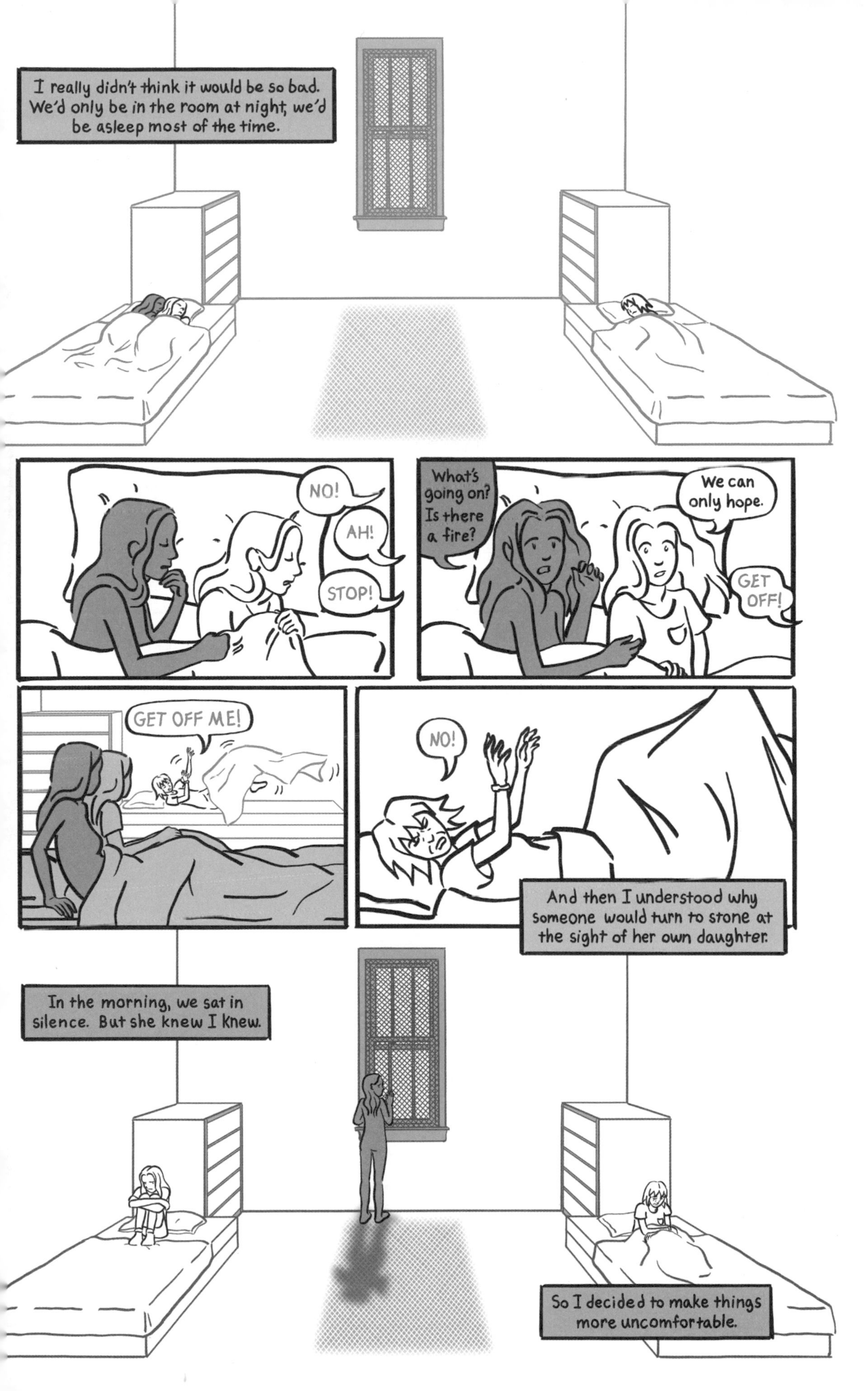
I really didn't think it would be so bad. We'd only be in the room at night, we'd be asleep most of the time.
NO!
AH!
STOP!
What's going on? Is there a fire?
We can only hope.
GET OFF!
GET OFF ME!
NO!
And then I understood why someone would turn to stone at the sight of her own daughter.
In the morning, we sat in silence. But she knew I knew.
So I decided to make things more uncomfortable.

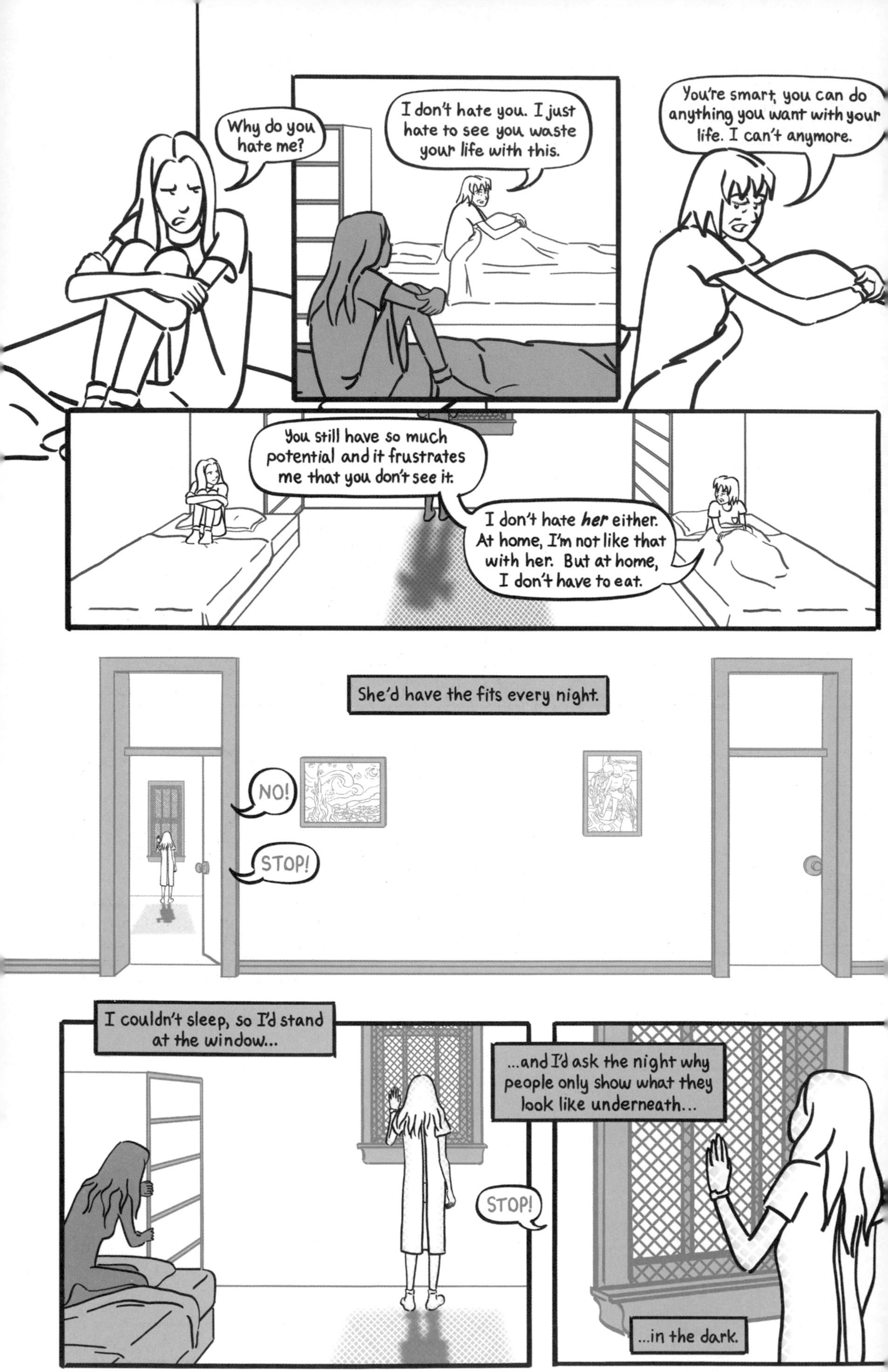
Why do you hate me?
I don't hate you. I just hate to see you waste your life with this.
You're smart, you can do anything you want with your life. I can't anymore.
You still have so much potential and it frustrates me that you don't see it.
I don't hate *her* either. At home, I'm not like that with her. But at home, I don't have to eat.
She'd have the fits every night.
NO!
STOP!
I couldn't sleep, so I'd stand at the window...
STOP!
...and I'd ask the night why people only show what they look like underneath...
...in the dark.

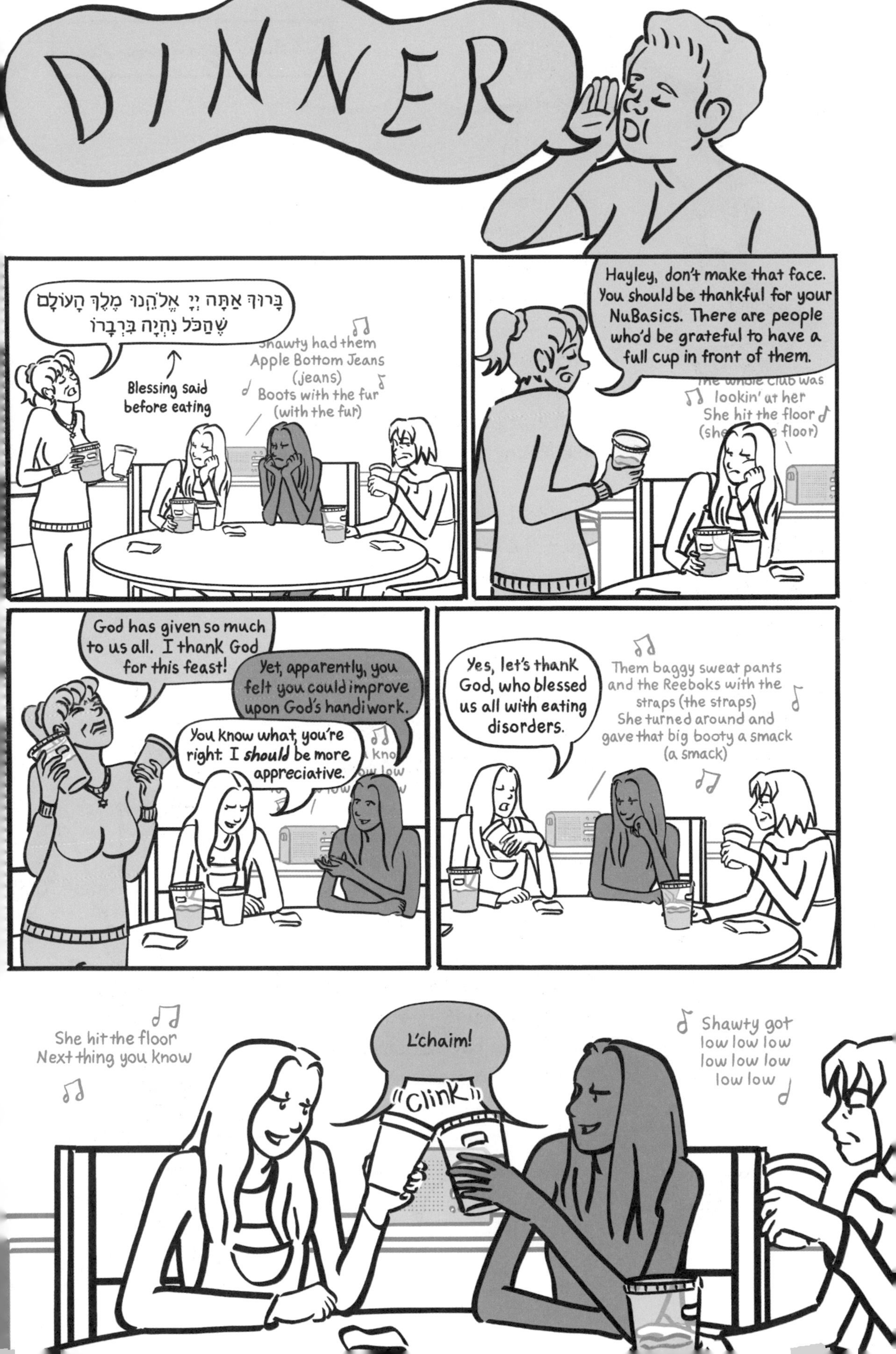
DINNER
בָּרוּךְ אַתָּה יְיָ אֱלֹהֵינוּ מֶלֶךְ הָעוֹלָם שֶׁהַכֹּל נִהְיָה בִּדְבָרוֹ
Blessing said before eating
Shawty had them Apple Bottom Jeans (jeans) Boots with the fur (with the fur)
Hayley, don't make that face. You should be thankful for your NuBasics. There are people who'd be grateful to have a full cup in front of them.
The whole club was lookin' at her She hit the floor
God has given so much to us all. I thank God for this feast!
Yet, apparently, you felt you could improve upon God's handiwork.
You know what, you're right. I *should* be more appreciative.
Yes, let's thank God, who blessed us all with eating disorders.
Them baggy sweat pants and the Reeboks with the straps (the straps) She turned around and gave that big booty a smack (a smack)
She hit the floor Next thing you know
L'chaim!
Clink
Shawty got low low low low low low low low

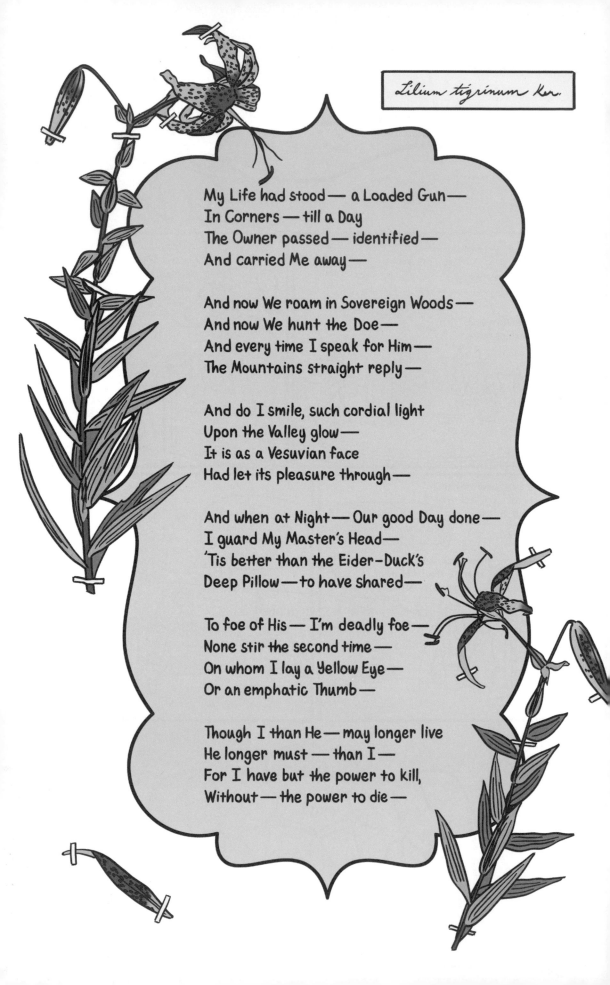

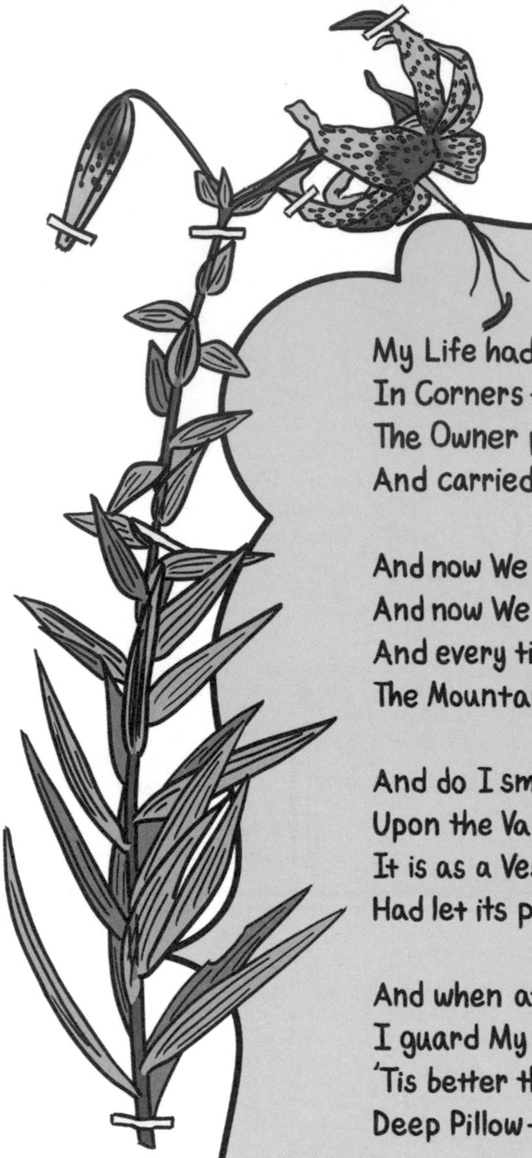
Lilium tigrinum Ker.

My Life had stood — a Loaded Gun —
In Corners — till a Day
The Owner passed — identified —
And carried Me away —

And now We roam in Sovereign Woods —
And now We hunt the Doe —
And every time I speak for Him —
The Mountains straight reply —

And do I smile, such cordial light
Upon the Valley glow —
It is as a Vesuvian face
Had let its pleasure through —

And when at Night — Our good Day done —
I guard My Master's Head —
'Tis better than the Eider-Duck's
Deep Pillow — to have shared —

To foe of His — I'm deadly foe —
None stir the second time —
On whom I lay a Yellow Eye —
Or an emphatic Thumb —

Though I than He — may longer live
He longer must — than I —
For I have but the power to kill,
Without — the power to die —

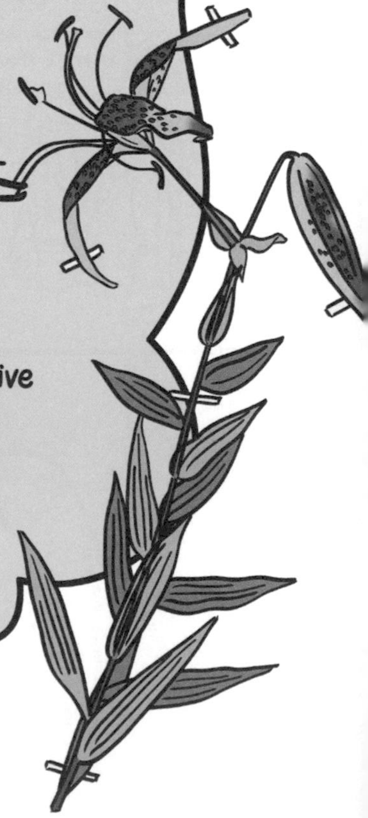

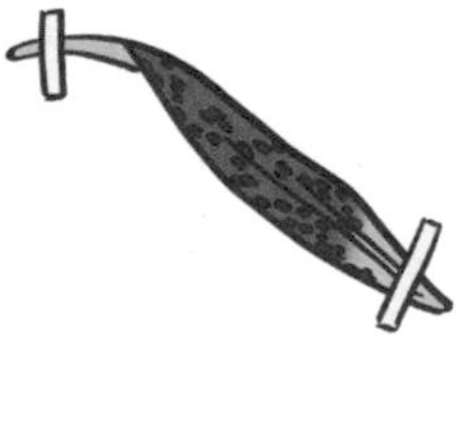

Chapter
5

Delusional

I used to like to draw, but not anymore. I used
to like to write, but I stopped liking that too. Even
jumping on the bed lost its appeal, because once I got
boobs, it hurt my chest. The only things I still liked were
puzzles, words, and numbers. But, since I *used* to like to
draw, I told Mom I wanted to go to art school. Being in
the hospital, I had no time to research schools or fill
out applications. So Mom did it for me...

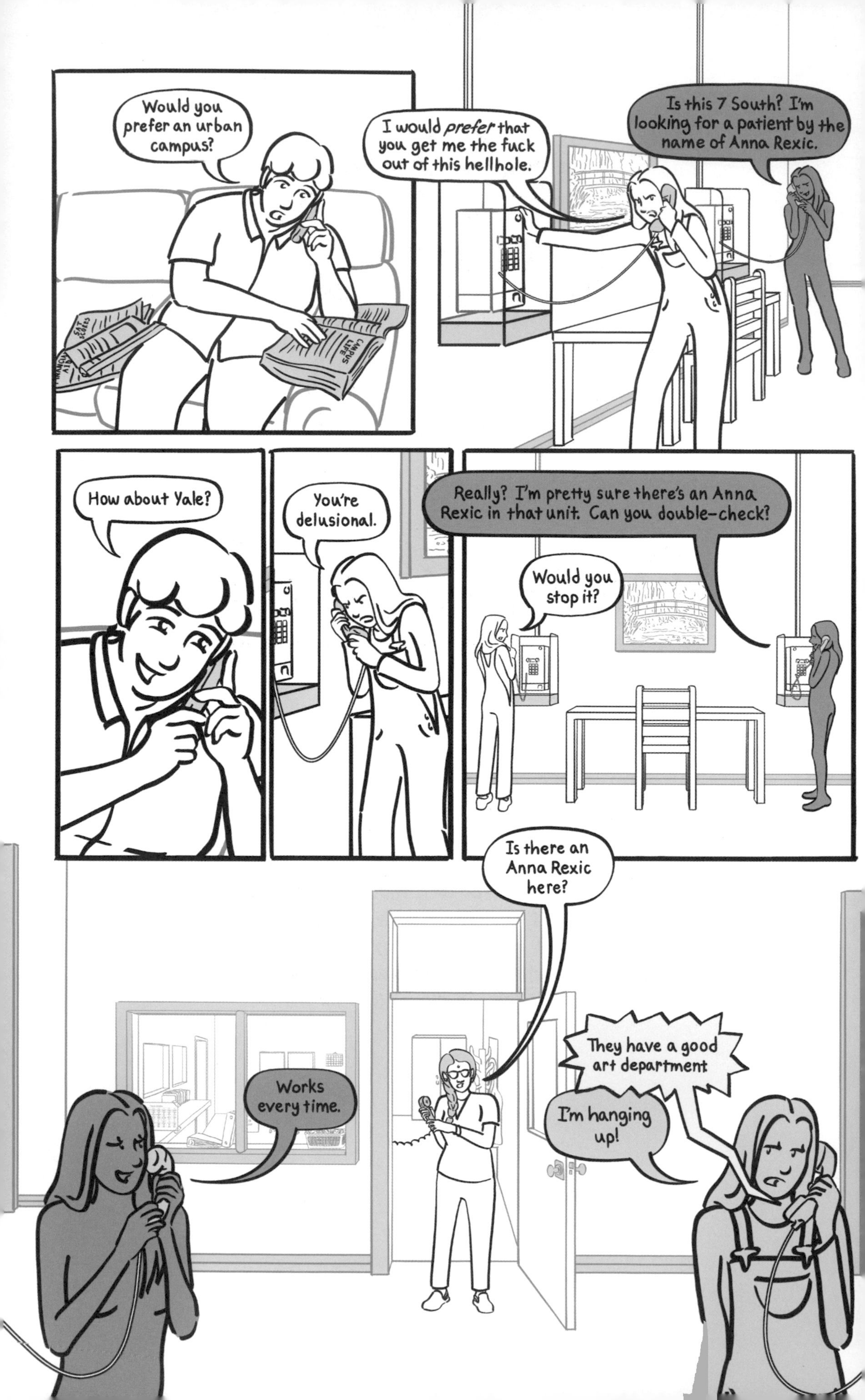
Would you prefer an urban campus?
SAT SCORES
CAMPUS LIFE
I would *prefer* that you get me the fuck out of this hellhole.
Is this 7 South? I'm looking for a patient by the name of Anna Rexic.
How about Yale?
You're delusional.
Really? I'm pretty sure there's an Anna Rexic in that unit. Can you double-check?
Would you stop it?
Is there an Anna Rexic here?
Works every time.
They have a good art department
I'm hanging up!

We eventually agreed upon an art school, which made all my AP credits a waste. I didn't attend most of those classes anyway (I was busy drinking NuBasics), but I still aced the tests. The words, the numbers— after I got out of Westchester they were everywhere, and they helped me cheat.

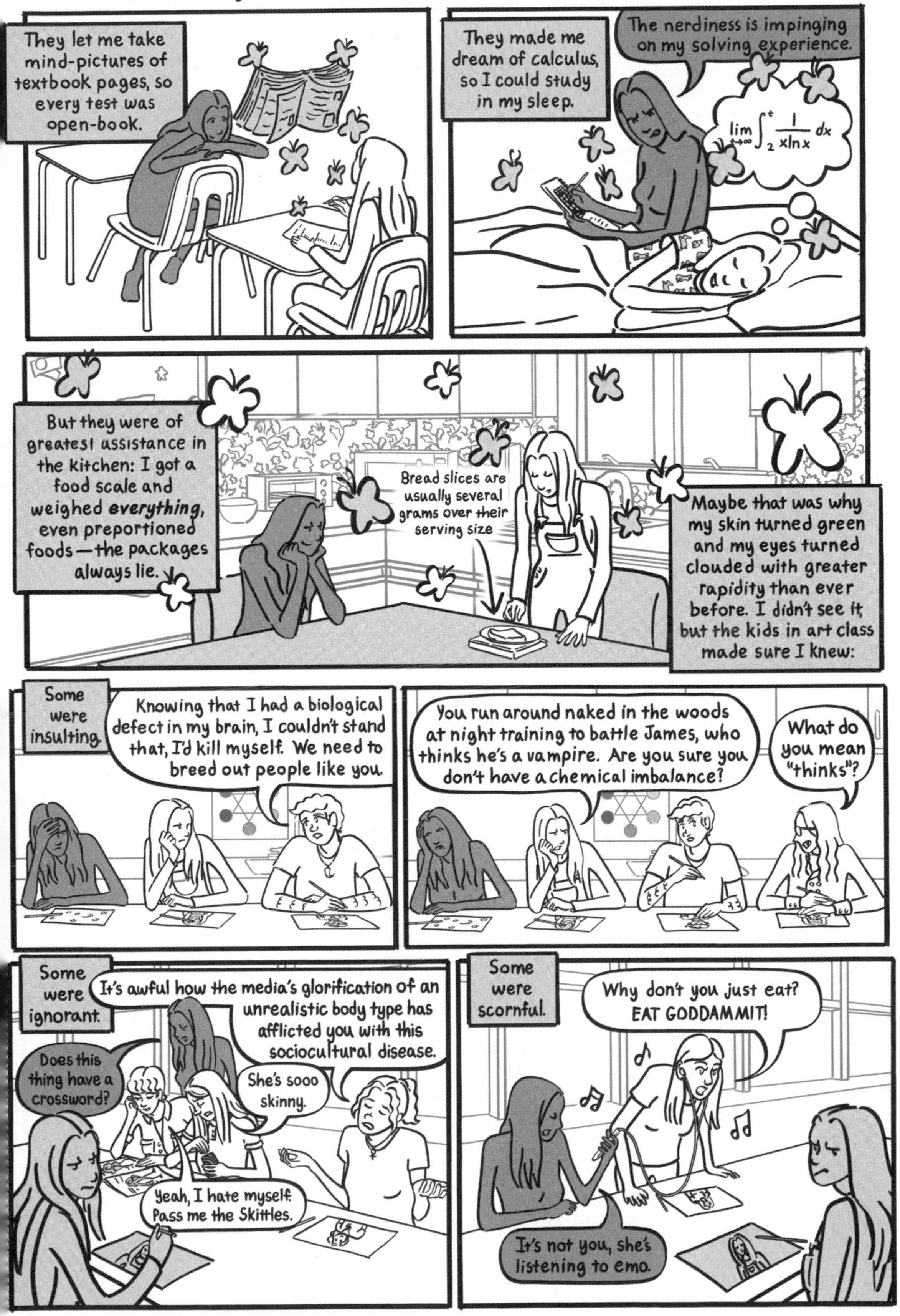

They let me take mind-pictures of textbook pages, so every test was open-book.
They made me dream of calculus, so I could study in my sleep.
The nerdiness is impinging on my solving experience.
$\lim_{t\to\infty}\int_2^t \frac{1}{x\ln x}\,dx$
But they were of greatest assistance in the kitchen: I got a food scale and weighed *everything*, even preportioned foods—the packages always lie.
Bread slices are usually several grams over their serving size
Maybe that was why my skin turned green and my eyes turned clouded with greater rapidity than ever before. I didn't see it, but the kids in art class made sure I knew:
Some were insulting.
Knowing that I had a biological defect in my brain, I couldn't stand that, I'd kill myself. We need to breed out people like you.
You run around naked in the woods at night training to battle James, who thinks he's a vampire. Are you sure you don't have a chemical imbalance?
What do you mean "thinks"?
Some were ignorant.
It's awful how the media's glorification of an unrealistic body type has afflicted you with this sociocultural disease.
Does this thing have a crossword?
She's sooo skinny.
Yeah, I hate myself. Pass me the Skittles.
Some were scornful.
Why don't you just eat? EAT GODDAMMIT!
It's not you, she's listening to emo.

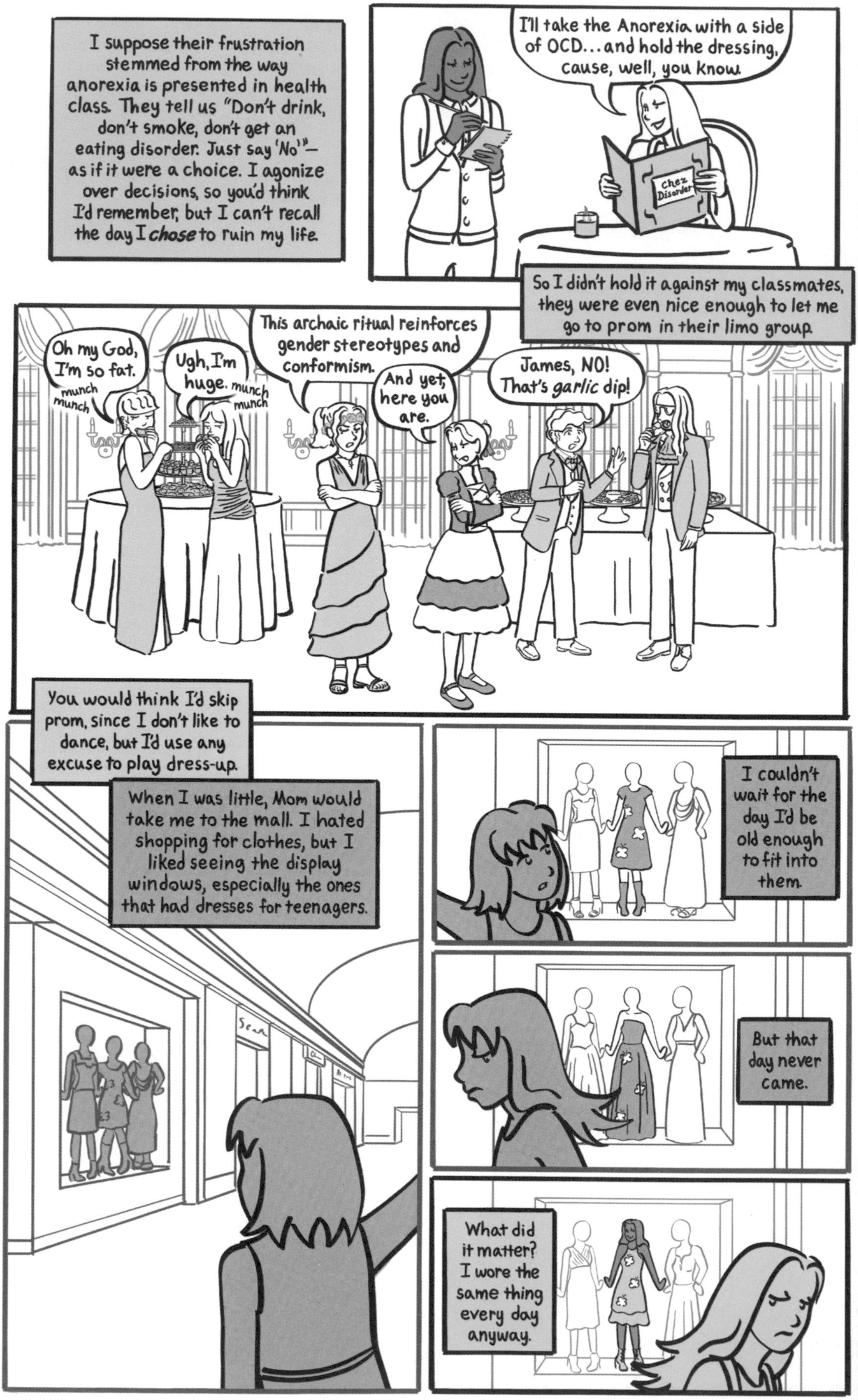
I suppose their frustration stemmed from the way anorexia is presented in health class. They tell us "Don't drink, don't smoke, don't get an eating disorder. Just say 'No'"—as if it were a choice. I agonize over decisions, so you'd think I'd remember, but I can't recall the day I *chose* to ruin my life.
I'll take the Anorexia with a side of OCD... and hold the dressing, cause, well, you know.
Chez Disorder
So I didn't hold it against my classmates, they were even nice enough to let me go to prom in their limo group.
Oh my God, I'm so fat.
munch munch
Ugh, I'm huge.
munch munch
This archaic ritual reinforces gender stereotypes and conformism.
And yet, here you are.
James, NO! That's *garlic* dip!
You would think I'd skip prom, since I don't like to dance, but I'd use any excuse to play dress-up.
When I was little, Mom would take me to the mall. I hated shopping for clothes, but I liked seeing the display windows, especially the ones that had dresses for teenagers.
I couldn't wait for the day I'd be old enough to fit into them.
But that day never came.
What did it matter? I wore the same thing every day anyway.

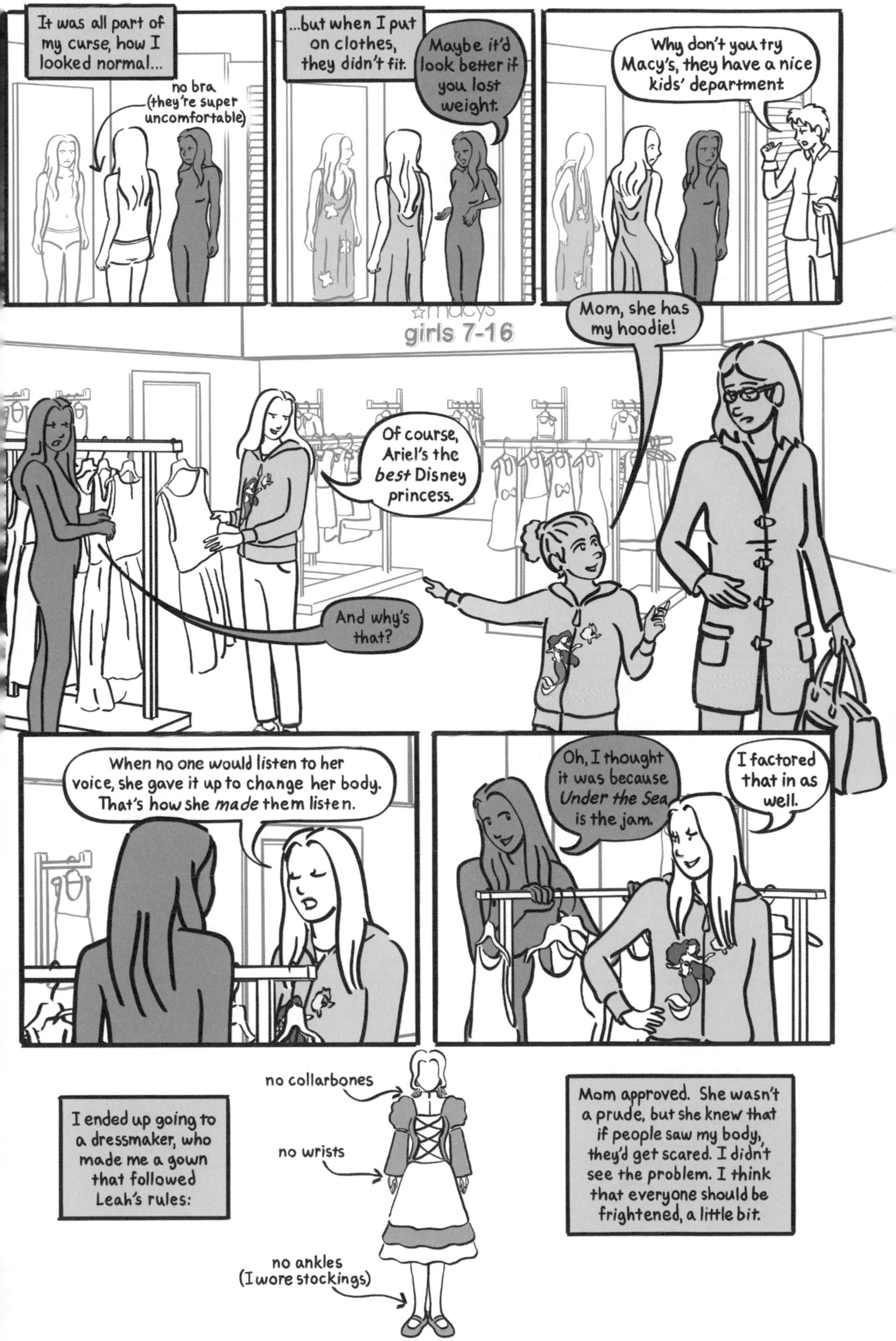

It was all part of my curse, how I looked normal...
no bra (they're super uncomfortable)
...but when I put on clothes, they didn't fit.
Maybe it'd look better if you lost weight.
Why don't you try Macy's, they have a nice kids' department.
macys
girls 7-16
Mom, she has my hoodie!
Of course, Ariel's the *best* Disney princess.
And why's that?
When no one would listen to her voice, she gave it up to change her body. That's how she *made* them listen.
Oh, I thought it was because *Under the Sea* is the jam.
I factored that in as well.
I ended up going to a dressmaker, who made me a gown that followed Leah's rules:
no collarbones
no wrists
no ankles (I wore stockings)
Mom approved. She wasn't a prude, but she knew that if people saw my body, they'd get scared. I didn't see the problem. I think that everyone should be frightened, a little bit.

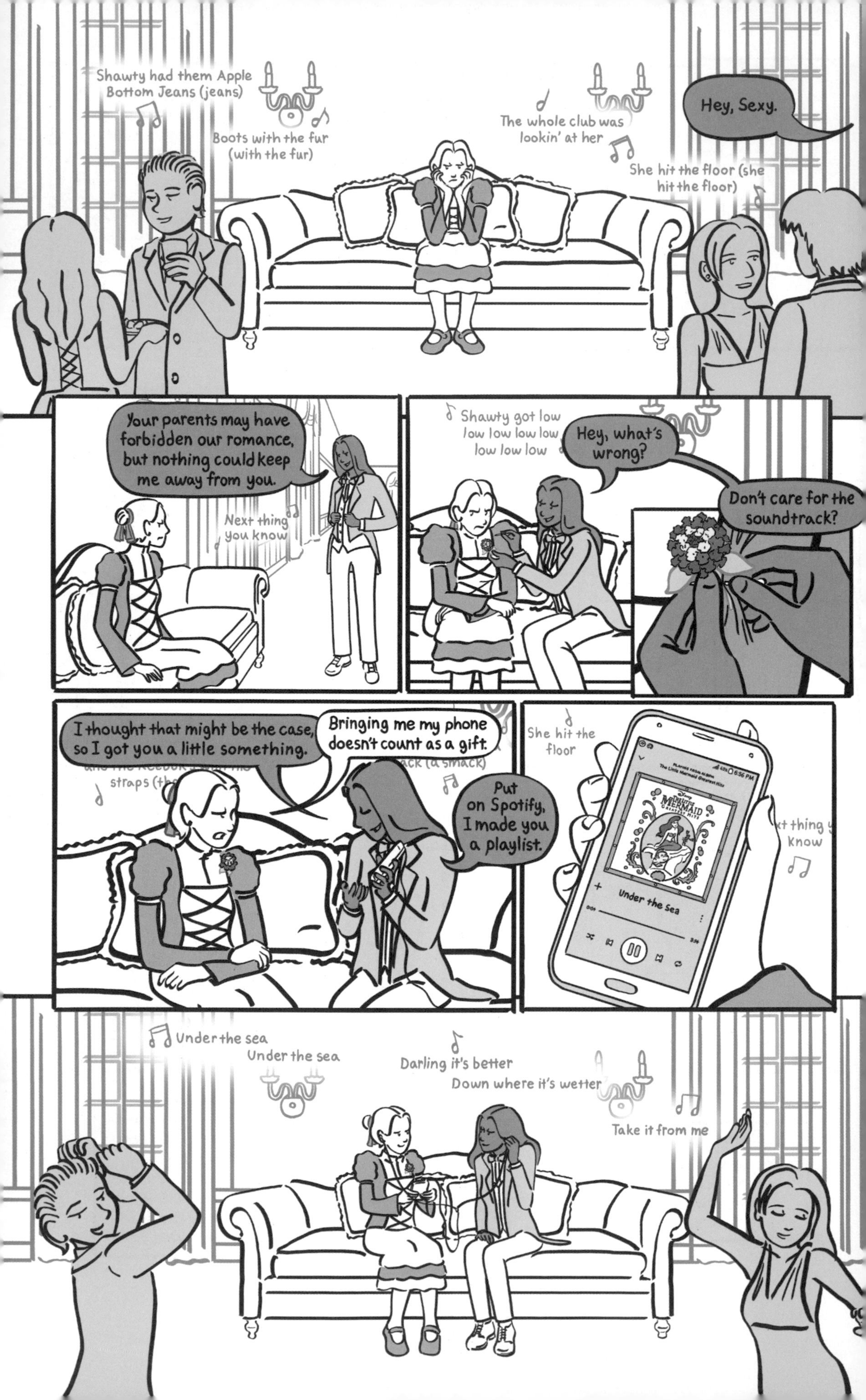

Shawty had them Apple Bottom Jeans (jeans)
Boots with the fur (with the fur)
The whole club was lookin' at her
Hey, Sexy.
She hit the floor (she hit the floor)
Your parents may have forbidden our romance, but nothing could keep me away from you.
Next thing you know
Shawty got low low low low low low low low
Hey, what's wrong?
Don't care for the soundtrack?
I thought that might be the case, so I got you a little something.
Bringing me my phone doesn't count as a gift.
Put on Spotify, I made you a playlist.
She hit the floor
The Little Mermaid
Under the Sea
Under the sea
Under the sea
Darling it's better
Down where it's wetter
Take it from me

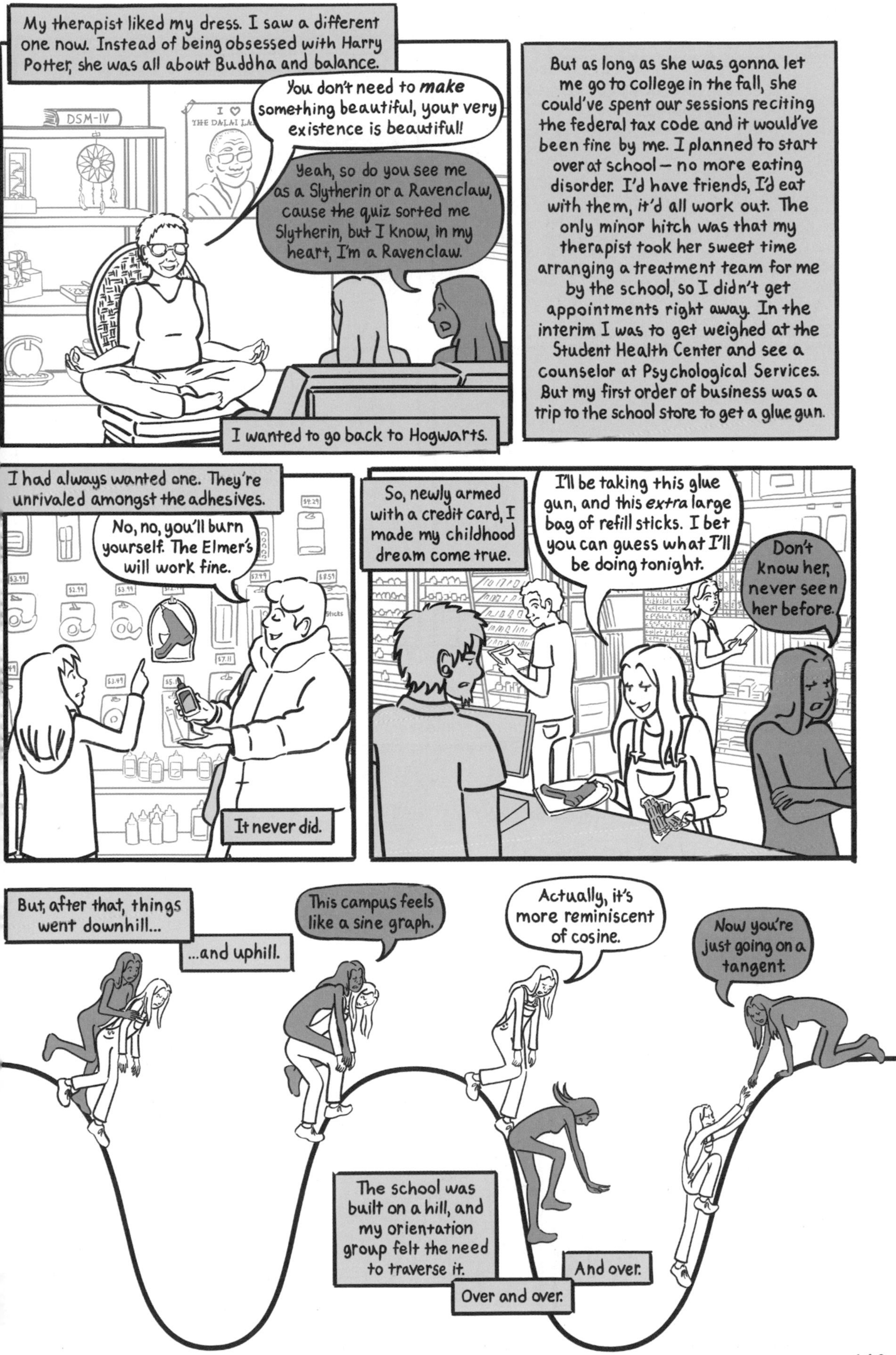

My therapist liked my dress. I saw a different one now. Instead of being obsessed with Harry Potter, she was all about Buddha and balance.
DSM-IV
I ♡ THE DALAI LA
You don't need to **make** something beautiful, your very existence is beautiful!
Yeah, so do you see me as a Slytherin or a Ravenclaw, cause the quiz sorted me Slytherin, but I know, in my heart, I'm a Ravenclaw.
I wanted to go back to Hogwarts.
But as long as she was gonna let me go to college in the fall, she could've spent our sessions reciting the federal tax code and it would've been fine by me. I planned to start over at school — no more eating disorder. I'd have friends, I'd eat with them, it'd all work out. The only minor hitch was that my therapist took her sweet time arranging a treatment team for me by the school, so I didn't get appointments right away. In the interim I was to get weighed at the Student Health Center and see a counselor at Psychological Services. But my first order of business was a trip to the school store to get a glue gun.
I had always wanted one. They're unrivaled amongst the adhesives.
No, no, you'll burn yourself. The Elmer's will work fine.
It never did.
So, newly armed with a credit card, I made my childhood dream come true.
I'll be taking this glue gun, and this *extra* large bag of refill sticks. I bet you can guess what I'll be doing tonight.
Don't know her, never seen her before.
But, after that, things went downhill...
...and uphill.
This campus feels like a sine graph.
Actually, it's more reminiscent of cosine.
Now you're just going on a tangent.
The school was built on a hill, and my orientation group felt the need to traverse it.
Over and over.
And over.

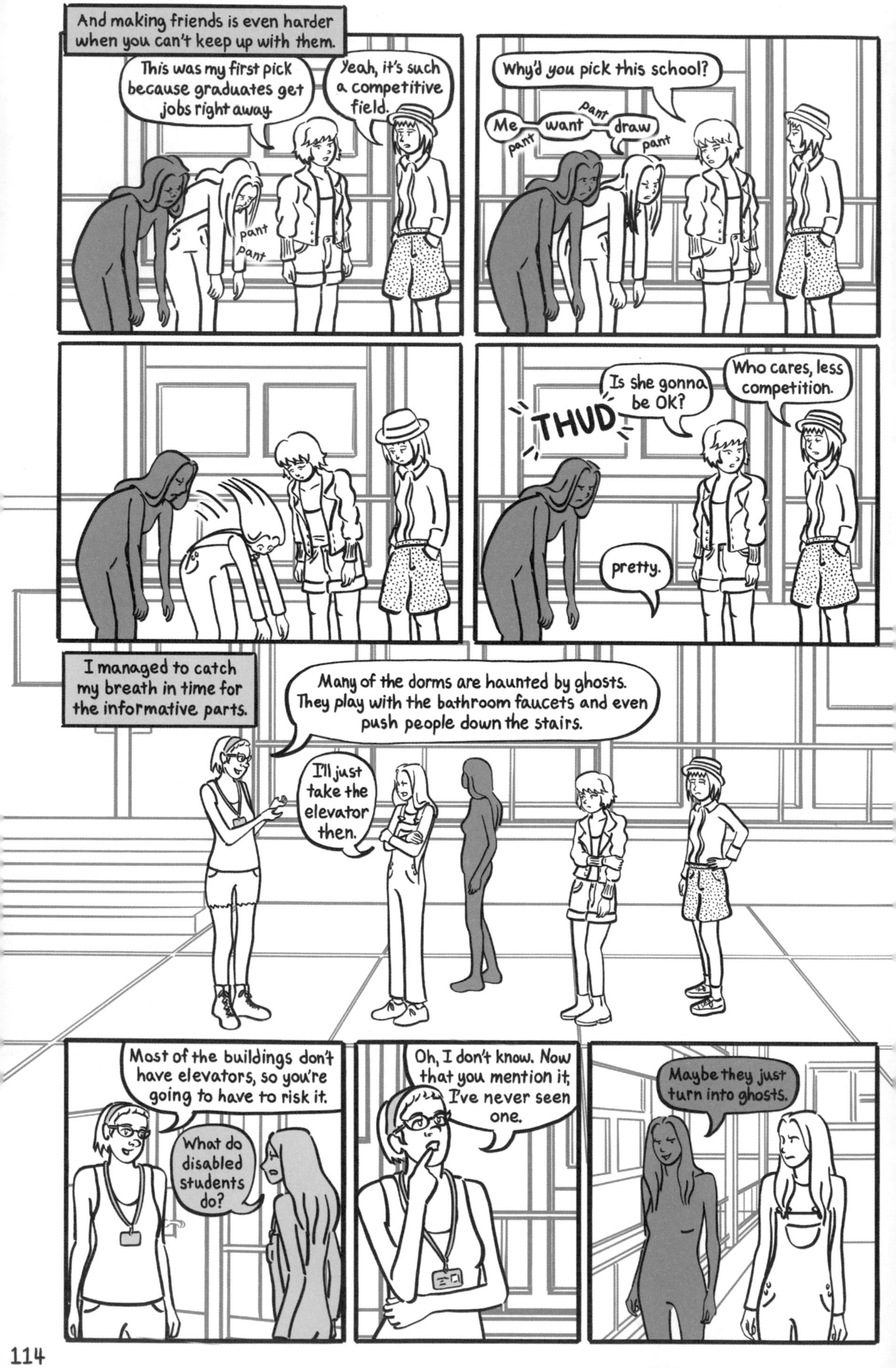

And making friends is even harder when you can't keep up with them.
This was my first pick because graduates get jobs right away.
Yeah, it's such a competitive field.
pant pant
Why'd you pick this school?
Me pant want pant draw pant
THUD
Is she gonna be OK?
Who cares, less competition.
pretty.
I managed to catch my breath in time for the informative parts.
Many of the dorms are haunted by ghosts. They play with the bathroom faucets and even push people down the stairs.
I'll just take the elevator then.
Most of the buildings don't have elevators, so you're going to have to risk it.
What do disabled students do?
Oh, I don't know. Now that you mention it, I've never seen one.
Maybe they just turn into ghosts.

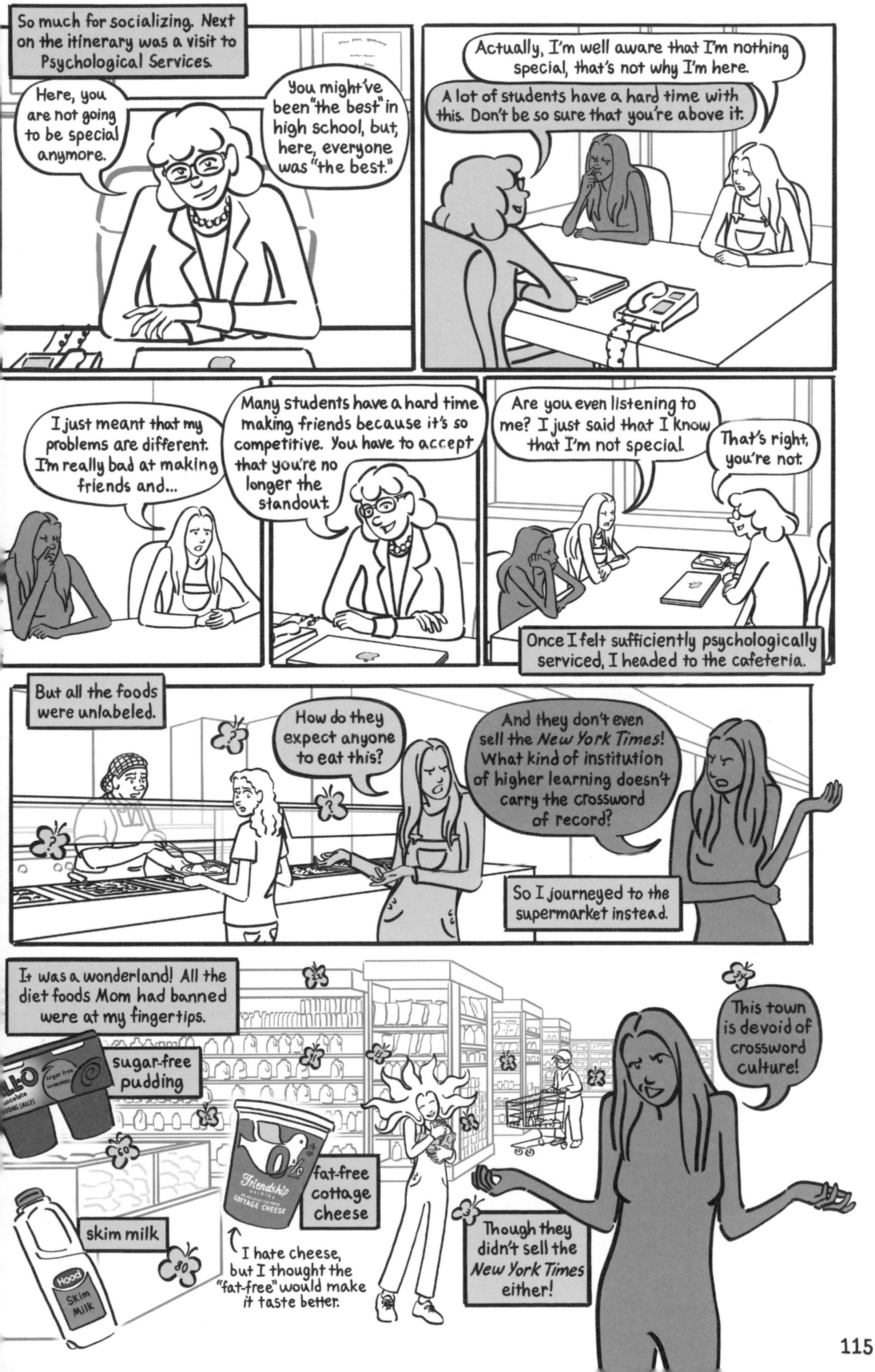
So much for socializing. Next on the itinerary was a visit to Psychological Services.
Here, you are not going to be special anymore.
You might've been "the best" in high school, but, here, everyone was "the best."
Actually, I'm well aware that I'm nothing special, that's not why I'm here.
A lot of students have a hard time with this. Don't be so sure that you're above it.
I just meant that my problems are different. I'm really bad at making friends and...
Many students have a hard time making friends because it's so competitive. You have to accept that you're no longer the standout.
Are you even listening to me? I just said that I know that I'm not special.
That's right, you're not.
Once I felt sufficiently psychologically serviced, I headed to the cafeteria.
But all the foods were unlabeled.
How do they expect anyone to eat this?
And they don't even sell the *New York Times*! What kind of institution of higher learning doesn't carry the crossword of record?
So I journeyed to the supermarket instead.
It was a wonderland! All the diet foods Mom had banned were at my fingertips.
sugar-free pudding
skim milk
fat-free cottage cheese
I hate cheese, but I thought the "fat-free" would make it taste better.
This town is devoid of crossword culture!
Though they didn't sell the *New York Times* either!

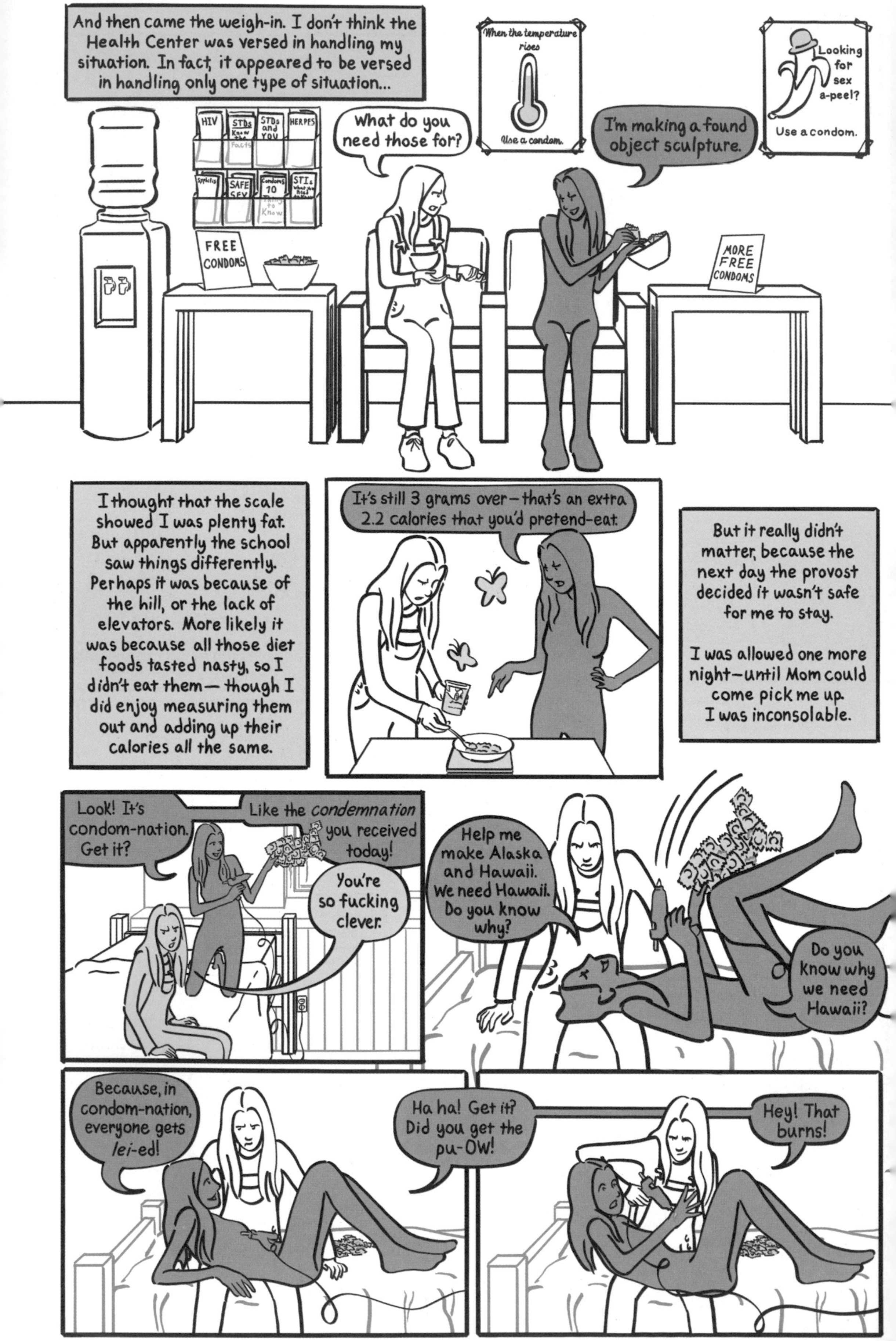

And then came the weigh-in. I don't think the Health Center was versed in handling my situation. In fact, it appeared to be versed in handling only one type of situation...
HIV
STDs
STDs and YOU
HERPES
Syphilis
SAFE SEX
Condoms 10
STIs
FREE CONDOMS
What do you need those for?
When the temperature rises
Use a condom.
I'm making a found object sculpture.
Looking for sex a-peel?
Use a condom.
MORE FREE CONDOMS
I thought that the scale showed I was plenty fat. But apparently the school saw things differently. Perhaps it was because of the hill, or the lack of elevators. More likely it was because all those diet foods tasted nasty, so I didn't eat them— though I did enjoy measuring them out and adding up their calories all the same.
It's still 3 grams over—that's an extra 2.2 calories that you'd pretend-eat.
But it really didn't matter, because the next day the provost decided it wasn't safe for me to stay.
I was allowed one more night—until Mom could come pick me up. I was inconsolable.
Look! It's condom-nation. Get it?
Like the *condemnation* you received today!
You're so fucking clever.
Help me make Alaska and Hawaii. We need Hawaii. Do you know why?
Do you know why we need Hawaii?
Because, in condom-nation, everyone gets *lei*-ed!
Ha ha! Get it? Did you get the pu-OW!
Hey! That burns!

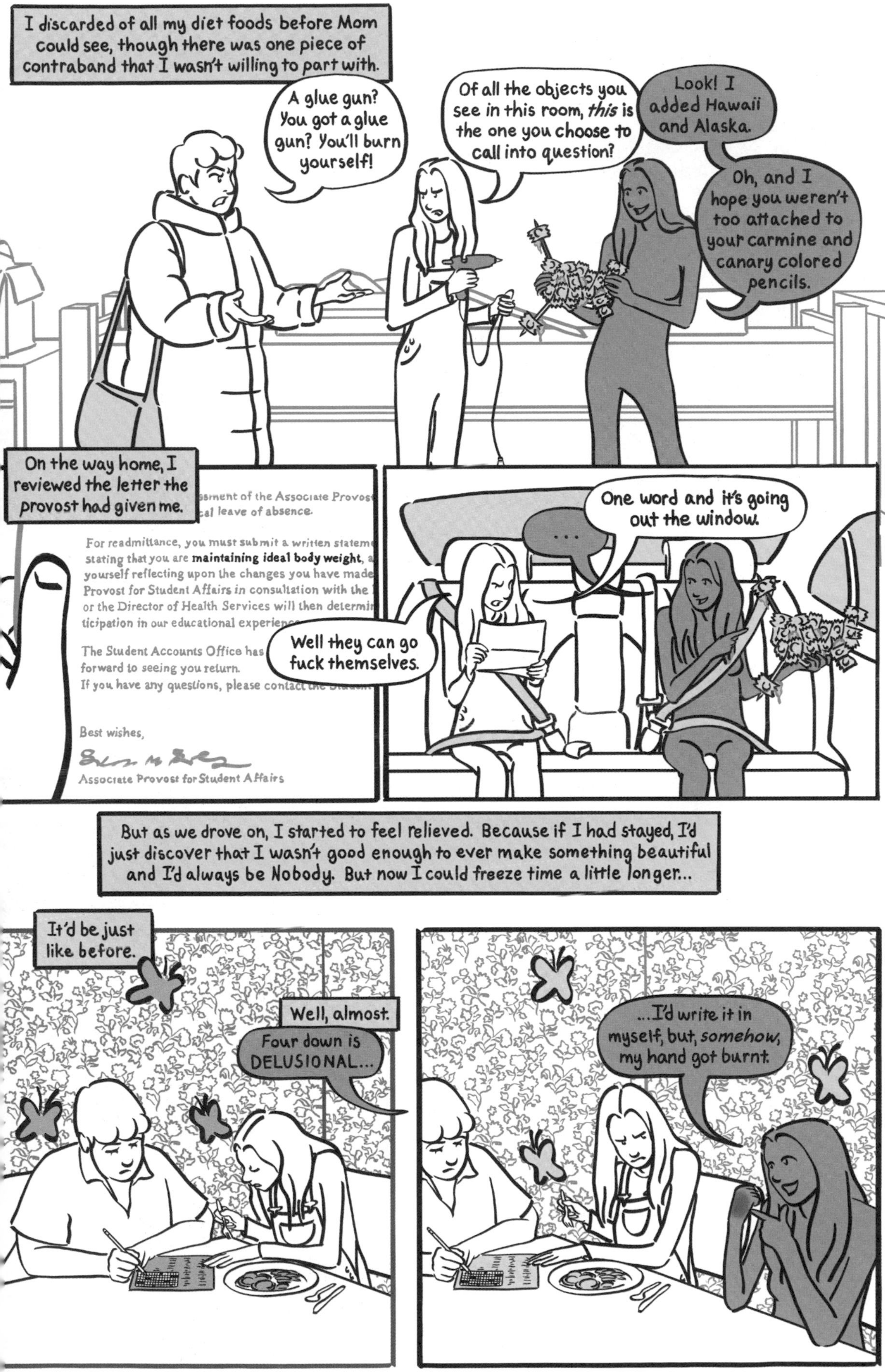
I discarded of all my diet foods before Mom could see, though there was one piece of contraband that I wasn't willing to part with.
A glue gun? You got a glue gun? You'll burn yourself!
Of all the objects you see in this room, *this* is the one you choose to call into question?
Look! I added Hawaii and Alaska.
Oh, and I hope you weren't too attached to your carmine and canary colored pencils.
On the way home, I reviewed the letter the provost had given me.
ssment of the Associate Provost
cal leave of absence.
For readmittance, you must submit a written stateme
stating that you are **maintaining ideal body weight**, a
yourself reflecting upon the changes you have made
Provost for Student Affairs in consultation with the
or the Director of Health Services will then determi
ticipation in our educational experienc
The Student Accounts Office has
forward to seeing you return.
If you have any questions, please contact
Best wishes,
Associate Provost for Student Affairs
...
One word and it's going out the window.
Well they can go fuck themselves.
But as we drove on, I started to feel relieved. Because if I had stayed, I'd just discover that I wasn't good enough to ever make something beautiful and I'd always be Nobody. But now I could freeze time a little longer...
It'd be just like before.
Well, almost.
Four down is DELUSIONAL...
...I'd write it in myself, but, *somehow*, my hand got burnt.

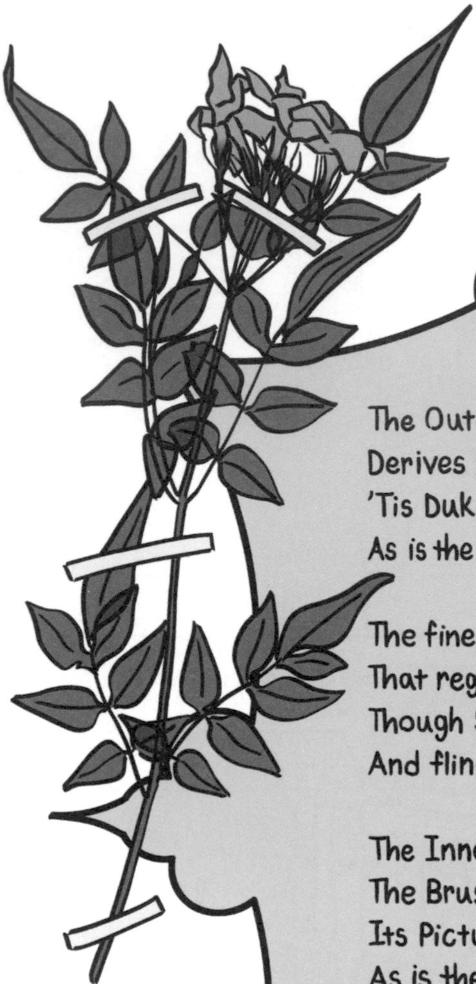

The Outer — from the Inner
Derives its Magnitude —
'Tis Duke, or Dwarf, according
As is the Central Mood —

The fine — unvarying Axis
That regulates the Wheel —
Though Spokes — spin — more conspicuous
And fling a dust — the while.

The Inner — paints the Outer —
The Brush without the Hand —
Its Picture publishes — precise —
As is the inner Brand —

On fine — Arterial Canvas —
A Cheek — perchance a Brow —
The Star's whole Secret — in the Lake —
Eyes were not meant to Know.

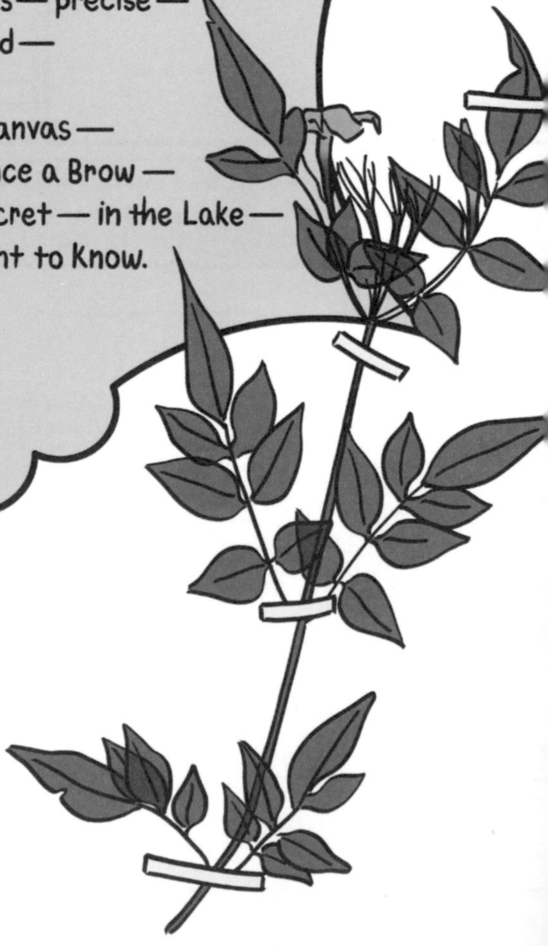

Jasminum Officinale L.

Chapter
6

The Underneath

A week after I came home my rabbit died.
But I didn't mind. He was a distraction. Everything
was a distraction — except for the puzzles, the food,
and Mom. So it was only when she refused to do the
crossword with me as I ate my daily plate of vegetables
that I agreed to see a doctor. But the doctor made me
go to the hospital, and the hospital shipped me to
another hospital in the faraway land of New Jersey —
but not before giving me a "temporary guardian."
He was a lawyer who had never met me and knew
nothing about eating disorders, but he would make
all medical decisions for me now. So, when I was
admitted to the hospital, I couldn't leave.

When I got there, they did 1,000 different tests on me—x-rays, ultrasounds. The transporter would take me to Radiology and leave me in my wheelchair as I waited to get my exam, my chart perched upon my lap, so I could freely peruse.

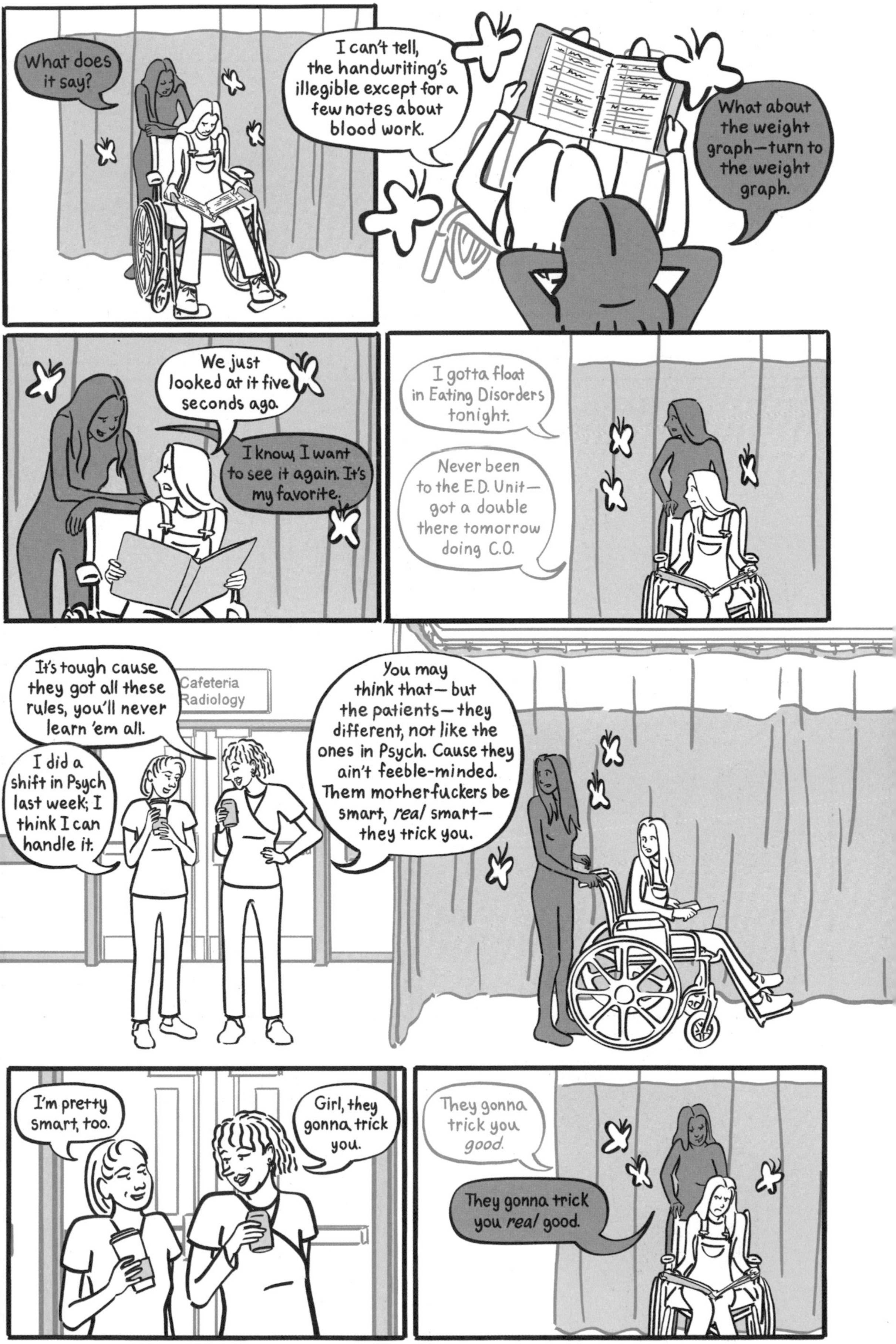
What does it say?
I can't tell, the handwriting's illegible except for a few notes about blood work.
What about the weight graph—turn to the weight graph.
We just looked at it five seconds ago.
I know, I want to see it again. It's my favorite.
I gotta float in Eating Disorders tonight.
Never been to the E.D. Unit—got a double there tomorrow doing C.O.
Cafeteria
Radiology
It's tough cause they got all these rules, you'll never learn 'em all.
I did a shift in Psych last week; I think I can handle it.
You may think that—but the patients—they different, not like the ones in Psych. Cause they ain't feeble-minded. Them motherfuckers be smart, *real* smart—they trick you.
I'm pretty smart, too.
Girl, they gonna trick you.
They gonna trick you *good.*
They gonna trick you *real* good.

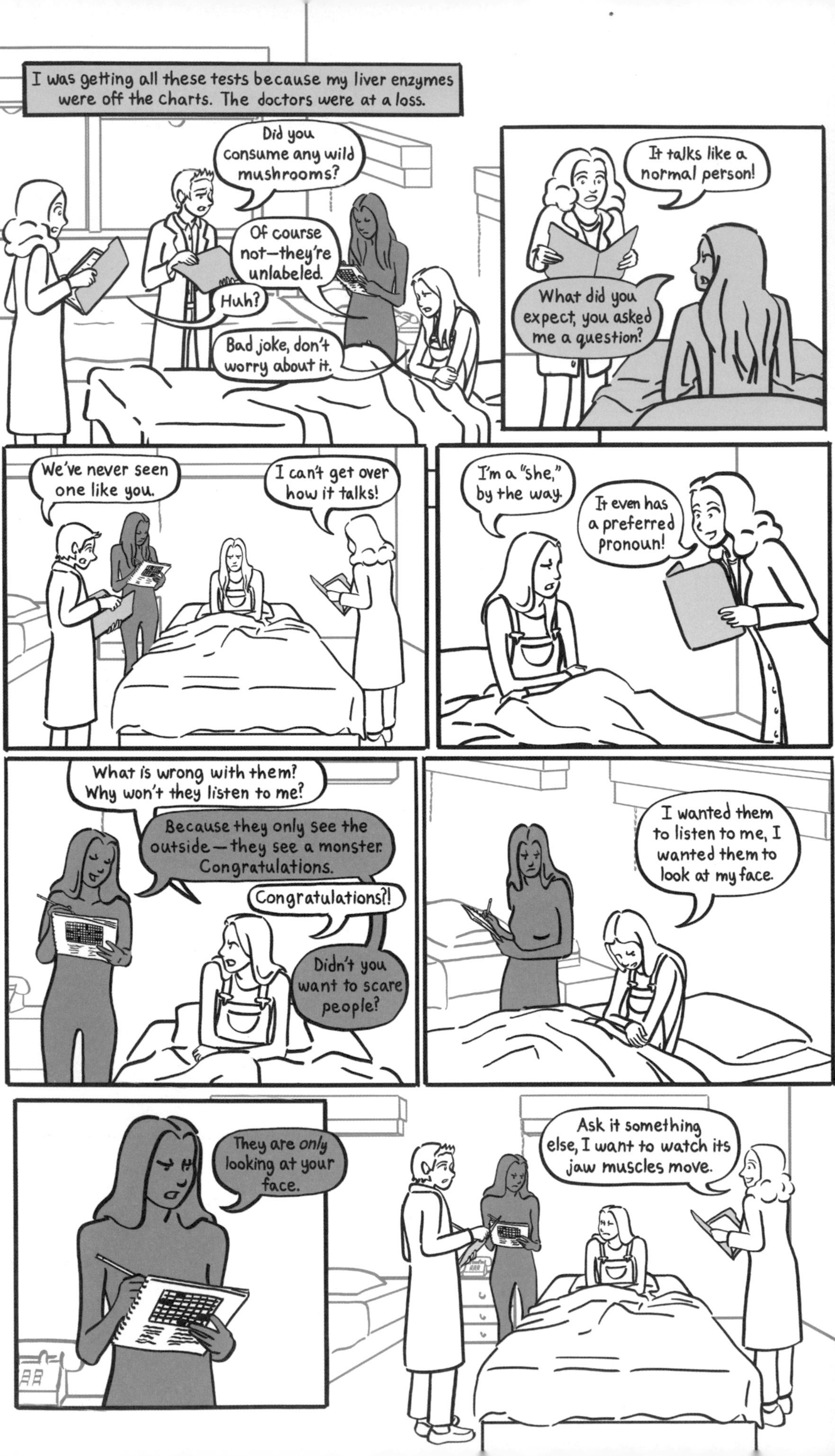
I was getting all these tests because my liver enzymes were off the charts. The doctors were at a loss.
Did you consume any wild mushrooms?
Of course not—they're unlabeled.
Huh?
Bad joke, don't worry about it.
It talks like a normal person!
What did you expect, you asked me a question?
We've never seen one like you.
I can't get over how it talks!
I'm a "she," by the way.
It even has a preferred pronoun!
What is wrong with them? Why won't they listen to me?
Because they only see the outside—they see a monster. Congratulations.
Congratulations?!
Didn't you want to scare people?
I wanted them to listen to me, I wanted them to look at my face.
They are *only* looking at your face.
Ask it something else, I want to watch its jaw muscles move.

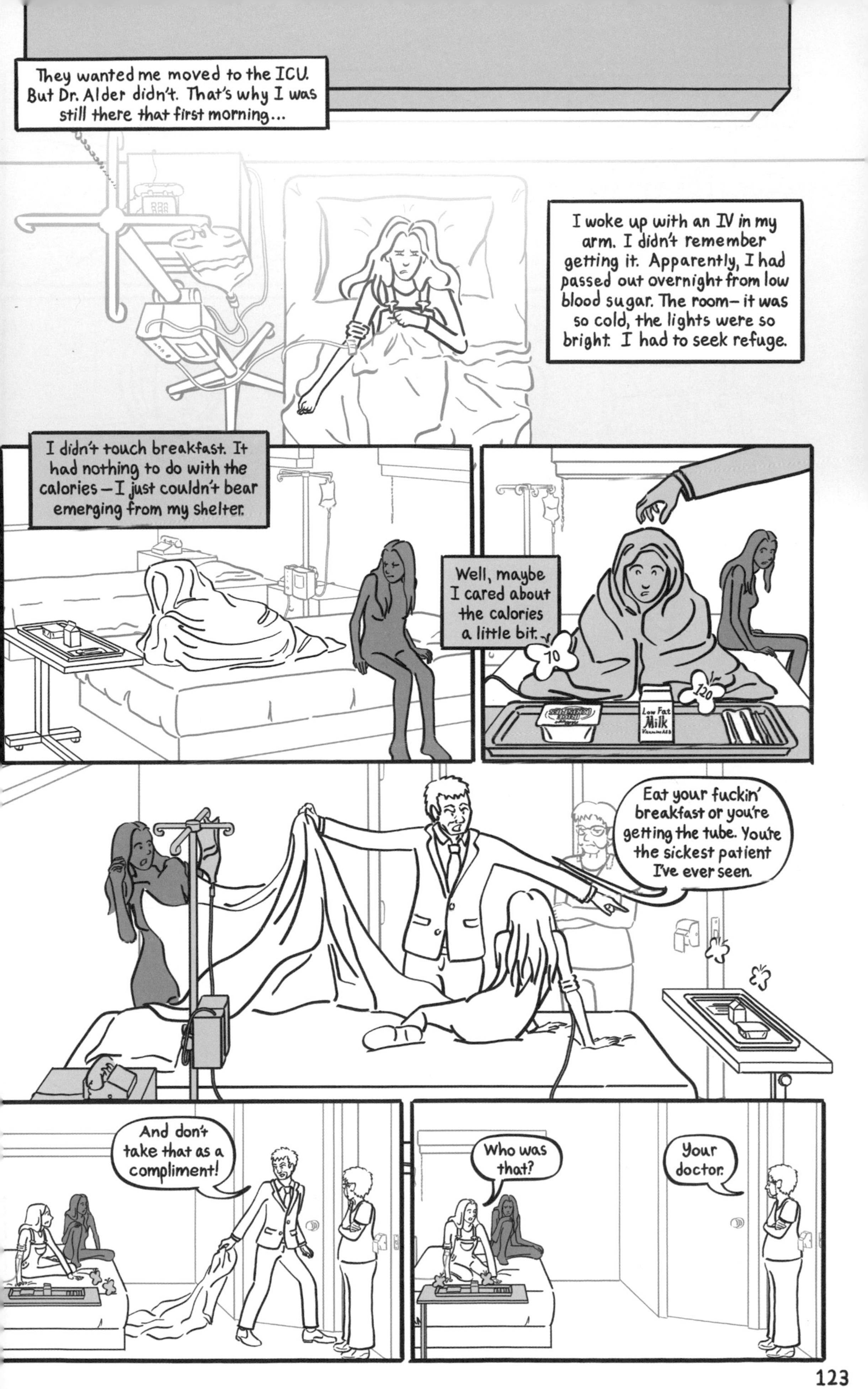
They wanted me moved to the ICU. But Dr. Alder didn't. That's why I was still there that first morning...
I woke up with an IV in my arm. I didn't remember getting it. Apparently, I had passed out overnight from low blood sugar. The room– it was so cold, the lights were so bright. I had to seek refuge.
I didn't touch breakfast. It had nothing to do with the calories—I just couldn't bear emerging from my shelter.
Well, maybe I cared about the calories a little bit.
70
120
Low Fat Milk
Eat your fuckin' breakfast or you're getting the tube. You're the sickest patient I've ever seen.
And don't take that as a compliment!
Who was that?
Your doctor.

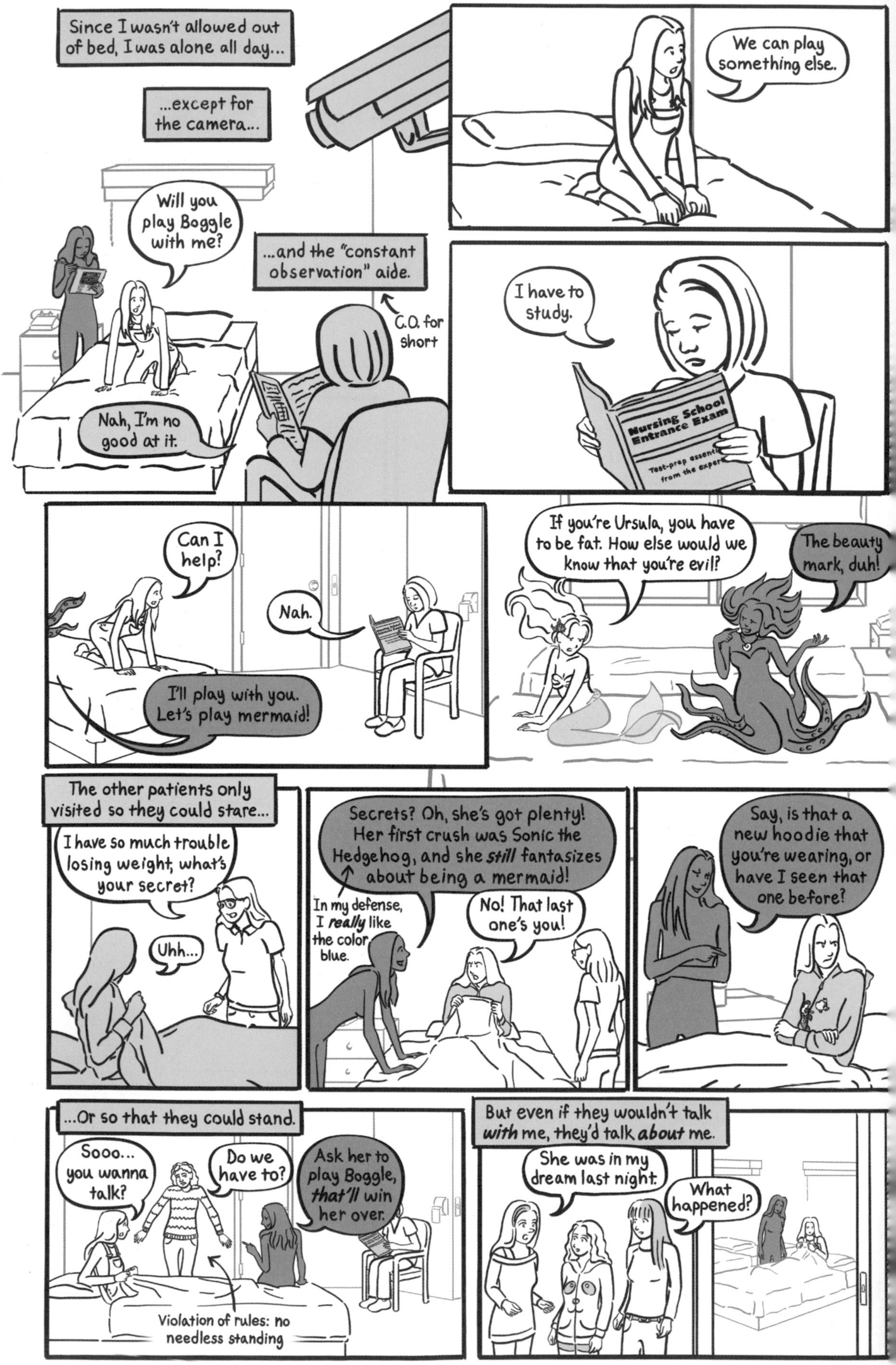
Since I wasn't allowed out of bed, I was alone all day...
...except for the camera...
We can play something else.
Will you play Boggle with me?
...and the "constant observation" aide.
C.O. for short
I have to study.
Nursing School Entrance Exam
Nah, I'm no good at it.
Can I help?
Nah.
I'll play with you. Let's play mermaid!
If you're Ursula, you have to be fat. How else would we know that you're evil?
The beauty mark, duh!
The other patients only visited so they could stare...
I have so much trouble losing weight, what's your secret?
Uhh...
Secrets? Oh, she's got plenty! Her first crush was Sonic the Hedgehog, and she *still* fantasizes about being a mermaid!
In my defense, I *really* like the color blue.
No! That last one's you!
Say, is that a new hoodie that you're wearing, or have I seen that one before?
...Or so that they could stand.
Sooo... you wanna talk?
Do we have to?
Ask her to play Boggle, *that'll* win her over.
Violation of rules: no needless standing
But even if they wouldn't talk *with* me, they'd talk *about* me.
She was in my dream last night.
What happened?

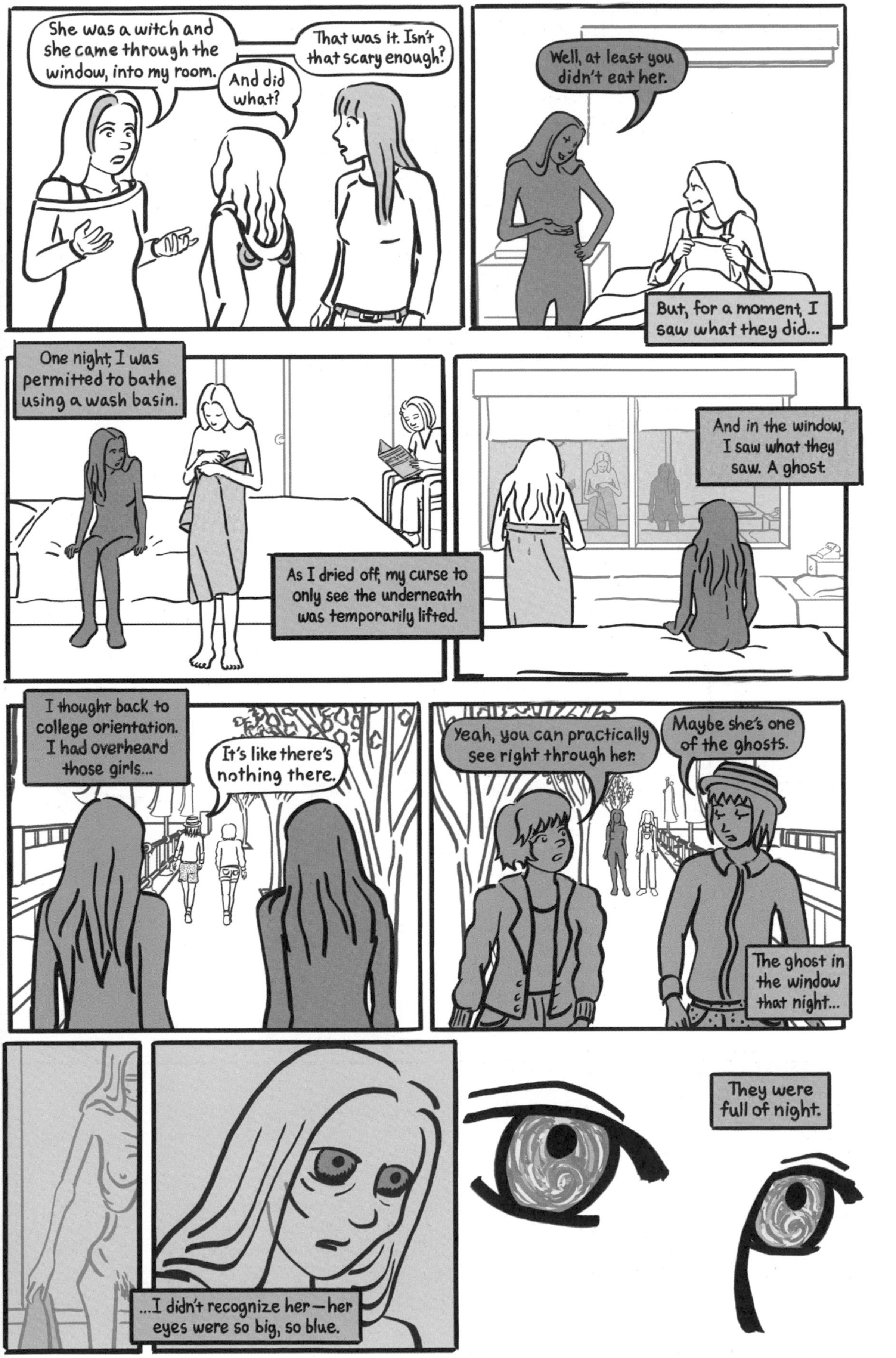
She was a witch and she came through the window, into my room.
And did what?
That was it. Isn't that scary enough?
Well, at least you didn't eat her.
But, for a moment, I saw what they did...
One night, I was permitted to bathe using a wash basin.
As I dried off, my curse to only see the underneath was temporarily lifted.
And in the window, I saw what they saw. A ghost.
I thought back to college orientation. I had overheard those girls...
It's like there's nothing there.
Yeah, you can practically see right through her.
Maybe she's one of the ghosts.
The ghost in the window that night...
...I didn't recognize her—her eyes were so big, so blue.
They were full of night.

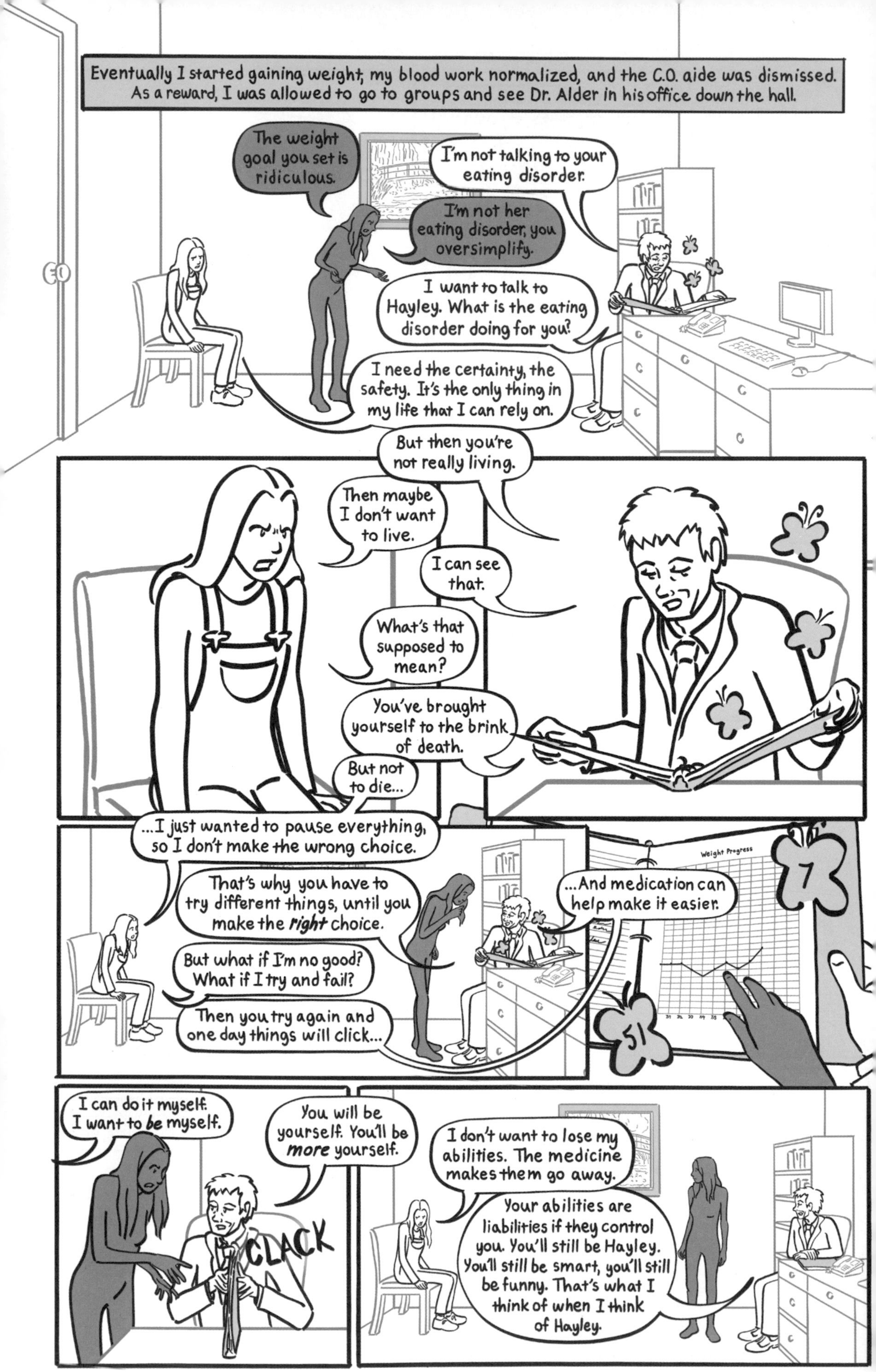
Eventually I started gaining weight, my blood work normalized, and the C.O. aide was dismissed. As a reward, I was allowed to go to groups and see Dr. Alder in his office down the hall.
The weight goal you set is ridiculous.
I'm not talking to your eating disorder.
I'm not her eating disorder, you oversimplify.
I want to talk to Hayley. What is the eating disorder doing for you?
I need the certainty, the safety. It's the only thing in my life that I can rely on.
But then you're not really living.
Then maybe I don't want to live.
I can see that.
What's that supposed to mean?
You've brought yourself to the brink of death.
But not to die...
...I just wanted to pause everything, so I don't make the wrong choice.
That's why you have to try different things, until you make the *right* choice.
But what if I'm no good? What if I try and fail?
Then you try again and one day things will click...
...And medication can help make it easier.
Weight Progress
7
51
I can do it myself. I want to *be* myself.
You will be yourself. You'll be *more* yourself.
CLACK
I don't want to lose my abilities. The medicine makes them go away.
Your abilities are liabilities if they control you. You'll still be Hayley. You'll still be smart, you'll still be funny. That's what I think of when I think of Hayley.

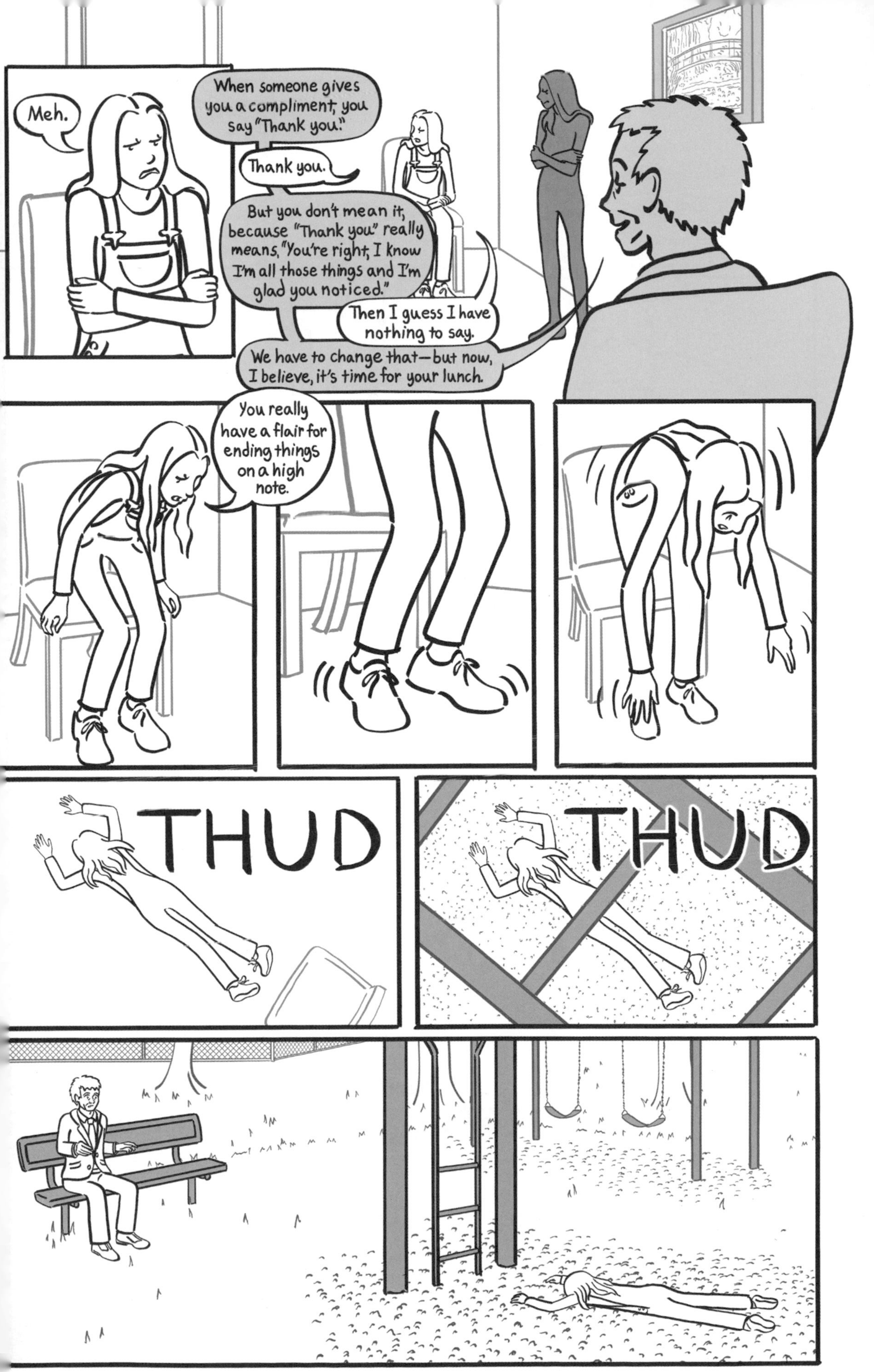
Meh.
When someone gives you a compliment, you say "Thank you."
Thank you.
But you don't mean it, because "Thank you" really means, "You're right, I know I'm all those things and I'm glad you noticed."
Then I guess I have nothing to say.
We have to change that—but now, I believe, it's time for your lunch.
You really have a flair for ending things on a high note.
THUD
THUD

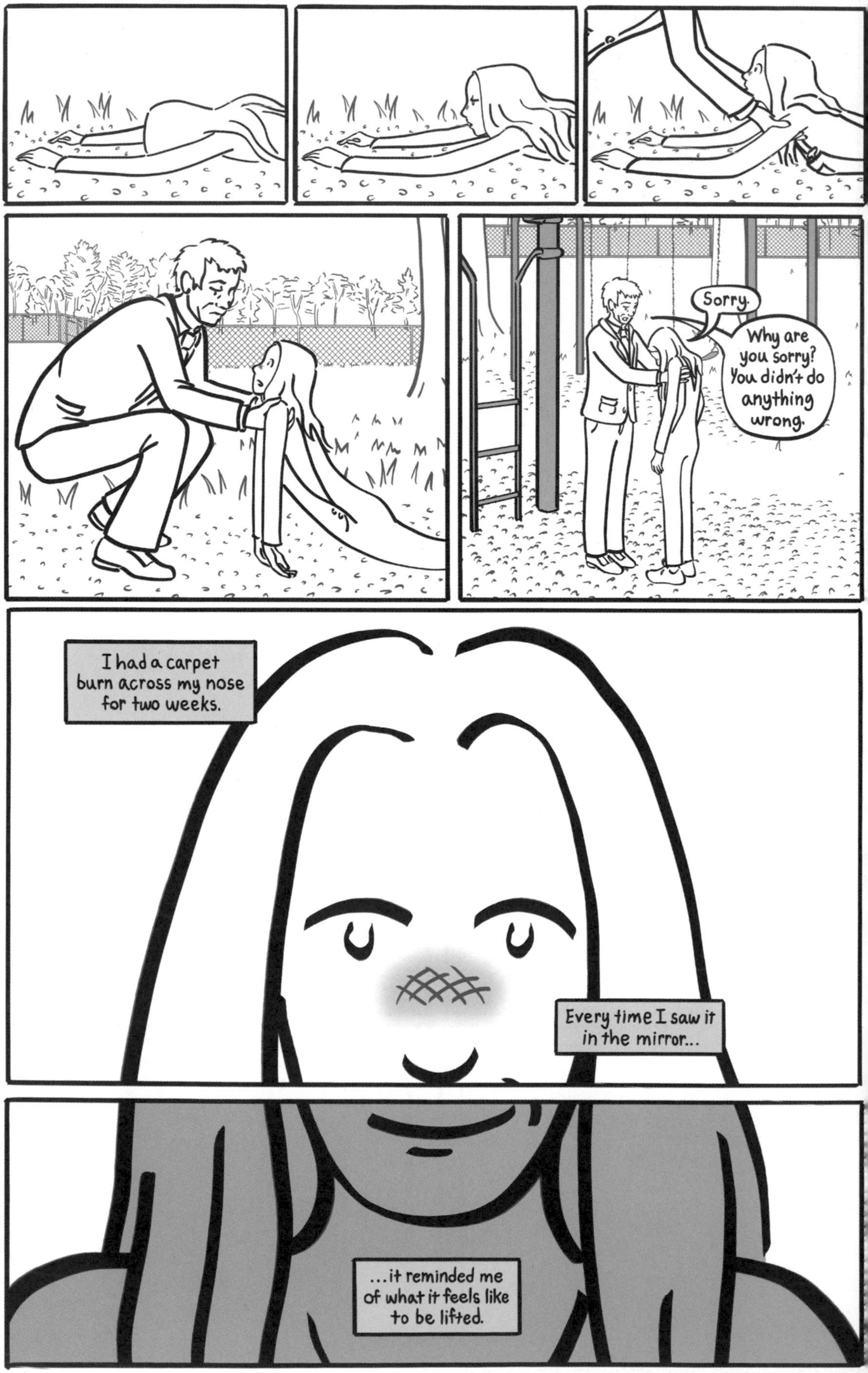
Sorry.
Why are you sorry? You didn't do anything wrong.
I had a carpet burn across my nose for two weeks.
Every time I saw it in the mirror...
...it reminded me of what it feels like to be lifted.

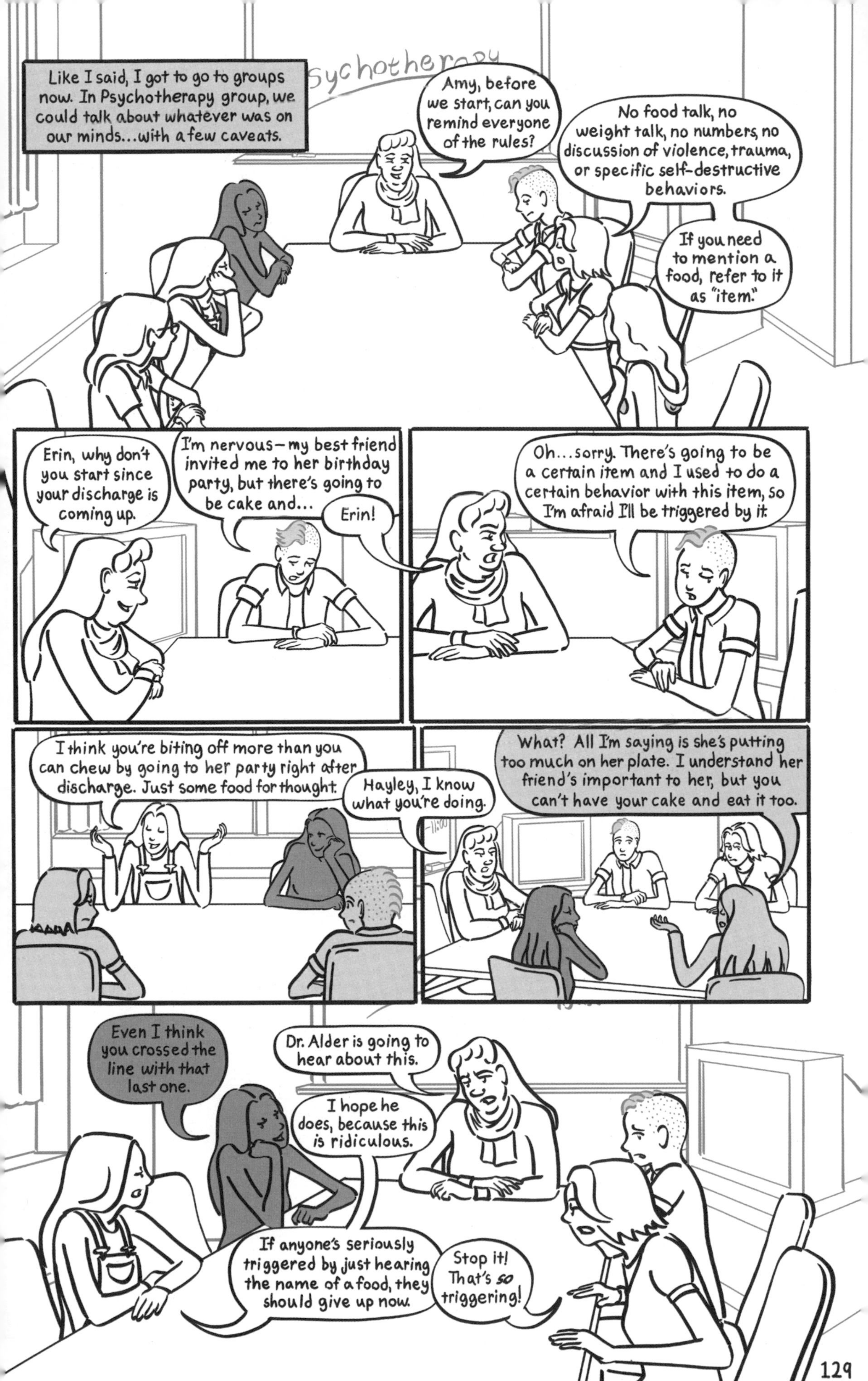
Like I said, I got to go to groups now. In Psychotherapy group, we could talk about whatever was on our minds...with a few caveats.
Psychotherapy
Amy, before we start, can you remind everyone of the rules?
No food talk, no weight talk, no numbers, no discussion of violence, trauma, or specific self-destructive behaviors.
If you need to mention a food, refer to it as "item."
Erin, why don't you start since your discharge is coming up.
I'm nervous—my best friend invited me to her birthday party, but there's going to be cake and...
Erin!
Oh...sorry. There's going to be a certain item and I used to do a certain behavior with this item, so I'm afraid I'll be triggered by it.
I think you're biting off more than you can chew by going to her party right after discharge. Just some food for thought.
Hayley, I know what you're doing.
What? All I'm saying is she's putting too much on her plate. I understand her friend's important to her, but you can't have your cake and eat it too.
Even I think you crossed the line with that last one.
Dr. Alder is going to hear about this.
I hope he does, because this is ridiculous.
If anyone's seriously triggered by just hearing the name of a food, they should give up now.
Stop it! That's *so* triggering!

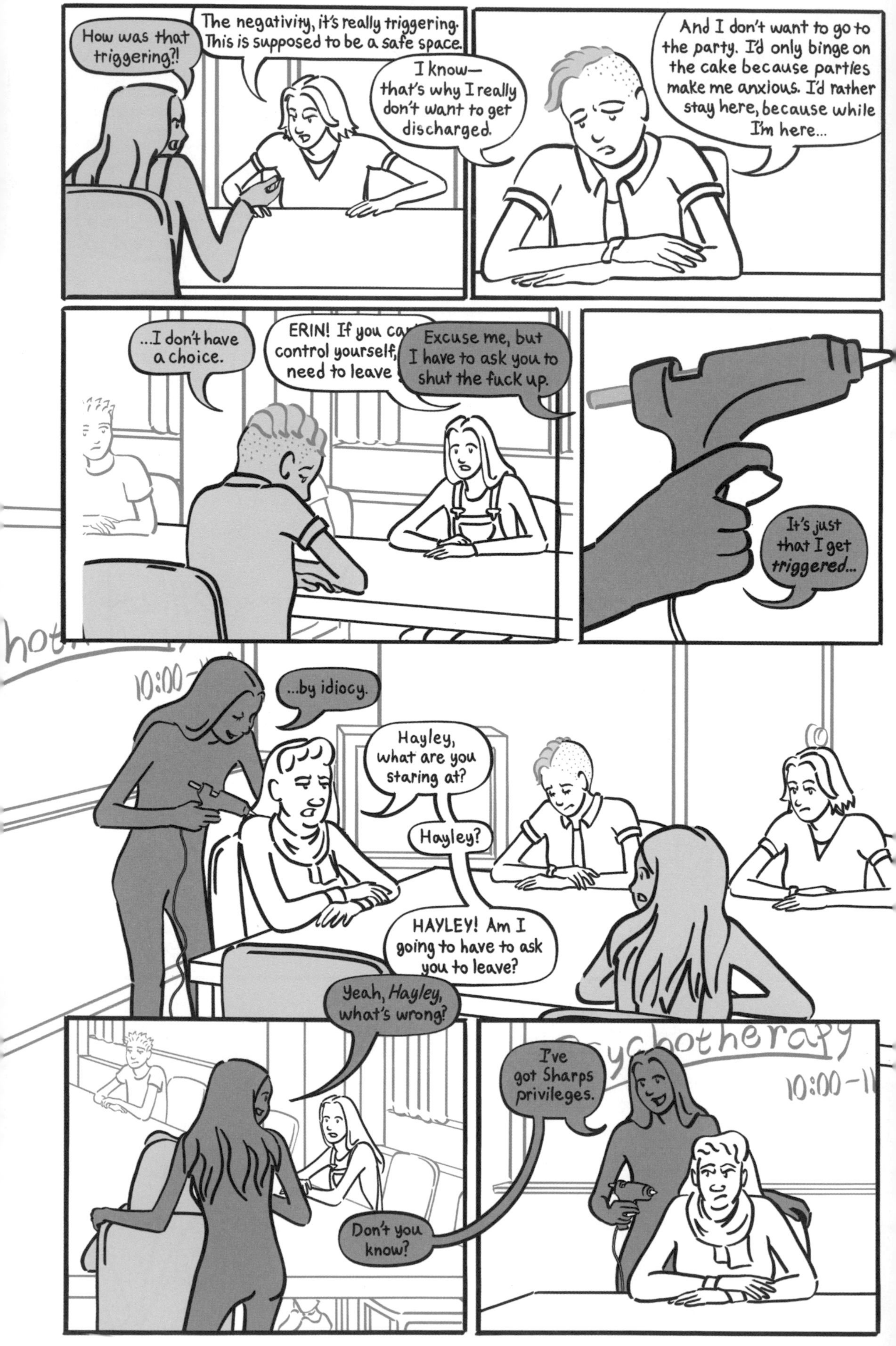

How was that triggering?!
The negativity, it's really triggering. This is supposed to be a safe space.
I know— that's why I really don't want to get discharged.
And I don't want to go to the party. I'd only binge on the cake because parties make me anxious. I'd rather stay here, because while I'm here...
...I don't have a choice.
ERIN! If you ca
control yourself,
need to leave
Excuse me, but I have to ask you to shut the fuck up.
It's just that I get *triggered*...
...by idiocy.
Hayley, what are you staring at?
Hayley?
HAYLEY! Am I going to have to ask you to leave?
Yeah, *Hayley*, what's wrong?
Don't you know?
I've got Sharps privileges.

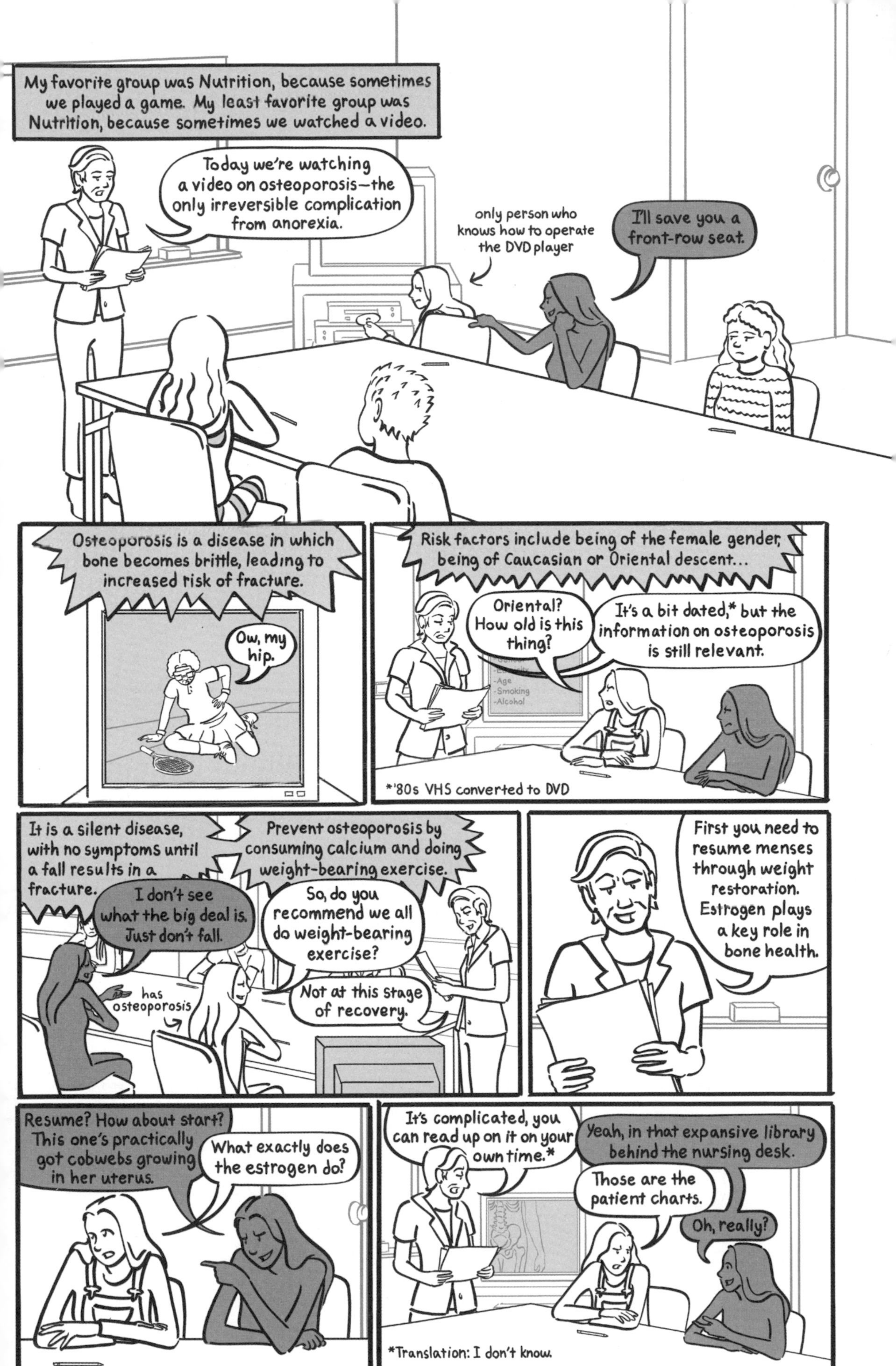
My favorite group was Nutrition, because sometimes we played a game. My least favorite group was Nutrition, because sometimes we watched a video.
Today we're watching a video on osteoporosis—the only irreversible complication from anorexia.
only person who knows how to operate the DVD player
I'll save you a front-row seat.
Osteoporosis is a disease in which bone becomes brittle, leading to increased risk of fracture.
Ow, my hip.
Risk factors include being of the female gender, being of Caucasian or Oriental descent...
Oriental? How old is this thing?
It's a bit dated,* but the information on osteoporosis is still relevant.
-Age
-Smoking
-Alcohol
*'80s VHS converted to DVD
It is a silent disease, with no symptoms until a fall results in a fracture.
Prevent osteoporosis by consuming calcium and doing weight-bearing exercise.
I don't see what the big deal is. Just don't fall.
has osteoporosis
So, do you recommend we all do weight-bearing exercise?
Not at this stage of recovery.
First you need to resume menses through weight restoration. Estrogen plays a key role in bone health.
Resume? How about start? This one's practically got cobwebs growing in her uterus.
What exactly does the estrogen do?
It's complicated, you can read up on it on your own time.*
Yeah, in that expansive library behind the nursing desk.
Those are the patient charts.
Oh, really?
*Translation: I don't know.

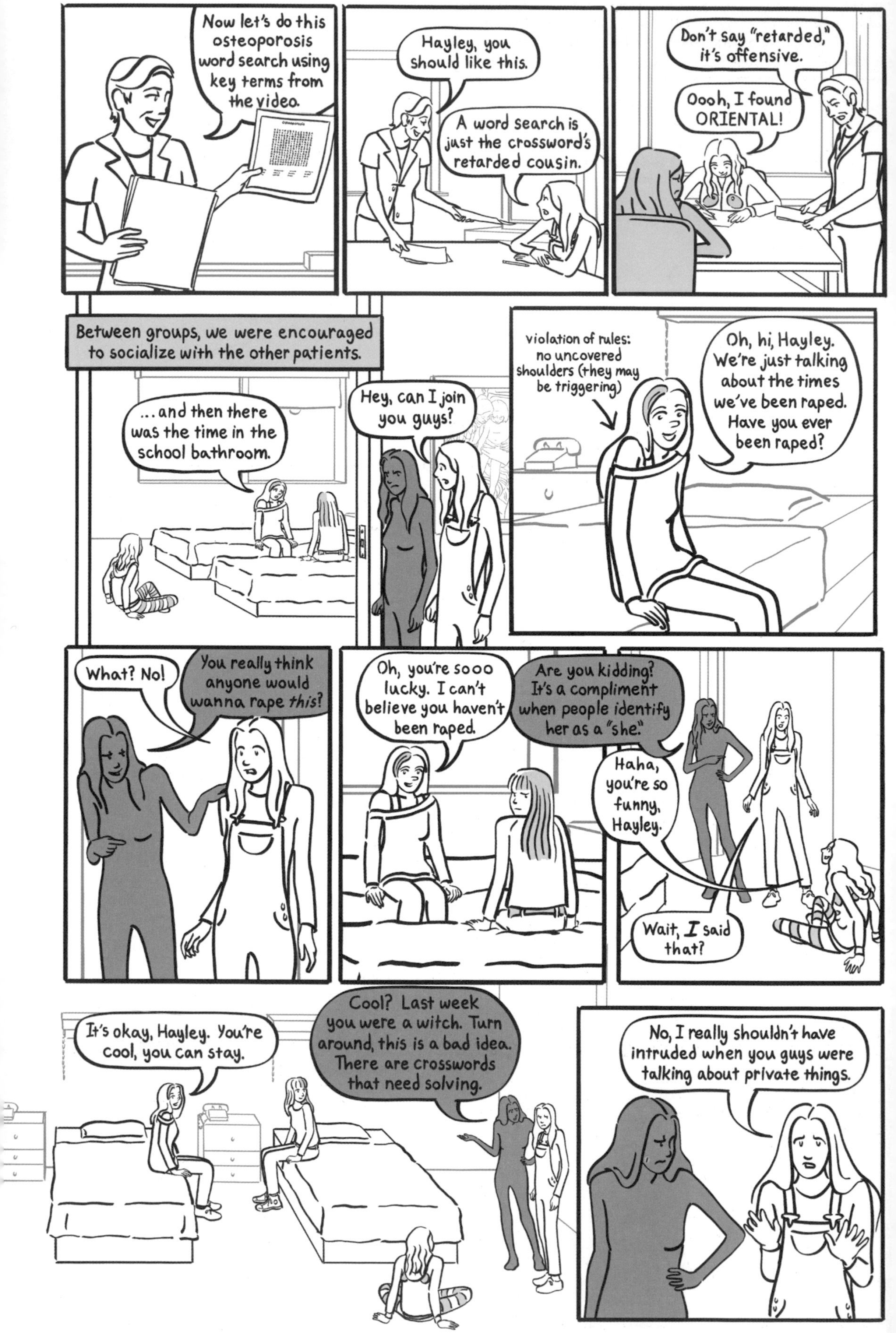
Now let's do this osteoporosis word search using key terms from the video.
Hayley, you should like this.
A word search is just the crossword's retarded cousin.
Don't say "retarded," it's offensive.
Oooh, I found ORIENTAL!
Between groups, we were encouraged to socialize with the other patients.
...and then there was the time in the school bathroom.
Hey, can I join you guys?
violation of rules: no uncovered shoulders (they may be triggering)
Oh, hi, Hayley. We're just talking about the times we've been raped. Have you ever been raped?
What? No!
You really think anyone would wanna rape *this*?
Oh, you're sooo lucky. I can't believe you haven't been raped.
Are you kidding? It's a compliment when people identify her as a "she."
Haha, you're so funny, Hayley.
Wait, *I* said that?
It's okay, Hayley. You're cool, you can stay.
Cool? Last week you were a witch. Turn around, this is a bad idea. There are crosswords that need solving.
No, I really shouldn't have intruded when you guys were talking about private things.

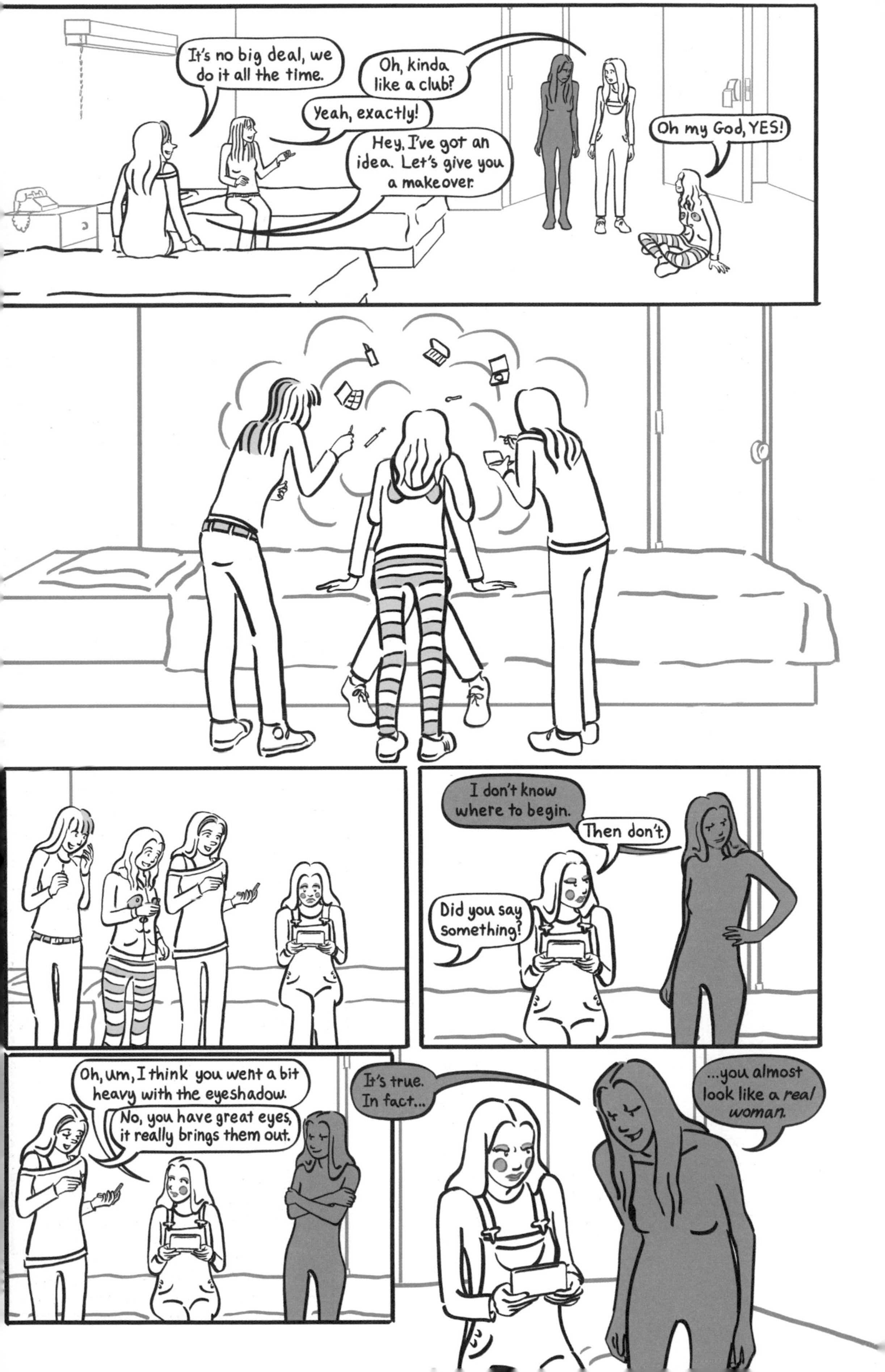

It's no big deal, we do it all the time.
Oh, kinda like a club?
Yeah, exactly!
Hey, I've got an idea. Let's give you a makeover.
Oh my God, YES!
I don't know where to begin.
Then don't.
Did you say something?
Oh, um, I think you went a bit heavy with the eyeshadow.
No, you have great eyes, it really brings them out.
It's true. In fact...
...you almost look like a *real woman*.

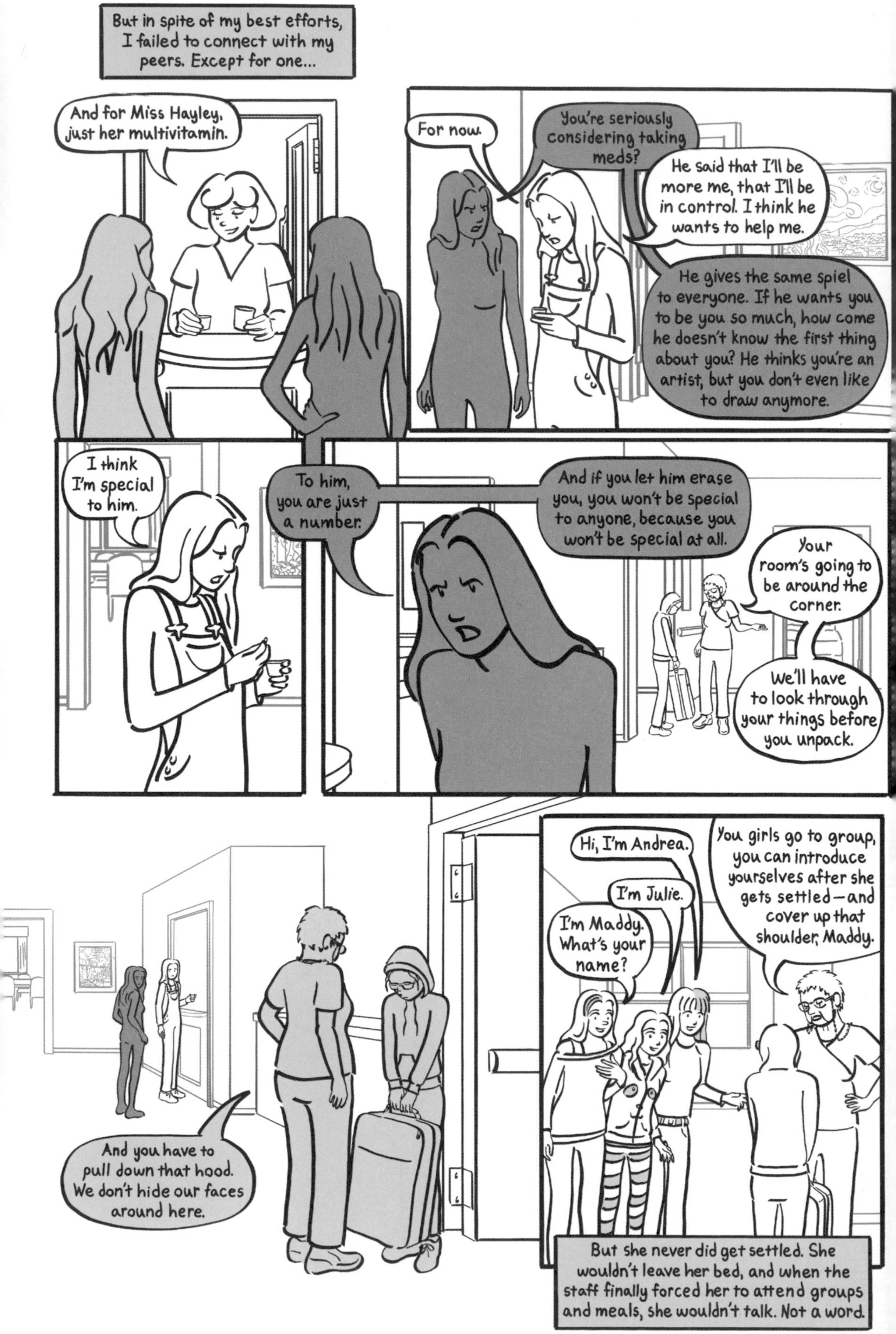

But in spite of my best efforts, I failed to connect with my peers. Except for one...
And for Miss Hayley, just her multivitamin.
For now.
You're seriously considering taking meds?
He said that I'll be more me, that I'll be in control. I think he wants to help me.
He gives the same spiel to everyone. If he wants you to be you so much, how come he doesn't know the first thing about you? He thinks you're an artist, but you don't even like to draw anymore.
I think I'm special to him.
To him, you are just a number.
And if you let him erase you, you won't be special to anyone, because you won't be special at all.
Your room's going to be around the corner.
We'll have to look through your things before you unpack.
And you have to pull down that hood. We don't hide our faces around here.
Hi, I'm Andrea.
I'm Julie.
I'm Maddy. What's your name?
You girls go to group, you can introduce yourselves after she gets settled—and cover up that shoulder, Maddy.
But she never did get settled. She wouldn't leave her bed, and when the staff finally forced her to attend groups and meals, she wouldn't talk. Not a word.

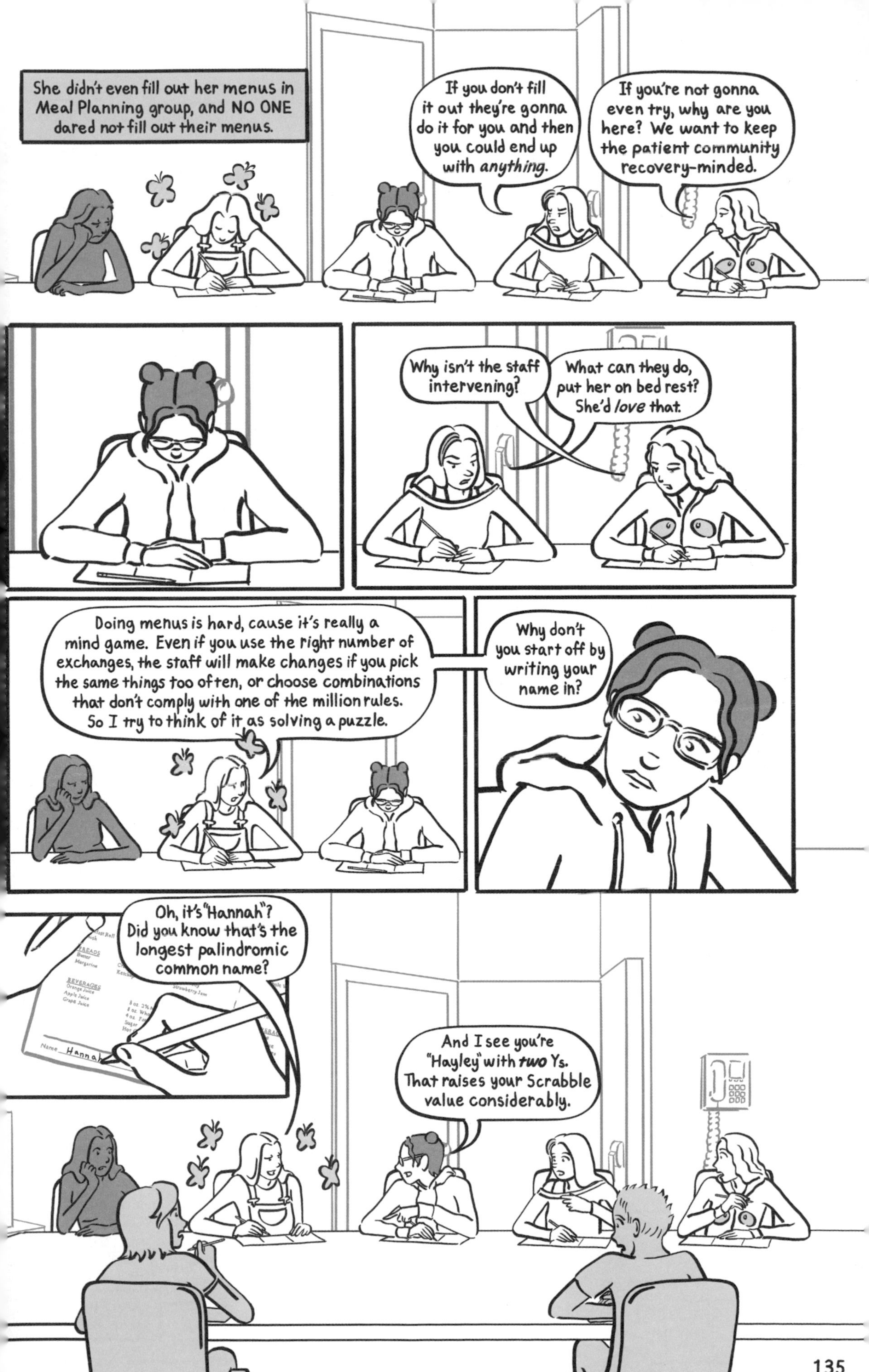

She didn't even fill out her menus in Meal Planning group, and NO ONE dared not fill out their menus.
If you don't fill it out they're gonna do it for you and then you could end up with *anything*.
If you're not gonna even try, why are you here? We want to keep the patient community recovery-minded.
Why isn't the staff intervening?
What can they do, put her on bed rest? She'd *love* that.
Doing menus is hard, cause it's really a mind game. Even if you use the right number of exchanges, the staff will make changes if you pick the same things too often, or choose combinations that don't comply with one of the million rules. So I try to think of it as solving a puzzle.
Why don't you start off by writing your name in?
Oh, it's "Hannah"? Did you know that's the longest palindromic common name?
And I see you're "Hayley" with ***two*** Ys. That raises your Scrabble value considerably.

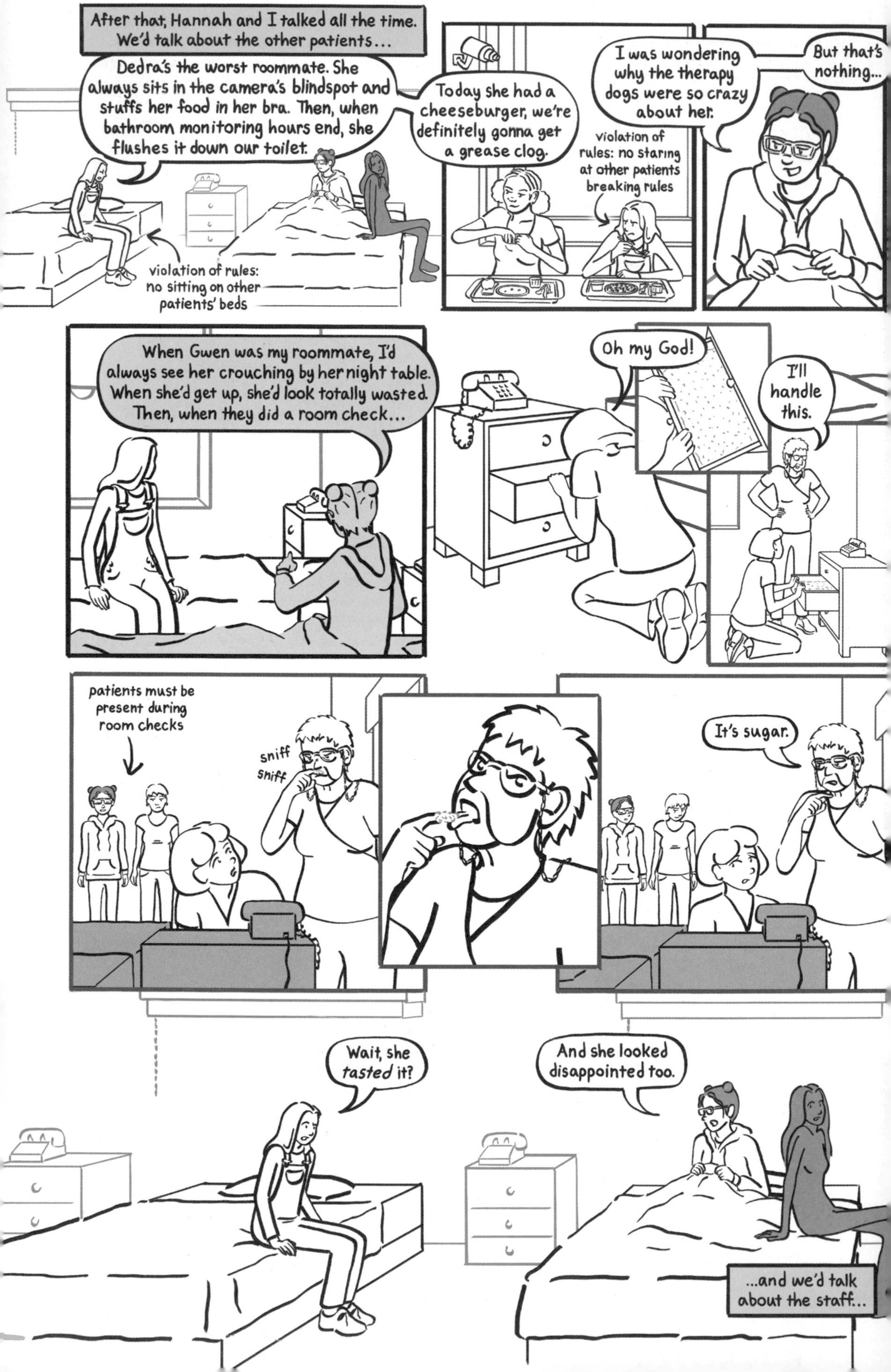
After that, Hannah and I talked all the time. We'd talk about the other patients...
Dedra's the worst roommate. She always sits in the camera's blindspot and stuffs her food in her bra. Then, when bathroom monitoring hours end, she flushes it down our toilet.
violation of rules: no sitting on other patients' beds
Today she had a cheeseburger, we're definitely gonna get a grease clog.
violation of rules: no staring at other patients breaking rules
I was wondering why the therapy dogs were so crazy about her.
But that's nothing...
When Gwen was my roommate, I'd always see her crouching by her night table. When she'd get up, she'd look totally wasted. Then, when they did a room check...
Oh my God!
I'll handle this.
patients must be present during room checks
sniff
sniff
It's sugar.
Wait, she *tasted* it?
And she looked disappointed too.
...and we'd talk about the staff...

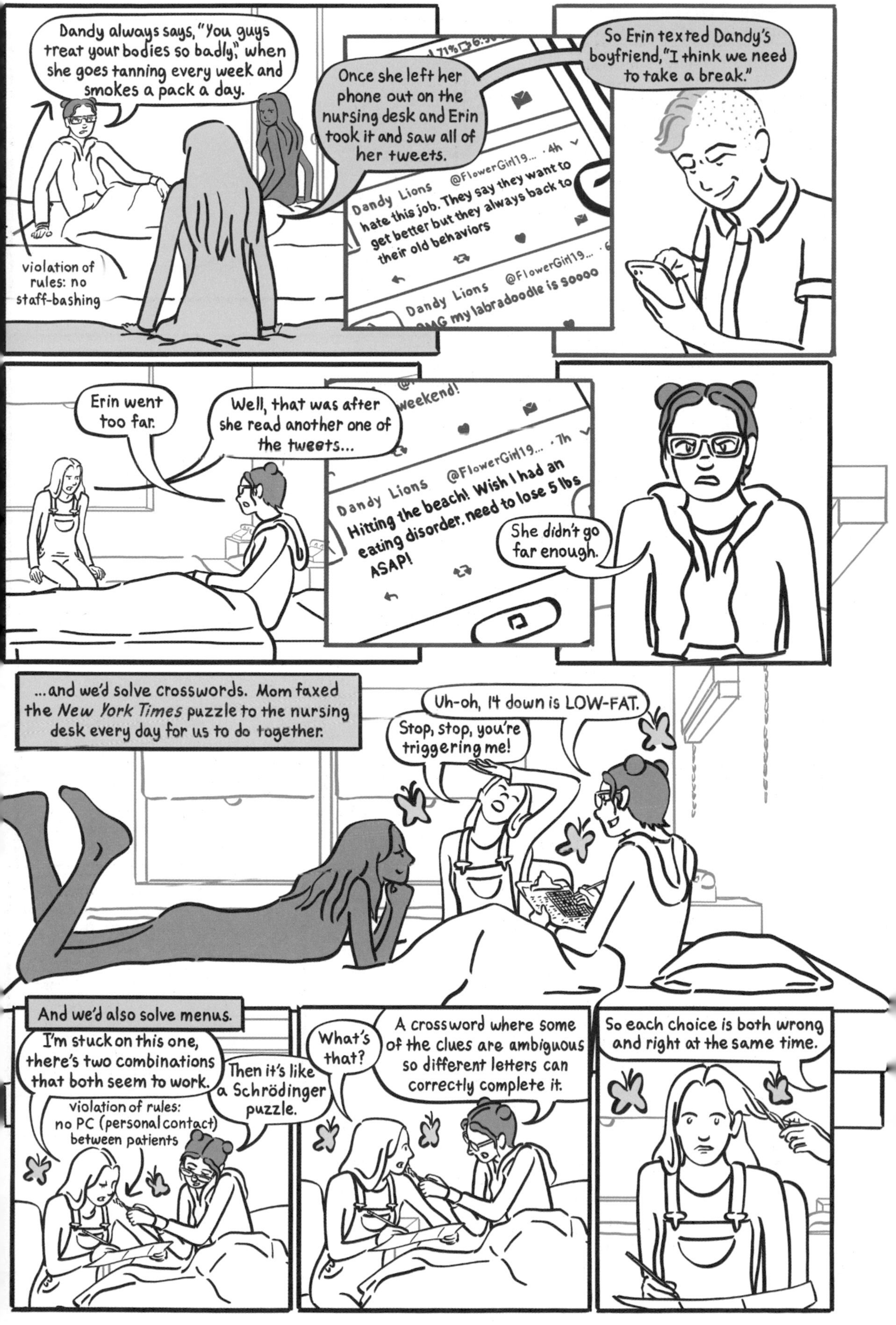
Dandy always says, "You guys treat your bodies so badly," when she goes tanning every week and smokes a pack a day.
violation of rules: no staff-bashing
Once she left her phone out on the nursing desk and Erin took it and saw all of her tweets.
Dandy Lions @FlowerGirl19... · 4h
hate this job. They say they want to get better but they always back to their old behaviors
Dandy Lions @FlowerGirl19...
OMG my labradoodle is soooo
So Erin texted Dandy's boyfriend, "I think we need to take a break."
Erin went too far.
Well, that was after she read another one of the tweets...
weekend!
Dandy Lions @FlowerGirl19... · 7h
Hitting the beach! Wish I had an eating disorder, need to lose 5 lbs ASAP!
She didn't go far enough.
...and we'd solve crosswords. Mom faxed the New York Times puzzle to the nursing desk every day for us to do together.
Uh-oh, 14 down is LOW-FAT.
Stop, stop, you're triggering me!
And we'd also solve menus.
I'm stuck on this one, there's two combinations that both seem to work.
violation of rules: no PC (personal contact) between patients
Then it's like a Schrödinger puzzle.
What's that?
A crossword where some of the clues are ambiguous so different letters can correctly complete it.
So each choice is both wrong and right at the same time.

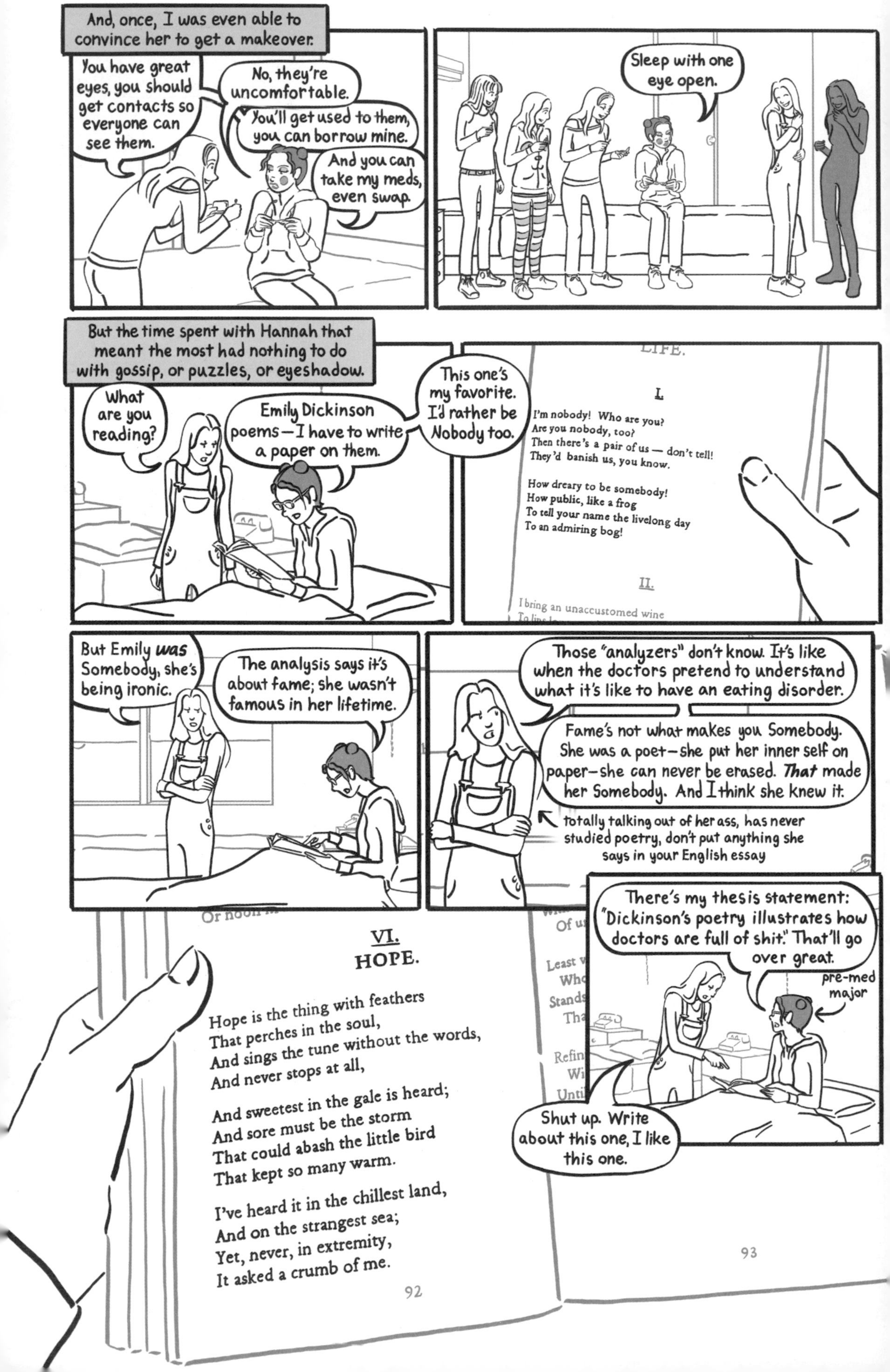

And, once, I was even able to convince her to get a makeover.
You have great eyes, you should get contacts so everyone can see them.
No, they're uncomfortable.
You'll get used to them, you can borrow mine.
And you can take my meds, even swap.
Sleep with one eye open.
But the time spent with Hannah that meant the most had nothing to do with gossip, or puzzles, or eyeshadow.
What are you reading?
Emily Dickinson poems—I have to write a paper on them.
This one's my favorite. I'd rather be Nobody too.
LIFE.
I.
I'm nobody! Who are you?
Are you nobody, too?
Then there's a pair of us — don't tell!
They'd banish us, you know.
How dreary to be somebody!
How public, like a frog
To tell your name the livelong day
To an admiring bog!
II.
I bring an unaccustomed wine
But Emily *was* Somebody, she's being ironic.
The analysis says it's about fame; she wasn't famous in her lifetime.
Those "analyzers" don't know. It's like when the doctors pretend to understand what it's like to have an eating disorder.
Fame's not what makes you Somebody. She was a poet—she put her inner self on paper—she can never be erased. *That* made her Somebody. And I think she knew it.
totally talking out of her ass, has never studied poetry, don't put anything she says in your English essay
VI.
HOPE.
Hope is the thing with feathers
That perches in the soul,
And sings the tune without the words,
And never stops at all,
And sweetest in the gale is heard;
And sore must be the storm
That could abash the little bird
That kept so many warm.
I've heard it in the chillest land,
And on the strangest sea;
Yet, never, in extremity,
It asked a crumb of me.
92
There's my thesis statement: "Dickinson's poetry illustrates how doctors are full of shit." That'll go over great.
pre-med major
Shut up. Write about this one, I like this one.
93

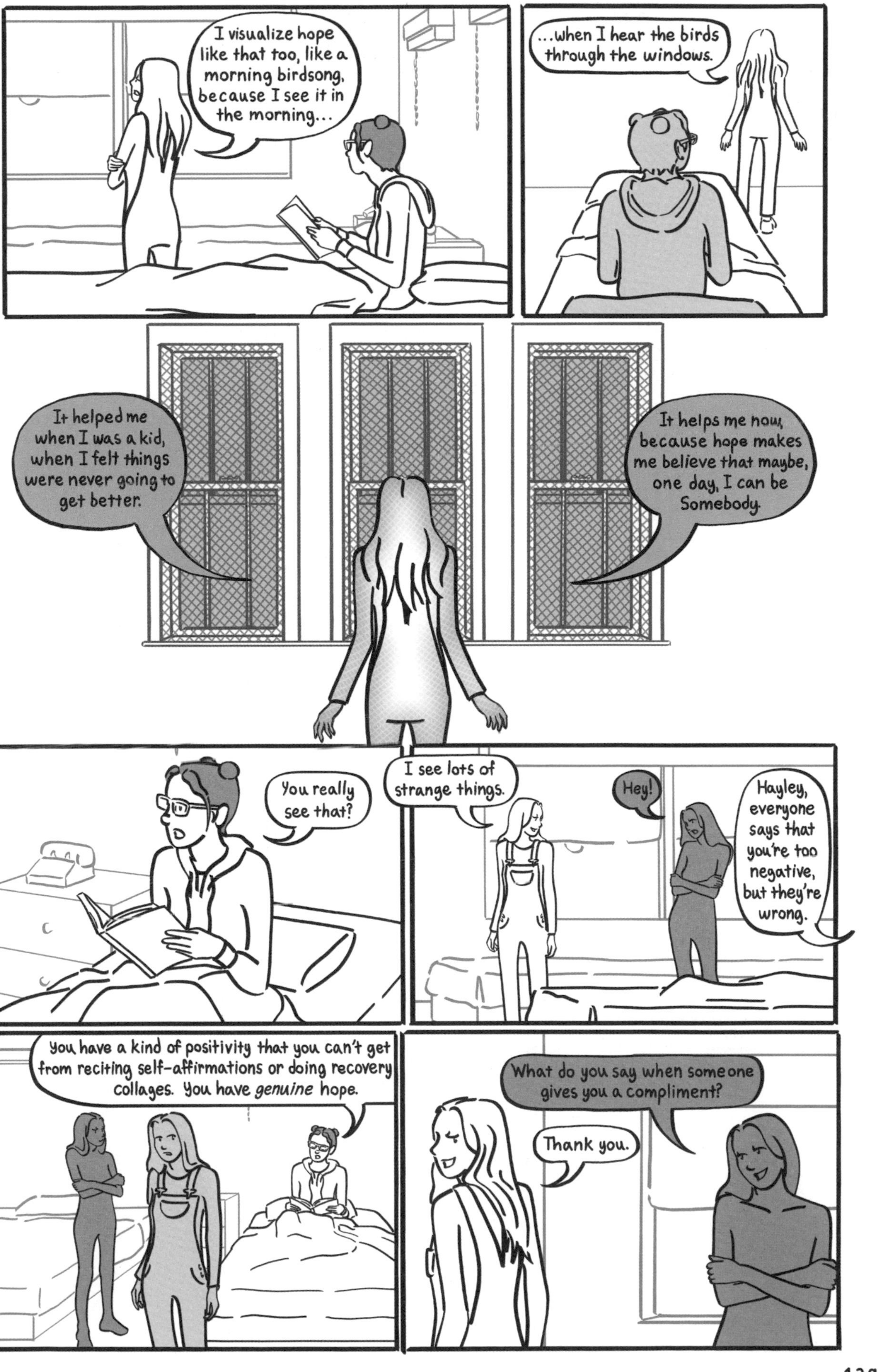
I visualize hope like that too, like a morning birdsong, because I see it in the morning...
...when I hear the birds through the windows.
It helped me when I was a kid, when I felt things were never going to get better.
It helps me now, because hope makes me believe that maybe, one day, I can be Somebody.
You really see that?
I see lots of strange things.
Hey!
Hayley, everyone says that you're too negative, but they're wrong.
You have a kind of positivity that you can't get from reciting self-affirmations or doing recovery collages. You have *genuine* hope.
What do you say when someone gives you a compliment?
Thank you.

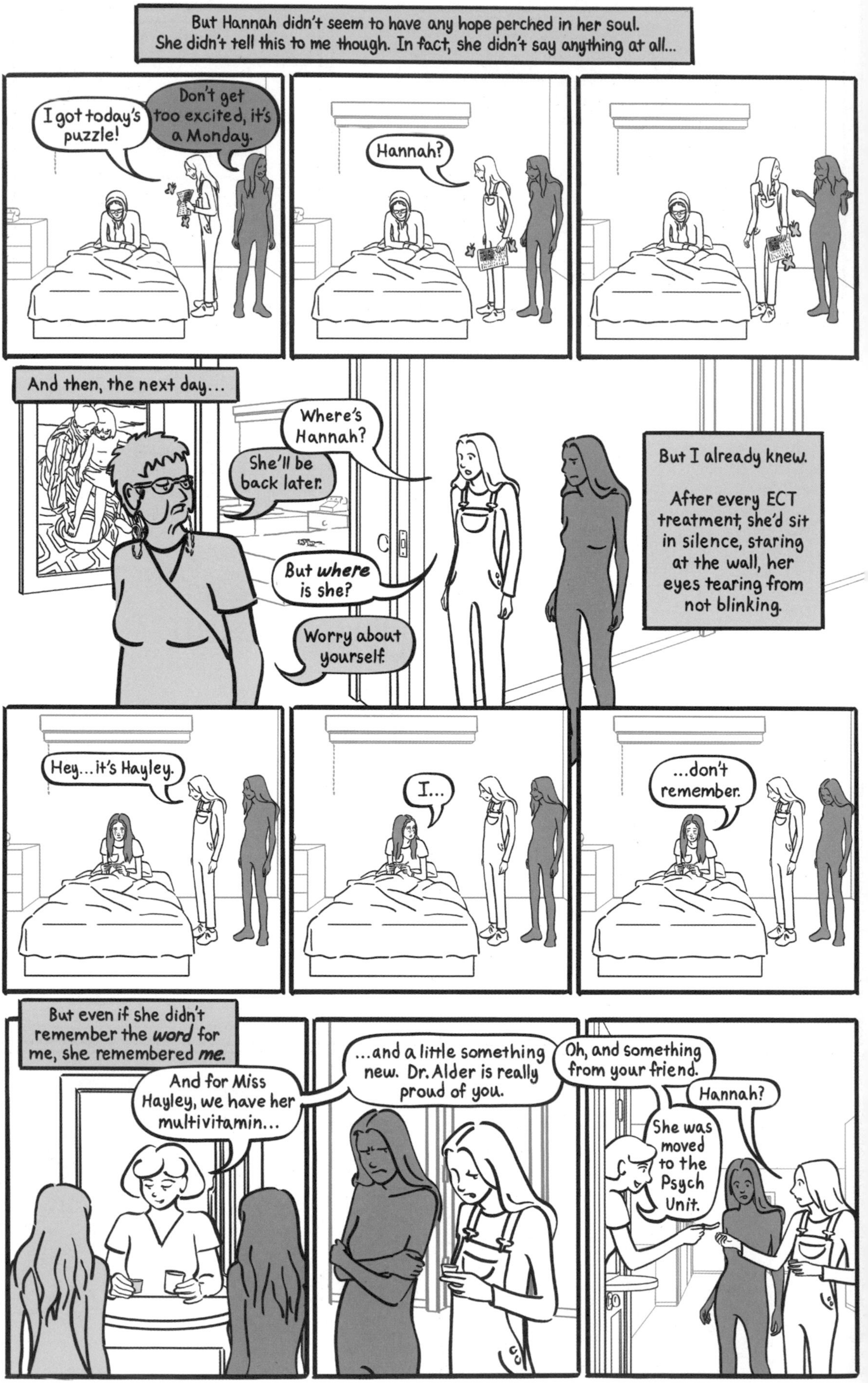

But Hannah didn't seem to have any hope perched in her soul. She didn't tell this to me though. In fact, she didn't say anything at all...
I got today's puzzle!
Don't get too excited, it's a Monday.
Hannah?
And then, the next day...
Where's Hannah?
She'll be back later.
But *where* is she?
Worry about yourself.
But I already knew.
After every ECT treatment, she'd sit in silence, staring at the wall, her eyes tearing from not blinking.
Hey... it's Hayley.
I...
...don't remember.
But even if she didn't remember the *word* for me, she remembered *me*.
And for Miss Hayley, we have her multivitamin...
...and a little something new. Dr. Alder is really proud of you.
Oh, and something from your friend.
Hannah?
She was moved to the Psych Unit.

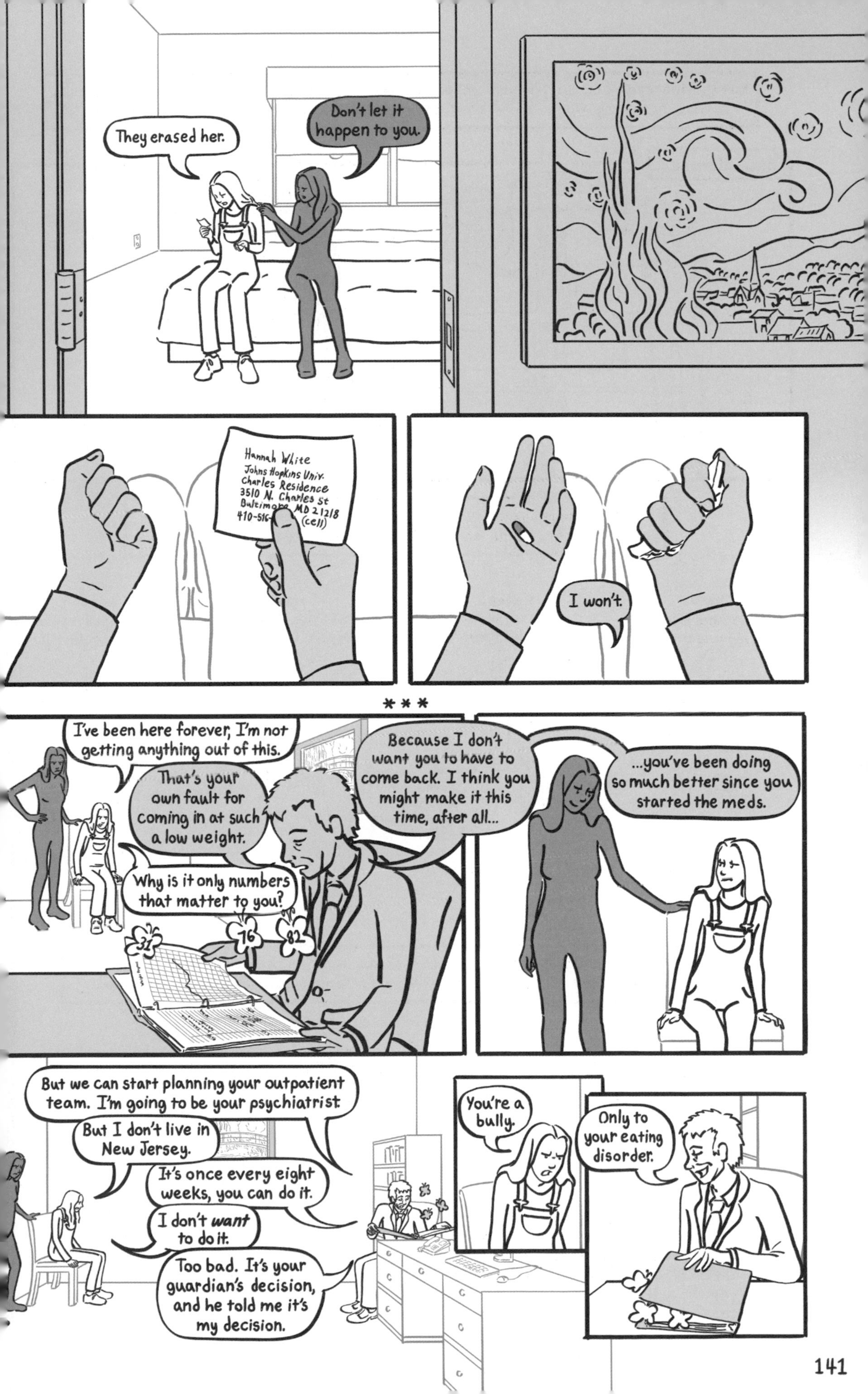
They erased her.
Don't let it happen to you.
Hannah White
Johns Hopkins Univ.
Charles Residence
3510 N. Charles St
MD 21218
(cell)
I won't.
* * *
I've been here forever, I'm not getting anything out of this.
That's your own fault for coming in at such a low weight.
Why is it only numbers that matter to you?
31
76
82
Because I don't want you to have to come back. I think you might make it this time, after all...
...you've been doing so much better since you started the meds.
But we can start planning your outpatient team. I'm going to be your psychiatrist.
But I don't live in New Jersey.
It's once every eight weeks, you can do it.
I don't *want* to do it.
Too bad. It's your guardian's decision, and he told me it's my decision.
You're a bully.
Only to your eating disorder.

But the therapist and nutritionist "we" picked were also in New Jersey, so every eight weeks turned into every week. And if I lost a single pound, he'd send me back to the hospital.
Back at home...
This is unfair unfair unfair.
You only have one way out.
To be fat?
No, you idiot. Wear weights.
I converted my savings into rolls of quarters (each roll weighs a half pound) and gradually increased how many I wore as my weight fell.
Layer 1
I stuffed them into a bra and my underwear...
bra purchased solely for this purpose
Layer 2
...and into the pockets of a light vest.
second pair of underwear to keep everything tucked in
Layer 3
Over that went the overalls, fully loaded.
Layer 4
Then I topped it all off wi
a jacket/robe hybrid.
a few pounds of water for extra insurance
headache from OD'ing on said water
outer pockets left empty-Do I look stupid to you?
no one suspects pink
As the number of weights increased, I needed help. Wearing the quarters for the car ride home was cutting off my circulation. Mom, for some reason, begrudgingly obliged.
I'd get weighed by my nutritionist.
Then I'd remove the weights in a Wendy's bathroom before seeing my therapist.
I'd emerge in fashionable clothes, since dressing nicely makes it seem like you care about yourself.
And Mom would tow away the quarters, since they were too heavy for me.
Wendy's
99¢

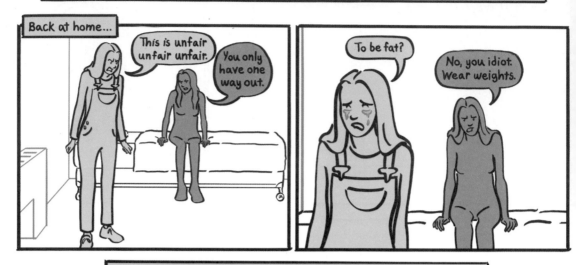

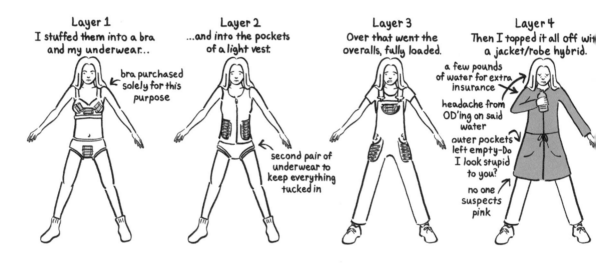

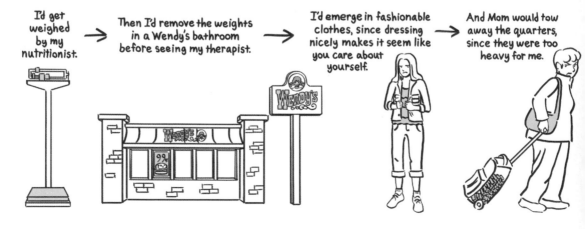

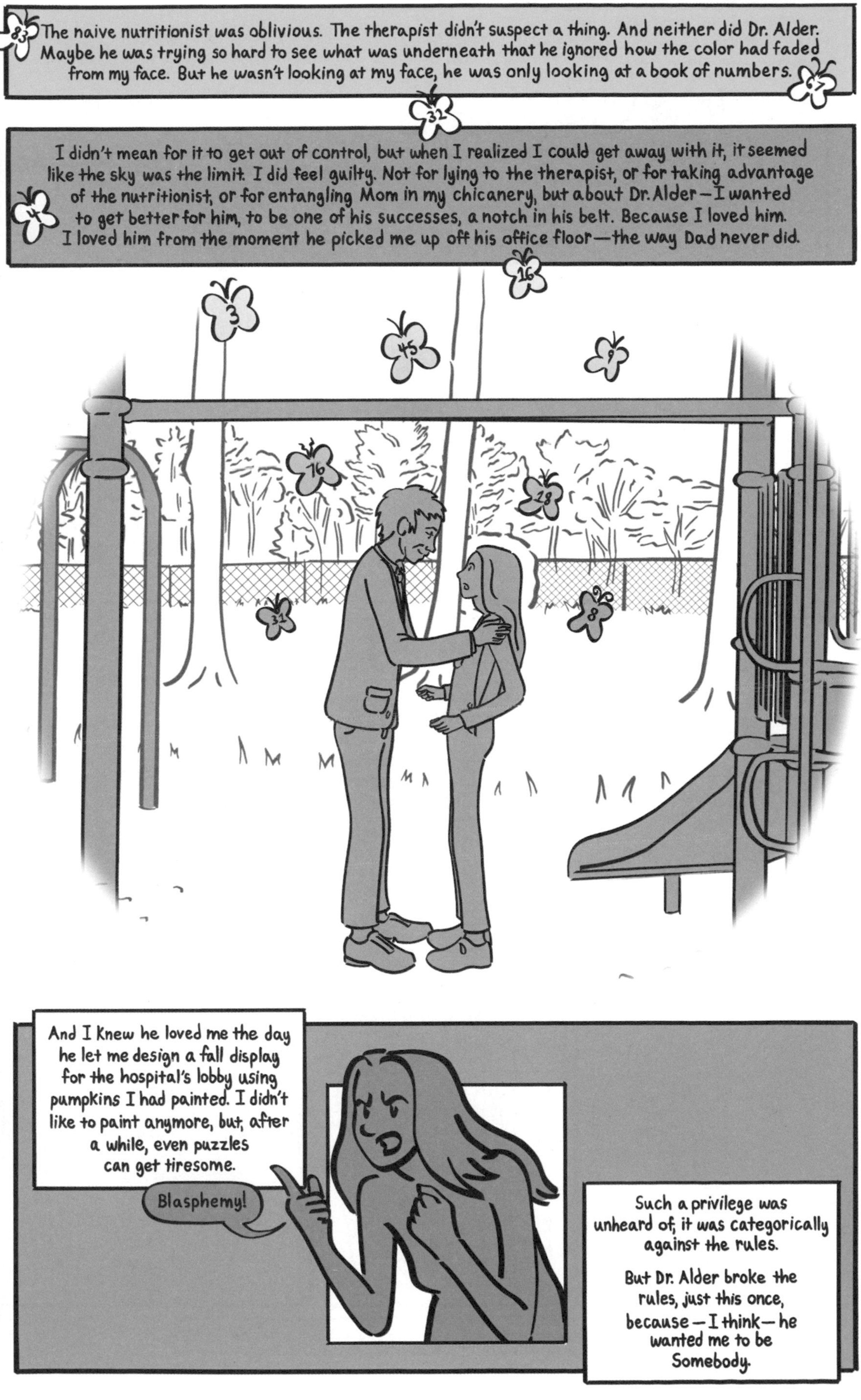
The naive nutritionist was oblivious. The therapist didn't suspect a thing. And neither did Dr. Alder. Maybe he was trying so hard to see what was underneath that he ignored how the color had faded from my face. But he wasn't looking at my face, he was only looking at a book of numbers.
I didn't mean for it to get out of control, but when I realized I could get away with it, it seemed like the sky was the limit. I did feel guilty. Not for lying to the therapist, or for taking advantage of the nutritionist, or for entangling Mom in my chicanery, but about Dr. Alder—I wanted to get better for him, to be one of his successes, a notch in his belt. Because I loved him. I loved him from the moment he picked me up off his office floor—the way Dad never did.
And I Knew he loved me the day he let me design a fall display for the hospital's lobby using pumpkins I had painted. I didn't like to paint anymore, but, after a while, even puzzles can get tiresome.
Blasphemy!
Such a privilege was unheard of, it was categorically against the rules.
But Dr. Alder broke the rules, just this once, because—I think—he wanted me to be Somebody.

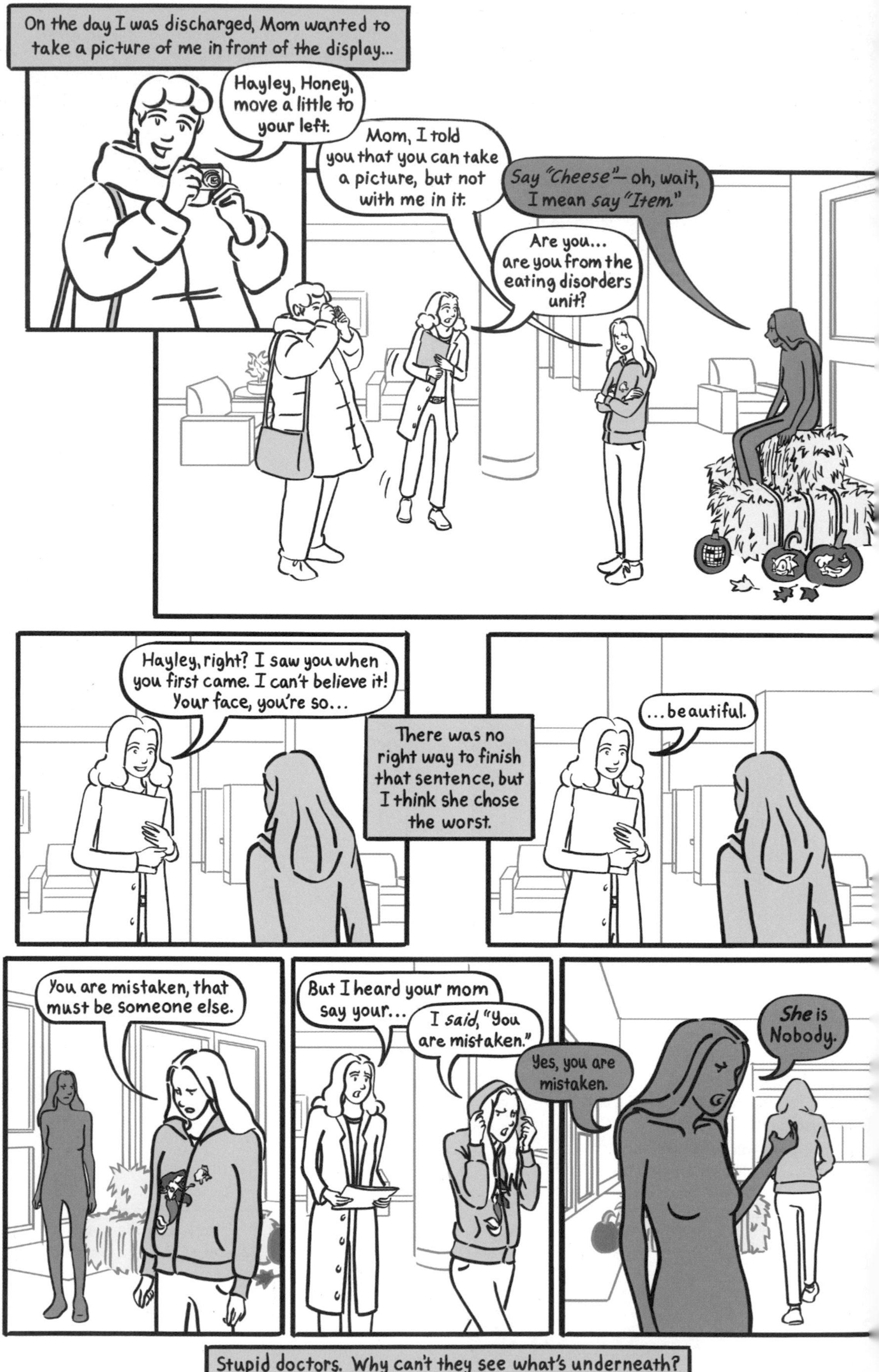
On the day I was discharged, Mom wanted to take a picture of me in front of the display...
Hayley, Honey, move a little to your left.
Mom, I told you that you can take a picture, but not with me in it.
Say "Cheese"— oh, wait, I mean say "Item."
Are you... are you from the eating disorders unit?
Hayley, right? I saw you when you first came. I can't believe it! Your face, you're so...
There was no right way to finish that sentence, but I think she chose the worst.
...beautiful.
You are mistaken, that must be someone else.
But I heard your mom say your...
I said, "You are mistaken."
Yes, you are mistaken.
She is Nobody.
Stupid doctors. Why can't they see what's underneath?

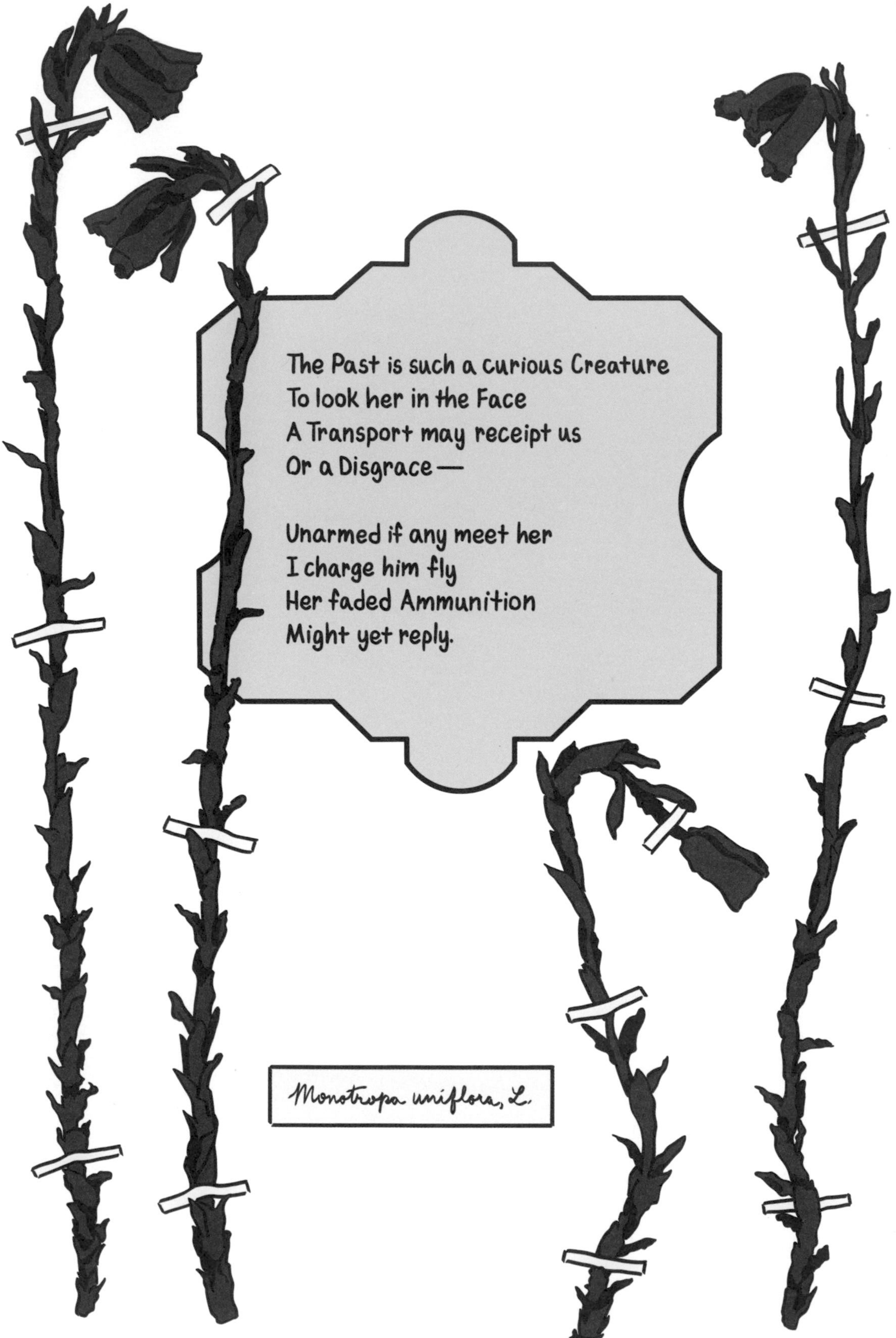

The Past is such a curious Creature
To look her in the Face
A Transport may receipt us
Or a Disgrace—

Unarmed if any meet her
I charge him fly
Her faded Ammunition
Might yet reply.

Monotropa uniflora, L.

Chapter

7

Coping Skills

After I got accepted to an art school in Manhattan,
where the terrain was flat and no provost cared how
much I weighed, Dr. Alder agreed to let me ditch him for
a local treatment team. I found a therapist and a
nutritionist. I didn't bother with a psychiatrist since
I wasn't actually taking my meds. And I got my
guardianship revoked, so I could never be locked up
again. I had finally gotten everything I wanted!

But it all seemed wrong. I was going to art school,
but I didn't like to draw. I'd be getting away from my
parents, but I still needed Mom on the phone to eat.
And class might as well have been a ceramic-disco-pizza
party flashback, because I somehow managed to
be the weirdo of art school.

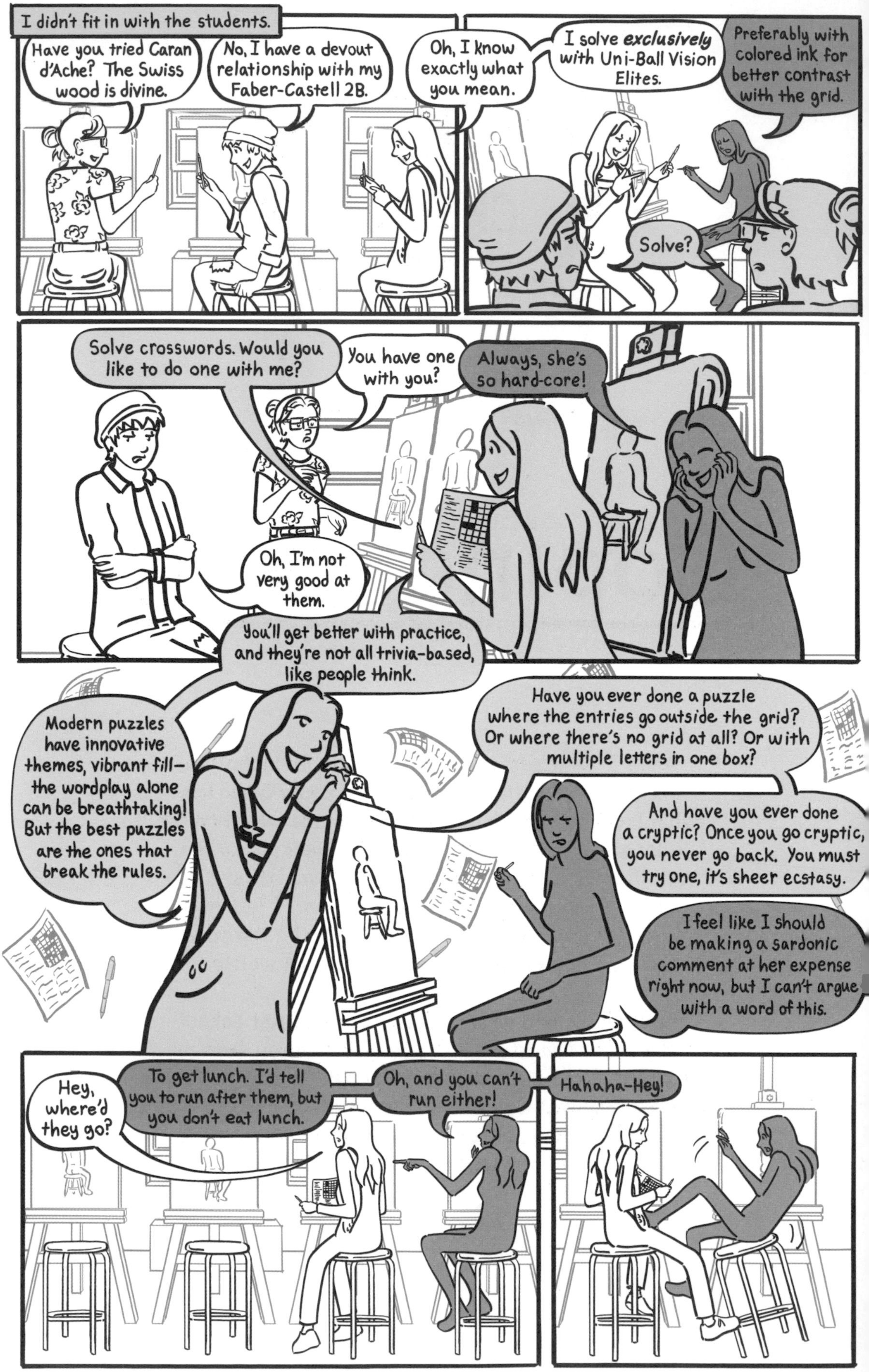

I didn't fit in with the students.
Have you tried Caran d'Ache? The Swiss wood is divine.
No, I have a devout relationship with my Faber-Castell 2B.
Oh, I know exactly what you mean.
I solve *exclusively* with Uni-Ball Vision Elites.
Preferably with colored ink for better contrast with the grid.
Solve?
Solve crosswords. Would you like to do one with me?
You have one with you?
Always, she's so hard-core!
Oh, I'm not very good at them.
You'll get better with practice, and they're not all trivia-based, like people think.
Modern puzzles have innovative themes, vibrant fill—the wordplay alone can be breathtaking! But the best puzzles are the ones that break the rules.
Have you ever done a puzzle where the entries go outside the grid? Or where there's no grid at all? Or with multiple letters in one box?
And have you ever done a cryptic? Once you go cryptic, you never go back. You must try one, it's sheer ecstasy.
I feel like I should be making a sardonic comment at her expense right now, but I can't argue with a word of this.
Hey, where'd they go?
To get lunch. I'd tell you to run after them, but you don't eat lunch.
Oh, and you can't run either!
Hahaha-Hey!

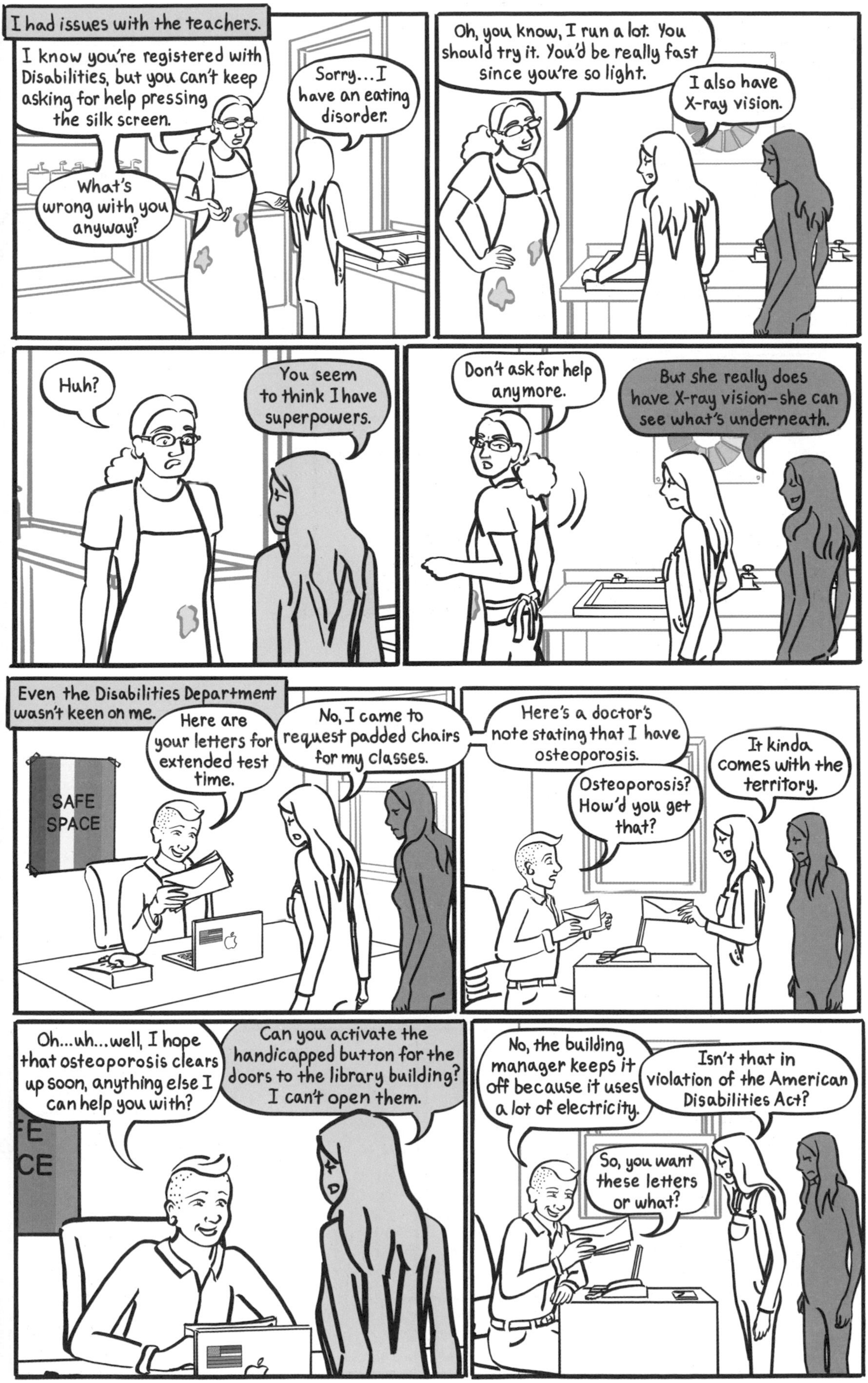

I had issues with the teachers.
I know you're registered with Disabilities, but you can't keep asking for help pressing the silk screen.
What's wrong with you anyway?
Sorry...I have an eating disorder.
Oh, you know, I run a lot. You should try it. You'd be really fast since you're so light.
I also have X-ray vision.
Huh?
You seem to think I have superpowers.
Don't ask for help anymore.
But she really does have X-ray vision—she can see what's underneath.
Even the Disabilities Department wasn't keen on me.
SAFE SPACE
Here are your letters for extended test time.
No, I came to request padded chairs for my classes.
Here's a doctor's note stating that I have osteoporosis.
Osteoporosis? How'd you get that?
It kinda comes with the territory.
Oh...uh...well, I hope that osteoporosis clears up soon, anything else I can help you with?
Can you activate the handicapped button for the doors to the library building? I can't open them.
No, the building manager keeps it off because it uses a lot of electricity.
Isn't that in violation of the American Disabilities Act?
So, you want these letters or what?

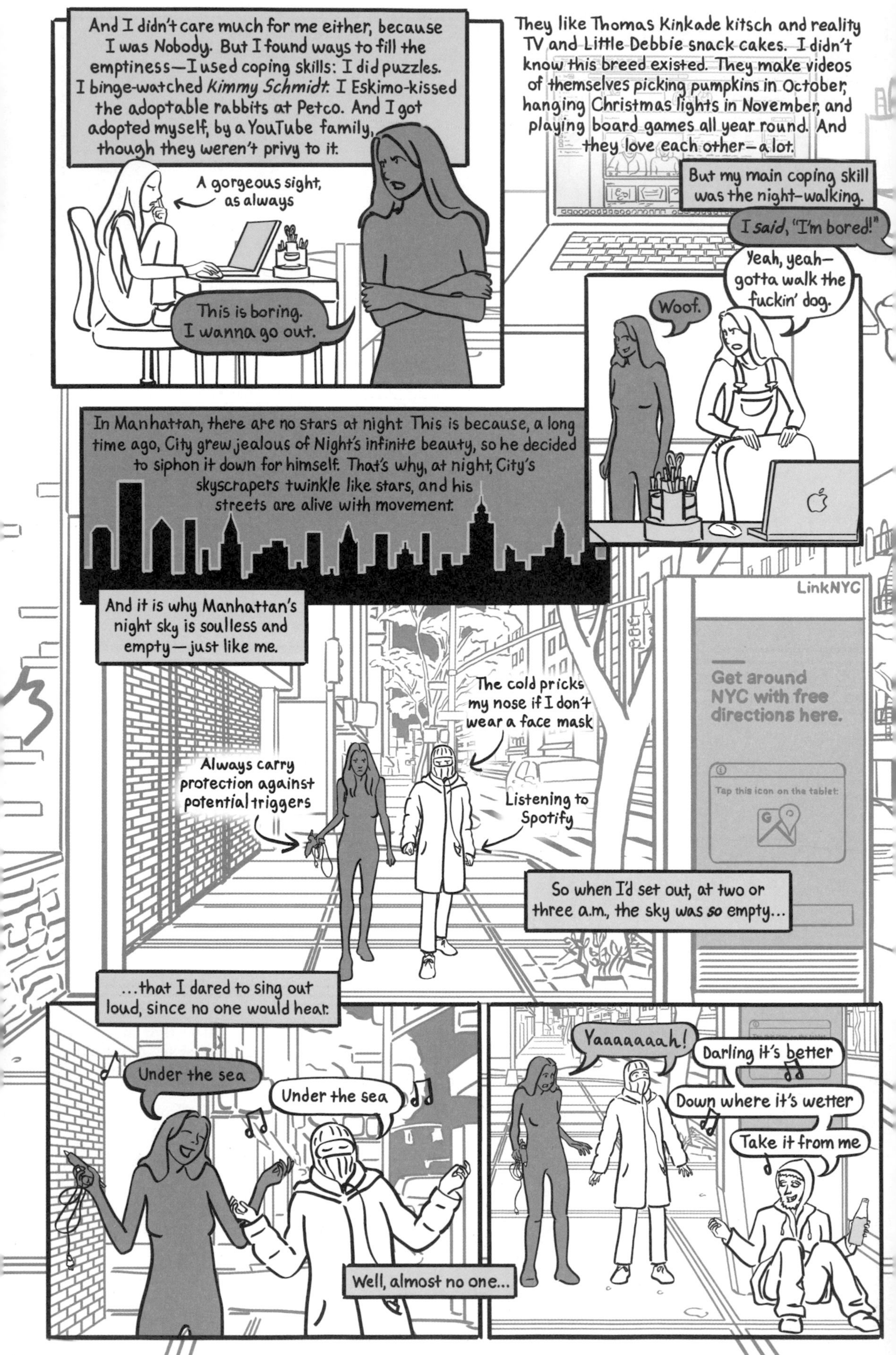

And I didn't care much for me either, because I was Nobody. But I found ways to fill the emptiness—I used coping skills: I did puzzles. I binge-watched *Kimmy Schmidt*. I Eskimo-kissed the adoptable rabbits at Petco. And I got adopted myself, by a YouTube family, though they weren't privy to it.
A gorgeous sight, as always
This is boring. I wanna go out.
They like Thomas Kinkade kitsch and reality TV and Little Debbie snack cakes. I didn't know this breed existed. They make videos of themselves picking pumpkins in October, hanging Christmas lights in November, and playing board games all year round. And they love each other—a lot.
But my main coping skill was the night-walking.
I *said*, "I'm bored!"
Yeah, yeah—gotta walk the fuckin' dog.
Woof.
In Manhattan, there are no stars at night. This is because, a long time ago, City grew jealous of Night's infinite beauty, so he decided to siphon it down for himself. That's why, at night, City's skyscrapers twinkle like stars, and his streets are alive with movement.
And it is why Manhattan's night sky is soulless and empty—just like me.
LinkNYC
Get around NYC with free directions here.
Tap this icon on the tablet:
The cold pricks my nose if I don't wear a face mask
Always carry protection against potential triggers
Listening to Spotify
So when I'd set out, at two or three a.m., the sky was *so* empty...
...that I dared to sing out loud, since no one would hear.
Under the sea
Under the sea
Well, almost no one...
Yaaaaaaah!
Darling it's better
Down where it's wetter
Take it from me

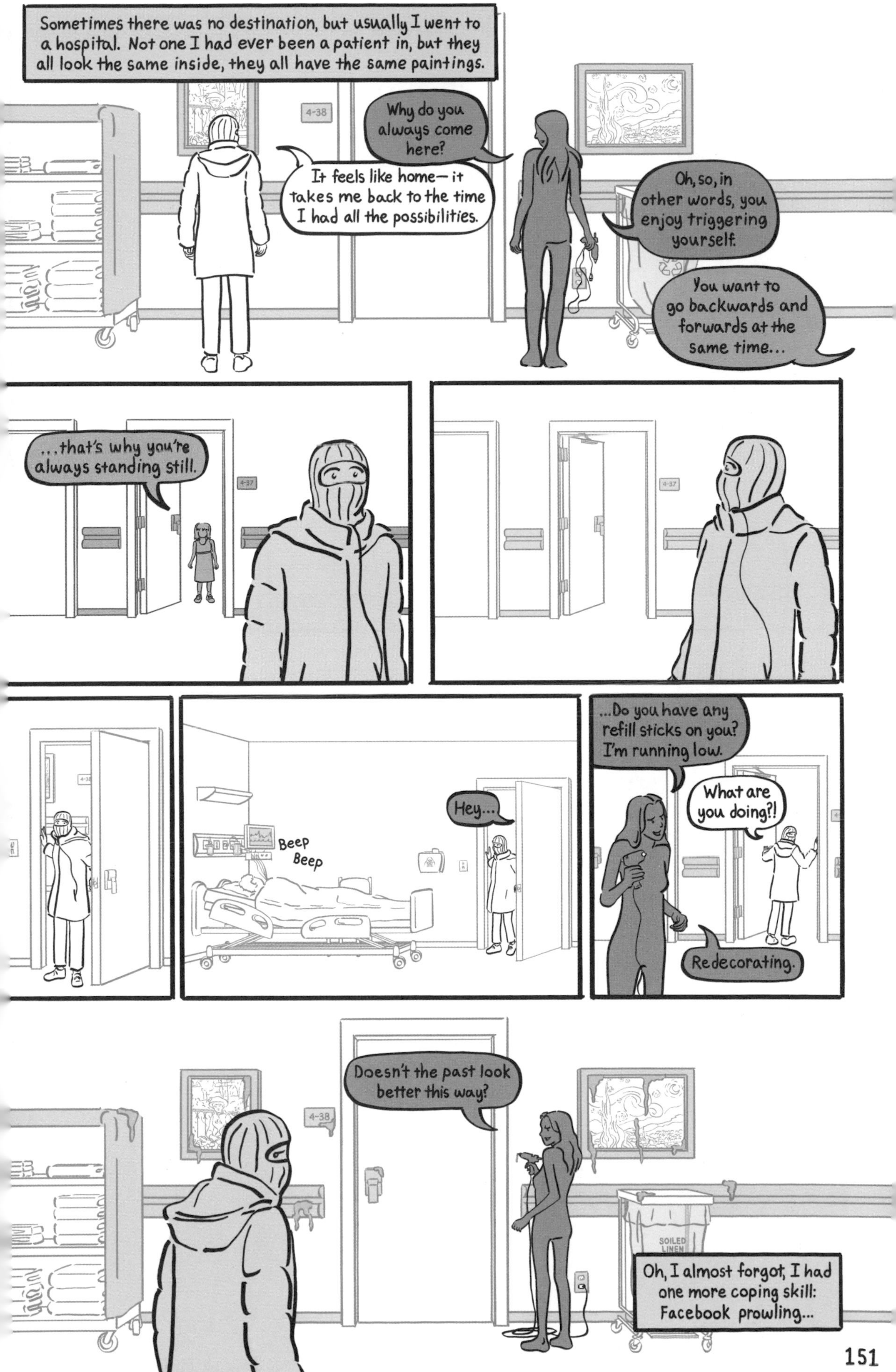
Sometimes there was no destination, but usually I went to a hospital. Not one I had ever been a patient in, but they all look the same inside, they all have the same paintings.
4-38
Why do you always come here?
It feels like home— it takes me back to the time I had all the possibilities.
Oh, so, in other words, you enjoy triggering yourself.
You want to go backwards and forwards at the same time...
...that's why you're always standing still.
4-37
4-37
Hey...
Beep
Beep
...Do you have any refill sticks on you? I'm running low.
What are you doing?!
Redecorating.
Doesn't the past look better this way?
4-38
SOILED LINEN
Oh, I almost forgot, I had one more coping skill: Facebook prowling...

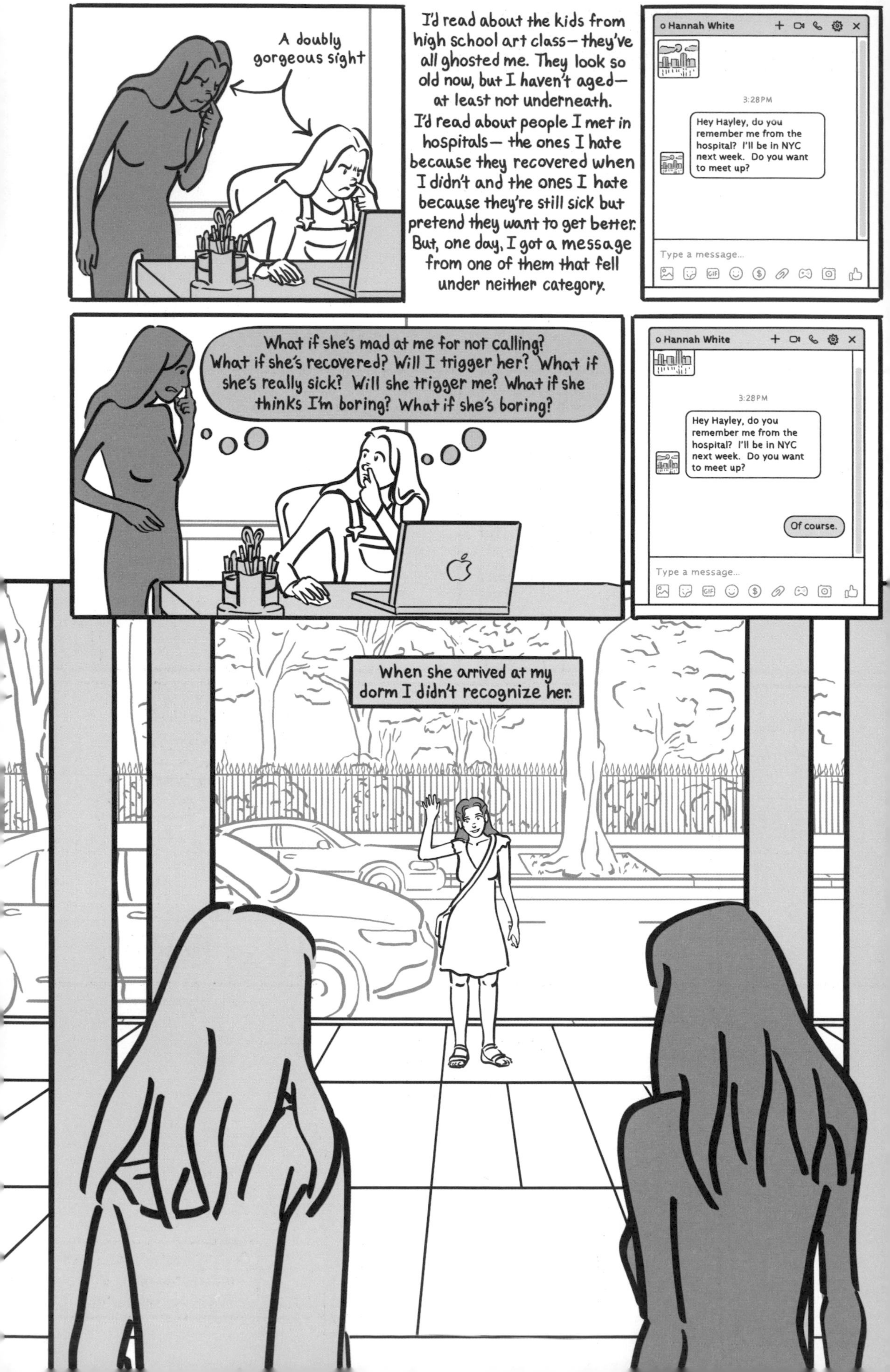
A doubly gorgeous sight
I'd read about the kids from high school art class— they've all ghosted me. They look so old now, but I haven't aged— at least not underneath.
I'd read about people I met in hospitals— the ones I hate because they recovered when I didn't and the ones I hate because they're still sick but pretend they want to get better.
But, one day, I got a message from one of them that fell under neither category.
Hannah White
3:28PM
Hey Hayley, do you remember me from the hospital? I'll be in NYC next week. Do you want to meet up?
Type a message...
What if she's mad at me for not calling? What if she's recovered? Will I trigger her? What if she's really sick? Will she trigger me? What if she thinks I'm boring? What if she's boring?
Hannah White
3:28PM
Hey Hayley, do you remember me from the hospital? I'll be in NYC next week. Do you want to meet up?
Of course.
Type a message...
When she arrived at my dorm I didn't recognize her.

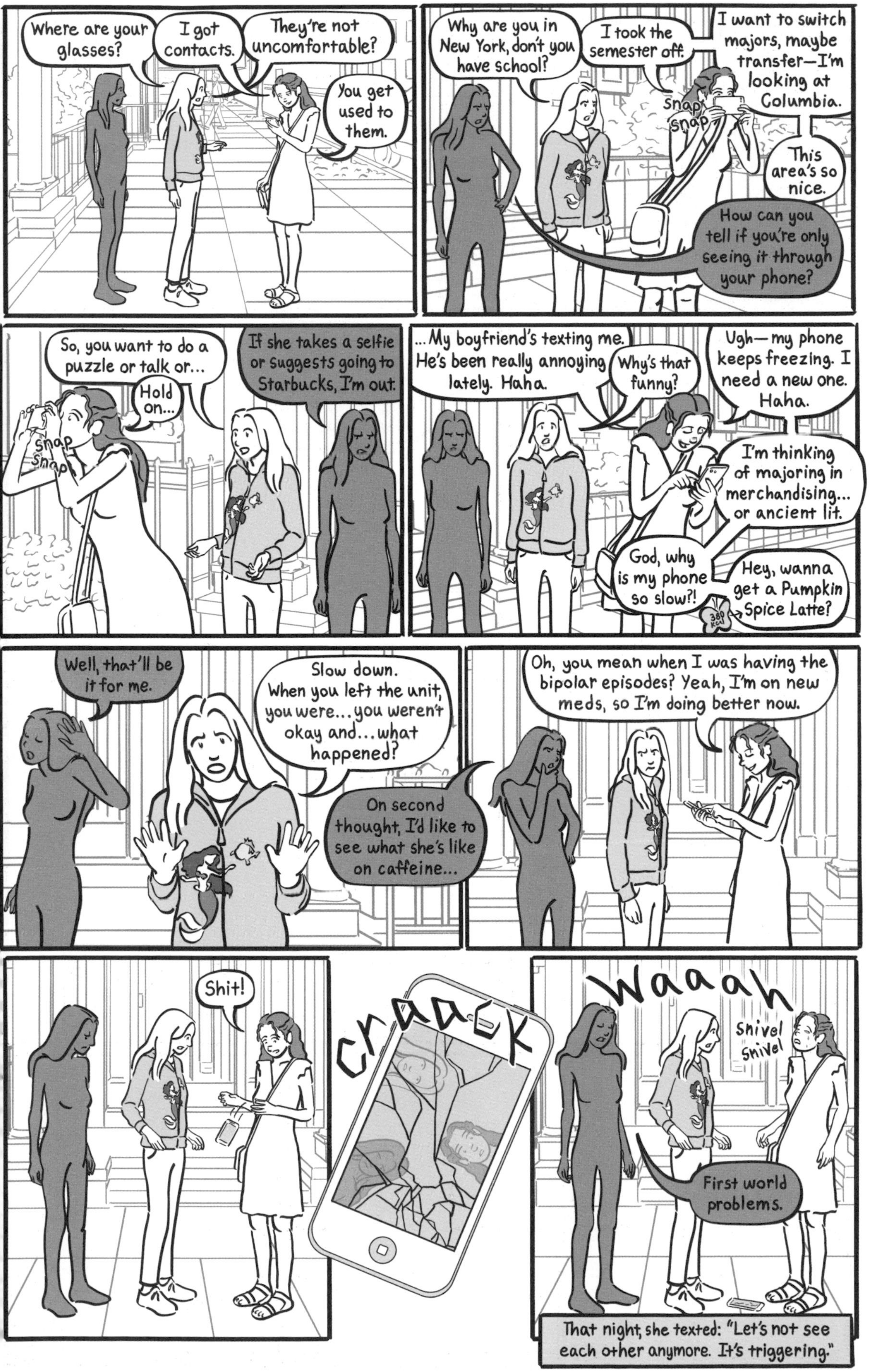

Where are your glasses?
I got contacts.
They're not uncomfortable?
You get used to them.
Why are you in New York, don't you have school?
I took the semester off.
I want to switch majors, maybe transfer—I'm looking at Columbia.
snap snap
This area's so nice.
How can you tell if you're only seeing it through your phone?
So, you want to do a puzzle or talk or...
Hold on...
snap snap
If she takes a selfie or suggests going to Starbucks, I'm out.
...My boyfriend's texting me. He's been really annoying lately. Haha.
Why's that funny?
Ugh—my phone keeps freezing. I need a new one. Haha.
I'm thinking of majoring in merchandising... or ancient lit.
God, why is my phone so slow?!
Hey, wanna get a Pumpkin Spice Latte?
380 kcal
Well, that'll be it for me.
Slow down. When you left the unit, you were... you weren't okay and... what happened?
On second thought, I'd like to see what she's like on caffeine...
Oh, you mean when I was having the bipolar episodes? Yeah, I'm on new meds, so I'm doing better now.
Shit!
CRAACK
Waaah
Snivel snivel
First world problems.
That night, she texted: "Let's not see each other anymore. It's triggering."

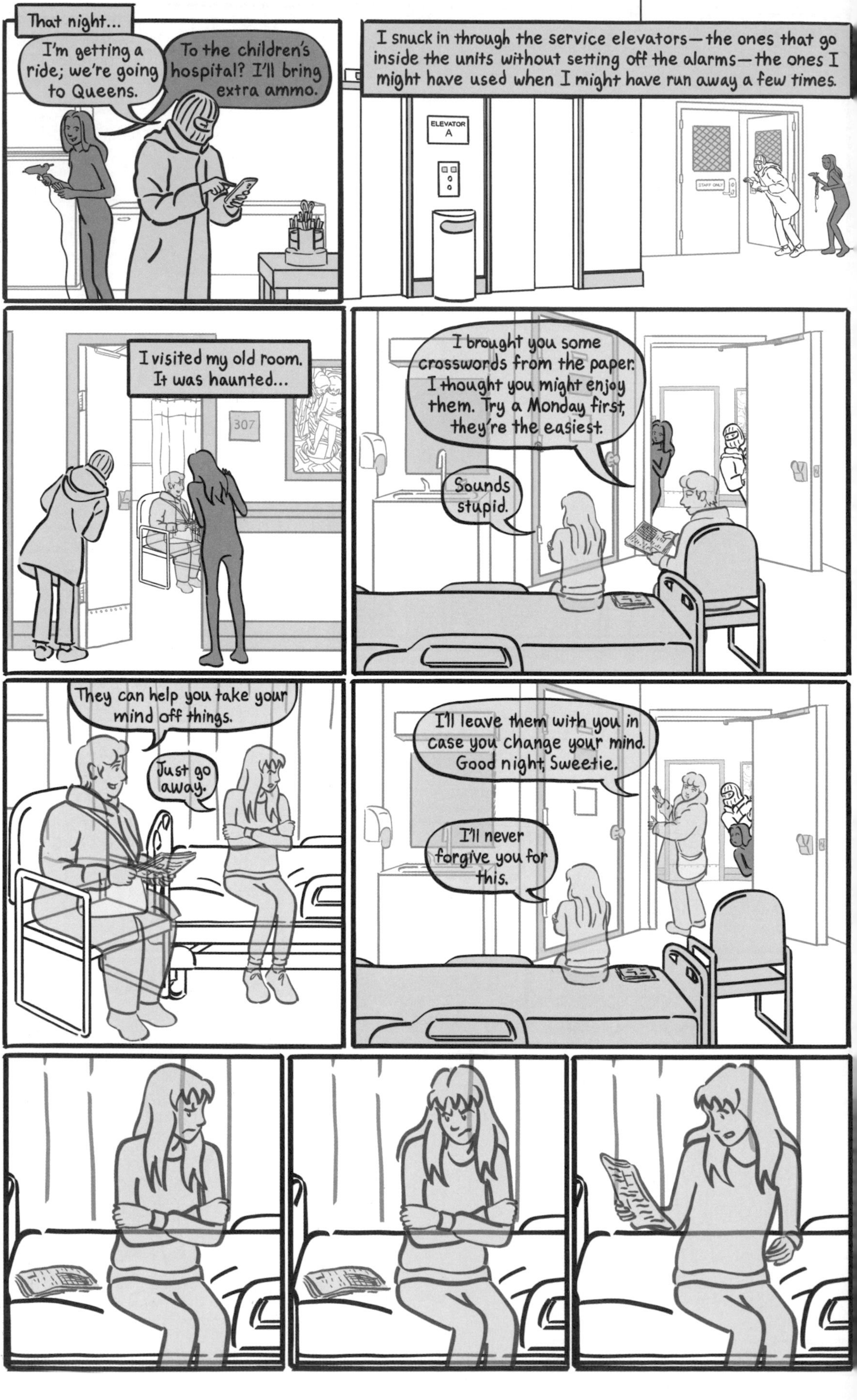

That night...
I'm getting a ride; we're going to Queens.
To the children's hospital? I'll bring extra ammo.
I snuck in through the service elevators—the ones that go inside the units without setting off the alarms—the ones I might have used when I might have run away a few times.
ELEVATOR A
I visited my old room. It was haunted...
307
I brought you some crosswords from the paper. I thought you might enjoy them. Try a Monday first, they're the easiest.
Sounds stupid.
They can help you take your mind off things.
Just go away.
I'll leave them with you in case you change your mind. Good night, Sweetie.
I'll never forgive you for this.

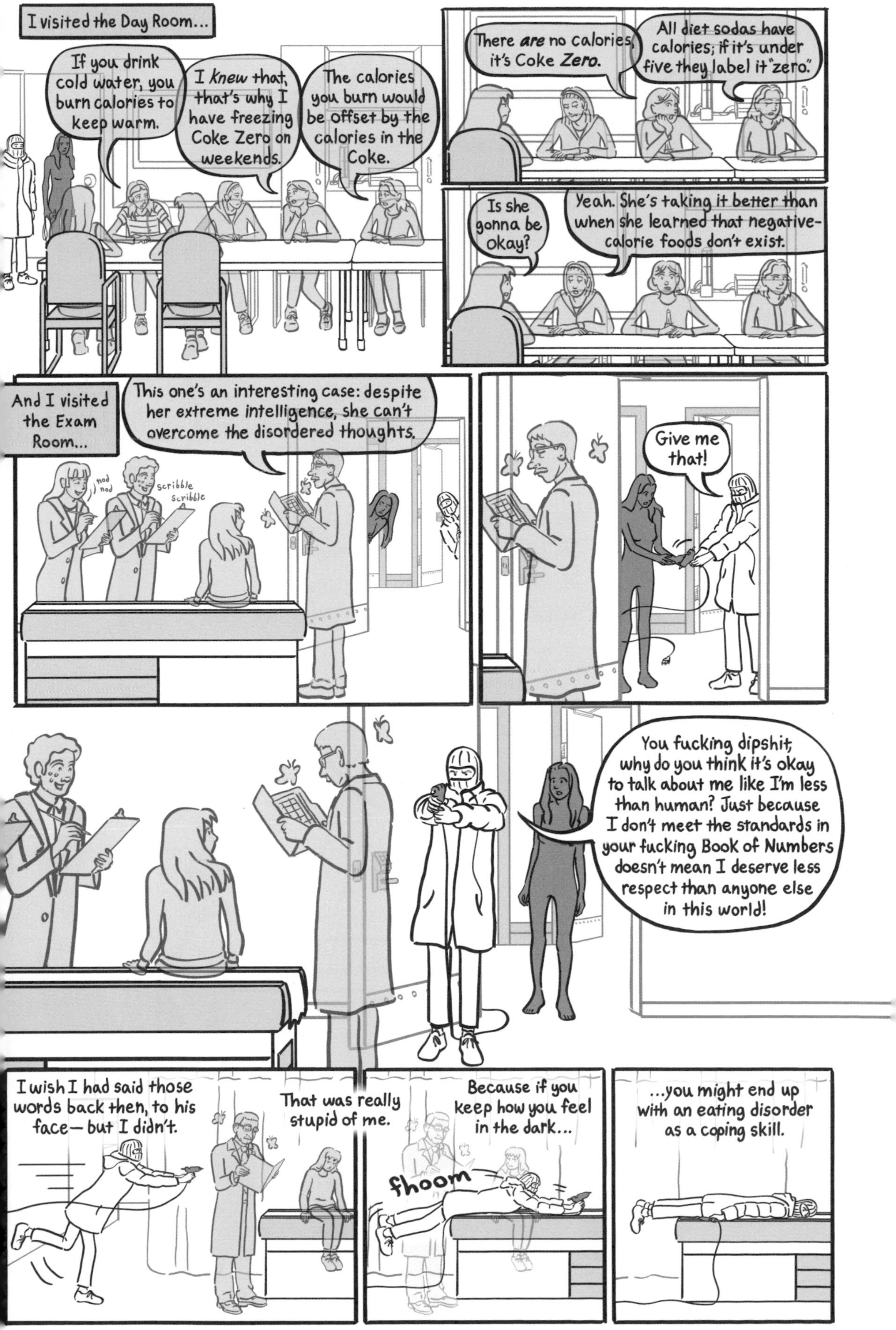
I visited the Day Room...
If you drink cold water, you burn calories to keep warm.
I *knew* that, that's why I have freezing Coke Zero on weekends.
The calories you burn would be offset by the calories in the Coke.
There *are* no calories, it's Coke *Zero*.
All diet sodas have calories; if it's under five they label it "zero."
Is she gonna be okay?
Yeah. She's taking it better than when she learned that negative-calorie foods don't exist.
And I visited the Exam Room...
This one's an interesting case: despite her extreme intelligence, she can't overcome the disordered thoughts.
nod nod
scribble scribble
Give me that!
You fucking dipshit, why do you think it's okay to talk about me like I'm less than human? Just because I don't meet the standards in your fucking Book of Numbers doesn't mean I deserve less respect than anyone else in this world!
I wish I had said those words back then, to his face—but I didn't.
That was really stupid of me.
Because if you keep how you feel in the dark...
fhoom
...you might end up with an eating disorder as a coping skill.

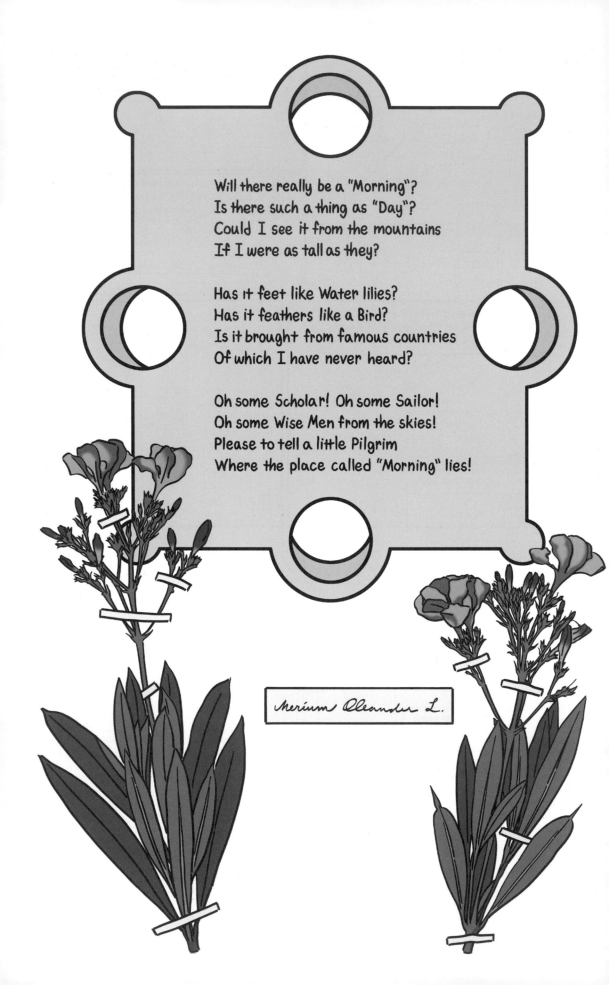

Will there really be a "Morning"?
Is there such a thing as "Day"?
Could I see it from the mountains
If I were as tall as they?

Has it feet like Water lilies?
Has it feathers like a Bird?
Is it brought from famous countries
Of which I have never heard?

Oh some Scholar! Oh some Sailor!
Oh some Wise Men from the skies!
Please to tell a little Pilgrim
Where the place called "Morning" lies!

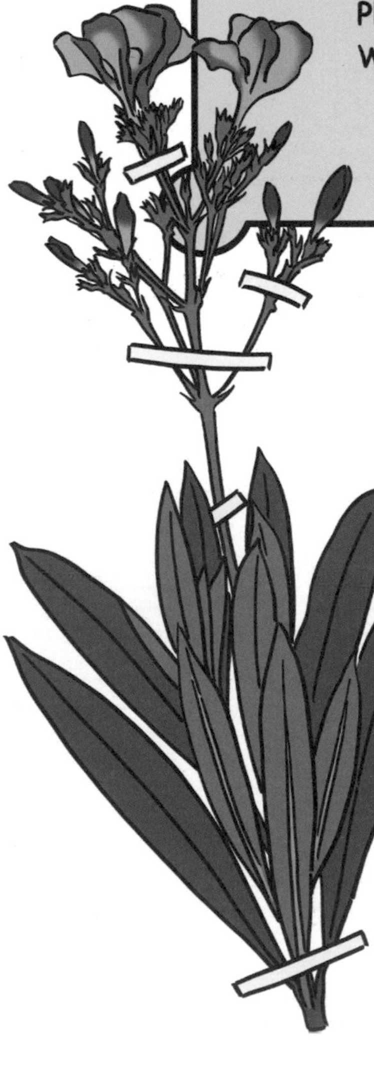

Nerium Oleander L.

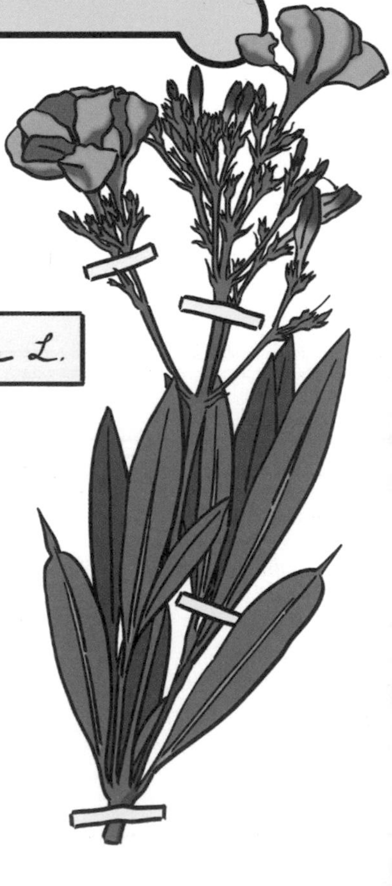

Chapter
8

Fractured

It started in my senior year of art school.
No. It started before then, but I was too deluded
to notice. But it was in my senior year that I started to
care, because, if I died, I would've never gotten to
make something beautiful. So, after graduation, I
immediately got an apartment and a full-time job:
seeing the doctor.

I started with the orthopedist. Every week, I came to him with something new.

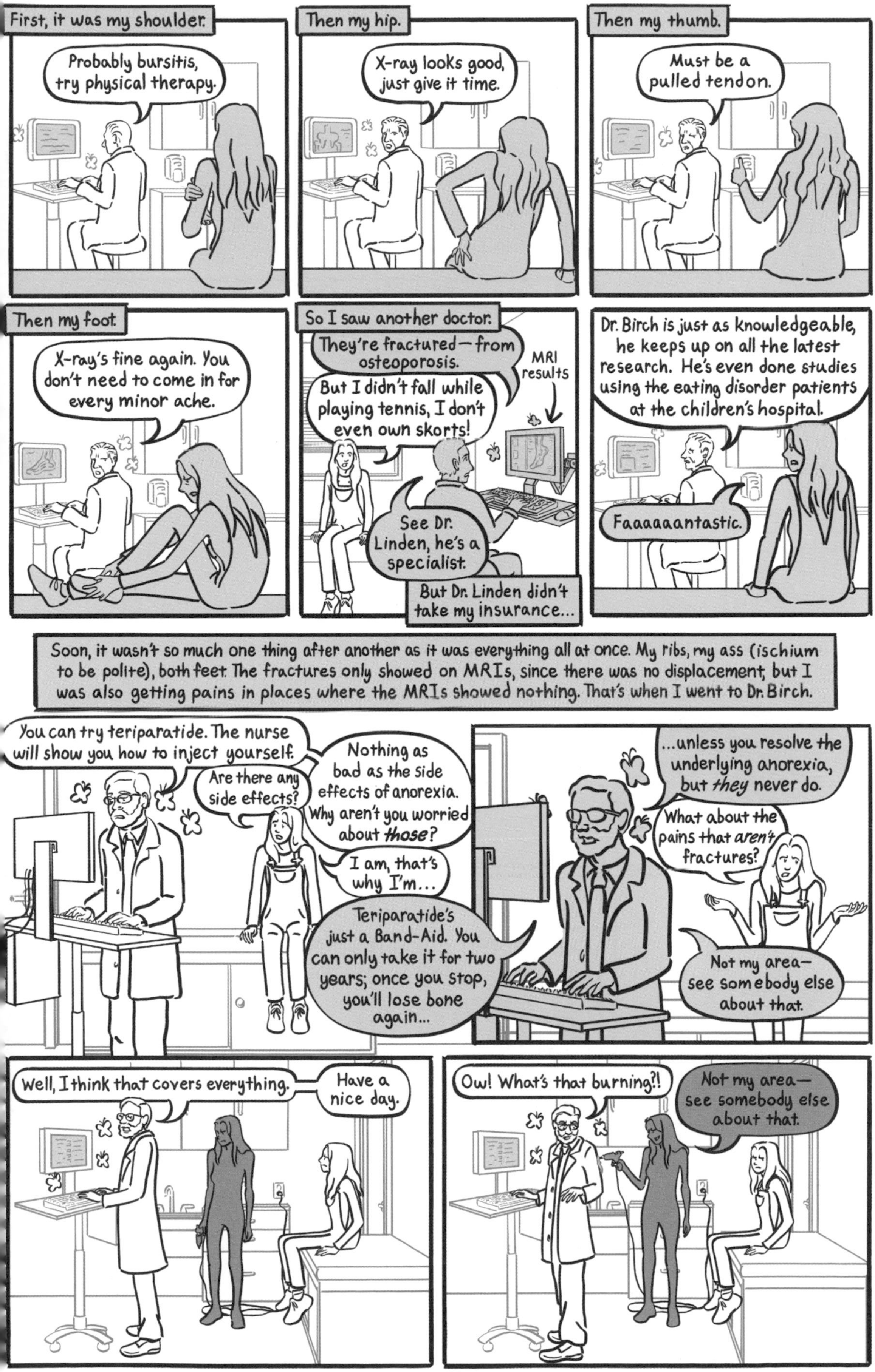
First, it was my shoulder.
Probably bursitis, try physical therapy.
Then my hip.
X-ray looks good, just give it time.
Then my thumb.
Must be a pulled tendon.
Then my foot.
X-ray's fine again. You don't need to come in for every minor ache.
So I saw another doctor.
They're fractured—from osteoporosis.
MRI results
But I didn't fall while playing tennis, I don't even own skorts!
See Dr. Linden, he's a specialist.
But Dr. Linden didn't take my insurance...
Dr. Birch is just as knowledgeable, he keeps up on all the latest research. He's even done studies using the eating disorder patients at the children's hospital.
Faaaaaantastic.
Soon, it wasn't so much one thing after another as it was everything all at once. My ribs, my ass (ischium to be polite), both feet. The fractures only showed on MRIs, since there was no displacement, but I was also getting pains in places where the MRIs showed nothing. That's when I went to Dr. Birch.
You can try teriparatide. The nurse will show you how to inject yourself.
Are there any side effects?
Nothing as bad as the side effects of anorexia. Why aren't you worried about *those*?
I am, that's why I'm...
Teriparatide's just a Band-Aid. You can only take it for two years; once you stop, you'll lose bone again...
...unless you resolve the underlying anorexia, but *they* never do.
What about the pains that *aren't* fractures?
Not my area—see somebody else about that.
Well, I think that covers everything.
Have a nice day.
Ow! What's that burning?!
Not my area—see somebody else about that.

* * *

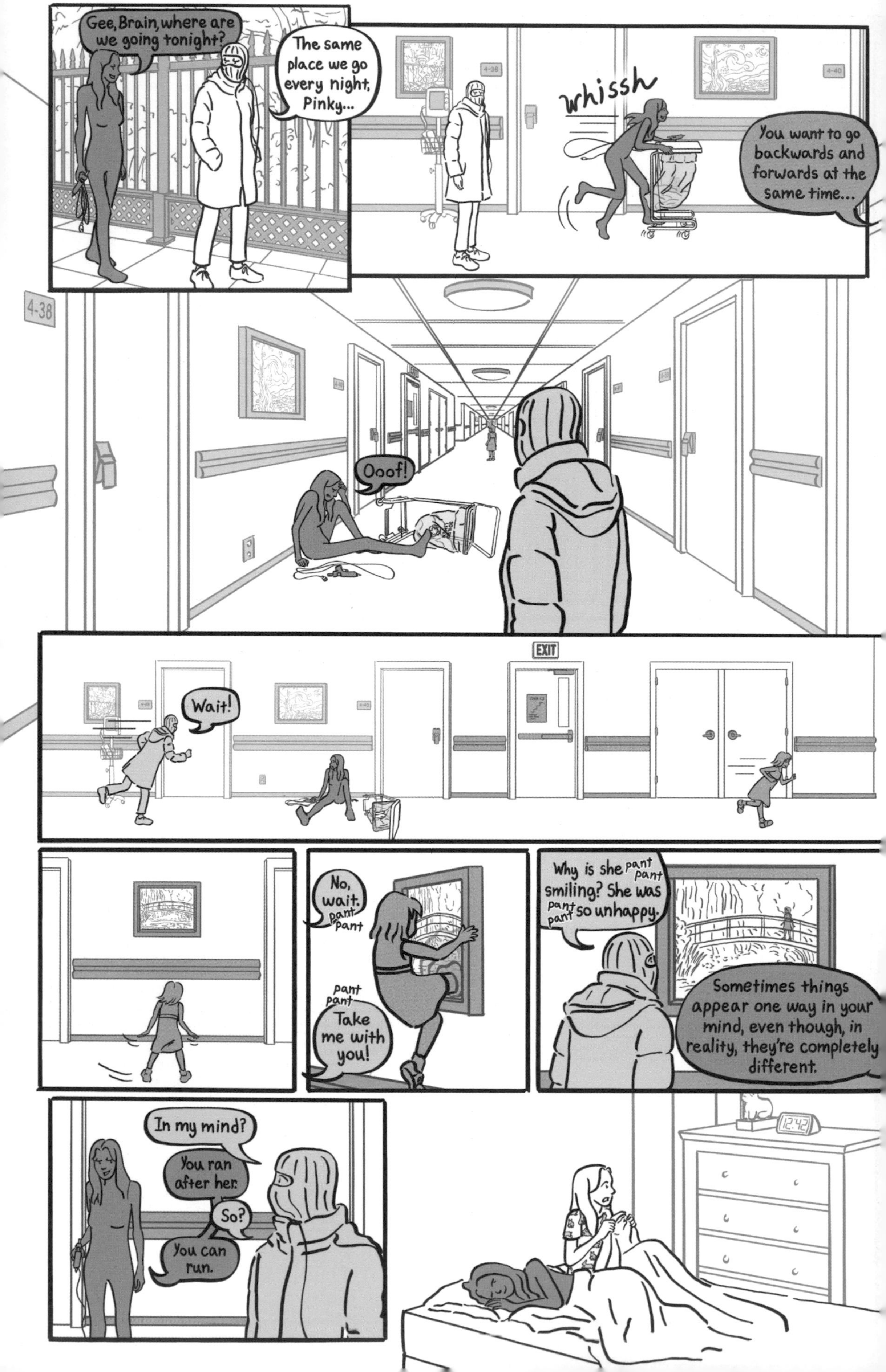
Gee, Brain, where are we going tonight?
The same place we go every night, Pinky...
4-38
whissh
4-40
You want to go backwards and forwards at the same time...
4-38
Ooof!
EXIT
Wait!
No, wait. pant pant
pant pant Take me with you!
Why is she pant pant smiling? She was pant pant so unhappy.
Sometimes things appear one way in your mind, even though, in reality, they're completely different.
In my mind?
You ran after her.
So?
You can run.
12:42

* * *

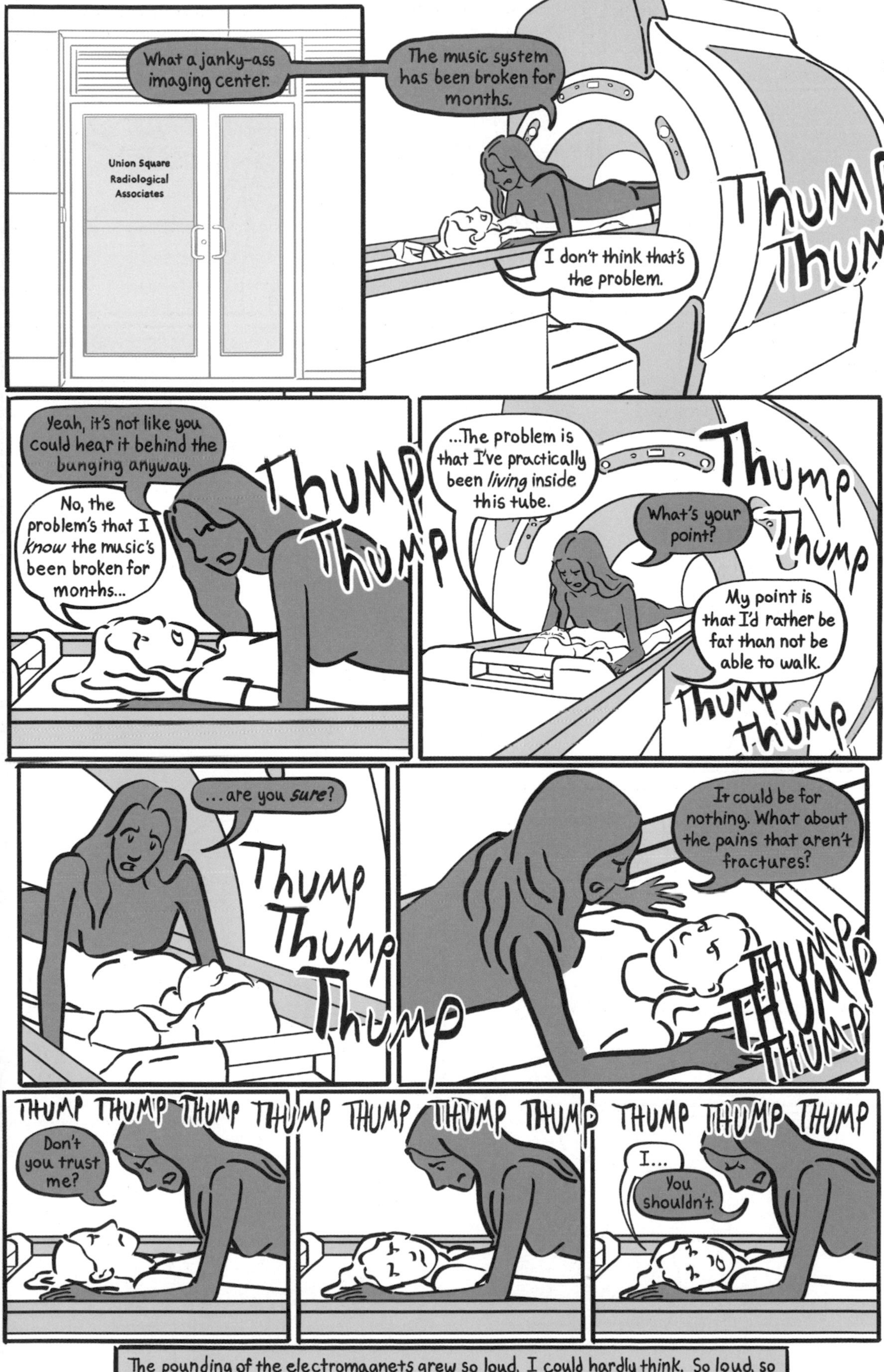
Union Square
Radiological
Associates
What a janky-ass imaging center.
The music system has been broken for months.
I don't think that's the problem.
THUMP
THUMP
Yeah, it's not like you could hear it behind the banging anyway.
No, the problem's that I *know* the music's been broken for months...
THUMP
THUMP
...The problem is that I've practically been *living* inside this tube.
THUMP
What's your point?
THUMP
My point is that I'd rather be fat than not be able to walk.
THUMP
THUMP
...are you *sure*?
Thump
Thump
Thump
It could be for nothing. What about the pains that aren't fractures?
THUMP
THUMP
THUMP
THUMP THUMP THUMP THUMP THUMP THUMP THUMP THUMP THUMP THUMP
Don't you trust me?
I...
You shouldn't.

The pounding of the electromagnets grew so loud, I could hardly think. So loud, so fast. Louder, faster. But it wasn't the magnets. It was time—it was speeding up.

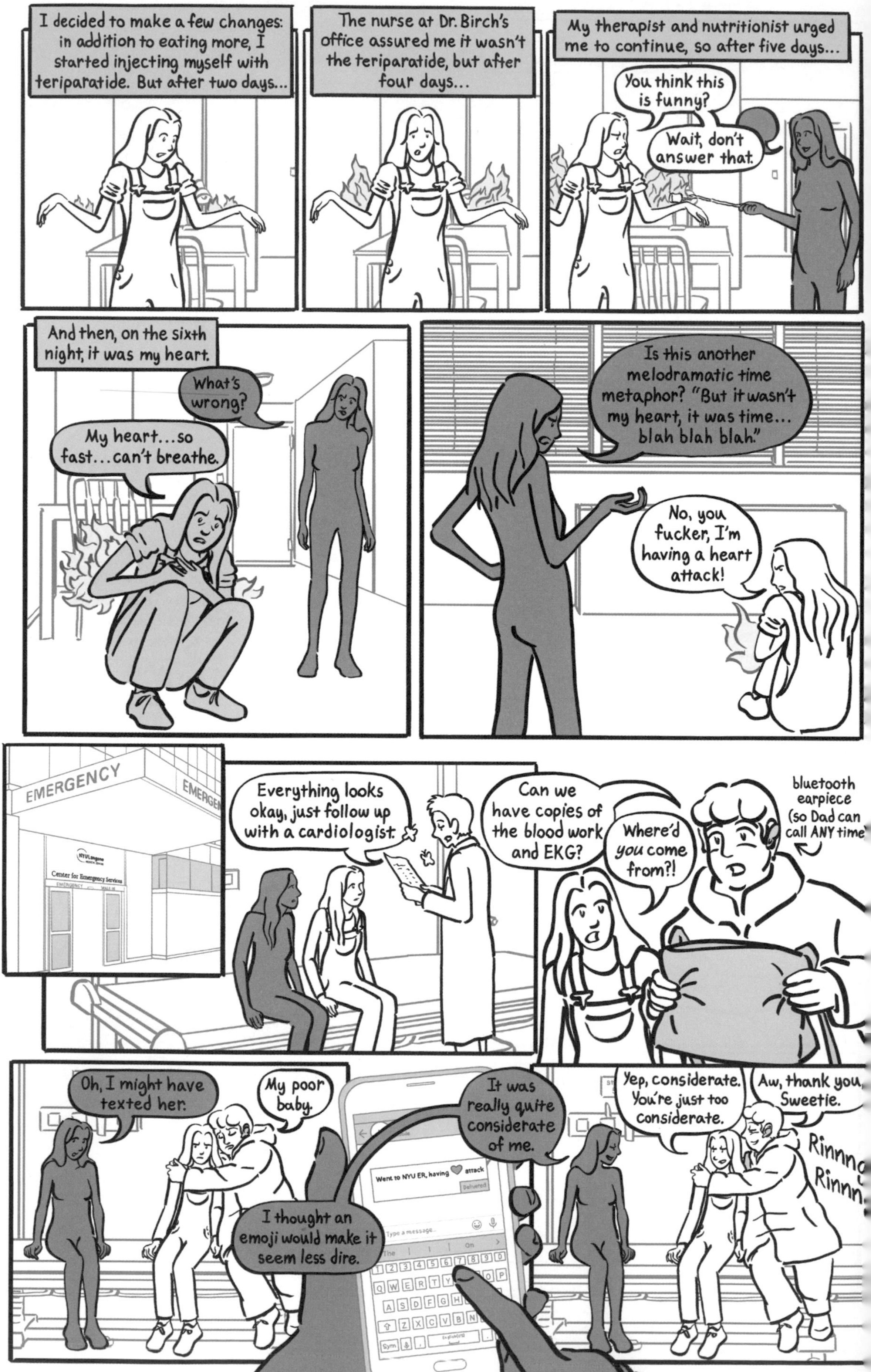
I decided to make a few changes: in addition to eating more, I started injecting myself with teriparatide. But after two days...
The nurse at Dr. Birch's office assured me it wasn't the teriparatide, but after four days...
My therapist and nutritionist urged me to continue, so after five days...
You think this is funny?
Wait, don't answer that.
And then, on the sixth night, it was my heart.
What's wrong?
My heart...so fast...can't breathe.
Is this another melodramatic time metaphor? "But it wasn't my heart, it was time... blah blah blah."
No, you fucker, I'm having a heart attack!
EMERGENCY
EMERGEN
Center for Emergency Services
Everything looks okay, just follow up with a cardiologist.
Can we have copies of the blood work and EKG?
Where'd *you* come from?!
bluetooth earpiece (so Dad can call ANY time)
Oh, I might have texted her.
My poor baby.
It was really quite considerate of me.
Went to NYU ER, having ♥ attack
Delivered
I thought an emoji would make it seem less dire.
Yep, considerate. You're just too considerate.
Aw, thank you, Sweetie.
Rinnng Rinnn

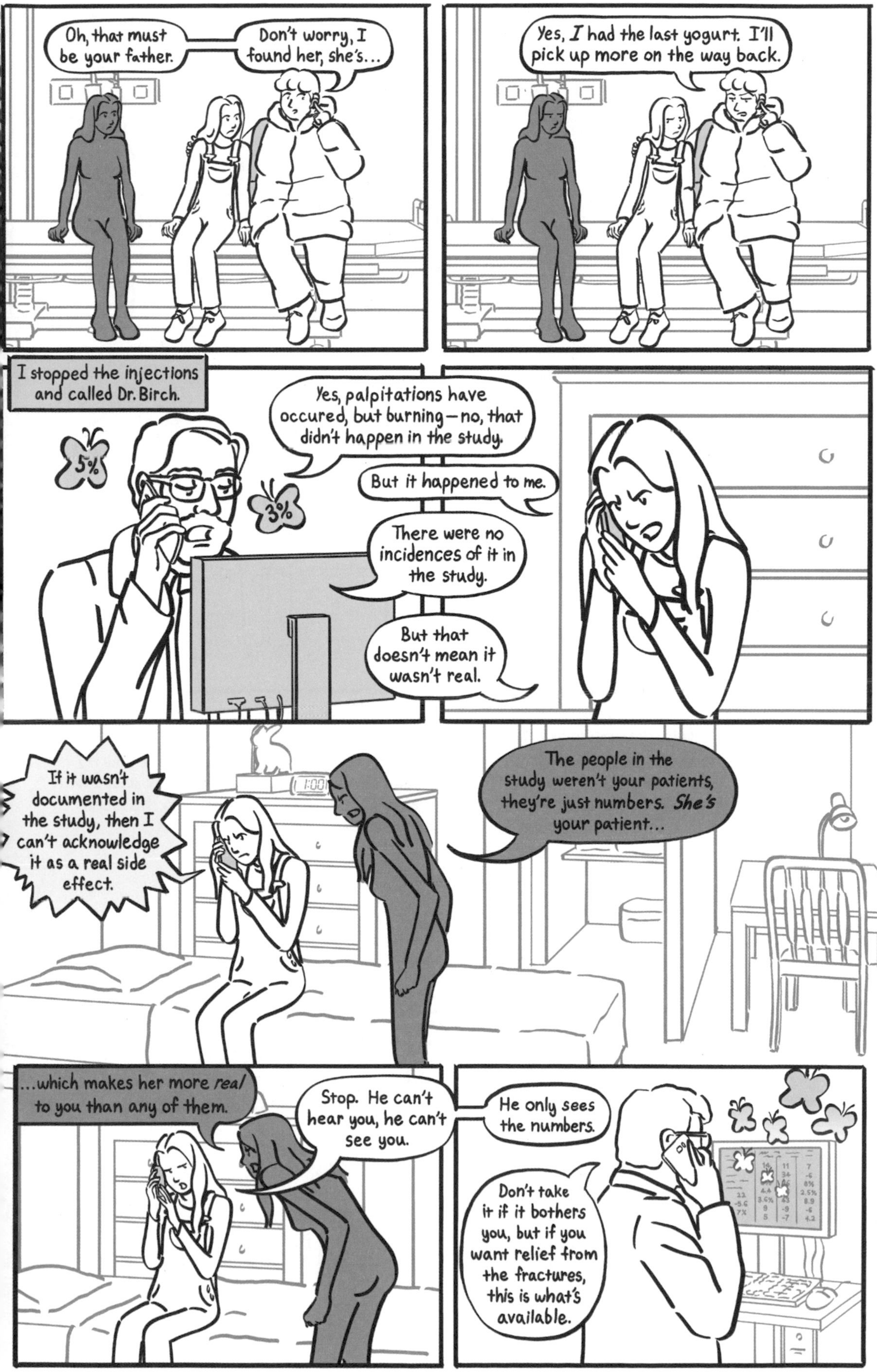
Oh, that must be your father.
Don't worry, I found her, she's...
Yes, *I* had the last yogurt. I'll pick up more on the way back.
I stopped the injections and called Dr. Birch.
5%
3%
Yes, palpitations have occured, but burning—no, that didn't happen in the study.
But it happened to me.
There were no incidences of it in the study.
But that doesn't mean it wasn't real.
If it wasn't documented in the study, then I can't acknowledge it as a real side effect.
The people in the study weren't your patients, they're just numbers. ***She's*** your patient...
...which makes her more *real* to you than any of them.
Stop. He can't hear you, he can't see you.
He only sees the numbers.
Don't take it if it bothers you, but if you want relief from the fractures, this is what's available.

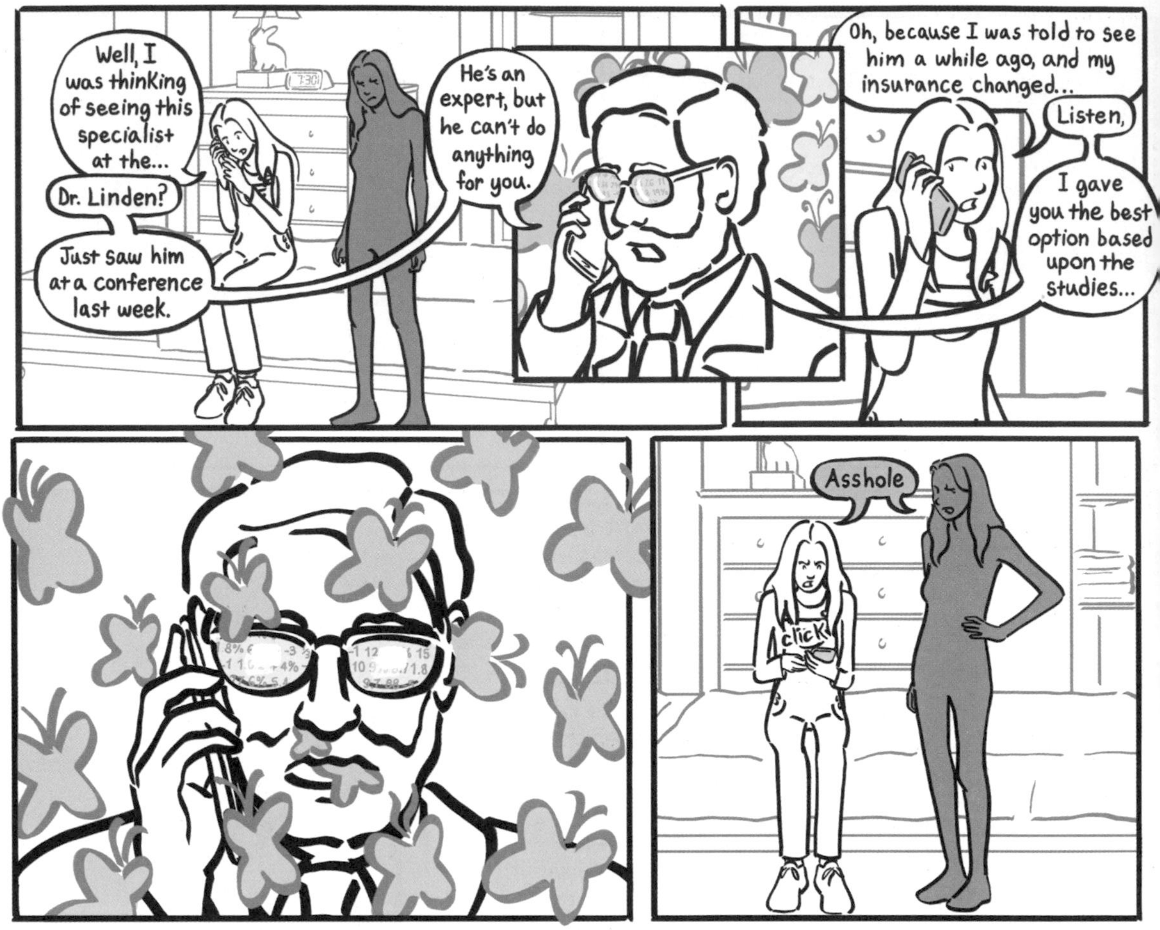
Well, I was thinking of seeing this specialist at the...
Dr. Linden?
Just saw him at a conference last week.
He's an expert, but he can't do anything for you.
Oh, because I was told to see him a while ago, and my insurance changed...
Listen,
I gave you the best option based upon the studies...
Asshole
click

I had gained weight, but my pains only grew: Every time I sat—knives. Every time I took a step—knives. At last, I had become the Little Mermaid. All I wanted was a pair of legs.

The doctors, they must've thought I wanted something else, because they'd all tell me how if I recovered, I could have babies. I guess it isn't just Leah's family—the whole world is obsessed with multiplying. Well, *I* don't want babies, there are already too many stupid people in this world. And when I go out at night, I see them all parading about...

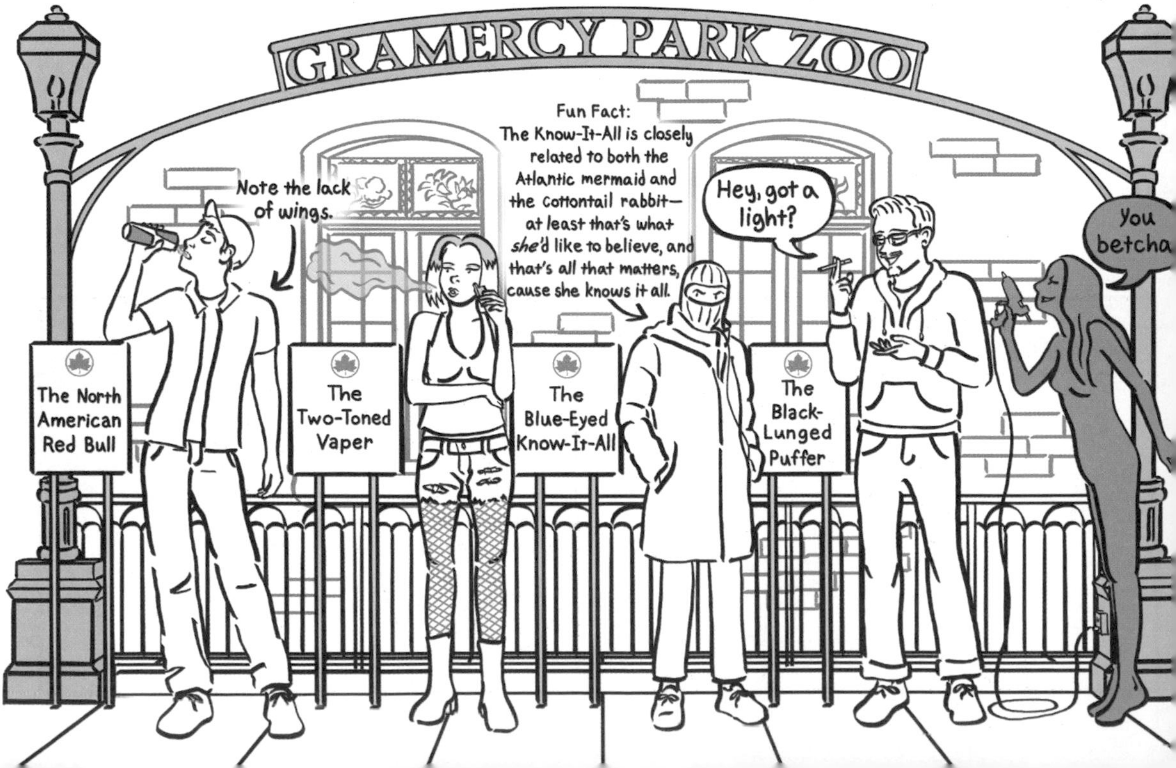
GRAMERCY PARK ZOO
Fun Fact:
The Know-It-All is closely related to both the Atlantic mermaid and the cottontail rabbit—at least that's what *she'd* like to believe, and that's all that matters, cause she knows it all.
Note the lack of wings.
Hey, got a light?
You betcha
The North American Red Bull
The Two-Toned Vaper
The Blue-Eyed Know-It-All
The Black-Lunged Puffer

But it's better than what's become of the daytime world. It's turned into a giant eating disorder unit, where everything is "triggering": words, thoughts, ideas— anything with the potential to upset is taboo. I hate this new world and I hate all its inhabitants. I hate how they all ask "How are you?" and you're supposed to say "Good" even though you're not. I hate how they say "Thank you" for every little thing, so you can't tell when they're actually thankful— though the answer is probably never. I hate how they say "Sorry" for no reason, like when you say "I'm sorry" to someone cause they have a cold. You didn't give them that cold, and you're not sorry, you're not sorry one bit. At least *I'm* not sorry, cause it's just a fucking cold.

And when I go out during the day, I see them all parading about...

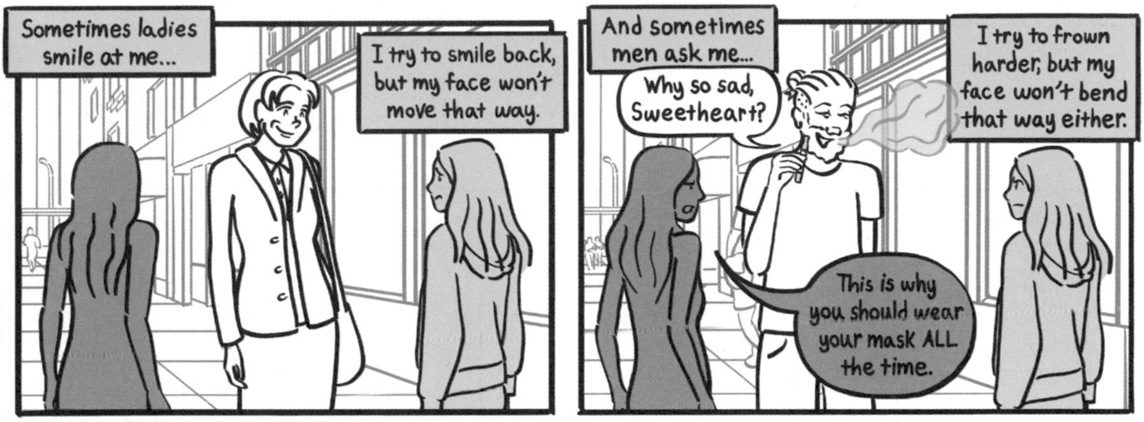
Sometimes ladies smile at me...
I try to smile back, but my face won't move that way.
And sometimes men ask me...
Why so sad, Sweetheart?
I try to frown harder, but my face won't bend that way either.
This is why you should wear your mask ALL the time.

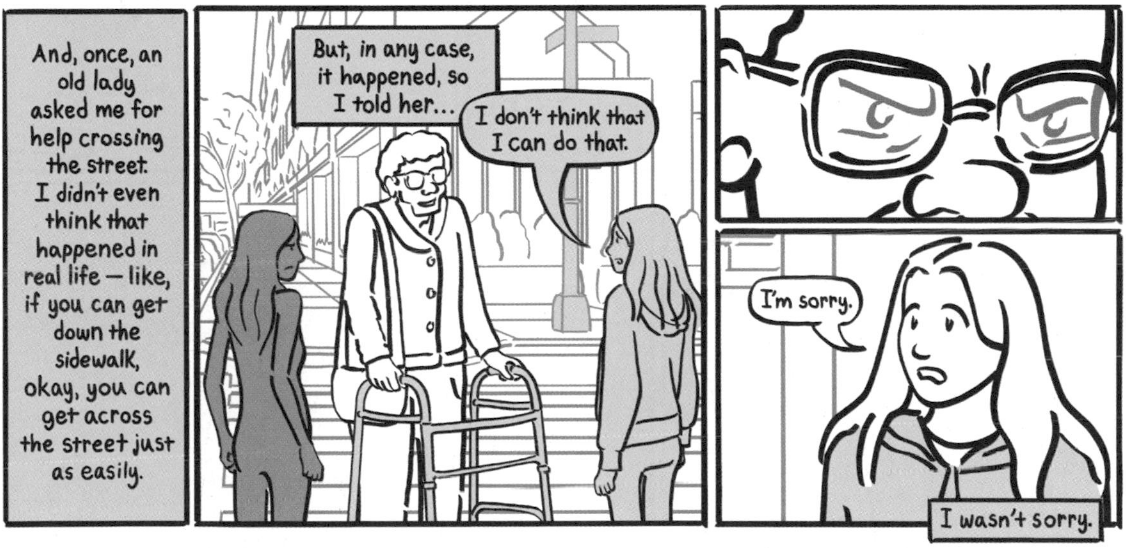
And, once, an old lady asked me for help crossing the street. I didn't even think that happened in real life — like, if you can get down the sidewalk, okay, you can get across the street just as easily.
But, in any case, it happened, so I told her...
I don't think that I can do that.
I'm sorry.
I wasn't sorry.

But I think the people I've come to hate the most are my therapist and nutritionist.

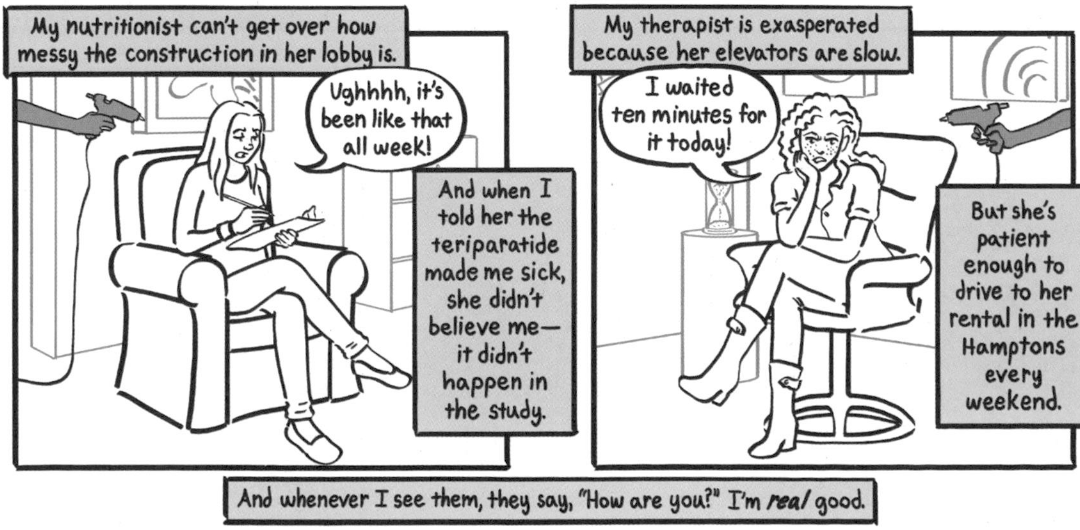
My nutritionist can't get over how messy the construction in her lobby is.
Ughhhh, it's been like that all week!
And when I told her the teriparatide made me sick, she didn't believe me— it didn't happen in the study.
My therapist is exasperated because her elevators are slow.
I waited ten minutes for it today!
But she's patient enough to drive to her rental in the Hamptons every weekend.
And whenever I see them, they say, "How are you?" I'm *real* good.

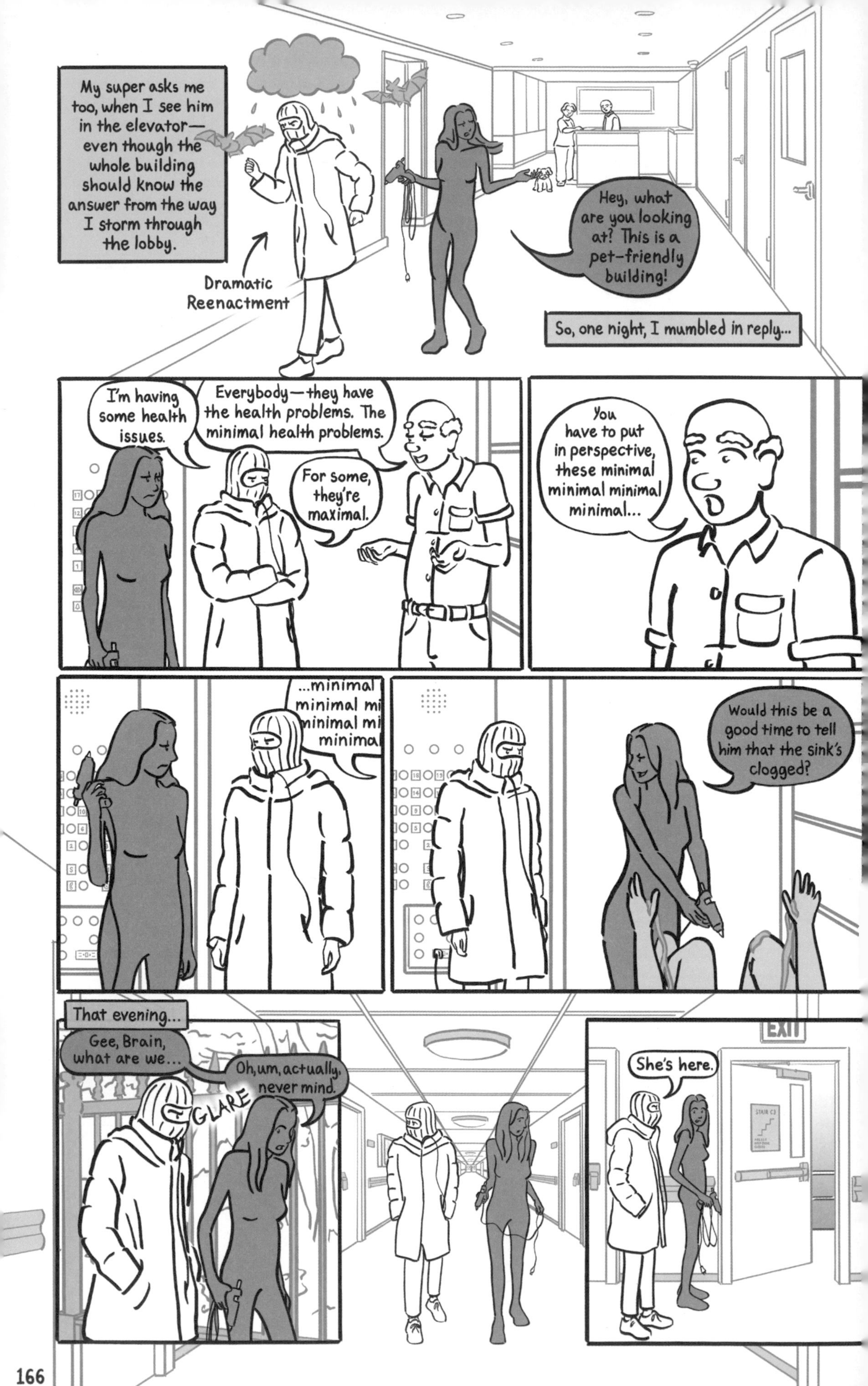
My super asks me too, when I see him in the elevator—even though the whole building should know the answer from the way I storm through the lobby.
Dramatic Reenactment
Hey, what are you looking at? This is a pet-friendly building!
So, one night, I mumbled in reply...
I'm having some health issues.
Everybody—they have the health problems. The minimal health problems.
For some, they're maximal.
You have to put in perspective, these minimal minimal minimal minimal...
...minimal
minimal mi
minimal mi
minimal
Would this be a good time to tell him that the sink's clogged?
That evening...
Gee, Brain, what are we...
GLARE
Oh, um, actually, never mind.
EXIT
She's here.

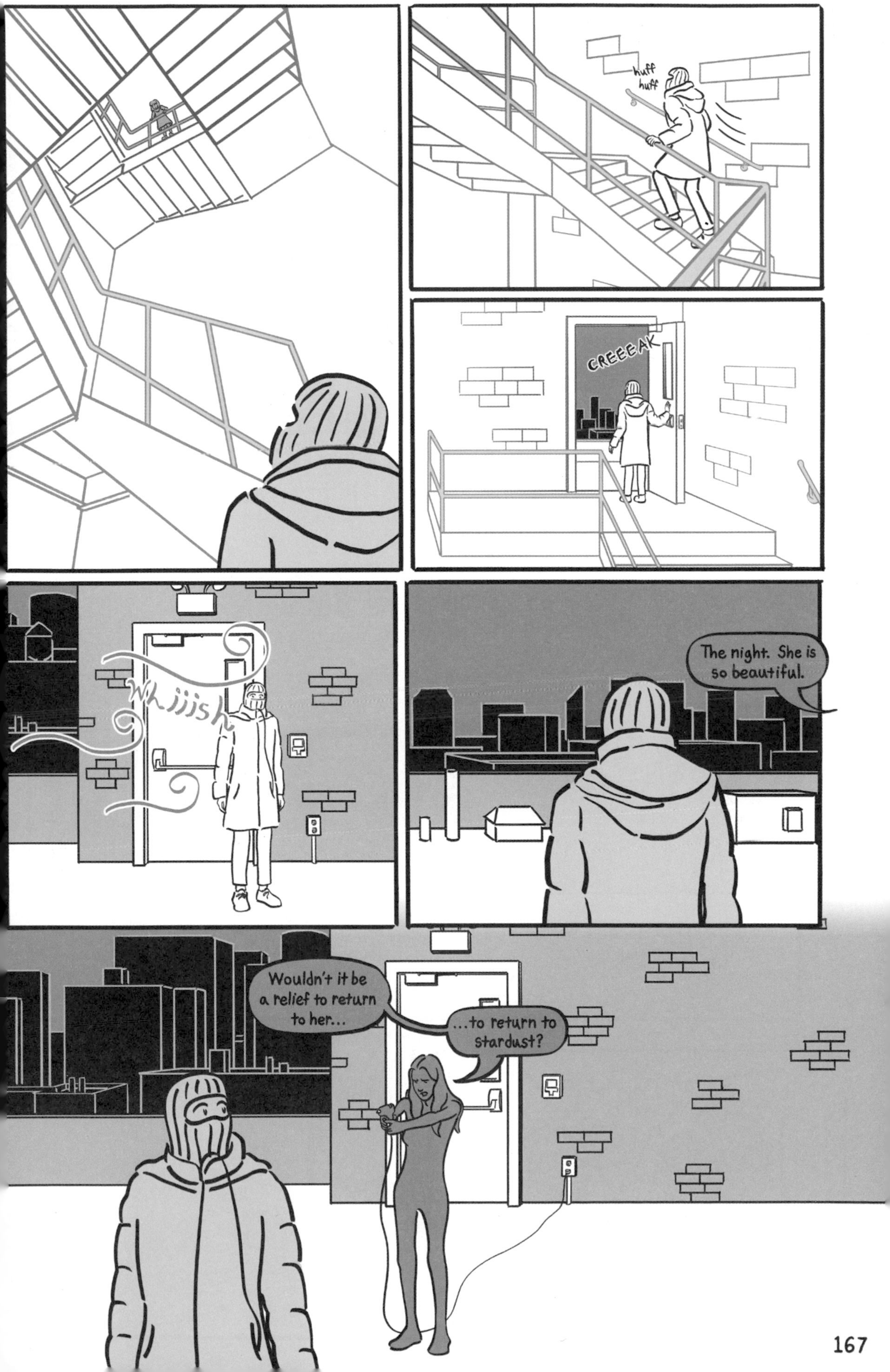
huff huff
CREEEAK
Whiiish
The night. She is so beautiful.
Wouldn't it be a relief to return to her...
...to return to stardust?

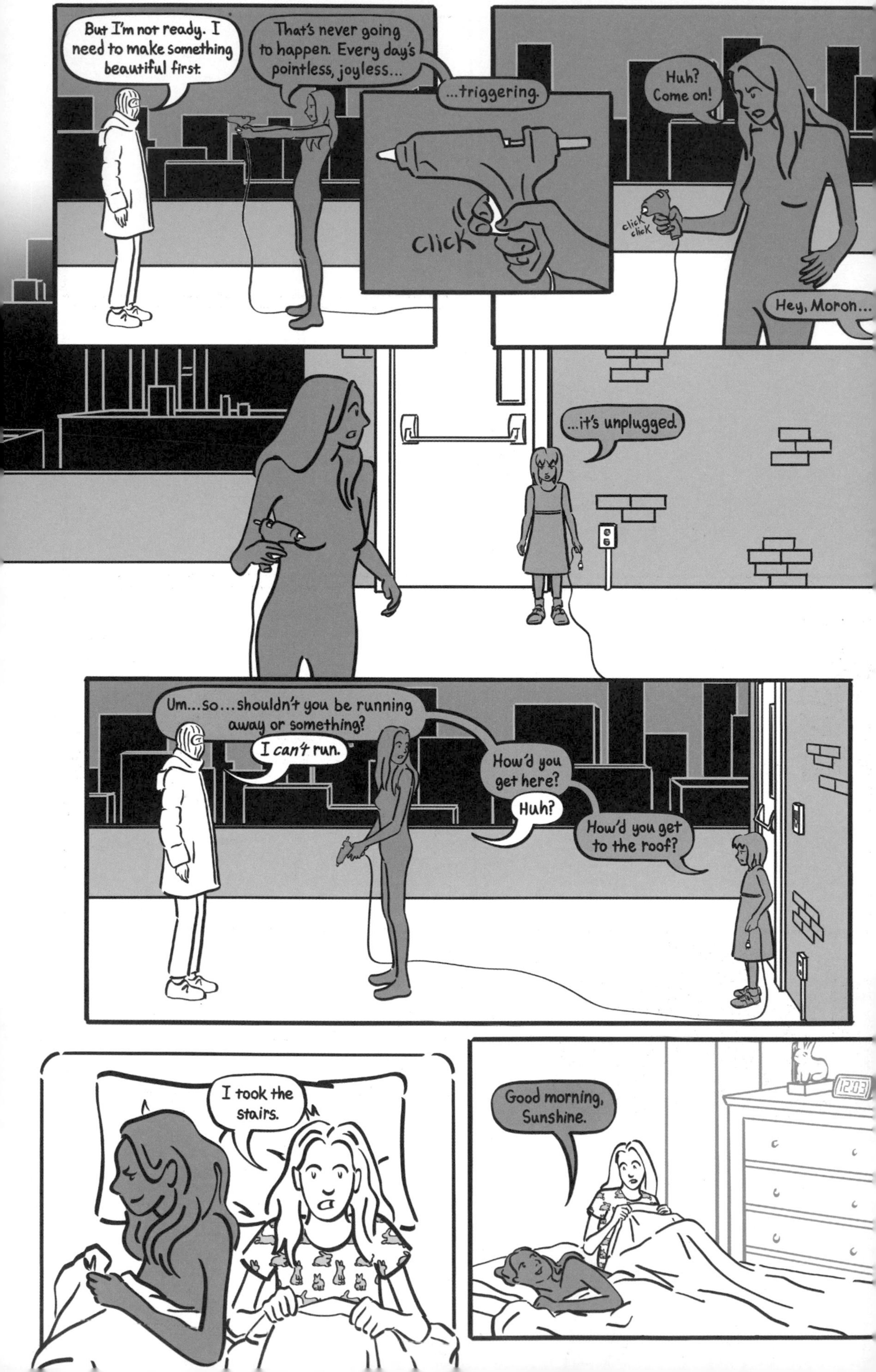
But I'm not ready. I need to make something beautiful first.
That's never going to happen. Every day's pointless, joyless...
...triggering.
Click
Huh? Come on!
click click
Hey, Moron...
...it's unplugged.
Um...so...shouldn't you be running away or something?
I can't run.
How'd you get here?
Huh?
How'd you get to the roof?
I took the stairs.
Good morning, Sunshine.
12:03

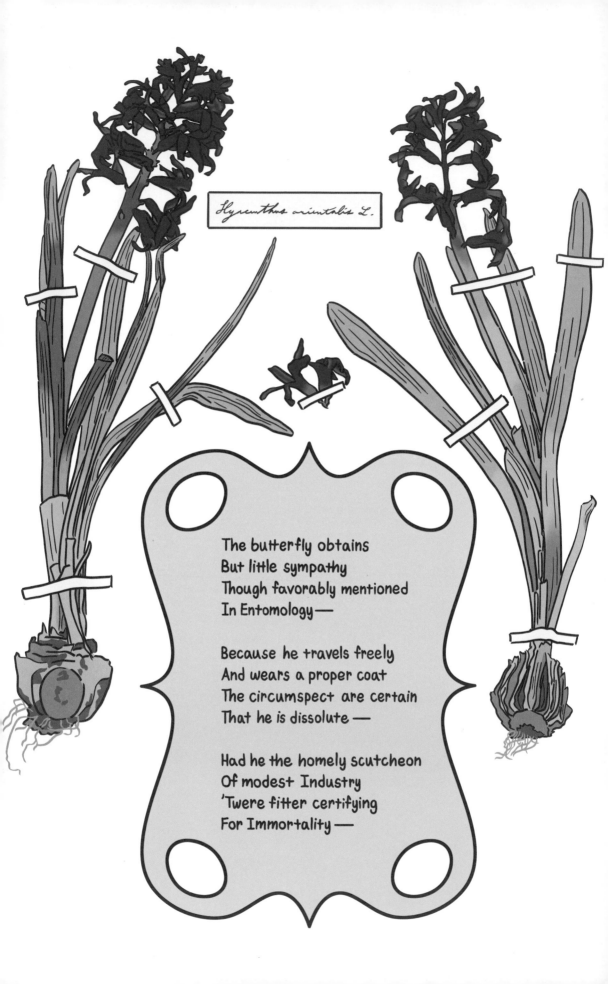

Hyacinthus orientalis L.

The butterfly obtains
But little sympathy
Though favorably mentioned
In Entomology —

Because he travels freely
And wears a proper coat
The circumspect are certain
That he is dissolute —

Had he the homely scutcheon
Of modest Industry
'Twere fitter certifying
For Immortality —

Chapter 9

The Old ~~Woman~~

As soon as my insurance plan switched over, I made an appointment with Dr. Linden. However, I still had to wait quite a while to see him. I didn't have trouble getting an appointment — his office overbooked — but I lost the better part of an afternoon to his waiting room.

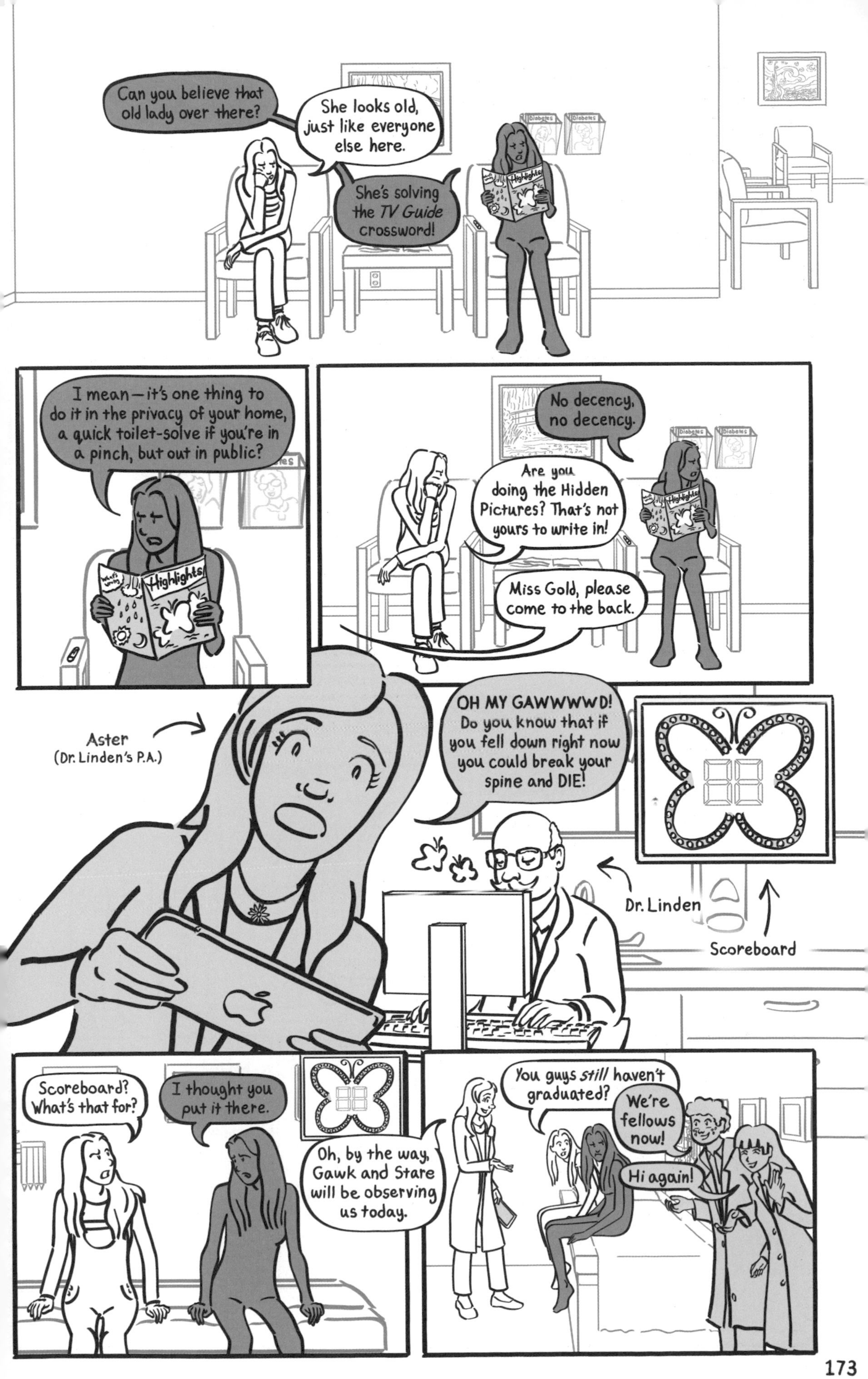

Can you believe that old lady over there?
She looks old, just like everyone else here.
She's solving the *TV Guide* crossword!
I mean—it's one thing to do it in the privacy of your home, a quick toilet-solve if you're in a pinch, but out in public?
No decency, no decency.
Are you doing the Hidden Pictures? That's not yours to write in!
Miss Gold, please come to the back.
Aster (Dr. Linden's P.A.)
OH MY GAWWWWD! Do you know that if you fell down right now you could break your spine and DIE!
Dr. Linden
Scoreboard
Scoreboard? What's that for?
I thought you put it there.
Oh, by the way, Gawk and Stare will be observing us today.
You guys *still* haven't graduated?
We're fellows now!
Hi again!

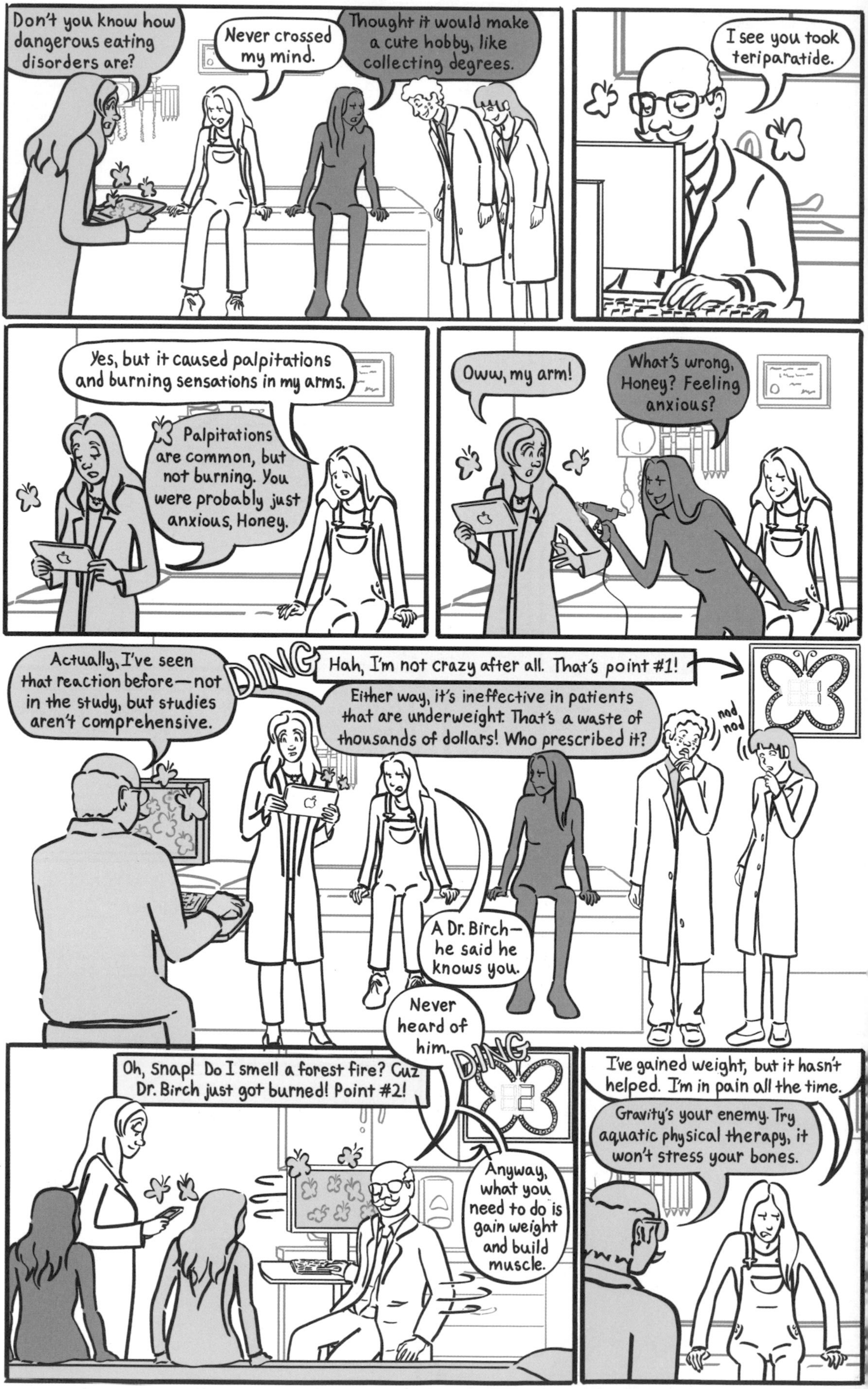
Don't you know how dangerous eating disorders are?
Never crossed my mind.
Thought it would make a cute hobby, like collecting degrees.
I see you took teriparatide.
Yes, but it caused palpitations and burning sensations in my arms.
Palpitations are common, but not burning. You were probably just anxious, Honey.
Oww, my arm!
What's wrong, Honey? Feeling anxious?
Actually, I've seen that reaction before—not in the study, but studies aren't comprehensive.
DING
Hah, I'm not crazy after all. That's point #1!
Either way, it's ineffective in patients that are underweight. That's a waste of thousands of dollars! Who prescribed it?
nod nod
A Dr. Birch—he said he knows you.
Never heard of him.
DING
Oh, snap! Do I smell a forest fire? Cuz Dr. Birch just got burned! Point #2!
Anyway, what you need to do is gain weight and build muscle.
I've gained weight, but it hasn't helped. I'm in pain all the time.
Gravity's your enemy. Try aquatic physical therapy, it won't stress your bones.

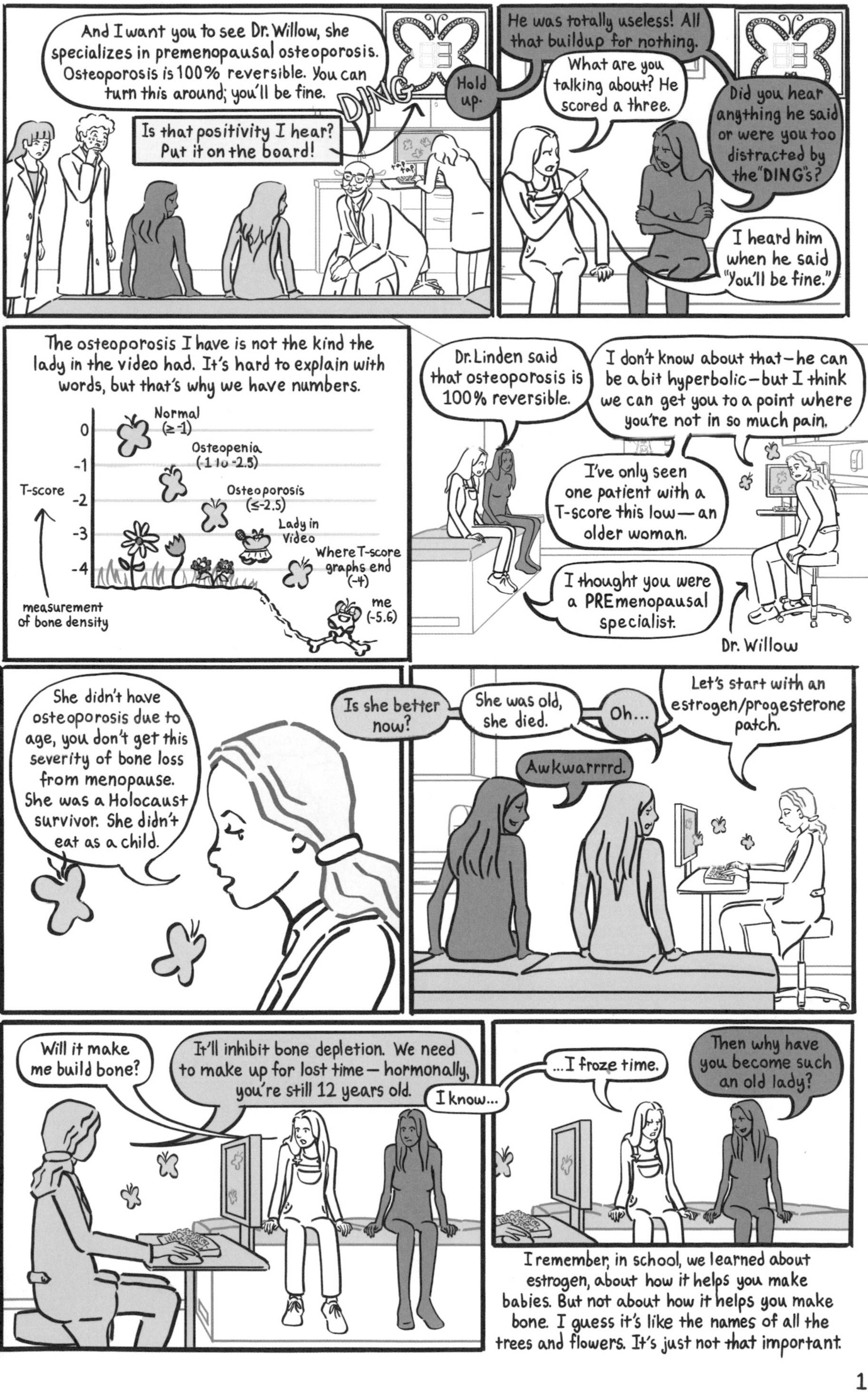
And I want you to see Dr. Willow, she specializes in premenopausal osteoporosis. Osteoporosis is 100% reversible. You can turn this around; you'll be fine.
DING
Is that positivity I hear? Put it on the board!
Hold up.
He was totally useless! All that buildup for nothing.
What are you talking about? He scored a three.
Did you hear anything he said or were you too distracted by the "DING"s?
I heard him when he said "You'll be fine."
The osteoporosis I have is not the kind the lady in the video had. It's hard to explain with words, but that's why we have numbers.
T-score
measurement of bone density
0
-1
-2
-3
-4
Normal (≥-1)
Osteopenia (-1 to -2.5)
Osteoporosis (≤-2.5)
Lady in video
Where T-score graphs end (-4)
me (-5.6)
Dr. Linden said that osteoporosis is 100% reversible.
I don't know about that—he can be a bit hyperbolic—but I think we can get you to a point where you're not in so much pain.
I've only seen one patient with a T-score this low—an older woman.
I thought you were a PREmenopausal specialist.
Dr. Willow
She didn't have osteoporosis due to age, you don't get this severity of bone loss from menopause. She was a Holocaust survivor. She didn't eat as a child.
Is she better now?
She was old, she died.
Oh...
Let's start with an estrogen/progesterone patch.
Awkwarrrrd.
Will it make me build bone?
It'll inhibit bone depletion. We need to make up for lost time—hormonally, you're still 12 years old.
I know...
...I froze time.
Then why have you become such an old lady?
I remember, in school, we learned about estrogen, about how it helps you make babies. But not about how it helps you make bone. I guess it's like the names of all the trees and flowers. It's just not that important.

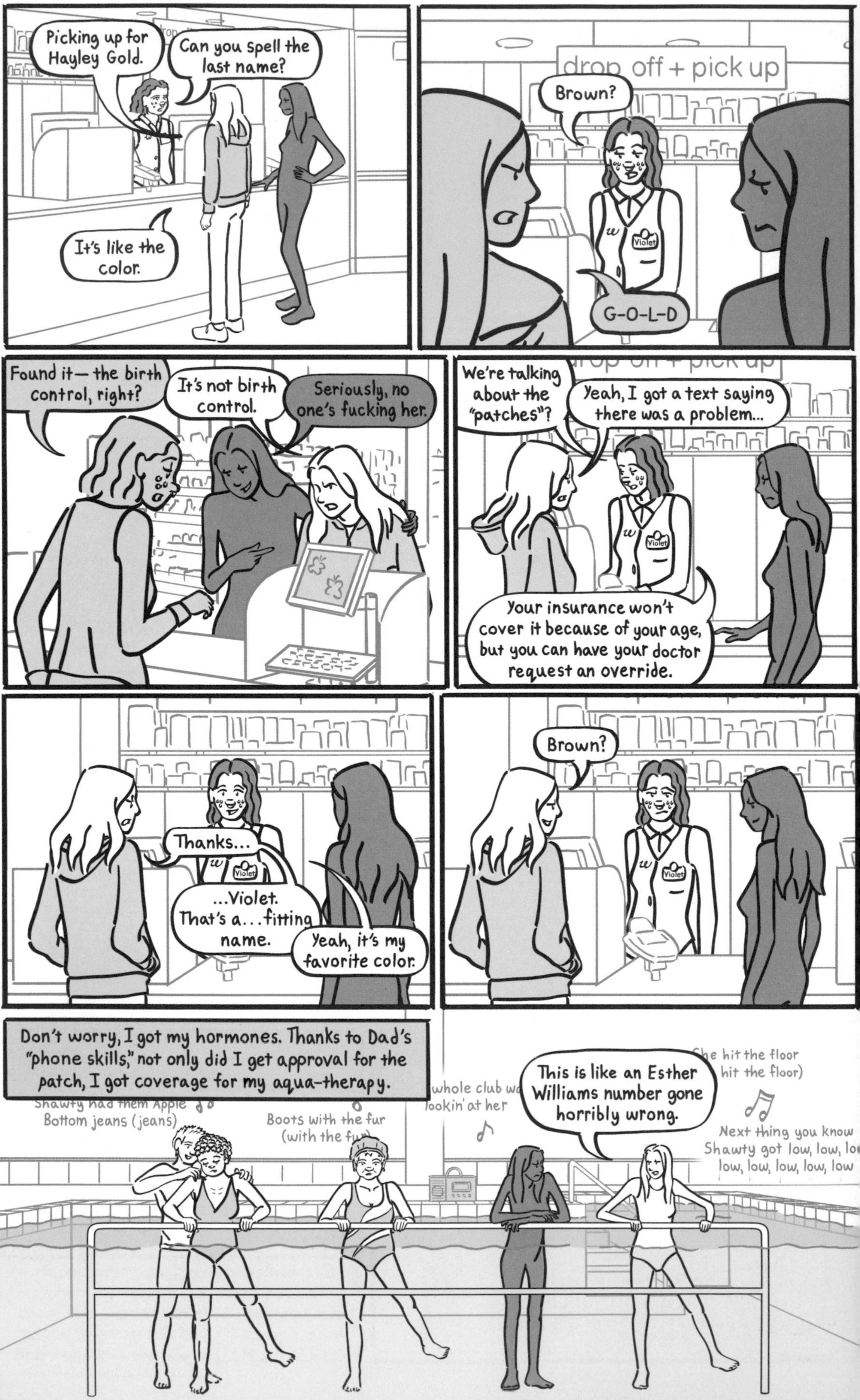
Picking up for Hayley Gold.
Can you spell the last name?
It's like the color.
drop off + pick up
Brown?
G-O-L-D
Violet
Found it— the birth control, right?
It's not birth control.
Seriously, no one's fucking her.
We're talking about the "patches"?
Yeah, I got a text saying there was a problem...
Your insurance won't cover it because of your age, but you can have your doctor request an override.
Thanks...
...Violet. That's a...fitting name.
Yeah, it's my favorite color.
Brown?
Don't worry, I got my hormones. Thanks to Dad's "phone skills," not only did I get approval for the patch, I got coverage for my aqua-therapy.
Bottom jeans (jeans)
Boots with the fur
lookin' at her
This is like an Esther Williams number gone horribly wrong.
hit the floor)
Next thing you know
low, low, low, low, low

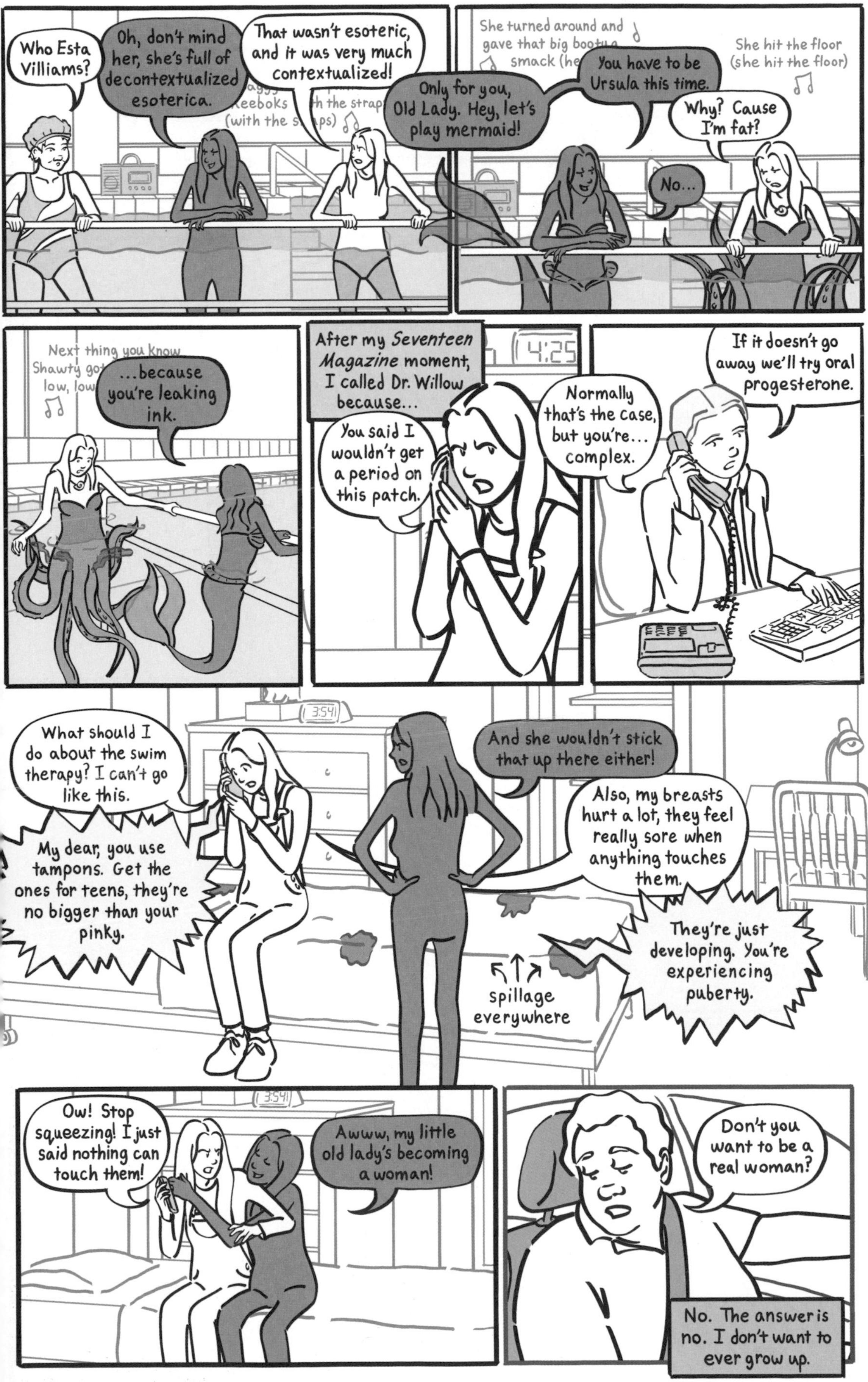

Who Esta Villiams?
Oh, don't mind her, she's full of decontextualized esoterica.
That wasn't esoteric, and it was very much contextualized!
Only for you, Old Lady. Hey, let's play mermaid!
She turned around and gave that big booty a
She hit the floor (she hit the floor)
You have to be Ursula this time.
Why? Cause I'm fat?
No...
Next thing you know
...because you're leaking ink.
After my *Seventeen Magazine* moment, I called Dr. Willow because...
You said I wouldn't get a period on this patch.
Normally that's the case, but you're... complex.
If it doesn't go away we'll try oral progesterone.
What should I do about the swim therapy? I can't go like this.
My dear, you use tampons. Get the ones for teens, they're no bigger than your pinky.
And she wouldn't stick that up there either!
Also, my breasts hurt a lot, they feel really sore when anything touches them.
They're just developing. You're experiencing puberty.
spillage everywhere
Ow! Stop squeezing! I just said nothing can touch them!
Awww, my little old lady's becoming a woman!
Don't you want to be a real woman?
No. The answer is no. I don't want to ever grow up.

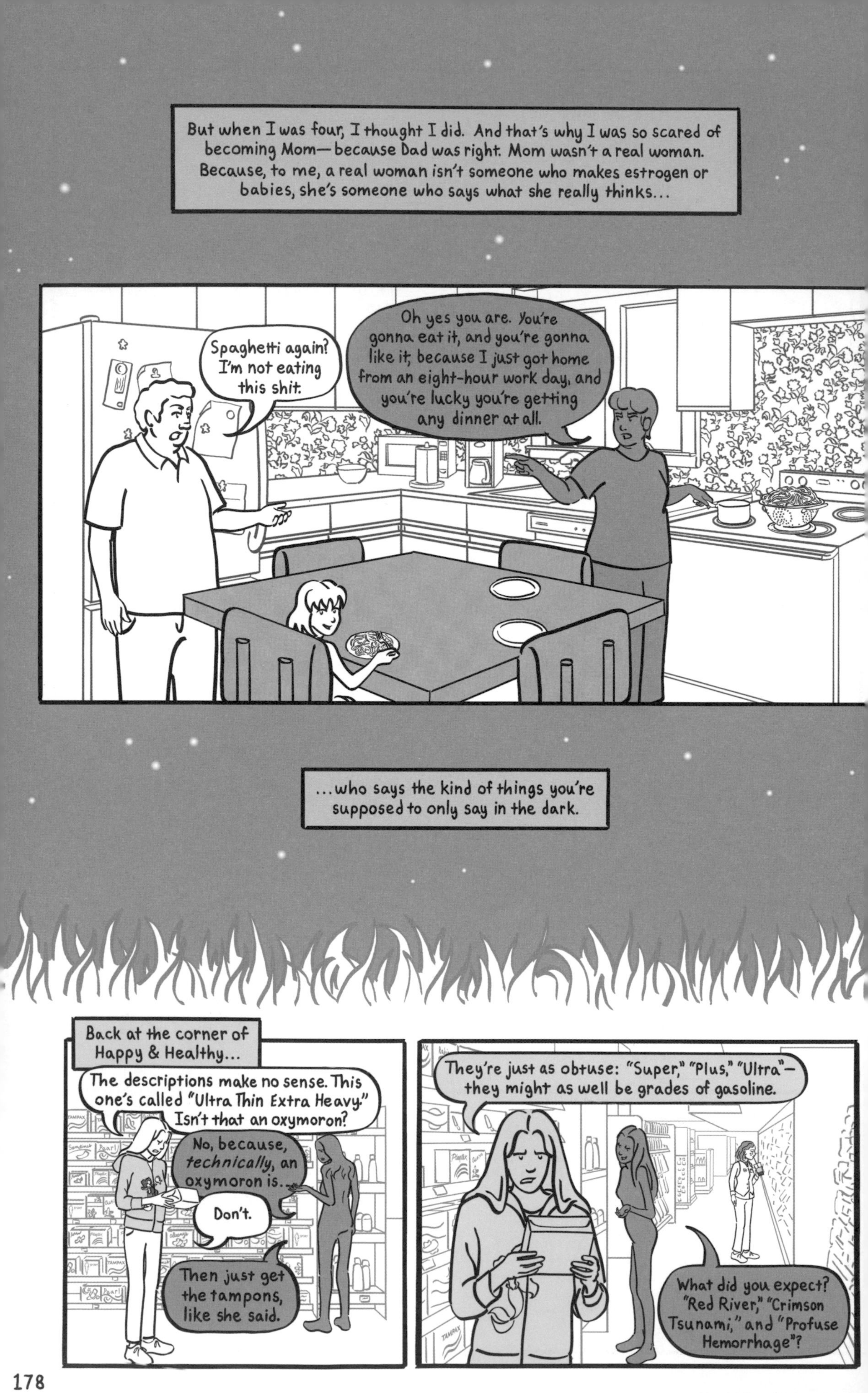

But when I was four, I thought I did. And that's why I was so scared of becoming Mom—because Dad was right. Mom wasn't a real woman. Because, to me, a real woman isn't someone who makes estrogen or babies, she's someone who says what she really thinks...
Spaghetti again? I'm not eating this shit.
Oh yes you are. You're gonna eat it, and you're gonna like it, because I just got home from an eight-hour work day, and you're lucky you're getting any dinner at all.
...who says the kind of things you're supposed to only say in the dark.
Back at the corner of Happy & Healthy...
The descriptions make no sense. This one's called "Ultra Thin Extra Heavy." Isn't that an oxymoron?
No, because, *technically*, an oxymoron is...
Don't.
Then just get the tampons, like she said.
They're just as obtuse: "Super," "Plus," "Ultra"—they might as well be grades of gasoline.
What did you expect? "Red River," "Crimson Tsunami," and "Profuse Hemorrhage"?

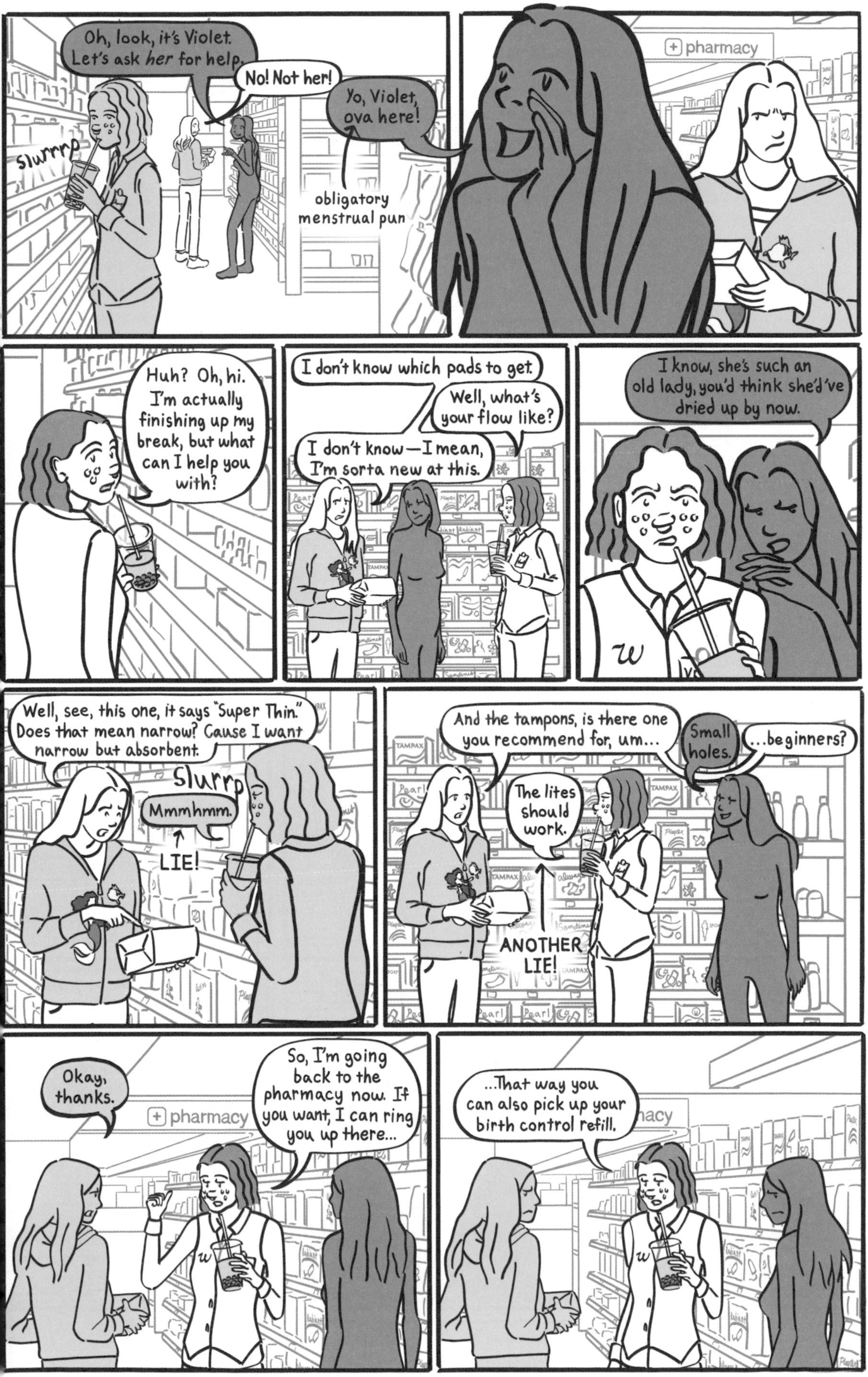
Oh, look, it's Violet. Let's ask *her* for help.
No! Not her!
Yo, Violet, ova here!
obligatory menstrual pun
Slurrrp
+ pharmacy
Huh? Oh, hi. I'm actually finishing up my break, but what can I help you with?
I don't know which pads to get.
Well, what's your flow like?
I don't know—I mean, I'm sorta new at this.
I know, she's such an old lady, you'd think she'd've dried up by now.
Well, see, this one, it says "Super Thin." Does that mean narrow? Cause I want narrow but absorbent.
Slurrp
Mmmhmm.
LIE!
And the tampons, is there one you recommend for, um...
Small holes.
...beginners?
The lites should work.
ANOTHER LIE!
Okay, thanks.
So, I'm going back to the pharmacy now. If you want, I can ring you up there...
+ pharmacy
...That way you can also pick up your birth control refill.

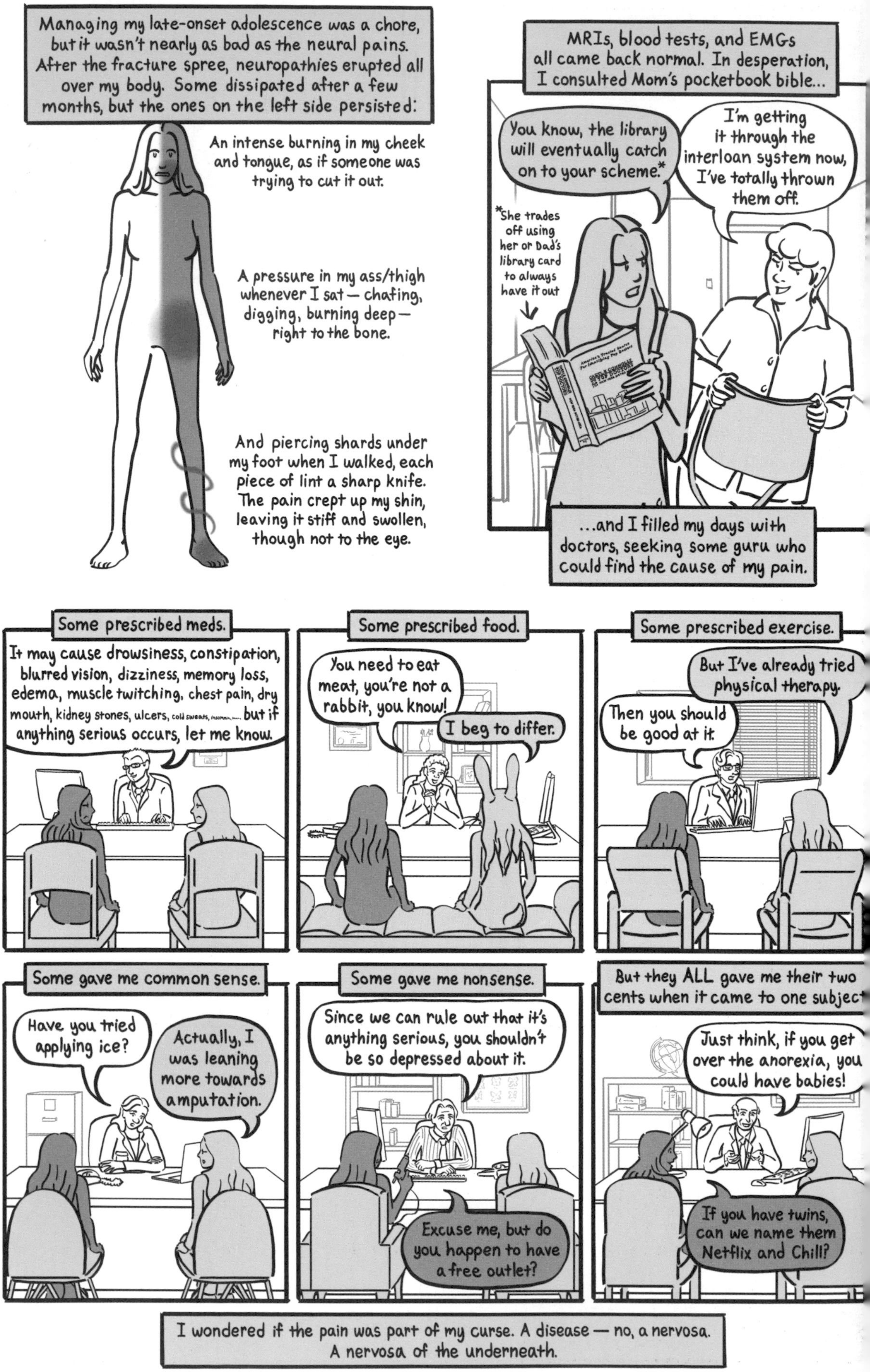
Managing my late-onset adolescence was a chore, but it wasn't nearly as bad as the neural pains. After the fracture spree, neuropathies erupted all over my body. Some dissipated after a few months, but the ones on the left side persisted:
An intense burning in my cheek and tongue, as if someone was trying to cut it out.
A pressure in my ass/thigh whenever I sat — chafing, digging, burning deep — right to the bone.
And piercing shards under my foot when I walked, each piece of lint a sharp knife. The pain crept up my shin, leaving it stiff and swollen, though not to the eye.
MRIs, blood tests, and EMGs all came back normal. In desperation, I consulted Mom's pocketbook bible...
You know, the library will eventually catch on to your scheme.*
I'm getting it through the interloan system now, I've totally thrown them off.
*She trades off using her or Dad's library card to always have it out
...and I filled my days with doctors, seeking some guru who could find the cause of my pain.
Some prescribed meds.
It may cause drowsiness, constipation, blurred vision, dizziness, memory loss, edema, muscle twitching, chest pain, dry mouth, kidney stones, ulcers, cold sweats, insomnia, but if anything serious occurs, let me know.
Some prescribed food.
You need to eat meat, you're not a rabbit, you know!
I beg to differ.
Some prescribed exercise.
But I've already tried physical therapy.
Then you should be good at it.
Some gave me common sense.
Have you tried applying ice?
Actually, I was leaning more towards amputation.
Some gave me nonsense.
Since we can rule out that it's anything serious, you shouldn't be so depressed about it.
Excuse me, but do you happen to have a free outlet?
But they ALL gave me their two cents when it came to one subject
Just think, if you get over the anorexia, you could have babies!
If you have twins, can we name them Netflix and Chill?
I wondered if the pain was part of my curse. A disease — no, a nervosa. A nervosa of the underneath.

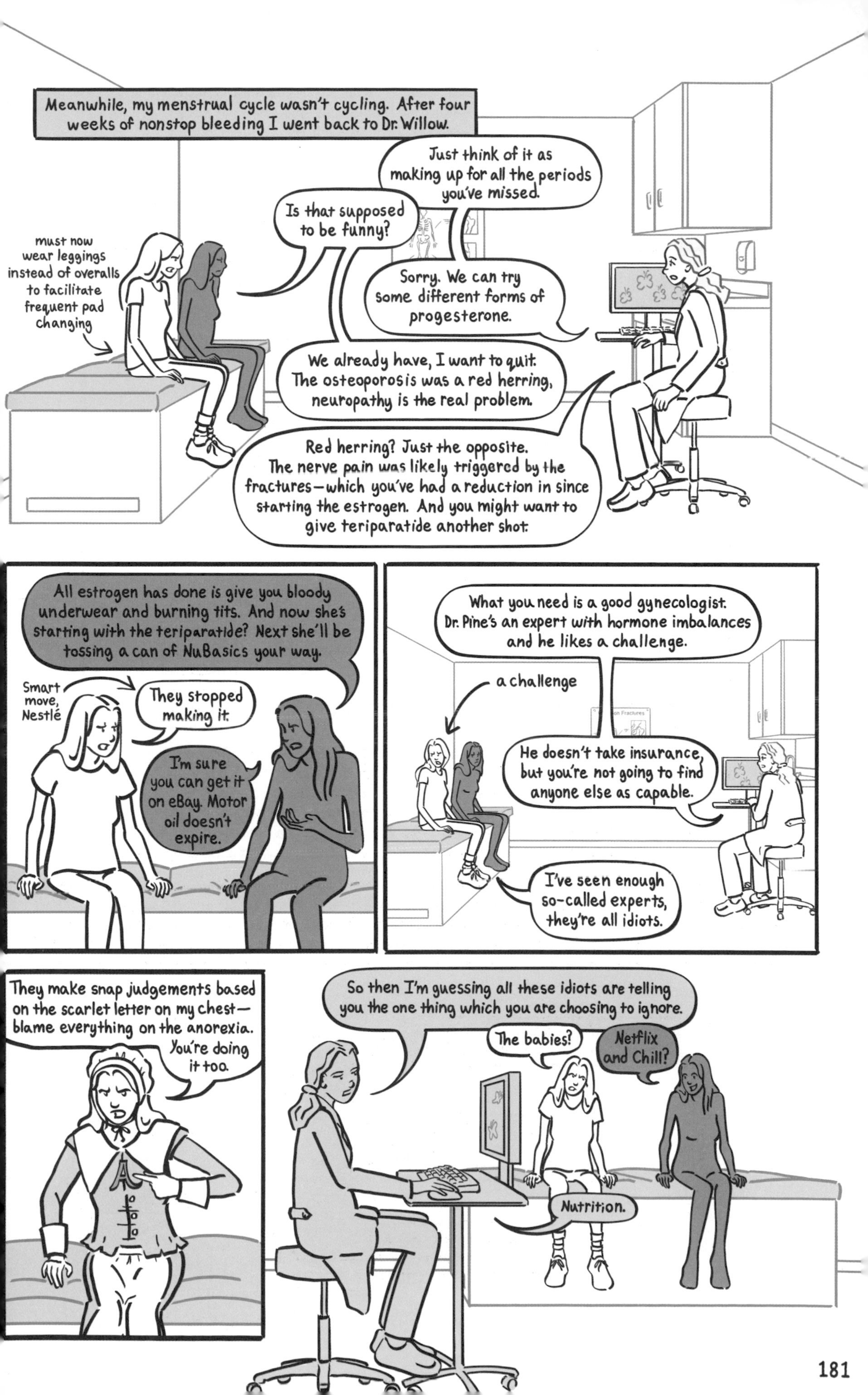
Meanwhile, my menstrual cycle wasn't cycling. After four weeks of nonstop bleeding I went back to Dr. Willow.
must now wear leggings instead of overalls to facilitate frequent pad changing
Just think of it as making up for all the periods you've missed.
Is that supposed to be funny?
Sorry. We can try some different forms of progesterone.
We already have, I want to quit. The osteoporosis was a red herring, neuropathy is the real problem.
Red herring? Just the opposite. The nerve pain was likely triggered by the fractures—which you've had a reduction in since starting the estrogen. And you might want to give teriparatide another shot.
All estrogen has done is give you bloody underwear and burning tits. And now she's starting with the teriparatide? Next she'll be tossing a can of NuBasics your way.
Smart move, Nestlé
They stopped making it.
I'm sure you can get it on eBay. Motor oil doesn't expire.
What you need is a good gynecologist. Dr. Pine's an expert with hormone imbalances and he likes a challenge.
a challenge
He doesn't take insurance, but you're not going to find anyone else as capable.
I've seen enough so-called experts, they're all idiots.
They make snap judgements based on the scarlet letter on my chest—blame everything on the anorexia. You're doing it too.
So then I'm guessing all these idiots are telling you the one thing which you are choosing to ignore.
The babies?
Netflix and Chill?
Nutrition.

They were always trying to scare us at the hospital, telling us we'd get dry skin, brittle nails, thinning hair. Stupid doctors. Anorexics don't care about their outsides. They only see the underneath.

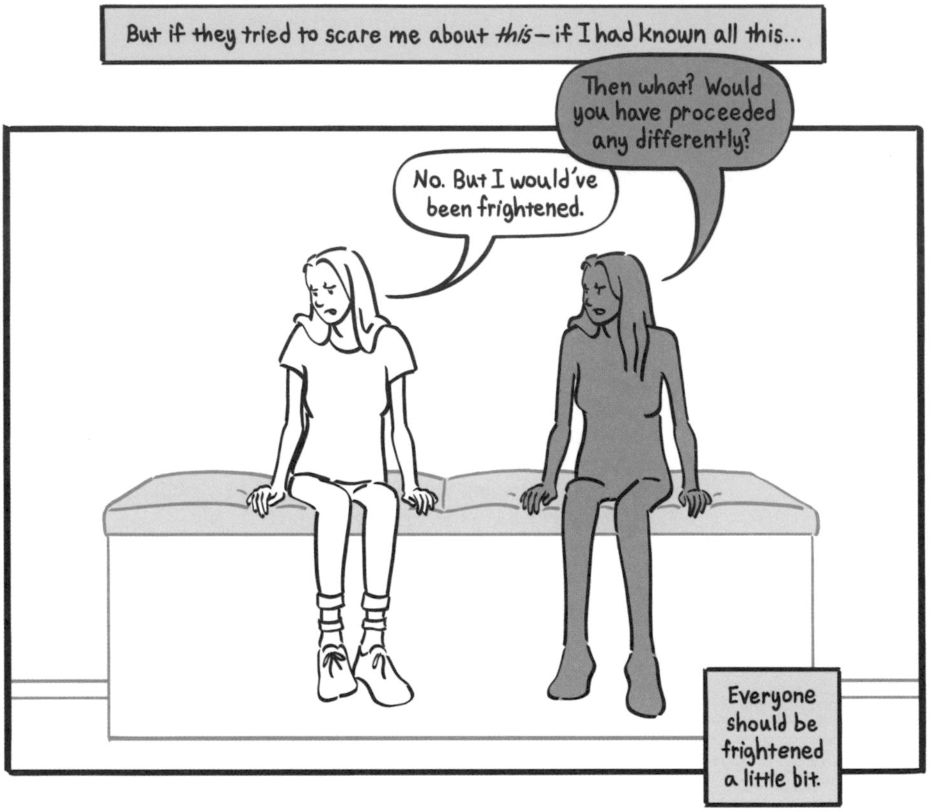

But if they tried to scare me about *this*—if I had known all this...
Then what? Would you have proceeded any differently?
No. But I would've been frightened.
Everyone should be frightened a little bit.

But fear works in strange ways: Mom told me that right before I left the hospital, Dr. Alder said to her, "If Hayley puts her body through this again, she's not going to make it." He never said it to me, because Dr. Alder wasn't actually stupid. He knew that telling me would be useless. The only way to convert an anorexic is by convincing them that there is greater happiness on the other side. But you can't see the other side until you've crossed into it. And, just like you, Stupid Reader, I only trust in what I can see.

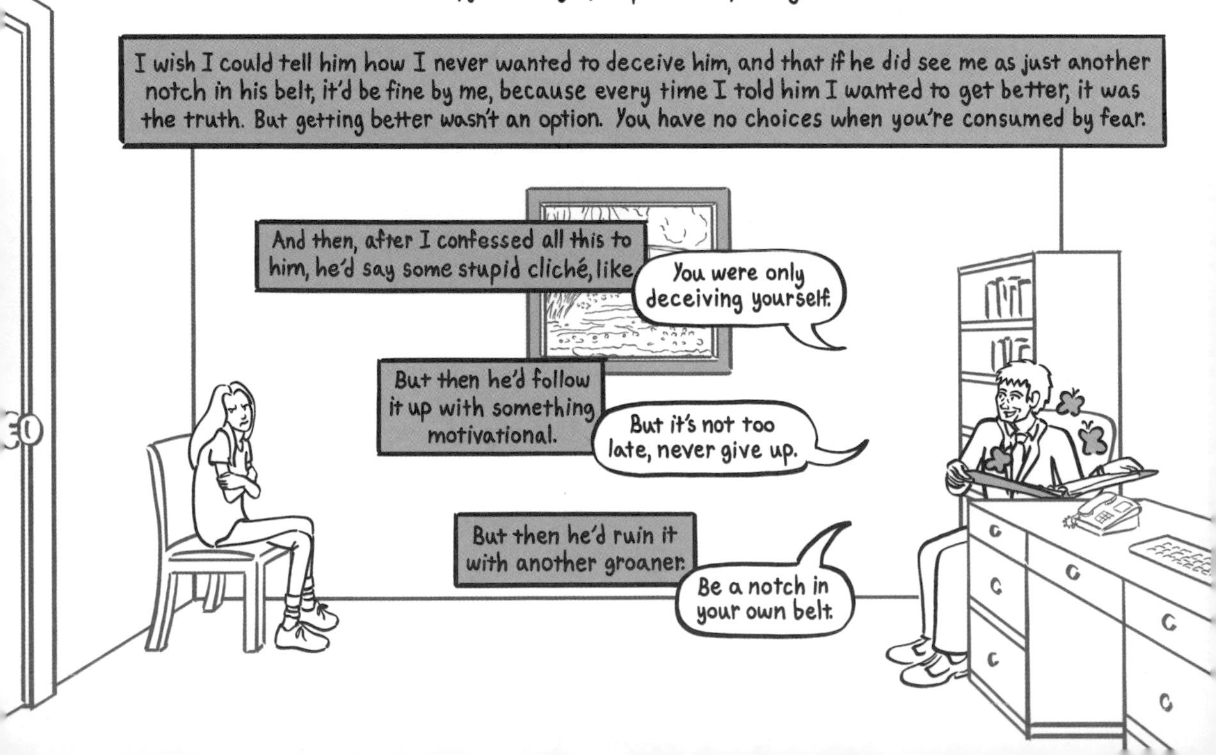

I wish I could tell him how I never wanted to deceive him, and that if he did see me as just another notch in his belt, it'd be fine by me, because every time I told him I wanted to get better, it was the truth. But getting better wasn't an option. You have no choices when you're consumed by fear.
And then, after I confessed all this to him, he'd say some stupid cliché, like
You were only deceiving yourself.
But then he'd follow it up with something motivational.
But it's not too late, never give up.
But then he'd ruin it with another groaner.
Be a notch in your own belt.

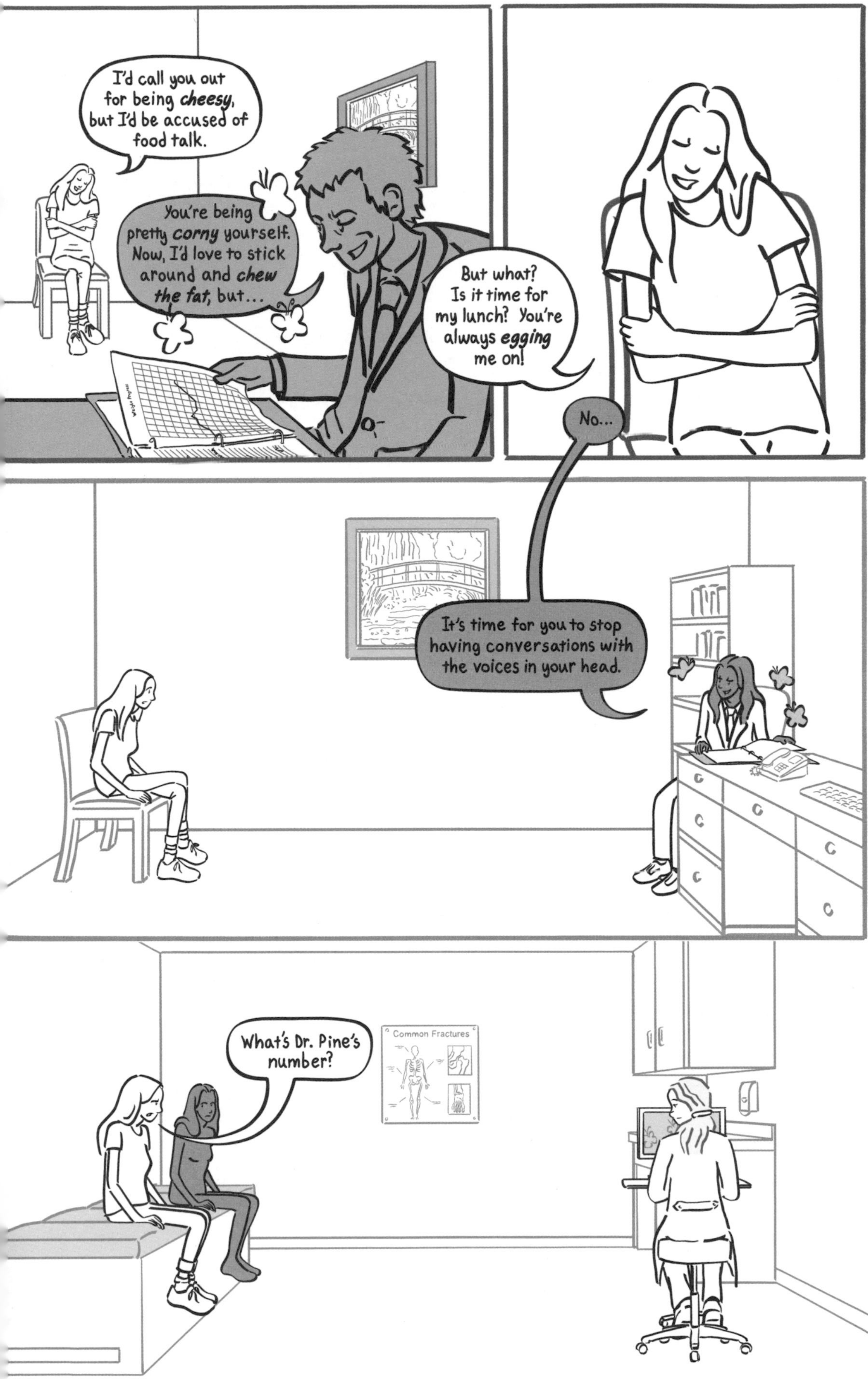
I'd call you out for being *cheesy*, but I'd be accused of food talk.
You're being pretty *corny* yourself. Now, I'd love to stick around and *chew the fat*, but...
But what? Is it time for my lunch? You're always *egging* me on!
No...
It's time for you to stop having conversations with the voices in your head.
What's Dr. Pine's number?
Common Fractures

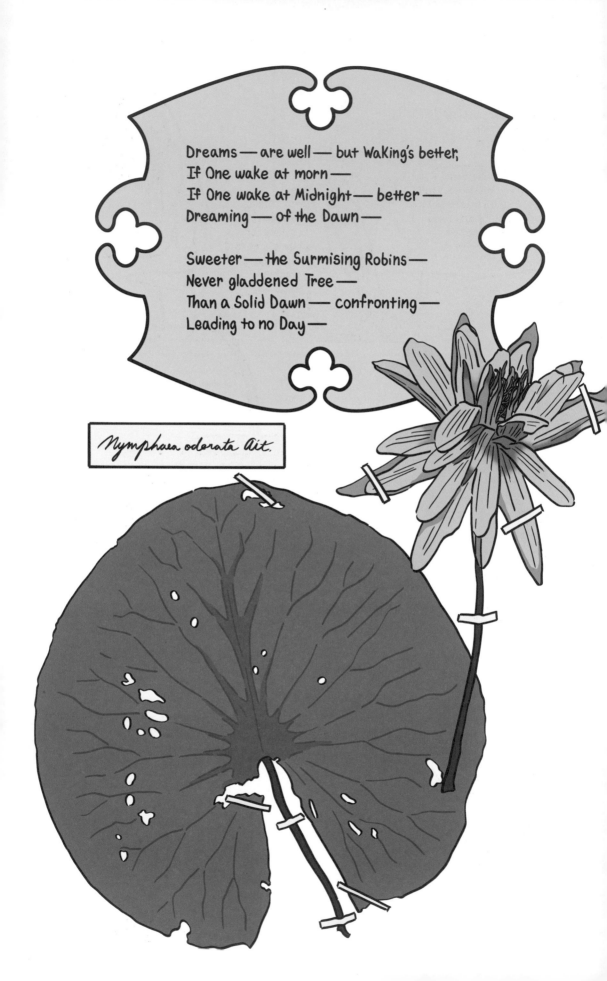

Dreams — are well — but Waking's better,
If One wake at morn —
If One wake at Midnight — better —
Dreaming — of the Dawn —

Sweeter — the Surmising Robins —
Never gladdened Tree —
Than a Solid Dawn — confronting —
Leading to no Day —

Nymphaea oderata Ait.

Chapter 10

Siren's Calling

Eventually I stopped seeking out doctors and
accepted that the nerve pain was never going to end.
All I had left to live for were the puzzles. I didn't need
Mom anymore. As long as I had the puzzles I could get
through my meals. They were all I could focus on—
all I wanted to focus on. Everything else was cloudy.
Like the world had been submerged in a deep fog
and every scene existed somewhere between dream
and reality. I'd sleep so much that I'd forget which was
which, as there was more life in my dreams than there
was in my waking. And, even when my dreams were
nightmares, as long as I was asleep,
I couldn't feel the pain.

Sometimes I dreamt about my classmates from high school. I'm sure I didn't exist in their heads anymore, but they were very much alive in mine. Sometimes I dreamt about the hospital. The doctors would come and find me and imprison me once again.

And sometimes the two dreams would blur together.

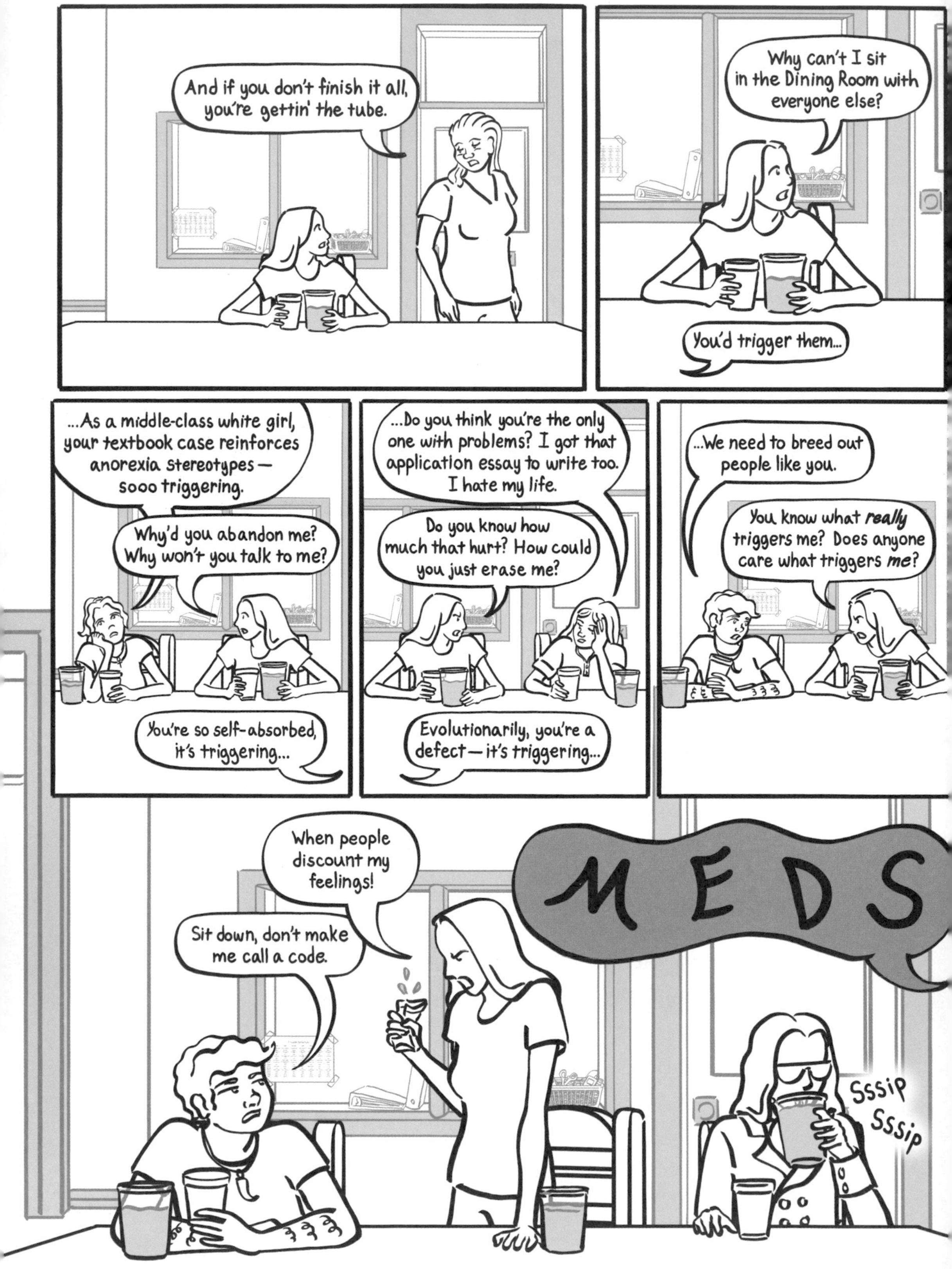
And if you don't finish it all, you're gettin' the tube.
Why can't I sit in the Dining Room with everyone else?
You'd trigger them...
...As a middle-class white girl, your textbook case reinforces anorexia stereotypes— sooo triggering.
Why'd you abandon me? Why won't you talk to me?
You're so self-absorbed, it's triggering...
...Do you think you're the only one with problems? I got that application essay to write too. I hate my life.
Do you know how much that hurt? How could you just erase me?
Evolutionarily, you're a defect—it's triggering...
...We need to breed out people like you.
You know what *really* triggers me? Does anyone care what triggers *me*?
When people discount my feelings!
Sit down, don't make me call a code.
MEDS
Sssip
Sssip

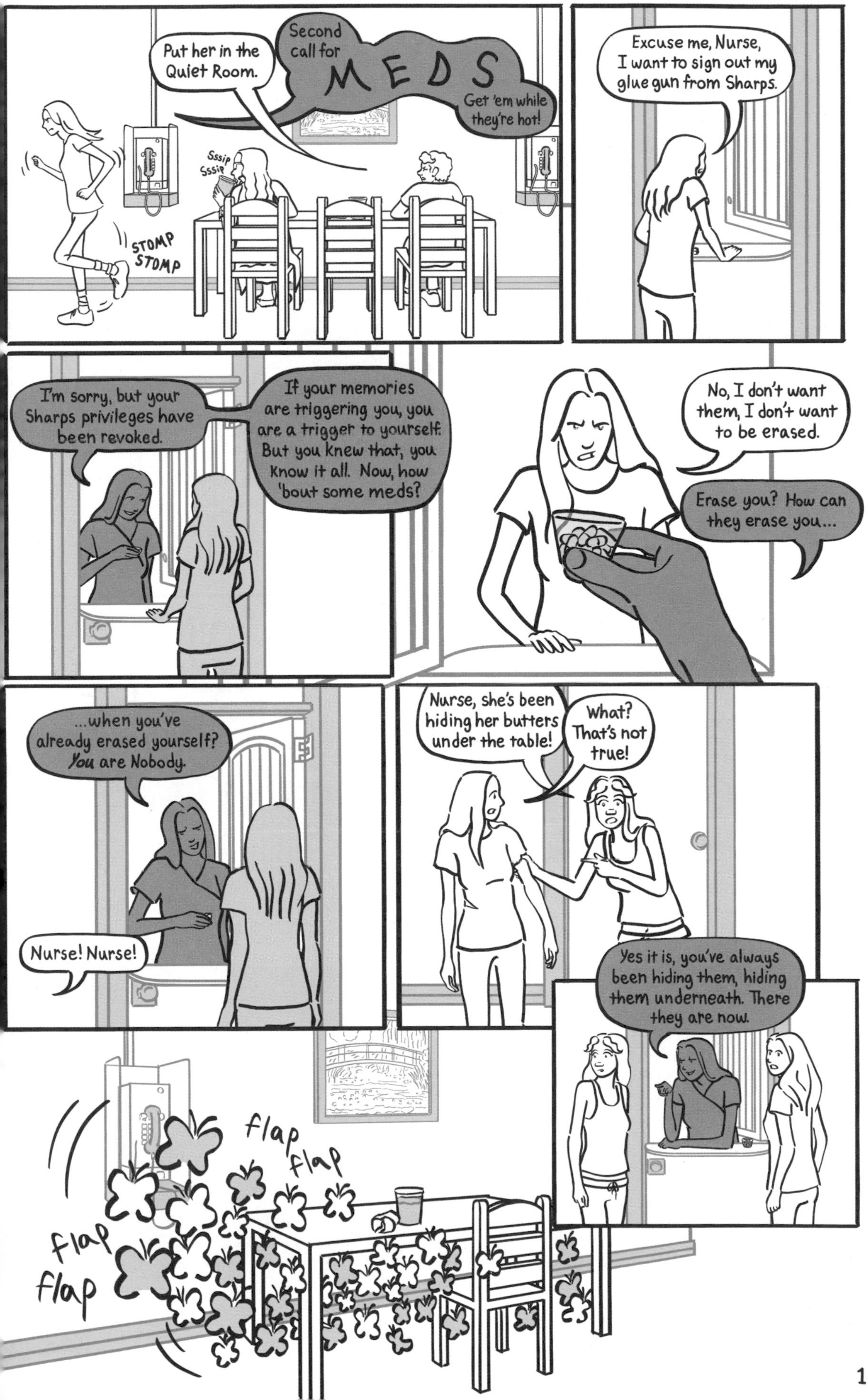
Put her in the Quiet Room.
Second call for MEDS Get 'em while they're hot!
Sssip Sssip
STOMP STOMP
Excuse me, Nurse, I want to sign out my glue gun from Sharps.
I'm sorry, but your Sharps privileges have been revoked.
If your memories are triggering you, you are a trigger to yourself. But you knew that, you know it all. Now, how 'bout some meds?
No, I don't want them, I don't want to be erased.
Erase you? How can they erase you...
...when you've already erased yourself? *You* are Nobody.
Nurse! Nurse!
Nurse, she's been hiding her butters under the table!
What? That's not true!
Yes it is, you've always been hiding them, hiding them underneath. There they are now.
flap flap
flap flap

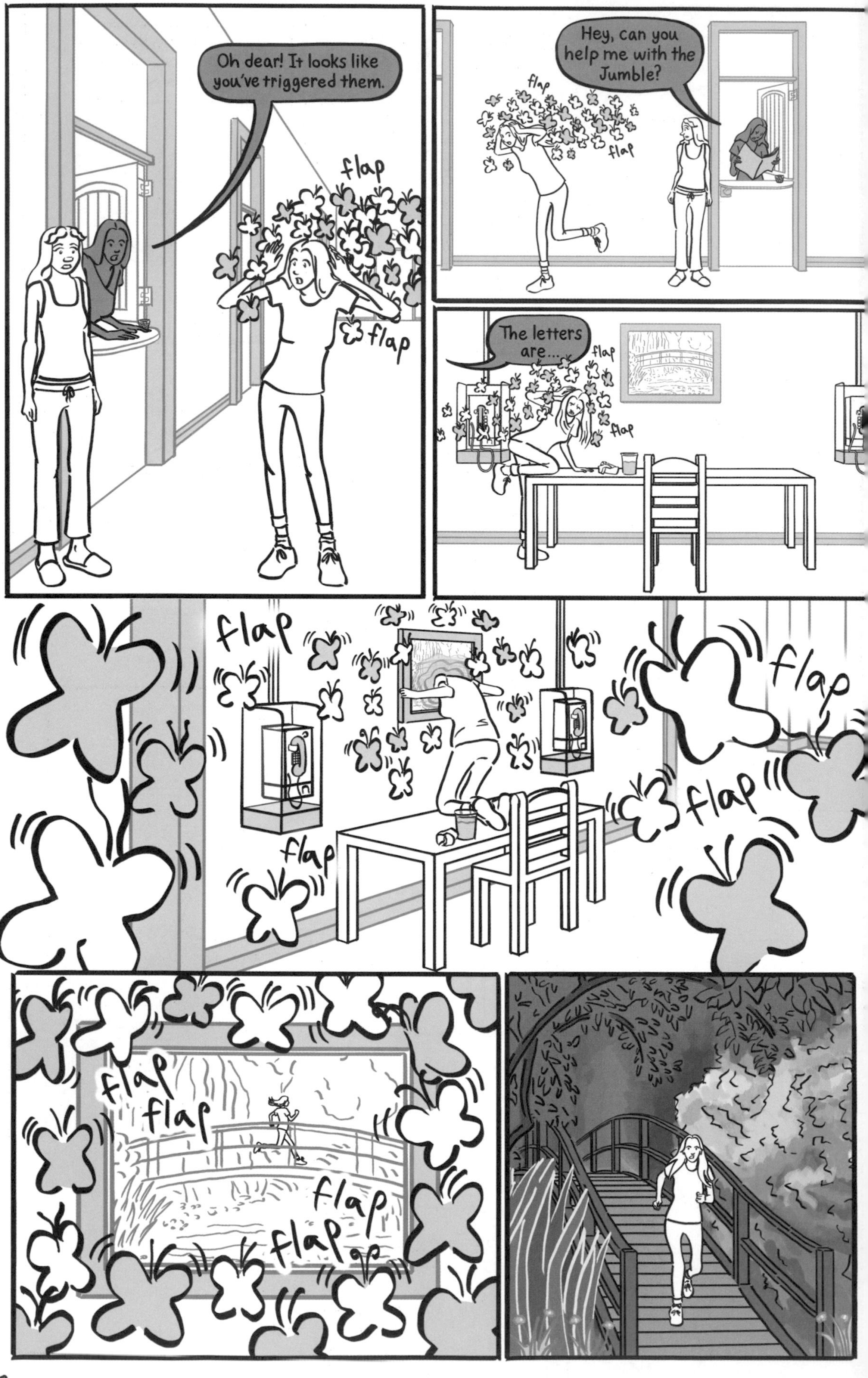
Oh dear! It looks like you've triggered them.
flap
flap
Hey, can you help me with the Jumble?
flap
flap
The letters are...
flap
flap
flap
flap
flap
flap
flap
flap
flap
flap
flap

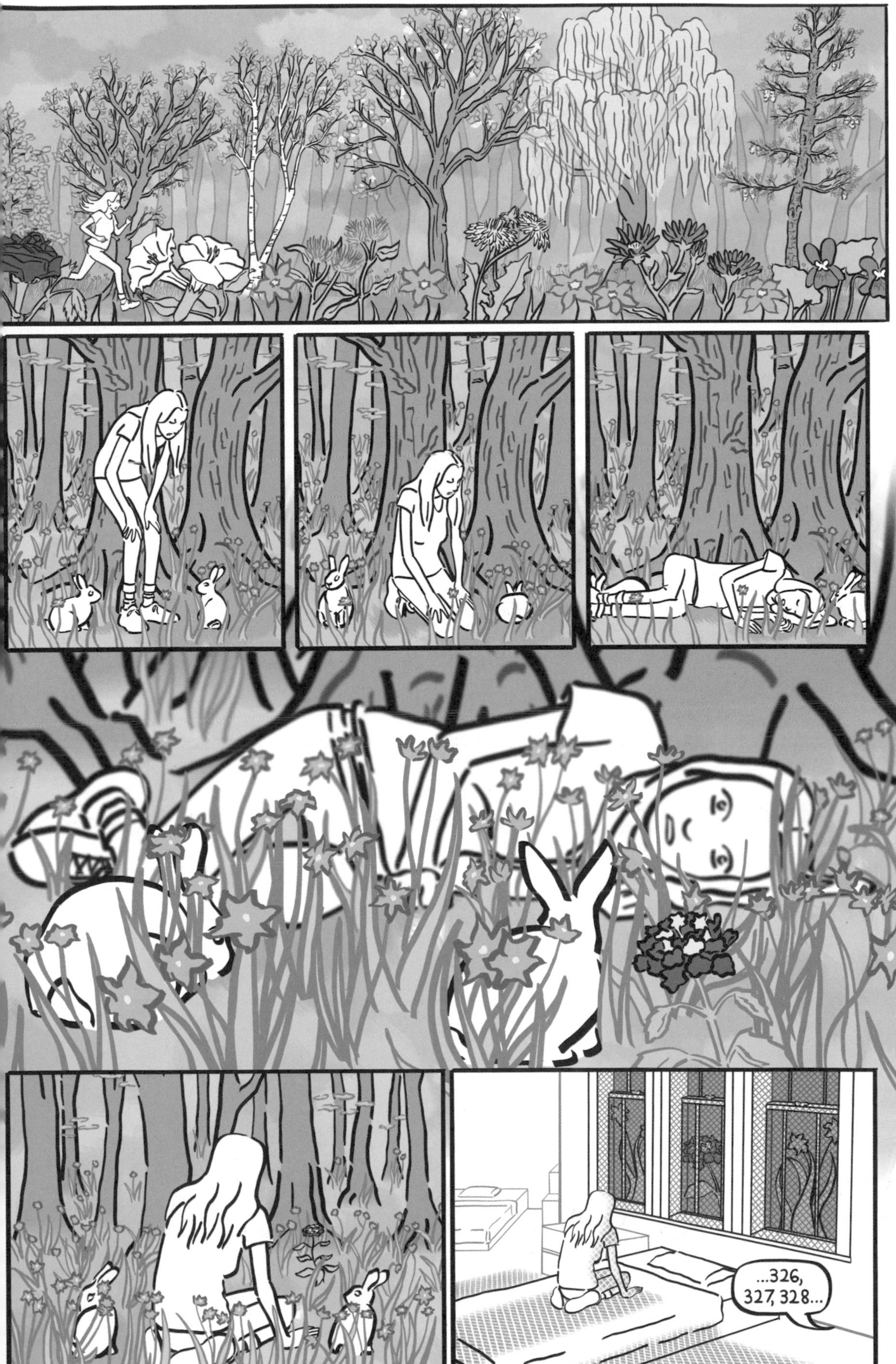
...326,
327, 328...

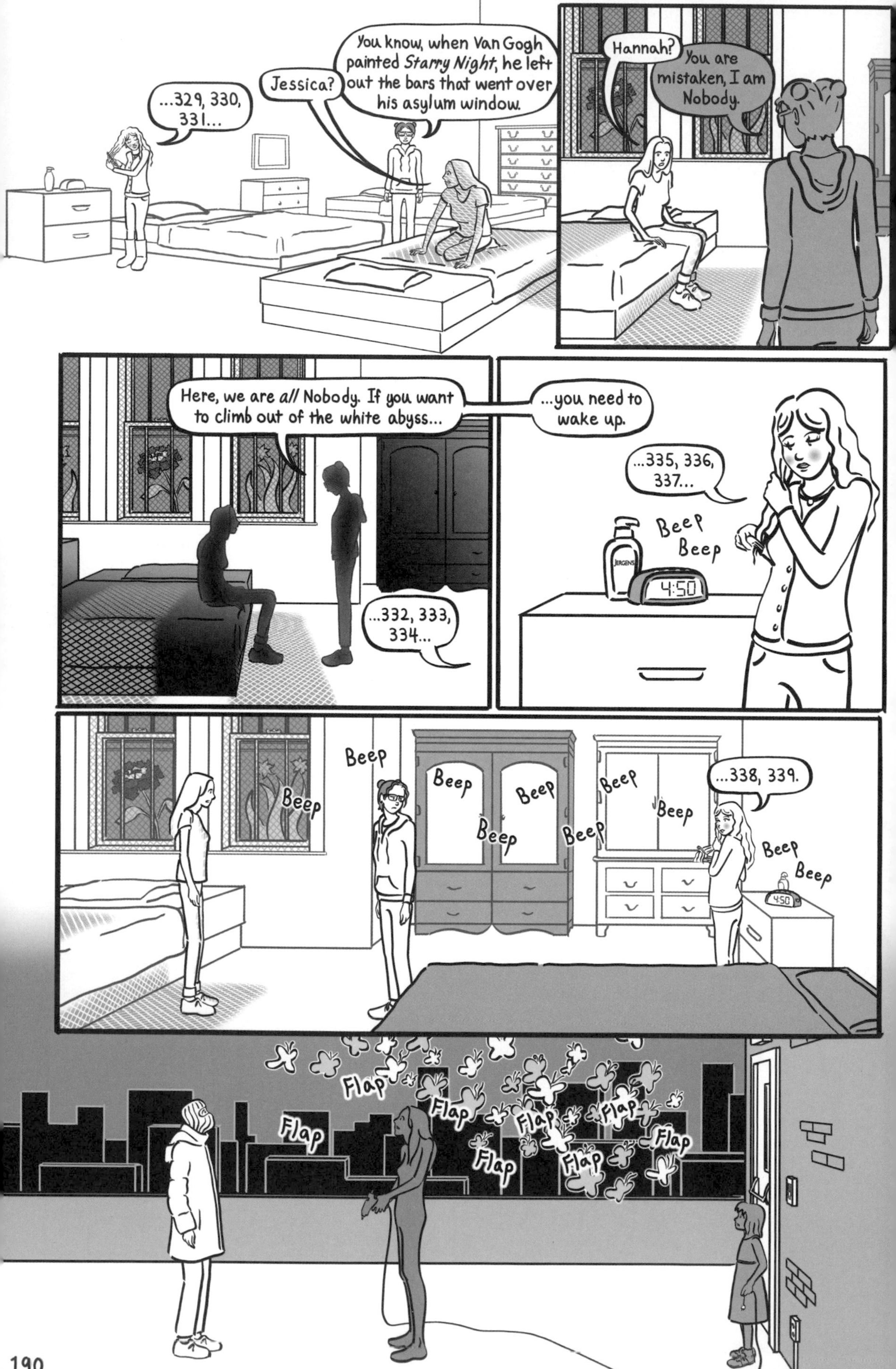
...329, 330, 331...
Jessica?
You know, when Van Gogh painted *Starry Night*, he left out the bars that went over his asylum window.
Hannah?
You are mistaken, I am Nobody.
Here, we are *all* Nobody. If you want to climb out of the white abyss...
...you need to wake up.
...332, 333, 334...
...335, 336, 337...
Beep
Beep
JERGENS
4:50
Beep
Beep
Beep
Beep
Beep
Beep
Beep
Beep
...338, 339.
Beep
Beep
Flap
Flap
Flap
Flap
Flap
Flap
Flap
Flap

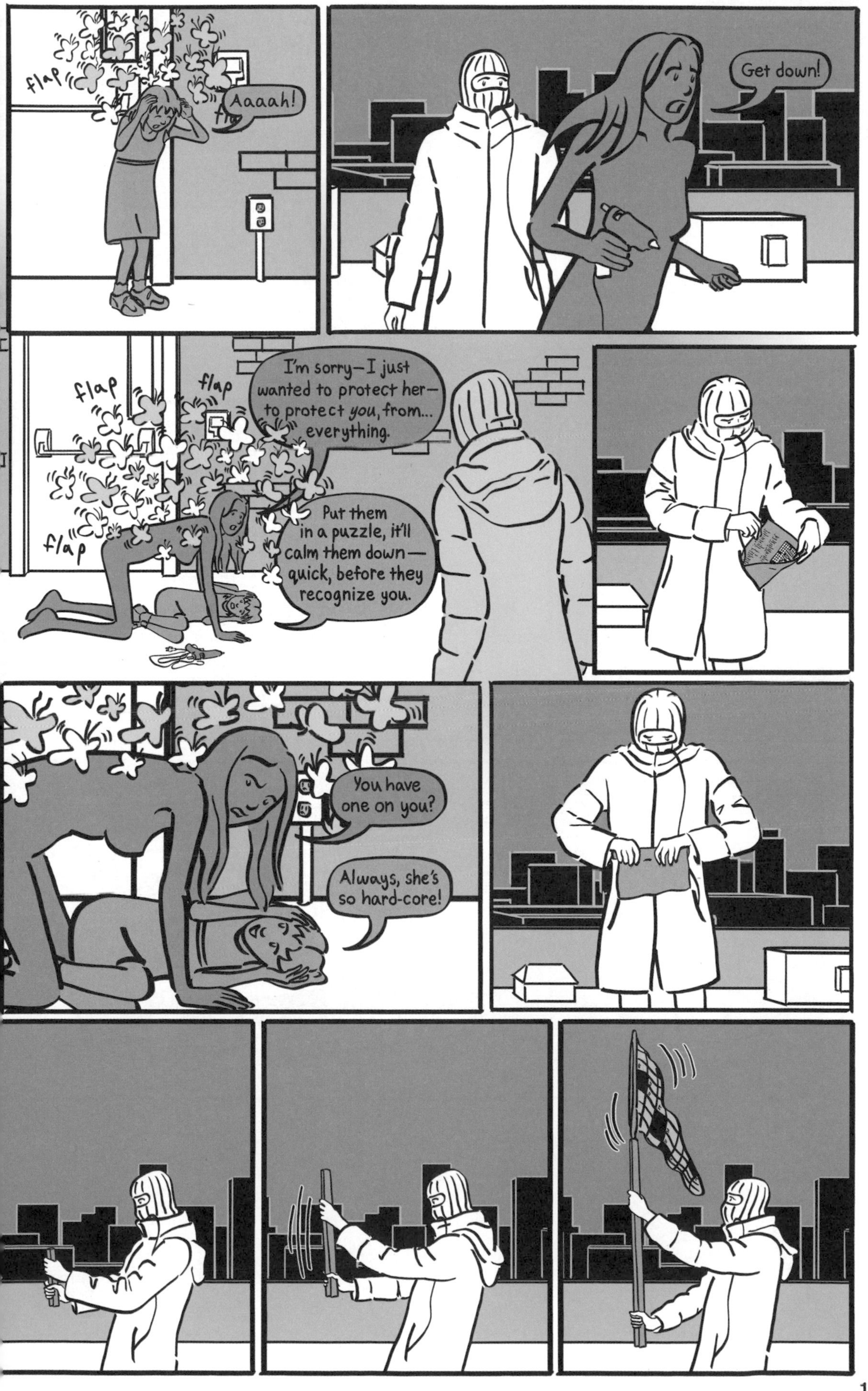
flap
Aaaah!
Get down!
flap
flap
flap
I'm sorry—I just wanted to protect her—to protect *you*, from... everything.
Put them in a puzzle, it'll calm them down—quick, before they recognize you.
You have one on you?
Always, she's so hard-core!

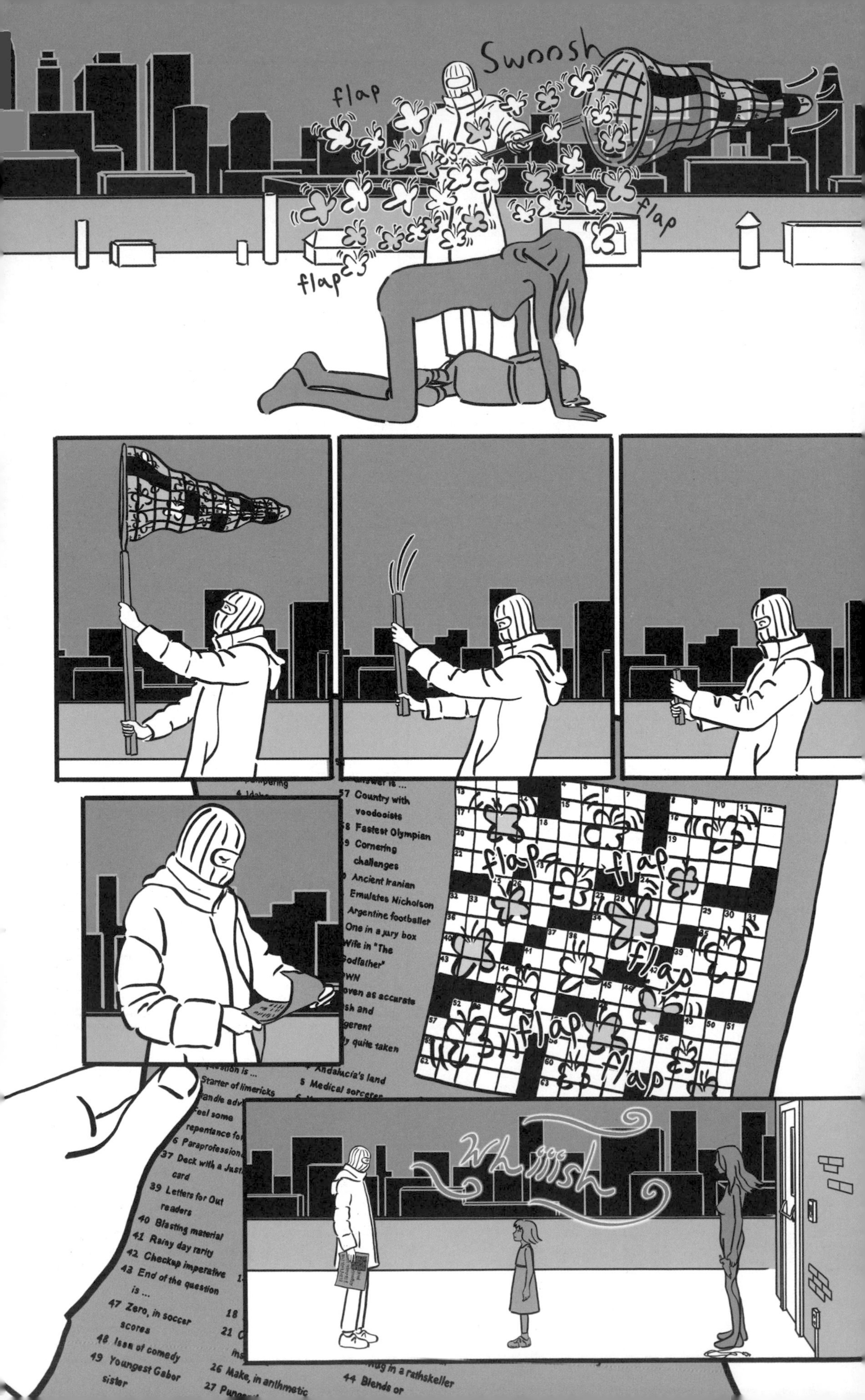

Swoosh
flap
flap
flap
57 Country with voodooists
Fastest Olympian
Cornering challenges
Ancient Iranian
Emulates Nicholson
Argentine footballer
One in a jury box
flap
flap
flap
flap
flap
Starter of limericks
39 Letters for Out readers
40 Blasting material
41 Rainy day rarity
42 Checkup imperative
43 End of the question is ...
47 Zero, in soccer scores
48 Issa of comedy
49 Youngest Gabor sister
Andalucía's land
5 Medical sorcerer
44 Blends or
Whiiish

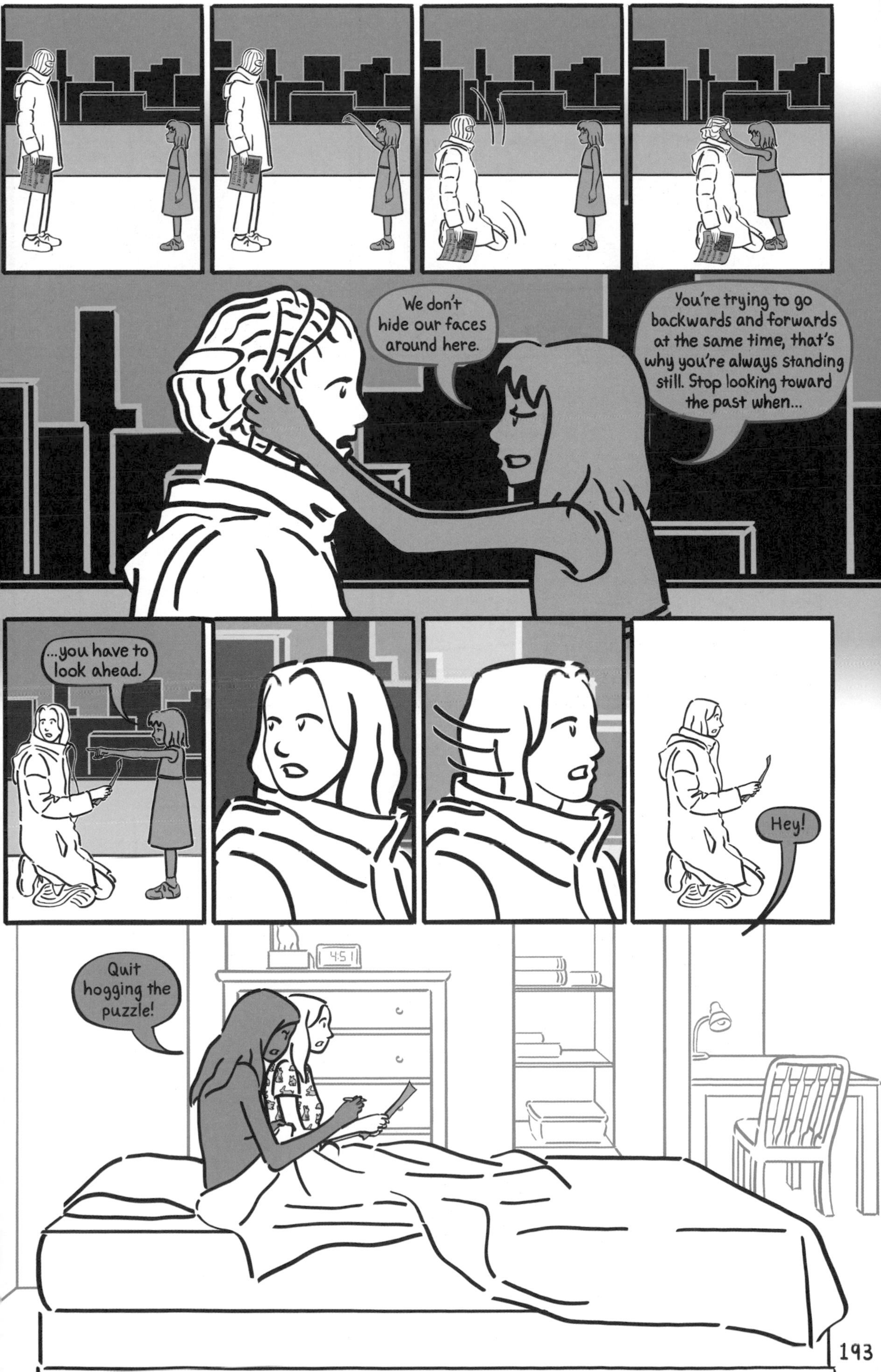
We don't hide our faces around here.
You're trying to go backwards and forwards at the same time, that's why you're always standing still. Stop looking toward the past when...
...you have to look ahead.
Hey!
Quit hogging the puzzle!

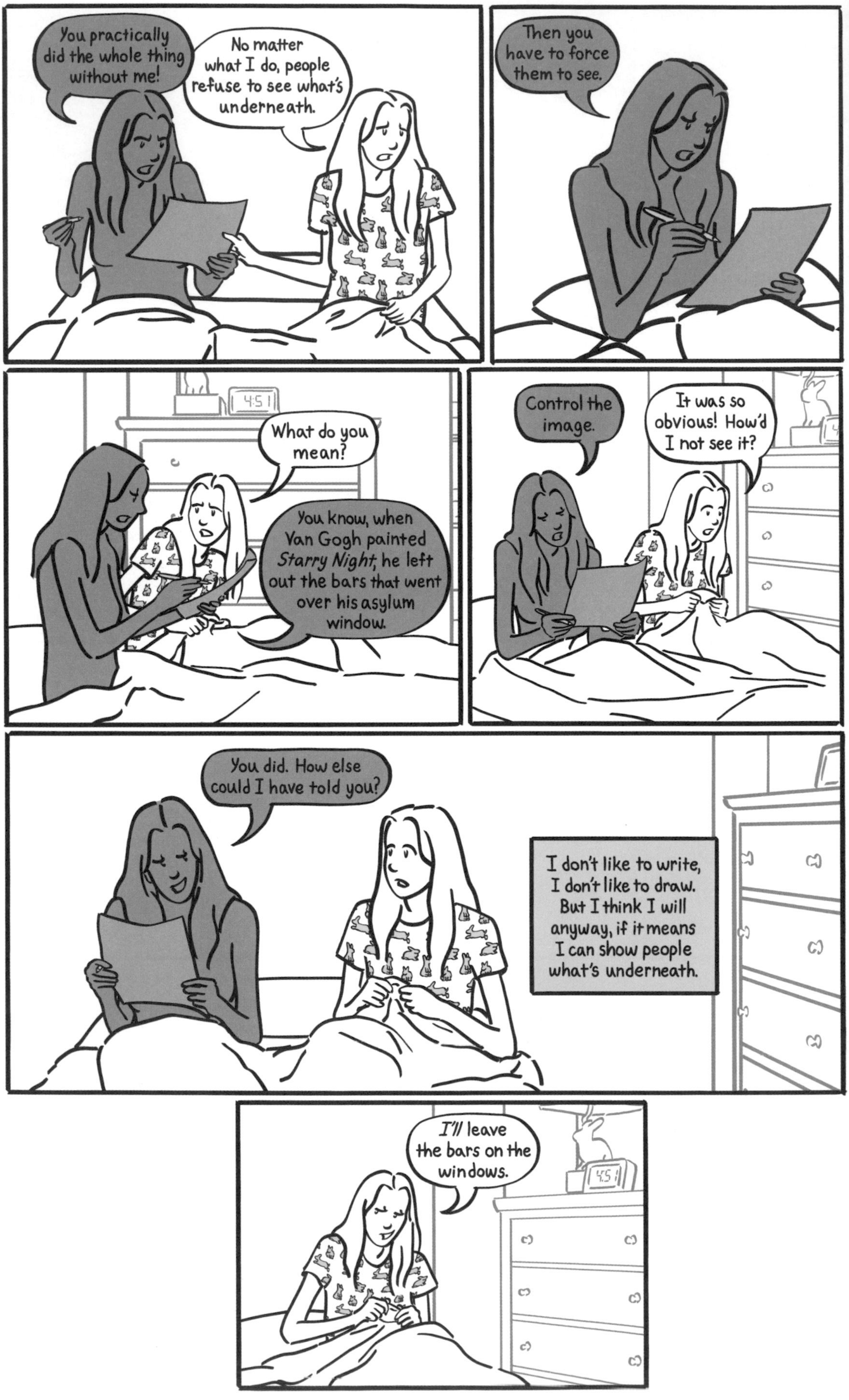
You practically did the whole thing without me!
No matter what I do, people refuse to see what's underneath.
Then you have to force them to see.
What do you mean?
You know, when Van Gogh painted *Starry Night*, he left out the bars that went over his asylum window.
4:51
Control the image.
It was so obvious! How'd I not see it?
You did. How else could I have told you?
I don't like to write, I don't like to draw. But I think I will anyway, if it means I can show people what's underneath.
I'll leave the bars on the windows.
4:51

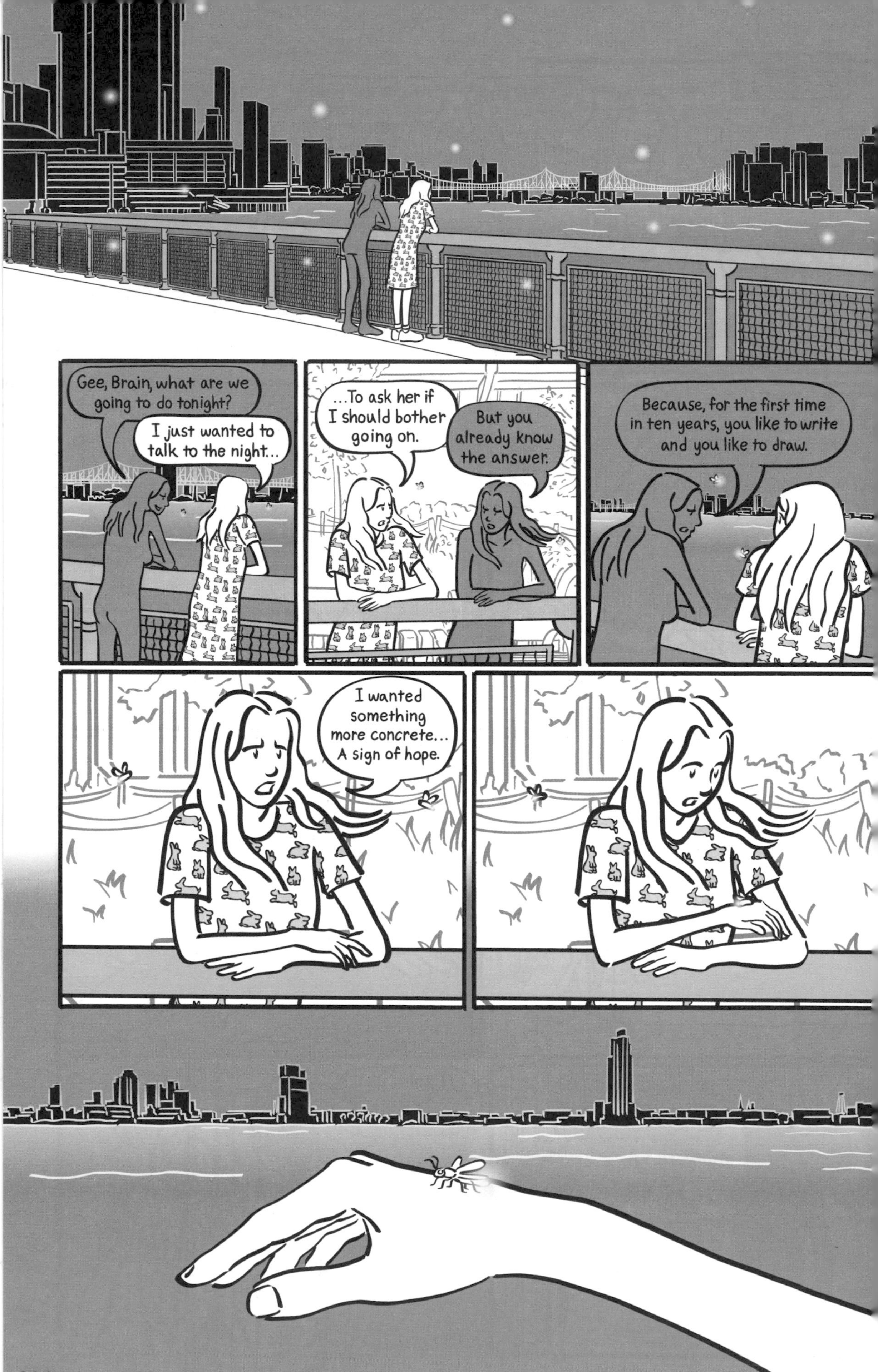
Gee, Brain, what are we going to do tonight?
I just wanted to talk to the night...
...To ask her if I should bother going on.
But you already know the answer.
Because, for the first time in ten years, you like to write and you like to draw.
I wanted something more concrete... A sign of hope.

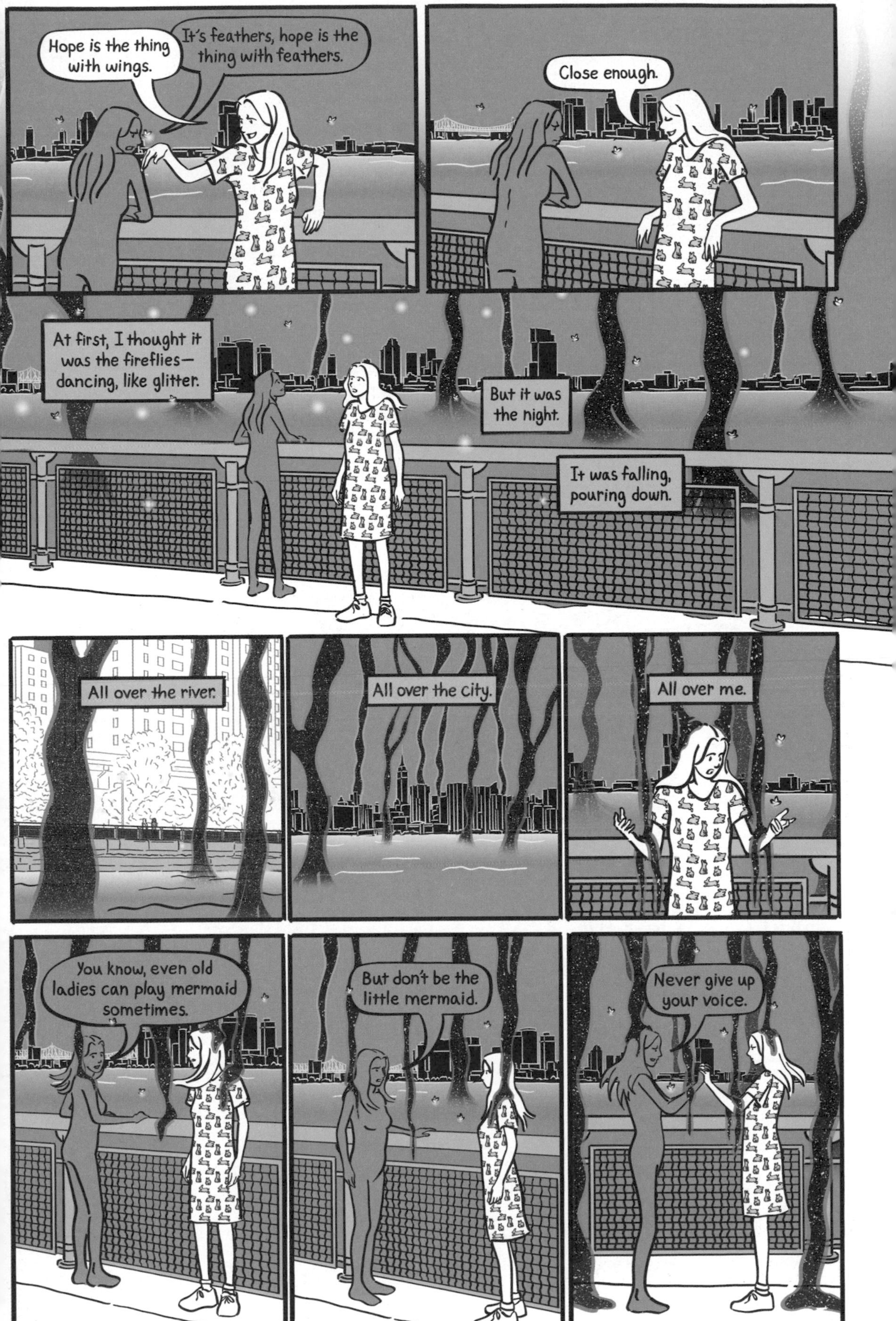
Hope is the thing with wings.
It's feathers, hope is the thing with feathers.
Close enough.
At first, I thought it was the fireflies— dancing, like glitter.
But it was the night.
It was falling, pouring down.
All over the river.
All over the city.
All over me.
You know, even old ladies can play mermaid sometimes.
But don't be the little mermaid.
Never give up your voice.

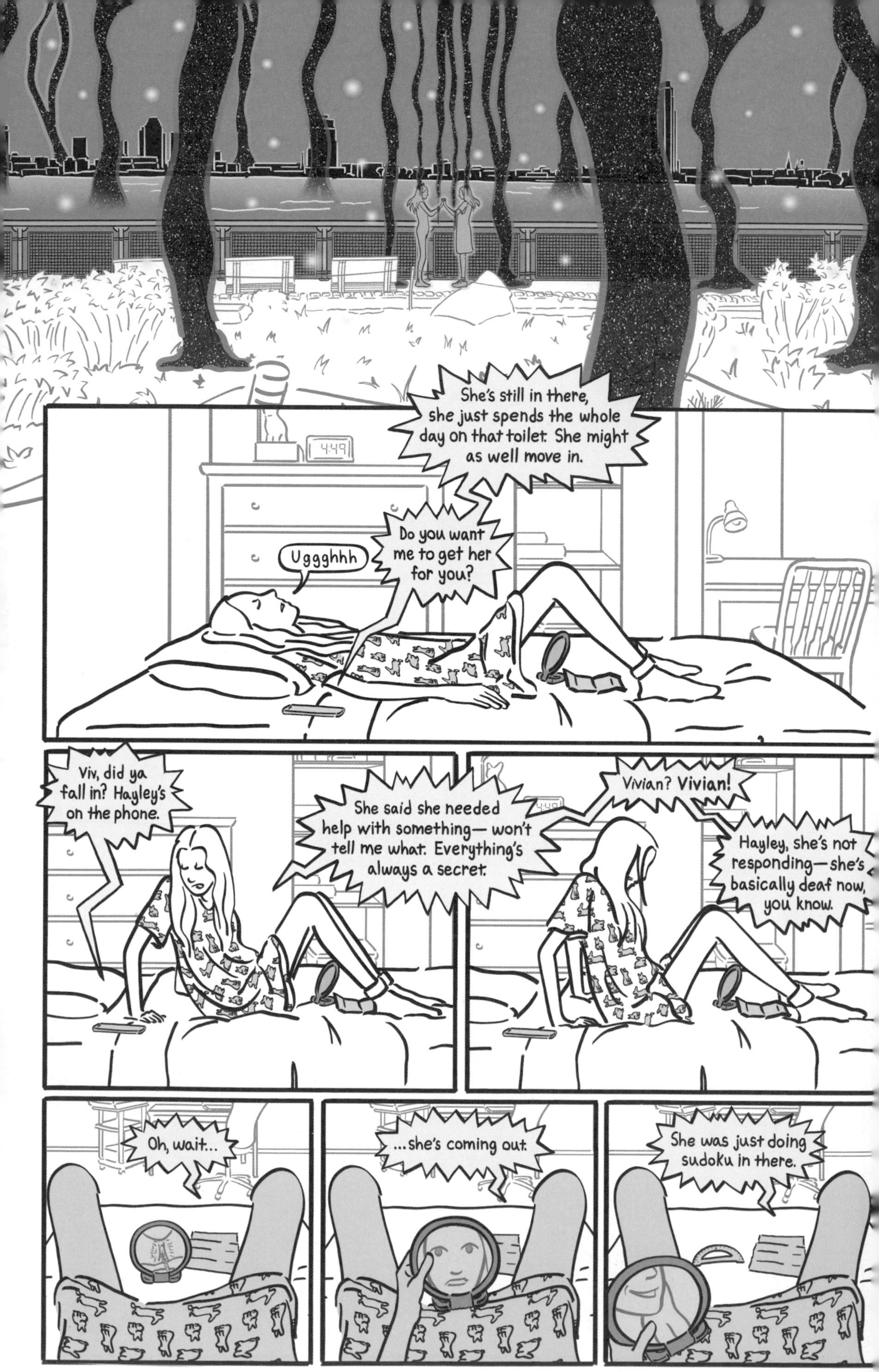
4:49
She's still in there, she just spends the whole day on that toilet. She might as well move in.
Uggghhh
Do you want me to get her for you?
Viv, did ya fall in? Hayley's on the phone.
She said she needed help with something— won't tell me what. Everything's always a secret.
Vivian? Vivian!
Hayley, she's not responding—she's basically deaf now, you know.
Oh, wait...
...she's coming out.
She was just doing sudoku in there.

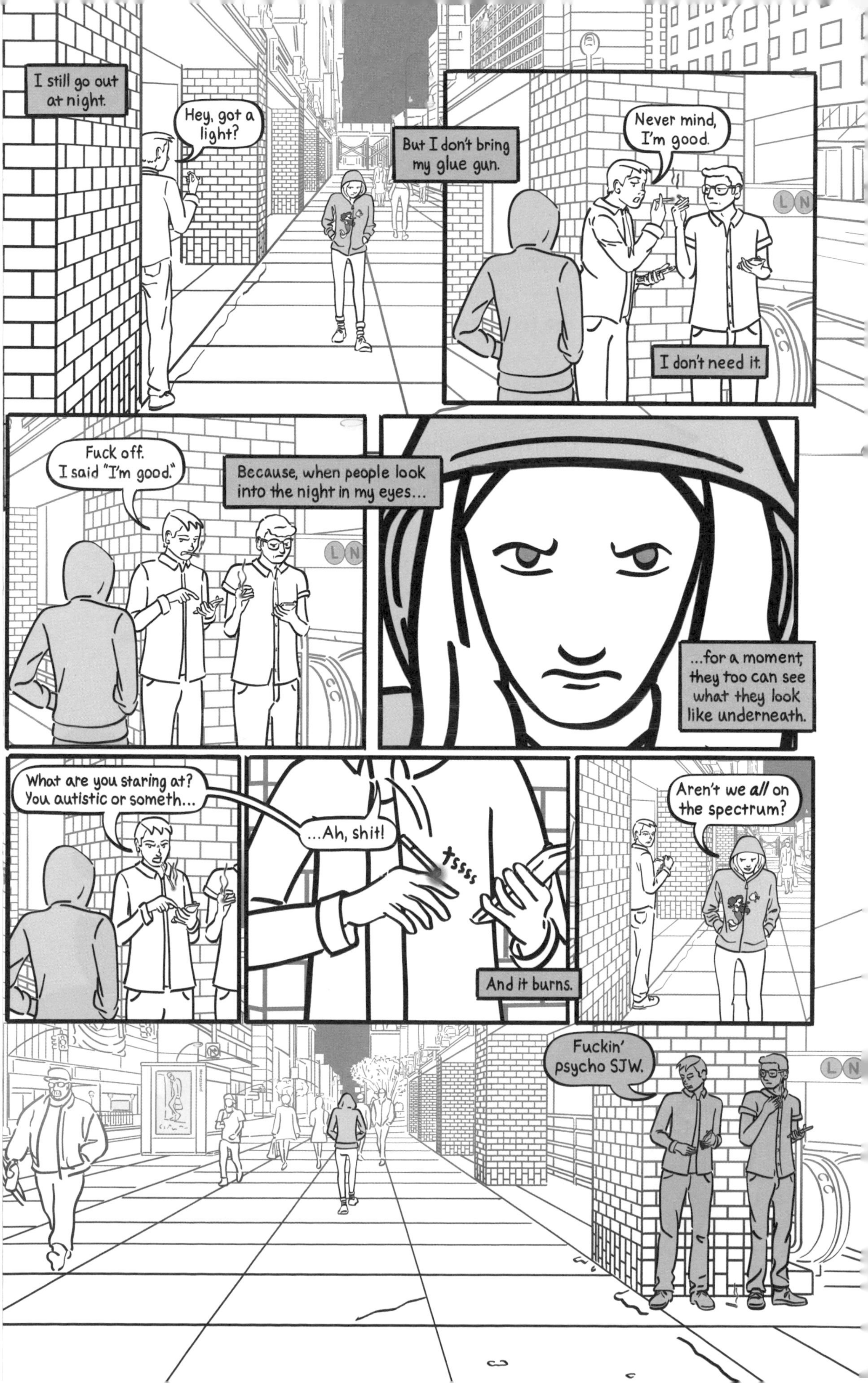
I still go out at night.
Hey, got a light?
But I don't bring my glue gun.
Never mind, I'm good.
I don't need it.
Fuck off. I said "I'm good."
Because, when people look into the night in my eyes...
...for a moment, they too can see what they look like underneath.
What are you staring at? You autistic or someth...
...Ah, shit!
tssss
And it burns.
Aren't we *all* on the spectrum?
Fuckin' psycho SJW.

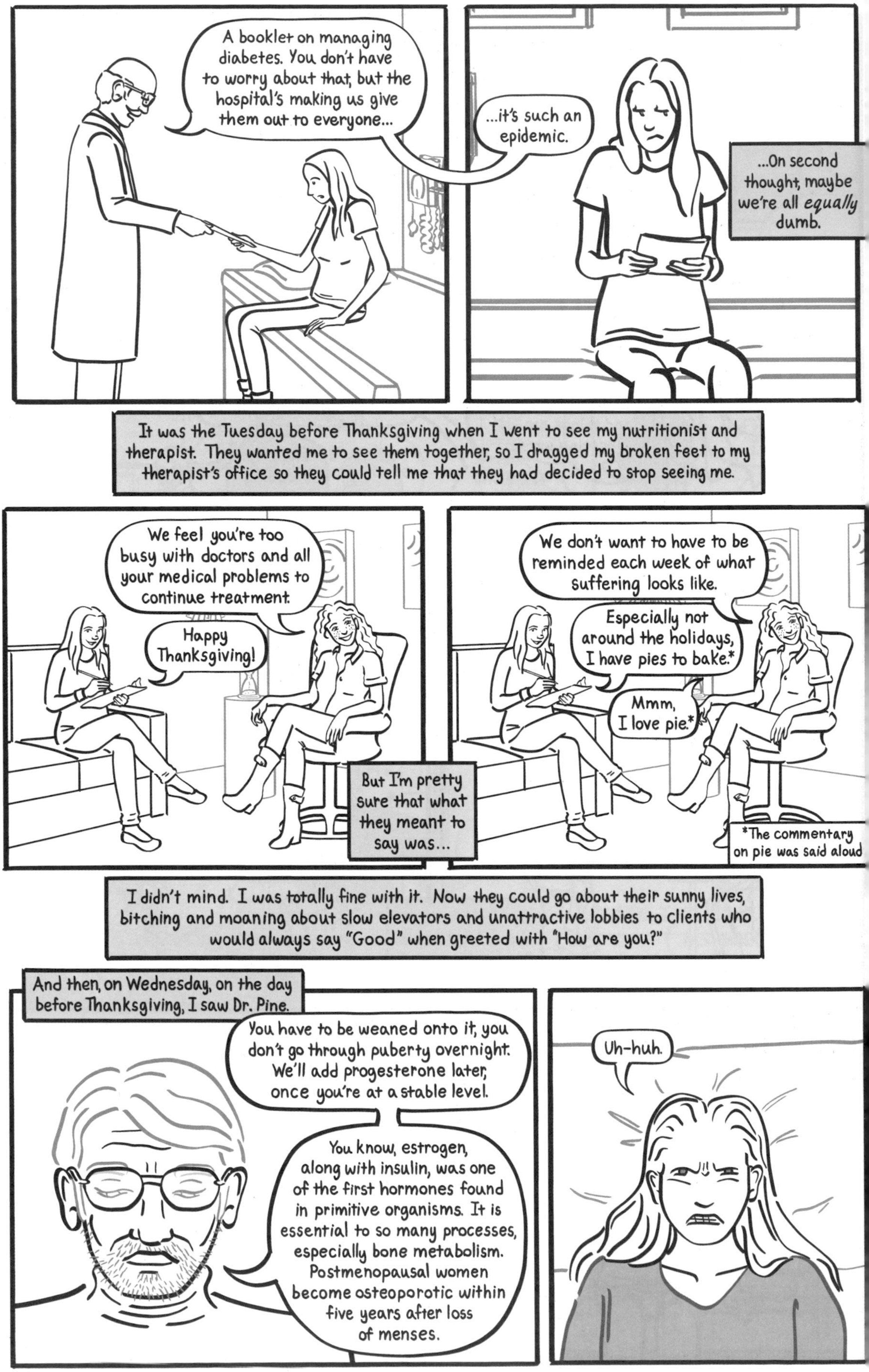
A booklet on managing diabetes. You don't have to worry about that, but the hospital's making us give them out to everyone...
...it's such an epidemic.
...On second thought, maybe we're all *equally* dumb.
It was the Tuesday before Thanksgiving when I went to see my nutritionist and therapist. They wanted me to see them together, so I dragged my broken feet to my therapist's office so they could tell me that they had decided to stop seeing me.
We feel you're too busy with doctors and all your medical problems to continue treatment.
Happy Thanksgiving!
But I'm pretty sure that what they meant to say was...
We don't want to have to be reminded each week of what suffering looks like.
Especially not around the holidays, I have pies to bake.*
Mmm, I love pie.*
*The commentary on pie was said aloud
I didn't mind. I was totally fine with it. Now they could go about their sunny lives, bitching and moaning about slow elevators and unattractive lobbies to clients who would always say "Good" when greeted with "How are you?"
And then, on Wednesday, on the day before Thanksgiving, I saw Dr. Pine.
You have to be weaned onto it, you don't go through puberty overnight. We'll add progesterone later, once you're at a stable level.
You know, estrogen, along with insulin, was one of the first hormones found in primitive organisms. It is essential to so many processes, especially bone metabolism. Postmenopausal women become osteoporotic within five years after loss of menses.
Uh-huh.

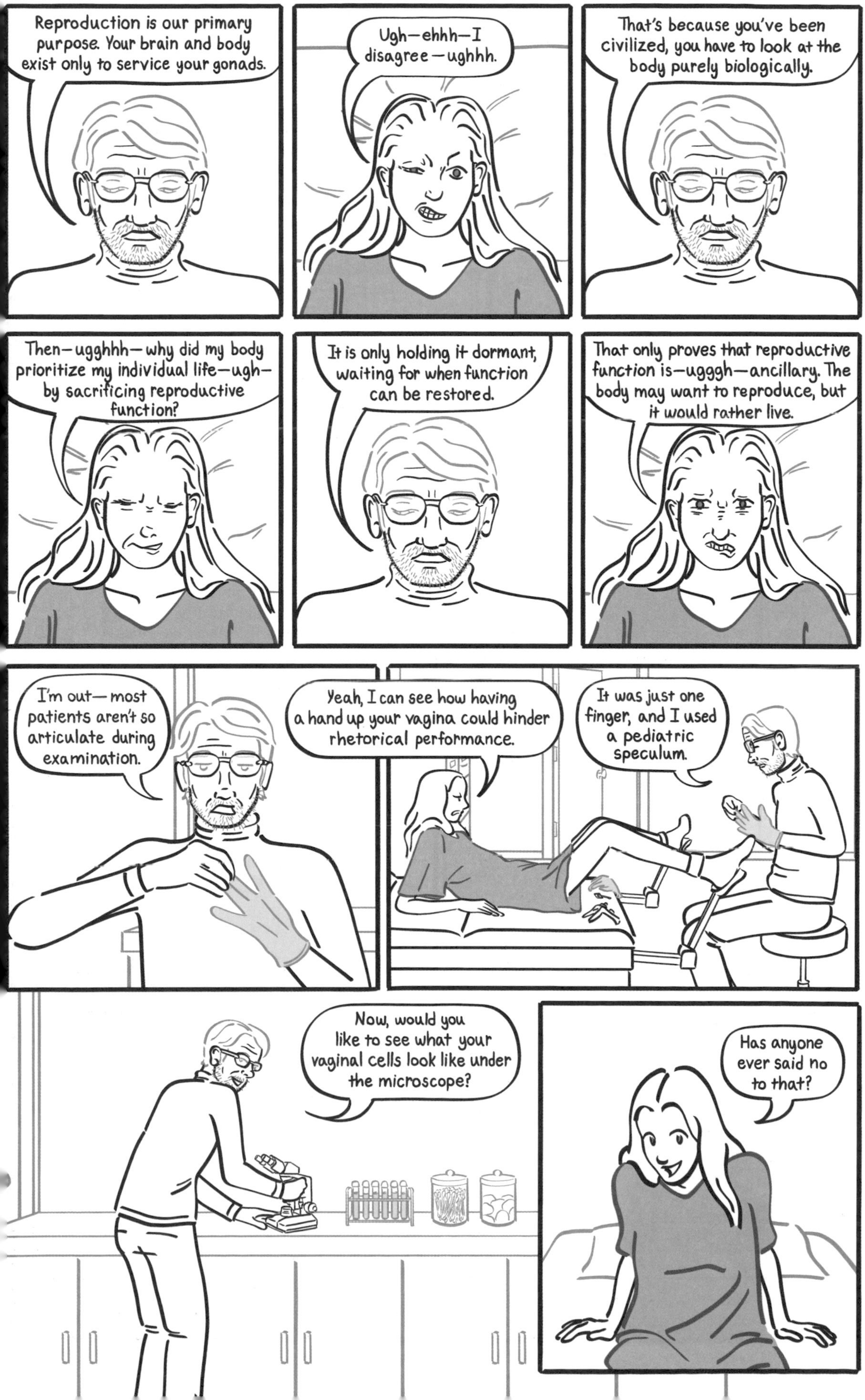
Reproduction is our primary purpose. Your brain and body exist only to service your gonads.
Ugh—ehhh—I disagree—ughhh.
That's because you've been civilized, you have to look at the body purely biologically.
Then—ugghhh—why did my body prioritize my individual life—ugh—by sacrificing reproductive function?
It is only holding it dormant, waiting for when function can be restored.
That only proves that reproductive function is—ugggh—ancillary. The body may want to reproduce, but it would rather live.
I'm out—most patients aren't so articulate during examination.
Yeah, I can see how having a hand up your vagina could hinder rhetorical performance.
It was just one finger, and I used a pediatric speculum.
Now, would you like to see what your vaginal cells look like under the microscope?
Has anyone ever said no to that?

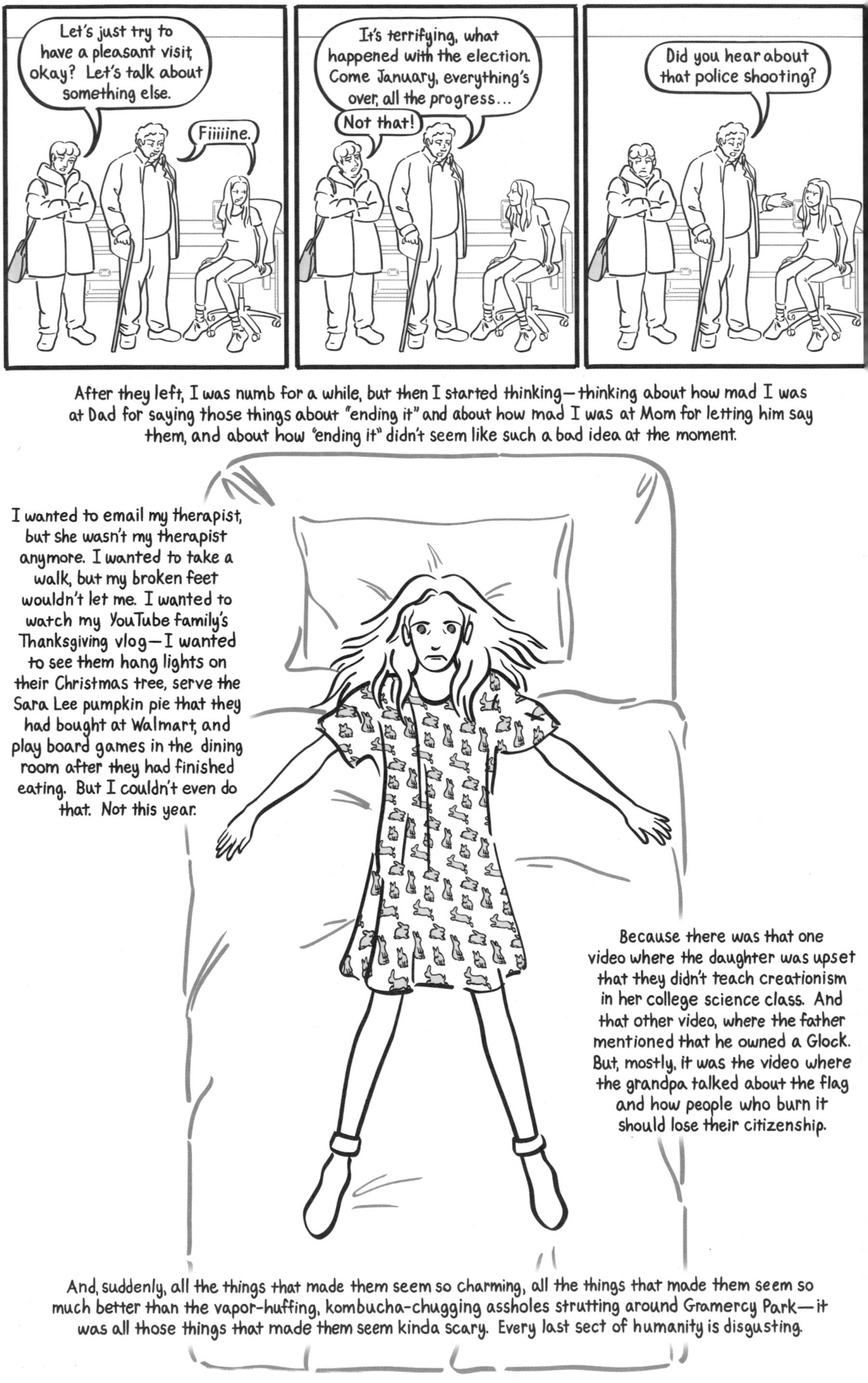
Let's just try to have a pleasant visit, okay? Let's talk about something else.
Fiiiiine.
It's terrifying, what happened with the election. Come January, everything's over, all the progress...
Not that!
Did you hear about that police shooting?
After they left, I was numb for a while, but then I started thinking—thinking about how mad I was at Dad for saying those things about "ending it" and about how mad I was at Mom for letting him say them, and about how "ending it" didn't seem like such a bad idea at the moment.
I wanted to email my therapist, but she wasn't my therapist anymore. I wanted to take a walk, but my broken feet wouldn't let me. I wanted to watch my YouTube family's Thanksgiving vlog—I wanted to see them hang lights on their Christmas tree, serve the Sara Lee pumpkin pie that they had bought at Walmart, and play board games in the dining room after they had finished eating. But I couldn't even do that. Not this year.
Because there was that one video where the daughter was upset that they didn't teach creationism in her college science class. And that other video, where the father mentioned that he owned a Glock. But, mostly, it was the video where the grandpa talked about the flag and how people who burn it should lose their citizenship.
And, suddenly, all the things that made them seem so charming, all the things that made them seem so much better than the vapor-huffing, kombucha-chugging assholes strutting around Gramercy Park—it was all those things that made them seem kinda scary. Every last sect of humanity is disgusting.

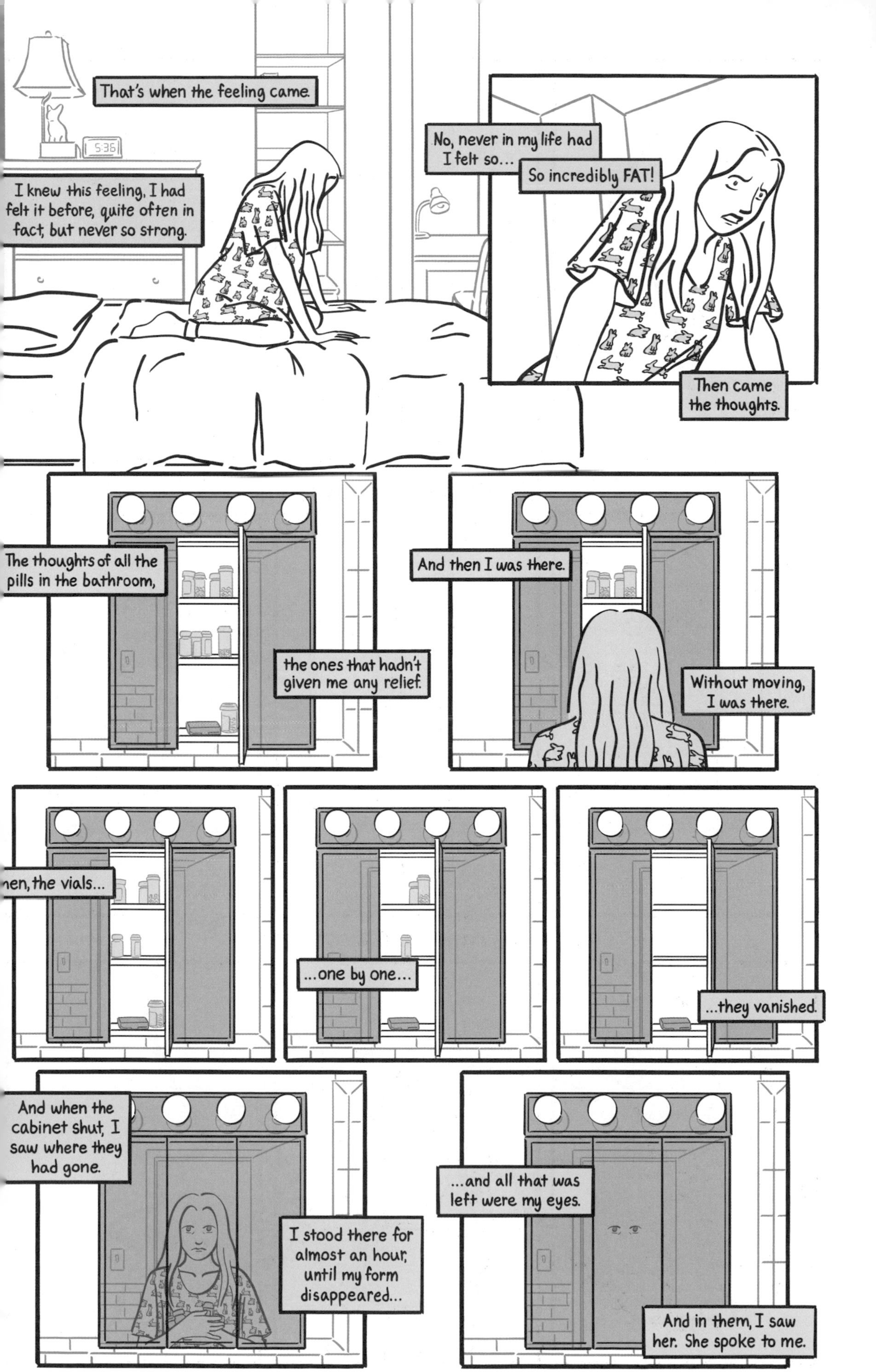

That's when the feeling came.
5:36
I knew this feeling, I had felt it before, quite often in fact, but never so strong.
No, never in my life had I felt so...
So incredibly FAT!
Then came the thoughts.
The thoughts of all the pills in the bathroom,
the ones that hadn't given me any relief.
And then I was there.
Without moving, I was there.
hen, the vials...
...one by one...
...they vanished.
And when the cabinet shut, I saw where they had gone.
I stood there for almost an hour, until my form disappeared...
...and all that was left were my eyes.
And in them, I saw her. She spoke to me.

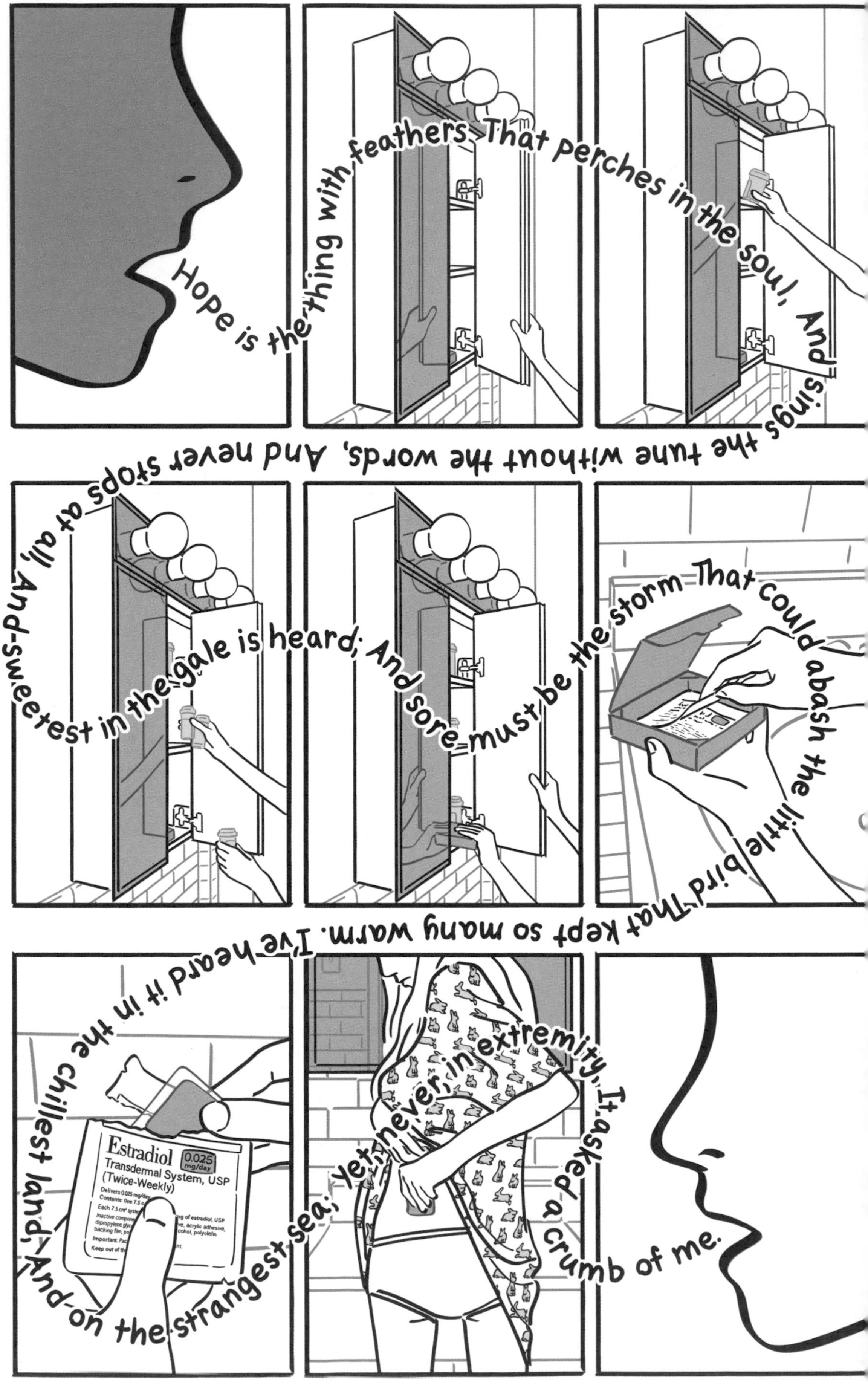

Hope is the thing with feathers That perches in the soul, And sings the tune without the words, And never stops at all, And sweetest in the gale is heard; And sore must be the storm That could abash the little bird That kept so many warm. I've heard it in the chillest land, And on the strangest sea; Yet, never, in extremity, It asked a crumb of me.
Estradiol
0.025 mg/day
Transdermal System, USP
(Twice-Weekly)

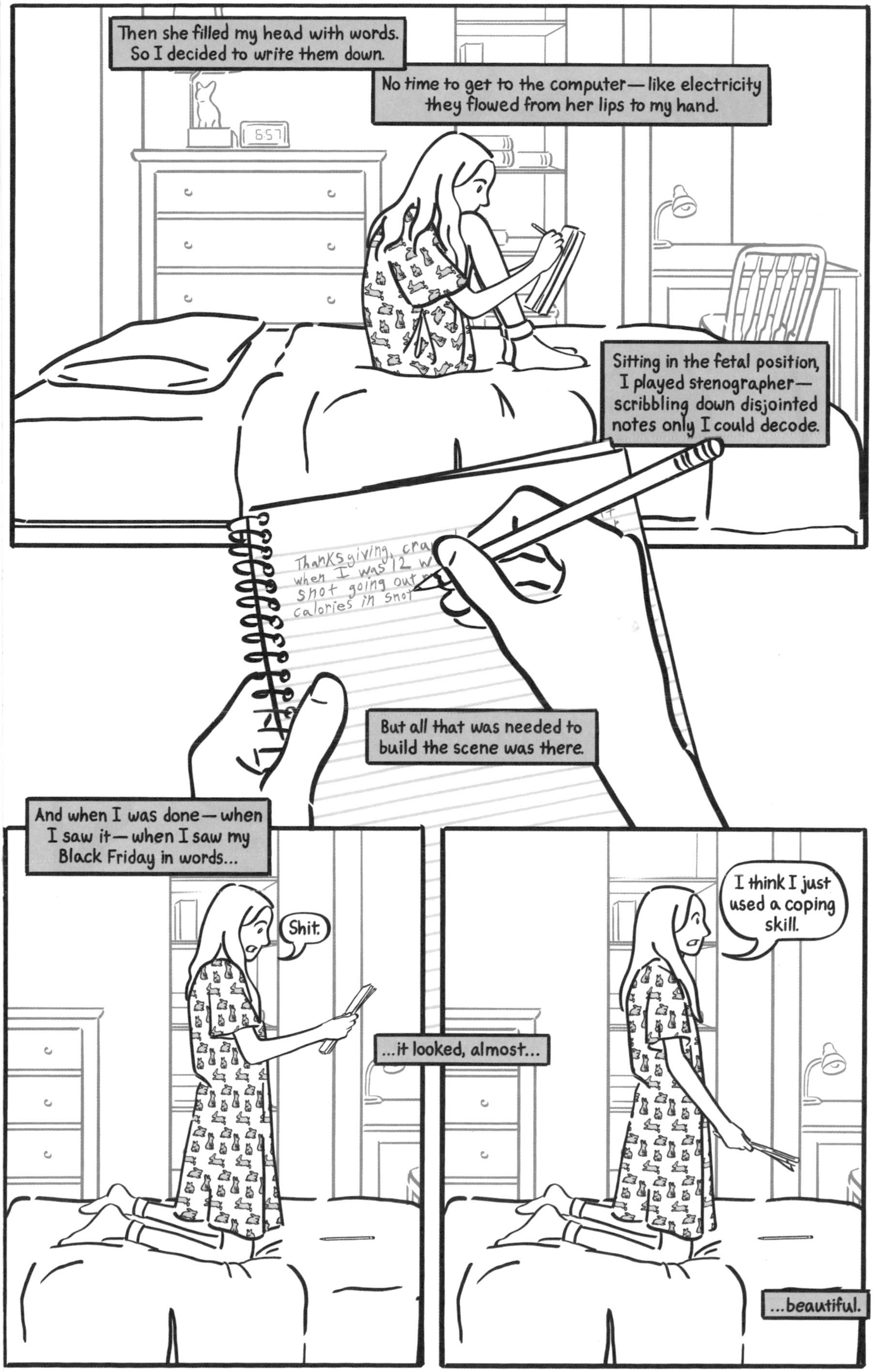
Then she filled my head with words. So I decided to write them down.
No time to get to the computer—like electricity they flowed from her lips to my hand.
6:57
Sitting in the fetal position, I played stenographer—scribbling down disjointed notes only I could decode.
But all that was needed to build the scene was there.
And when I was done—when I saw it—when I saw my Black Friday in words...
Shit.
...it looked, almost...
I think I just used a coping skill.
...beautiful.

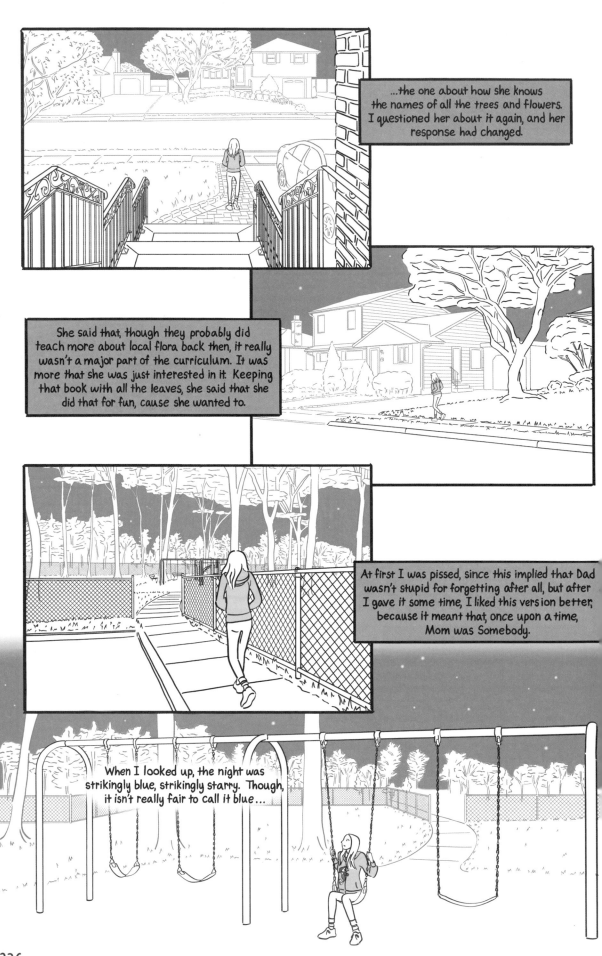

...the one about how she knows the names of all the trees and flowers. I questioned her about it again, and her response had changed.

She said that, though they probably did teach more about local flora back then, it really wasn't a major part of the curriculum. It was more that she was just interested in it. Keeping that book with all the leaves, she said that she did that for fun, cause she wanted to.

At first I was pissed, since this implied that Dad wasn't stupid for forgetting after all, but after I gave it some time, I liked this version better, because it meant that, once upon a time, Mom was Somebody.

When I looked up, the night was strikingly blue, strikingly starry. Though, it isn't really fair to call it blue...

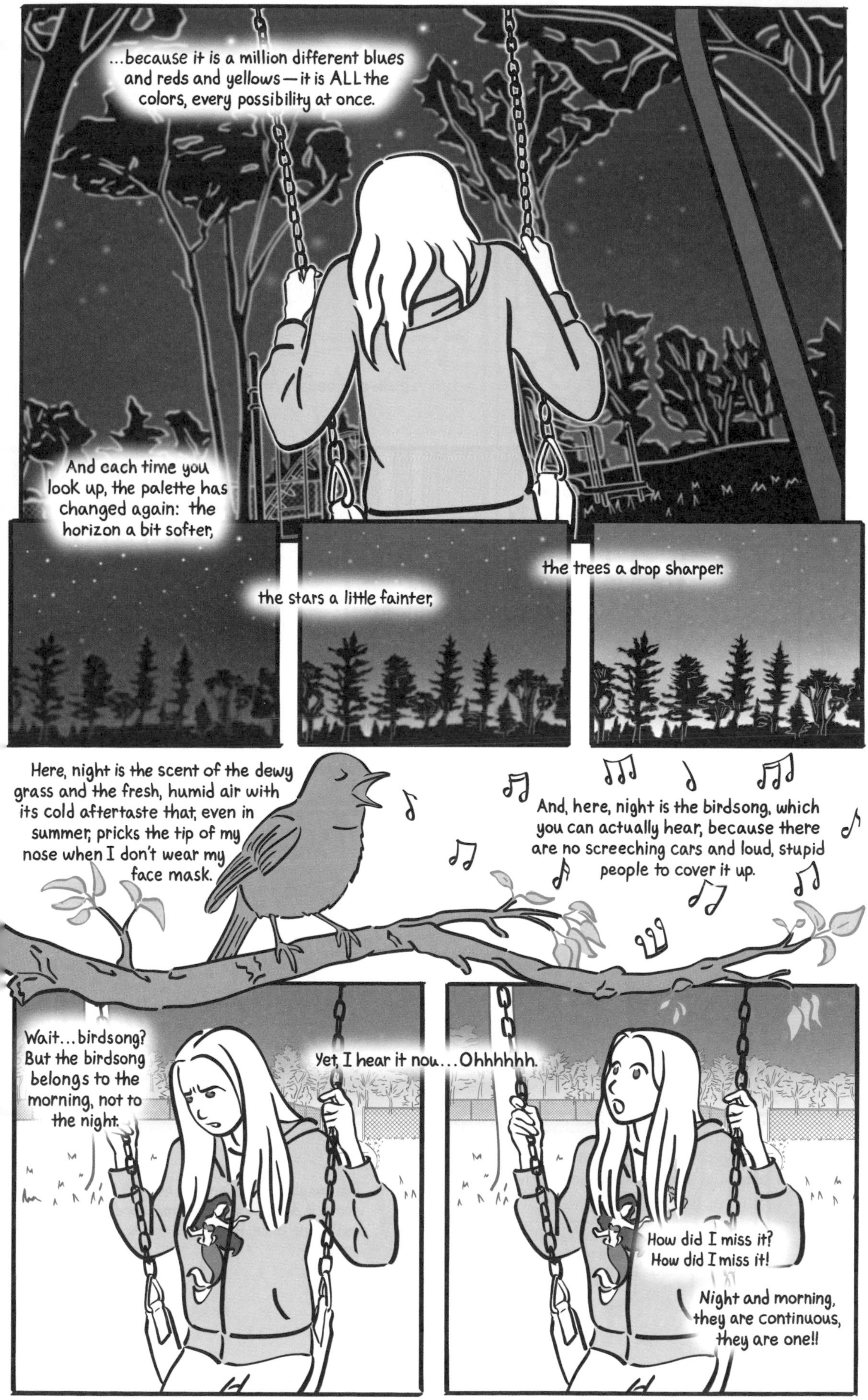
...because it is a million different blues and reds and yellows—it is ALL the colors, every possibility at once.
And each time you look up, the palette has changed again: the horizon a bit softer,
the stars a little fainter,
the trees a drop sharper.
Here, night is the scent of the dewy grass and the fresh, humid air with its cold aftertaste that, even in summer, pricks the tip of my nose when I don't wear my face mask.
And, here, night is the birdsong, which you can actually hear, because there are no screeching cars and loud, stupid people to cover it up.
Wait...birdsong? But the birdsong belongs to the morning, not to the night.
Yet, I hear it now...Ohhhhhh.
How did I miss it? How did I miss it!
Night and morning, they are continuous, they are one!!

It was given to me by the Gods—
When I was a little Girl—
They give us Presents most — you know—
When we are new — and small.
I kept it in my Hand—
I never put it down—
I did not dare to eat — or sleep—
For fear it would be gone—
I heard such words as "Rich"—
When hurrying to school—
From lips at Corners of the Streets—
And wrestled with a smile.
Rich! 'Twas Myself — was rich—
To take the name of Gold—
And Gold to own — in solid Bars—
The Difference —made me bold—

Viburnum Lantana L.